T0301725

MONETARY THEORY AND POLICY FROM HUME
AND SMITH TO WICKSELL

This book provides a comprehensive survey of the major developments in monetary theory and policy from David Hume and Adam Smith to Walter Bagehot and Knut Wicksell. In particular, it seeks to explain why it took so long for a theory of central banking to penetrate mainstream thought.

The book investigates how major monetary theorists understood the roles of the invisible and visible hands in money, credit, and banking; what they thought about rules and discretion and the role played by commodity-money in their conceptualizations; whether or not they distinguished between the two different roles carried out via the financial system – making payments efficiently within the exchange process and facilitating intermediation in the capital market; how they perceived the influence of the monetary system on macroeconomic aggregates such as the price level, output, and accumulation of wealth; and finally, what they thought about monetary policy. The book explores the analytical dimensions in the various monetary theories while emphasizing their policy consequences.

The book highlights the work of a number of pioneering theoreticians. Among these Henry Thornton stands out, primarily because of his innovative analysis of the complicated phenomena that developed after the introduction of an inconvertible monetary system in 1797. A major question addressed by the book is why theoreticians and policy makers were so resistant to his ideas for so many years.

Arie Arnon is Associate Professor of Economics at Ben-Gurion University and Head of the Economics and Society Program at Van Leer Jerusalem Institute, Israel. Professor Arnon's areas of research include the history of economic thought, macroeconomics, and monetary theory. His books include *Thomas Tooke: A Pioneer of Monetary Theory* (1991); *The Palestinian Economy: Between Imposed Integration and Voluntary Separation* (1997, coauthored with I. Luski, A. Spivak, and J. Weinblatt); and *The Open Economy Macromodel: Past, Present, and Future* (2002, coedited with W. Young).

Professor Arnon has published articles in *History of Political Economy, Oxford Economic Papers*, the *Economic Journal*, and *Middle East Journal*. He has served on the editorial boards of the *European Journal of the History of Economic Thought*, the *Economic Quarterly*, and the *Journal of Welfare and Social Security Studies*. He has held visiting positions at the University of California, Berkeley; Stanford University; the University of Pennsylvania; The New School; and the School of Oriental and African Studies, University of London. He has also served as a Senior Economist in the Research Department of the Bank of Israel and as a consultant to the World Bank.

Since 2002, Professor Arnon has been the coordinator of the Israeli team in the Aix Group, where experts from the Palestinian Authority, Israel, and the international community discuss various economic aspects of the conflict and develop scenarios and policy alternatives for a permanent peace settlement. A recent publication of the group is entitled *Economic Dimensions of a Two-State Agreement between Israel and Palestine* (2007).

HISTORICAL PERSPECTIVES ON MODERN ECONOMICS

General Editor: Craufurd D. Goodwin, Duke University

This series contains original works that challenge and enlighten historians of economics. For the profession as a whole, it promotes better understanding of the origin and content of modern economics

Other Books in the Series:

Continued after Index

Monetary Theory and Policy from Hume and Smith to Wicksell

Money, Credit, and the Economy

ARIE ARNON

Department of Economics,
Ben-Gurion University
of the Negev, Beer-Sheva, Israel
and
Head, Economics and Society Program,
Van Leer Jerusalem Institute

CAMBRIDGE UNIVERSITY PRESS
Cambridge, New York, Melbourne, Madrid, Cape Town,
Singapore, São Paulo, Delhi, Mexico City

Cambridge University Press
32 Avenue of the Americas, New York, NY 10013-2473, USA

www.cambridge.org
Information on this title: www.cambridge.org/9781107642737

First published 2011
Reprinted 2011 (twice)
First paperback edition 2012

A catalog record for this publication is available from the British Library.

Library of Congress Cataloging in Publication Data

Monetary theory and policy from Hume and Smith to Wicksell : money,
credit, and the economy / Arie Arnon.
    p.   cm. – (Historical perspectives on modern economics)
Includes bibliographical references and index.
ISBN 978-0-521-19113-5 (hardback)
1. Monetary policy – History.   2. Banks and banking, Central – History.
3. Economists.   I. Title.   II. Series.
HG230.3.A684 2011
339.5'3–dc22   2010037658

ISBN 978-0-521-19113-5 Hardback
ISBN 978-1-107-64273-7 Paperback

To Ruth, my greatest love;
Yes, more than the history of monetary thought and
Peace in the Middle East.

Contents

Contents

Illustrations

Tables

Preface

I was first attracted to the history of monetary thought many years ago, puzzled by an enduring question: What is the right balance between the visible and invisible hands in economics? I thought then, and still think, that the appeal of the invisible hand is even less convincing in the fields of money and banking than in other fields. The necessity of interventions in money and banking, and more generally in finance, seem so obvious that I assumed that such interventions had a long history. I was surprised to learn that this was not the case. Rather, I soon learned that the classical conventional wisdom, represented by David Hume, by Adam Smith, and by David Ricardo in most of his writings, unreservedly adopted the invisible hand/no policy approach.

Most of the eighteenth- and nineteenth-century scholars who thought about the subject believed that the "natural order," organized spontaneously around the precious metals, would suffice to establish a well-functioning monetary system. As we shall see, there were some dissenting views, but they had little influence. Rather, for many years, the dissenters were almost completely ignored. The recognition that it is up to society to regulate and direct the monetary system came to take center stage only toward the end of the nineteenth century.

The slow rise of a theory of monetary policy is the story told in this book. Understanding this story also means understanding the obstacles and stiff resistance that for so long delayed recognition of the failure of the invisible hand. The debate over the correct balance between the two hands is far from over, both in banking and in spheres outside of banking. Therefore, understanding the obstacles that stood in the way of a theory of central banking may help in present-day and future debates over similar issues. In any case, that is the constant hope of those of us who would study the history of thought not just for its own sake, but in the belief that important lessons can be gained from it.

My personal route to studying the history of monetary theory took me
from Karl Marx back to those who most influenced his thinking about
the sphere of money and banking: the Banking School, and primarily
Thomas Tooke. In an effort to understand Tooke, I looked further back to
the canonical figures of classical monetary theory. Although my journey
moved backwards through time, the present book naturally begins with the
state of monetary theory in the mid-eighteenth century; in other words,
with Hume and Smith, who define the "state of the art" at the time. In the
first part of the book, I also briefly review the institutional setup, a decentralized banking system linked to the precious metals. In the last chapter in
Part One (Chapter 4), entitled "'Monetary Theories of Credit' in Exchange,"
I present an analytical summary of a system based on gold, wherein other
debts and credits are linked to that anchor. Part Two of the book deals with
an exciting period when the sovereign purposefully decided to give up the
gold anchor. The Restriction Period (1797–1821) brings us to an amazing
group of thinkers, most notably Henry Thornton (Chapter 7). Chapters
6 and 8 introduce Walter Boyd and David Ricardo on the one hand, and
Francis Baring and Charles Bosanquet on the other hand, arguing on opposite sides of the famous Bullionist–anti-Bullionist divide. Chapter 9, entitled "'Credit Theories of Money' in Exchange and Intermediation," presents
the analytical perspective most suited to understanding Henry Thornton,
the most original thinker. His analytical framework will reappear with Knut
Wicksell. Readers less interested in the analytical framework can skip this
chapter but might be tempted to return to it (and to Chapter 4) after perusal
of the rest of the book.

Part Three covers the years after the 1821 Resumption, when Great
Britain was back on gold. Although the famous debates between the
Currency and Banking Schools about bank reform are well known, I link
them both not only to the phenomenon of reoccurring crises, but also to
a relatively neglected aspect of our story: the different roles of the monetary system in exchange and intermediation. The slow rise of a theory of
monetary policy and the hegemony of the Currency School for so many
years in the mid-nineteenth century are clearly two sides of the same coin,
as we shall see. In Part Four, we encounter Walter Bagehot, one of the
better-known scholars who helped to speed up the slow rise of discretionary monetary policy, though in a restricted form. I argue that Bagehot's
achievements were both less original than many think and less comprehensive than those of Thornton, seventy years earlier. Wicksell, covered
in the last part of the book, is the scholar who closed the circle that began
with Thornton.

In a few of the chapters, I draw on material from published papers. I wish to thank Duke University Press and the *History of Political Economy* for permission to use materials from:

Arnon, A. (1984), "The Transformation in Thomas Tooke's Monetary Theory Reconsidered," *History of Political Economy* 16, pp. 311–326.

Arnon, A. (1984), "Marx's Theory of Money – The Formative Years," *History of Political Economy* 16, pp. 555–575.

Arnon, A. (1999), "Free (and Not So Free) Banking Theories among the Classicals or Classical Forerunners of Free Banking and Why They Have Been Neglected," *History of Political Economy* 31, pp. 79–107.

Arnon, A. (2009), "Reexamination of Thornton's Innovative Monetary Analysis: The Bullion Debate during the Restriction Once Again," *History of Political Economy* 41, pp. 545–574.

I wish to thank the Verlag Wirtschaft und Finanzen for permission to draw from:

Arnon, A. (1997), "Thomas Tooke, The Currency Principle and the 1844 Bank Act," Introductory Essay to Tooke's "An Inquiry into the Currency Principle," reissued in 'Klassiker der Nationalokonomie' series, B. Schefold, (Ed).

I wish to thank Oxford University Press and *Oxford Economic Papers* for permission to use:

Arnon, A. (1987), "Banking Between the Invisible and Visible Hands: A Reinterpretation of Ricardo's Place within the Classical School," *Oxford Economic Papers* 39, pp. 268–281.

During my many years of study of the major monetary scholars in the British tradition, I received, directly and indirectly, much help from many persons both deceased and alive. Although experience has taught me that listing one's debts is a dangerous mission, it is a risk well taken. I owe special thanks to Laurence Harris, who guided me during my first steps in this field. Sam Hollander provided advice in many instances, both when he was in Toronto and more recently, when we are closer in Beer Sheva. Neil Skaggs, David Laidler, Cristina Marcuzzo, Bob Dimand, Jerome de Boyer, and Mauro Boianovsky all discussed with me, at various stages, the ideas covered in the book. Three anonymous referees of Cambridge provided excellent and constructive criticism at different stages of writing. I wish to thank all of them for their advice and contributions. None of them is responsible for the views expressed in the book; any remaining errors are, of course, mine alone.

I wrote most of this book between 2006 and 2009, drawing on drafts written through many years of study and teaching of the history of monetary theory. I spent a sabbatical year in 2006–2007 at UC Berkeley, where I remained in 2008–2009 as the Helen Diller Visiting Israeli Professor in the Department of Economics, the Center of Middle Eastern Studies (CMES), and the Institute for Research on Labor and Employment (IRLE). I thank the Institute and especially its director Michael Reich for their hospitality and intellectually stimulating environment.

Throughout the work on the final drafts, I enjoyed the excellent editing assistance of Wendy Schor-Haim, for which I am very grateful. At Cambridge University Press, the consistent good advice and encouragement of Scott Parris were indispensable.

Last, but not least, I wish to thank my partner in life, Ruth. She and I know well why.

Introduction

Monetary theories, Sir John Hicks taught us, are always closely related to monetary histories, even more than general economic theory is related to economic facts. The institutions making up the monetary system the mediums used in a nonbarter economy, the preconceptions of the participants in the various transactions as to what does and does not constitute money, and even the observers' prejudices all play crucial roles in constructing theories. Monetary theories have obvious consequences for policy, so much so that positions on the right policies also have significant effect on theoretical discussions.

Monetary Theory and Policy from Hume and Smith to Wicksell: Money, Credit, and the Economy surveys the major developments in monetary theory and associated positions on policy. The book begins with David Hume and Adam Smith, moves through Henry Thornton and David Ricardo, and ends with Walter Bagehot and Knut Wicksell. The period covers the one hundred years of the Classical School, from the 1770s to the 1870s, with a brief look before, at Hume, and a look beyond, to Alfred Marshall and Wicksell.

The book covers the period's major monetary theorists and asks: What role did commodity-money, and in particular gold and silver, play in their conceptualizations? How did they explain the roles of the invisible and visible hands in money, credit, and banking? What did they think about rules and discretion? Did they distinguish between the two different roles of the financial system – making payments efficiently within the exchange process and facilitating intermediation in the capital market? How did they perceive the influence of the monetary system on macroeconomic aggregates, whether nominal, such as the price level and exchange rates, or real, such as output, employment, and the accumulation of wealth? And finally – and crucially – what did they think about monetary policy? In

1

particular, a central issue we address throughout this book concerns the puzzlingly slow development of a theory of central banking.

Henry Thornton stands out among the major figures whose ideas shaped monetary theory, primarily for his innovative analysis of the complicated phenomena that were just taking shape after the introduction of an inconvertible monetary system in 1797. Thornton drew unprecedented conclusions about monetary policy and about the links between money, credit, and the "real" economy. Perhaps most important in the present context, he developed a theory of central banking. For reasons which will be discussed in the book, Thornton's influence was limited. He was not able to convince contemporaries to look beyond the conventional wisdom at the turn of the nineteenth century as defined by Hume and Smith, the founding fathers of classical monetary theory. To Hume, contemporaries owed the analytical apparatus – known as the Price-Specie-Flow mechanism – that linked the internal money supply to automatic, international forces and relieved analysts from any worries about its determination. To Smith, contemporaries owed the extension of the "invisible hand" argument to money, credit, and finance. Later theoreticians became indebted also to Ricardo for turning the Quantity Theory into the cornerstone of monetary theory. The book will elaborate on the founding fathers' respective roles in blocking Thornton's path-breaking ideas on both monetary policy and the feasibility of a well-functioning inconvertible system.

The first part of this book discusses the analytical foundations of classical monetary theory. We survey the monetary theories of Hume, Smith, and Ricardo, which assumed convertible monetary systems where bank notes could, in principle, be exchanged for commodity-money; in other words, these were theoretical discussions of the gold and silver standards. We start our journey by exploring the state of monetary theory in the mid-eighteenth century through the important contributions of Hume. The common view that classical monetary thought was "metallist" owes much to Hume's conceptualization. We then address the major message of Adam Smith's monetary theory, namely, that the invisible hand should rule in money and the payments system as well as in credit creation and intermediation, as it should rule elsewhere. Smith's theoretical approach, though not explicitly reliant on Hume, did not depart from the conventional wisdom associated with Hume. Thus, Smith accepted convertibility, granting gold a pivotal role, and supported free trade in banking and finance. The ideas of Hume and Smith influenced many, though by no means all, of the well-known schools that followed.

In this book we argue that the classical hegemonic thinking of Hume and Smith became, in fact, a serious obstacle to the development of monetary theory and stood in direct contrast to Thornton's innovative ideas. The similar theoretical structure used by Hume and Smith concerning money and credit was typical of what came to be termed, after Schumpeter, a "monetary theory of credit." Their theories were based on the unique role of commodity-money; these theories provided the cornerstone of Ricardo's thinking, although his monetary theory must be read against the background of the Restriction Period (1797–1821), when bank notes became inconvertible, whereas Hume and Smith analyzed convertible systems. After describing the background for and the basic economic facts of the Restriction, we discuss the critical early round (1800–1802) of the post-1797 debate between the Bullionists and anti-Bullionists, and argue that important lessons relevant for later classical and modern debates concerning monetary control can already be found in this early period. We will analyze the early Bullion Debate through the ideas of two of its famous contenders, the Bullionist Walter Boyd and the anti-Bullionist Francis Baring.

The Bullion Debate provides a context in which to understand Thornton, the most outstanding monetary theoretician of the time and a pragmatic visionary neglected by economists for many years – but no longer. A major section of the book covers Thornton's innovative ideas and emphasizes his contributions both to the refutation of the invisible hand approach in banking associated with Smith, and to the critique of the Price-Specie-Flow mechanism and the Quantity Theory associated with Hume and later with Ricardo. Perhaps because Thornton's theories were ahead of their time, his impact, though significant, was only indirect; it was felt mainly through the reliance of later economists on his compelling ideas. Thornton formulated many of the elements of modern monetary theory, including a compelling argument advocating central banking; what is surprising is that his groundbreaking ideas did not enter mainstream thinking until the twentieth century. In the concluding sections of this book we try to explain why.

Returning to the major persona, we then devote some attention to Ricardo's well-known contributions to economic theory, beginning with his appearance on the scene in 1809 during the famous second round of the Bullion Debate. Ricardo helped shape classical monetary theory in the tradition of Hume. Unlike Smith, he pushed it in the direction of the Quantity Theory of Money, a well-known and deeply rooted approach. The Quantity Theory has since become such a basic tenet of monetary theory that many scholars believe it to be *the* monetary theory. We will try to convince readers (a difficult job indeed) that Ricardo's uncritical attitude toward the Quantity

Theory became the third obstacle to the development of monetary theory beyond Hume's adoption of the Price-Specie-Flow mechanism and Smith's adoption of the concept of free trade in banking matters.

The Resumption of cash (gold) payments, that is, the return to convertibility, finally took place in 1821. We will follow some aspects of the development of the monetary system from 1821 to the end of the nineteenth century. Since the Resumption, inconvertibility had become a side issue, attracting the interest of only a few economists. The focus of the post-Restriction debates concerned various reforms in banking, both in the Bank of England and the other banks. The continuing crises in the economy, in particular those of 1825 and 1836–1837, shaped the debate about country banking, small notes, and joint-stock banking as well as the major debate around the renewal of the Bank charter in 1832. This led to the famous and defining exchange between the Currency School, represented by Samuel J. Loyd, Robert Torrens, and George W. Norman, and the Banking School, represented by Thomas Tooke, John Fullarton, and James Wilson that culminated in the Currency School's victory with the 1844 Bank Act. We will also present some of the figures who belonged to neither school, like Thomas Joplin and Henry Parnell, the latter of the so-called Free Banking School. We shall see how this period brought to the forefront the tensions between Laissez-Faire, Rules, and Discretion that have played out in arguments about monetary policy ever since.

We next discuss the work of Walter Bagehot, who introduced a consistent discretionary policy role for the Bank of England. The major aims of this policy were to maintain convertibility and provide stability. However, we will argue that even though Bagehot is commonly presented as the "father" of modern central banking, his conception of the Bank's role fell short not only of a modern, active theory of monetary policy, but also of Thornton's formulations. We then turn to two more political economists, Karl Marx and Alfred Marshall. The former has been strangely neglected in the spheres of money and banking; in our discussion, we attempt to answer the question of how he fits into our story. We will see that his ideas on money and banking drew heavily from the Banking School, though his metallic view of money is tied to his real analysis and is not linked to the Currency School. We will then review the positions of Marshall and address the issue of bimetallism that bothered economists in the last quarter of the nineteenth century, and that likely had an important impact on our last, but certainly not least, scholar.

Our review of major figures ends with an examination of Wicksell's contribution to the development of monetary economics, with a particular focus on his innovative articulation of an "active central banking" concept similar both to the one raised by Thornton one hundred years earlier and to that used today. We will show how Wicksell clearly distinguished between financial systems based on commodity-money and those based on pure credit (the "pure credit system"). The achievements of Wicksell and the progress made by those before him who slowly came closer to active central banking are explained in part by the emphasis on the role of the monetary system, not just in supporting the exchange process, but also in facilitating intermediation.

By this point, we would have laid the groundwork for an analysis of the slow rise of central banking. To this end, we introduce a distinction between what we term "defensive" and "active" monetary policies, policies that differ both from one another and from what is commonly known as the central authority's role as Lender of Last Resort. I will argue that defensive central banking was first roughly articulated by the Banking School and then, famously and clearly, in the work of Walter Bagehot, who introduced a consistent discretionary policy role for the Bank of England. The major aims of this policy were to maintain convertibility and provide stability; it thus fell short of a fully developed active monetary policy such as that which we know today. Most interesting, we shall see that Thornton had already developed a theory of active central banking a full seventy years earlier than Bagehot.

The book concludes by bringing together the major themes raised by the Thornton–Banking School–Bagehot–Wicksell link, especially those concerning monetary policy. The clear distinction drawn between the two functions fulfilled by the financial sector – one in the exchange process and the other in intermediation – and the different theoretical structures developed to explain these functions are typical of these scholars. Because the two functions deal with very different processes, we emphasize the distinctions theoreticians should have drawn between them, both in Thornton's era and after. This final chapter assesses the reasons for the slow rise of central banking, distinguishing between more ideological obstacles and more theoretical ones, which together delayed an earlier understanding of the importance and contribution of intervention in banking to the economy's real performance. The explanations for the slow rise of a theory of central banking follow the tensions – ideological, theoretical, and political – throughout the nineteenth century between Laissez-Faire, Rules, and Discretion as dominant concepts for analyzing the financial system. These obstacles still seem to be with us today, as those in the field of economics struggle to understand the structural weaknesses in the modern financial system. A better understanding of the past can hopefully contribute to overcoming our present difficulties.

PART ONE

ANALYTICAL AND HISTORICAL
FOUNDATIONS

ONE

Monetary Theory circa 1750

David Hume

Introduction

David Hume's (1711–1776) writings on economics are found primarily in the collection of essays published in 1752 as *Political Discourses*. As we will see, this relatively short work became a benchmark analysis in later years; references to Hume's monetary theory appear repeatedly in later discussions of monetary issues. Hence, Hume's monetary theory and the analytical framework he used are natural starting points for our journey into the debates concerning monetary theories.[1] Although many scholars who have studied the subject (Viner [1937], Rist [1940], Schumpeter [1954]) agree that none of the major analytical tenets of Hume's thought constitute a "discovery" but rather could be found among the writings of others at the time; the impact of his monetary ideas and the unique position that they came to assume are beyond doubt. This is probably due both to Hume's other major achievements as a philosopher and historian and to the comprehensive character of his economic formulations. Most important, Hume's monetary theory distanced him from the Mercantilist perspective on money, which was still very influential in the mid-eighteenth century; he clearly contributed significantly to its decline.

The Mercantilists, as is well known, associated the wealth of a society with the stock of money it held. In particular, this school of thought held the view that not only were the precious metals a good measure for wealth,

[1] For studies of Hume's economic writings see Rotwein's (1955) detailed introduction to a volume in which Hume's economic texts can be found; Skinner (1996); Wennerlind (2001, 2005); Wennerlind and Schabas (2008) and many references therein, as well as in the more general studies of Vickers (1959, chapter 11) and Taylor (1965, part 1, chapter 3 and part 2, Chapter 3). As Rotwein (1955) observes, "monetary theory...is the most extensive and detailed part of [Hume's] political economy" (p. lv). For a more general view on moral philosophy and political economy in Scotland, see Hutchison (1988) and Skinner (1996).

but also that accumulating a bigger stock of precious metals would serve to increase the wealth of a country.[2] Hence, the Mercantilists supported policies that were intended to create a surplus in the balance of payments; the resulting surplus was supposed to be maintained consistently over time. The comprehensive interventionist measures that the Mercantilists advocated, with a view to achieving surpluses, culminated in a set of policies directed at both internal economic affairs and external trade (for a review of Mercantilism, see Angell [1926], Viner [1937], and Magnusson [1994], as well as many references therein). Hume and other critics of Mercantilism rejected the fundamental argument of the Mercantilists on two accounts: First, they proposed a different conceptualization of wealth than what the Mercantilists adopted; and second, on a more technical level, though not less influential, they pointed out a flaw concerning a logical inconsistency in the Mercantilist argument. We will address the first argument briefly in the chapter on Smith and will present later an analysis of the second critique, the "logical flaw," as Hume presented it in 1752, because developments in monetary theory cannot be understood without it.

In brief, Hume argued that it was impossible to permanently achieve a surplus in the balance of payments as the Mercantilists hoped, because the surplus would create counter-forces that would abolish the surplus. Thus, the Mercantilist policy recommendations were inherently inconsistent. While developing this critique of Mercantilism, Hume provided us with a sophisticated monetary theory that attracted the attention of contemporaries, including that of his Scottish friend Adam Smith.

"Of Money" and Commodity-Money

In "Of Money," one of the better known and often quoted of Hume's texts, the first paragraph states:

Money is not, properly speaking, one of the subjects of commerce; but only the instrument which men have agreed upon to facilitate the exchange of one commodity for another. It is none of the wheels of trade: It is the oil which renders the motion of the wheels more smooth and easy. If we consider any one kingdom by itself, it is evident, that the greater or less plenty of money is of no consequence; since the prices of commodities are always proportioned to the plenty of money ... (Hume [1752] "Of Money," p. 33; references are to Hume's texts as appear in Rotwein [1955])

---

[2]   See Thornton (2007) on Hume and a critique of Mercantilism as well as on the difficulties surrounding the definition of Mercantilism. See also Magnusson (1994) and Coleman (1969).

Thus, money serves exchange as oil helps the wheels' movements: Neither, it seems, is contributing to the creation of genuine new value or more energy via their quantity, but the presence of money, as of oil, significantly improves the functioning of their respective wheels. In fact, the two are necessary conditions for the systems to work efficiently. The usage of money in the economy's exchange process transforms the economy from a less efficient regime of exchange – barter – to the more efficient regime of a monetary economy; the existence and use of money is of course essential, but the *quantity* of money in itself has no significance in this transformation. Some commentators have perceived this conclusion as relevant only to the case of a "closed economy." However, as we will see later, Hume extended the argument about the limited importance of the quantity of money per se to the "open economy" case as well.

The relationship between Hume's philosophical and economic writings, particularly the ability to analyze the latter separately from the former, has been a subject of continuing debate over the years. Skinner (1996) quotes Rotwein's valuable introduction to *David Hume: Writings on Economics* (1955) approvingly to remind students of the importance of Hume's philosophy to his economic discussions and the dependence of his economic writings on the "science of Man."[3] Nakano (2006) similarly emphasizes the importance of Hume's "philosophy of social science in his philosophical works" to his "economic theory."[4] Hume perceived the individual as an interacting person and attributed to institutions an important role in shaping behavior. Thus, argues Nakano, "for Hume, individuals could not act together without pre-existing, socially shared symbols. ... Hume's interactionism is shown in his discussion of conventions." A convention, Hume writes,

gives us a confidence of the future regularity of their conduct: And 'tis only on the expectation of this, that our moderation and abstinence are founded. In like manner are languages gradually establish'd by human conventions without any promise. *In like manner do gold and silver become the common measures of exchange*, and are esteem'd sufficient payment for what is of hundred times their value. (Nakano quotes Hume's *A Treatise of Human Nature* [1739–1740], p. 490; emphasis mine)

On the basis of such quotes, many have described Hume as a "metallist." Wennerlind (2001, 2005), who studied Hume's philosophical and economic writings carefully, disagreed with Schumpeter (1954), Vickers

---

[3] See Skinner (1996, p. 233) quoted from Rotwein (1955, p. 4).
[4] Nakano lists Schumpeter and others as agreeing with him, but strangely does not quote Rotwein (1955). The other position, which "examine[s] Hume's economic writings" without linking the examination to his philosophy, is rejected by Nakano.

(1959), and many others who have described Hume as a "theoretical metallist." Wennerlind argues that in Book 3 of Hume's *A Treatise of Human Nature*, in a section entitled "Of the Obligation of Promises," Hume "prefigures a monetary theory." The theory seeks to explain how individuals can exchange beyond barter.[5] According to Wennerlind, Hume's solution "was a conventional agreement in which a particular symbol or sign would function as a guarantor of the promise." Moreover, "[o]nly if an efficient mechanism for keeping promises is established, can the transition from a barter economy to one with monetized markets occur" (Wennerlind 2001, p. 146). Thus, Wennerlind goes all the way to argue that "Hume's exposition moves towards a fiduciary concept of money," wherein a symbol can act as money. Though he admits that "Hume did not explicitly state that a symbol was money per se," he insists – wrongly, I believe – that Hume "proposed a monetary theory centered around fiduciary money" (2001, p. 147). Clearly, however, the money Hume discusses is gold coins. Gold coins are not considered "fiduciary money" by most accounts.

Caffenzis (2008) makes an even stronger argument than Wennerlind's against the idea that Hume based his monetary theory on commodity-money (and therefore against Hume as a metallist). Caffenzis draws on Hume's philosophical distinctions between natural and artificial fictions to make the case that for Hume, the differences between metallic money and paper money are "philosophical" rather than just "technical" (p. 165). Hume describes metallic money as "fictitious" whereas paper money earns the title "counterfeit." The former results from conventions whereas the latter results from promises, distinctions that are rooted in Hume's general philosophy of Man. Hence, both lead, with due differences, to a view of the monetary, nonbarter economy as a fiduciary – rather than metal-based – monetary system. In any case, even Wennerlind accepts that Hume was a "practical metallist," if not a "theoretical" one.[6] As we shall argue later, in Hume's monetary theory, "money" cannot be understood unless it functions in international transactions, a sphere in which fiduciary money did not function and was not accepted. According to Hume, the use of money transforms society and the economy from barter to a monetary economy wherein commerce becomes well developed. Commerce is important to the sovereign, to individuals, and to the public at large:

---

[5] Although problems already exist in a nonpure barter economy when "trading goods of unequal value, services to be discharged in the future, and general, as opposed to particular, commodities." See Wennerlind (2001, p. 143).

[6] For a somewhat different version, closer to what we present here, see Wennerlind (2008, pp. 108–113).

The greatness of a state, and the happiness of its subjects, how independent soever they may be supposed in some respects, are commonly allowed to be inseparable with regard to commerce; and as private men receive greater security, in the possession of their trade and riches, from the power of the public, so the public becomes powerful in proportion to the opulence and extensive commerce of private men. ("Of Commerce," p. 5)

Thus commerce, both internally and internationally, is a key concept in understanding the process of wealth creation, and the role of money in promoting commerce is crucial. However, Hume argues that the role played by the quantity of money in the economy, particularly in the process of wealth creation, had been misunderstood by the Mercantilists. An increase in money in a society will only change the prices of commodities, which are in turn determined as a ratio of, or at least by the quantity of, money. The level of prices, though, is of no significance to the wealth of a nation; the "real" factors, in modern jargon, are important: the number of people, their industry, and so forth. These are some of Hume's core ideas; however, the opening statement in "Of Money" adds many qualifications. Some of the famous, long-standing disagreements concerning Hume's monetary thought concern these qualifications, among them Hume's stance on the neutrality of money. Further on in this study, we will examine Hume's writings to see whether or not we can find statements concerning the long-term and short-term neutrality of money.

Hume's analysis in "Of Money" continues with his observations concerning open economies, and more specifically with how money and prices affect relations between countries that are at different stages of development. The more developed nation has an advantage in trade "because of the superior industry and skill ... which enable them to trade on so much smaller profits":

But these advantages are compensated, in some measure, by the low price of labor in every nation which has not an extensive commerce, and does not much abound in gold and silver. Manufactures, therefore gradually shift their places, leaving those countries and provinces which they have already enriched, and flying to others, whither they are allured by the cheapness of provisions and labour; till they have enriched these also, and are again banished by the same causes. And, in general, we may observe, that the dearness of every thing, *from plenty of money,* is a disadvantage, which attends an established commerce, and sets bounds to it in every country, by enabling the poorer states to undersell the richer in all foreign markets. ("Of Money," pp. 34–35; emphasis added)

In both "Of Commerce" and "Of Money," as in his other writings, Hume uses economic history to strengthen and support his analytical arguments. The analysis is dynamic and relates to complex changes over time in various

economic variables in the different economies. Thus, the move from barter to a monetary economy is presented as of utmost importance for commerce and development, although the specific quantity of money, as we
have argued, is of little or even no importance. The disadvantages to the
rich countries caused by high prices raised doubts in Hume's mind as to the
benefits of paper money and banking, and his analysis here reveals some of
his fundamental thinking on monetary theory:

> This has made me entertain a doubt concerning the benefit of *banks* and *paper-
> credit*, which are so generally esteemed advantageous to every nation. That provi-
> sions and labour should become dear by the encrease of trade and money, is, in
> many respects, an inconvenience; but an inconvenience that is unavoidable, and
> the effect of that public wealth and prosperity which are the end of all our wishes.
> It is compensated by the advantages, which we reap from the possession of these
> precious metals, and the weight, which they give the nation in all foreign wars and
> negociations. But there appears no reason for encreasing that inconvenience by a
> counterfeit money, which foreigners will not accept of in any payment, and which
> any great disorder in the state will reduce to nothing. ("Of Money," p. 35)

Thus, his argument as to the disadvantages of paper-credit and banks draws
on paper-credit being "counterfeit money," not acceptable in international
transactions and whose value depends upon the stability of the state. Hume
does not deny the advantages of banks, especially for those who have money
and seek secure and cheap methods of transferring it. Thus, he distinguishes
between "public" and "private" banking, explaining that if there is no public
bank to supply the demand for paper-credit, then a private bank will step
in.[7] However, the analysis of society as a whole – the macroeconomic analysis – is the major issue in "Of Money":

> But to endeavour artificially to encrease such a credit, can never be the interest of
> any trading nation; but must lay them under disadvantages, by encreasing money
> beyond its natural proportion to labour and commodities, and thereby heightening
> their price to the merchant and manufacturer. And in this view, it must be allowed,
> that no bank could be more advantageous, than such a one as locked up all the
> money it received, and never augmented the circulating coin, as is usual, by return-
> ing part of its treasure into commerce. A public bank, by this expedient, might
> cut off much of the dealings of private bankers and money-jobbers; and though
> the state bore the charge of salaries to the directors and tellers of this bank (for,

---

[7] "There are, it is true, many people in every rich state, who having large sums of money, would
prefer paper with good security; as being of more easy transport and more safe custody. If
the public provide not a bank, private bankers will take advantage of this circumstance; as
the goldsmiths formerly did in LONDON, or as the bankers do at present in DUBLIN: And
therefore it is better, it may be thought, that a public company should enjoy the benefit of that
paper-credit, which always will have place in every opulent kingdom" ("Of Money," p. 35).

according to the preceding supposition, it would have no profit from its dealings), the national advantage, resulting from the low price of labour and the destruction of paper-credit, would be a sufficient compensation. Not to mention, that so large a sum, lying ready at command, would be a convenience in times of great public danger and distress; and what part of it was used might be replaced at leisure, when peace and tranquility was restored to the nation. ("Of Money," pp. 35–36)

The argument here is about "public interest" and how it will be served; the considerations are not motivated by profit. The public bank will present a "national advantage" because it will keep prices at a lower level and provide security in the form of a large reserve in times of danger. Thus, although Hume has been associated with a monetary approach characterized by "automatism," we shall see that a hint at policy and a clear distinction between private and public interests can be found in his writings.

Hume concludes "Of Money" with what he describes as "two observations, which may, perhaps, serve to employ the thought of our speculative politicians." The first observation relates to the debate on the impact money may have on the economy. It starts with what we may call a closed economy ("a nation within itself"; see Note 8), where money plays the role of a measure of value, and the level of prices depends on the quantity of money relative to transactions and is only nominally important.[8] However, after touching on the closed economy, Hume immediately goes on to the more realistic and interesting case of the open economy, a case that provides the essential framework for his monetary analysis. He mentions the historical record that shows more gold coming from the newly discovered gold mines in America leading to the creation of more wealth, that is, "real" and not just "nominal" effect:

Since the discovery of the mines in AMERICA, industry has encreased in all the nations of EUROPE, except in the possessors of those mines; and this may justly be ascribed, amongst other reasons, to the encrease of gold and silver. Accordingly we find, that, in every kingdom, into which money begins to flow in greater

---

[8] "It was a shrewd observation of ANACHARSIS the SCYTHIAN, who had never seen money in his own country, that gold and silver seemed to him of no use to the GREEKS, but to assist them in numeration and arithmetic. It is indeed evident, that money is nothing but the representation of labour and commodities, and serves only as a method of rating or estimating them. Where coin is in greater plenty; as a greater quantity of it is required to represent the same quantity of goods; it can have no effect, either good or bad, taking a nation within itself; any more than it would make an alteration on a merchant's books, if, instead of the ARABIAN method of notation, which requires few characters, he should make use of the ROMAN, which requires a great many. Nay, the greater quantity of money, like the ROMAN characters, is rather inconvenient, and requires greater trouble both to keep and transport it" ("Of Money," pp. 36–37).

abundance than formerly, every thing takes a new face: labour and industry gain life; the merchant becomes more enterprising, the manufacturer more diligent and skilful, and even the farmer follows his plough with greater alacrity and attention. This is not easily to be accounted for, if we consider only the influence which a greater abundance of coin has in the kingdom itself, by heightening the price of Commodities, and obliging every one to pay a greater number of these little yellow or white pieces for every thing he purchases. And as to foreign trade, it appears that great plenty of money is rather disadvantageous, by raising the price of every kind of labour.

To account, then, for this phenomenon, we must consider, that though the high price of commodities be a necessary consequence of the encrease of gold and silver, yet it follows not immediately upon that encrease; but some time is required before the money circulates through the whole state, and makes its effect be felt on all ranks of people. At first, no alteration is perceived; by degrees the price rises, first of one commodity, then of another; till the whole at last reaches a just proportion with the new quantity of specie which is in the kingdom. In my opinion, it is only in this interval or intermediate situation, between the acquisition of money and rise of prices, that the encreasing quantity of gold and silver is favourable to industry. ("Of Money," pp. 37–38)

This discussion is the source for the argument that Hume advocated the non-neutrality of money in the short run, although it is only in the context of the discussion of the open economy that Hume raises this argument. The mechanism that makes this non-neutrality work relates to conditions typical of an economy out of equilibrium.[9] Thus, although Hume starts the analysis by emphasizing the view that the effect of more (or less) money on prices is nominal, in the oft-quoted text, Hume raises the possibility that the changes in the quantity of money will have some "real" effects. This

---

[9] "When any quantity of money is imported into a nation, it is not at first dispersed into many hands; but is confined to the coffers of a few persons, who immediately seek to employ it to advantage. Here are a set of manufacturers or merchants, we shall suppose, who have received returns of gold and silver for goods which they sent to CADIZ. They are thereby enabled to employ more workmen than formerly, who never dream of demanding higher wages, but are glad of employment from such good paymasters. If workmen become scarce, the manufacturer gives higher wages, but at first requires an encrease of labour; and this is willingly submitted to by the artisan, who can now eat and drink better, to compensate his additional toil and fatigue. He carries his money to market, where he, finds every thing at the same price as formerly, but returns with greater quantity and of better kinds, for the use of his family. The farmer and gardener, finding, that all their commodities are taken off, apply themselves with alacrity to the raising more; and at the same time can afford to take better and more cloths from their tradesmen, whose price is the same as formerly, and their industry only whetted by so much new gain. It is easy to trace the money in its progress through the whole commonwealth; where we shall find, that it must first quicken the diligence of every individual, before it encrease the price of labour" ("Of Money," p. 38). See also Perlman (1987) for a discussion of the transitory effects of changes in the quantity of money discussed in the quoted passage.

aspect of his thoughts concerning the neutrality of money in the short run
has received repeated contradictory interpretations.

The Price-Specie-Flow Mechanism

The second observation that Hume makes in the conclusion of "Of Money"
concerns a more detailed analysis of the determination of prices in a monetary
economy. On the one hand, one has to observe the volume of transactions
that are part of the monetary exchange, that is, that are characterized by the
exchange of money for commodities; on the other hand, one has to assess the
quantity of effective money, that is, that money that is not hoarded but that
participates in the exchange process. An overly restricted monetary economy
leads to difficulties for the sovereign in raising taxes. It is also reflected sometimes in high prices due to the relation between money and restricted usages:

It is the proportion between the circulating money, and the commodities in the market, which determines the prices. Goods, that are consumed at home, or exchanged
with other goods in the neighbourhood, never come to market; they affect not in the
least the current specie; with regard to it they are as if totally annihilated; and consequently this method of using them sinks the proportion on the side of the commodities, and encreases the prices. But after money enters into all contracts and sales, and
is every where the measure of exchange, the same national cash has a much greater
task to perform; all commodities are then in the market; the sphere of circulation is
enlarged; it is the same case as if that individual sum were to serve a larger kingdom;
and therefore, the proportion being here lessened on the side of the money, every
thing must become cheaper, and the prices gradually fall. ("Of Money," p. 43)

The most important part of Hume's monetary analysis is contained in "Of
the Balance of Trade." There Hume presents what is known as the Price-
Specie-Flow mechanism, or sometimes as the Quantity Theory Price-
Specie-Flow (QT PSF) mechanism.[10] This argument considers the long-run,
steady-state conditions of countries that are partners in trade. In cases of
imbalances – surpluses or deficits – in the balance of trade, these countries
use money that is accepted internationally, usually in a form that represents coins, to pay the imbalances. When these flows passed in or out of a

---

[10] This argument first appeared in a letter to Montesquieu. "It appears that we are, in England,
too much concerned about the balance of trade. It is difficult for a loss of balance to reach
the point where it will do considerable harm to a nation. If half the money in England were
suddenly destroyed, labour and goods would suddenly become so cheap that there would
suddenly follow a great quantity of exports which would attract to us the money of all our
neighbours. If half the money which is in England were suddenly doubled, goods would
suddenly become more expensive, imports would rise to the disadvantage of exports and

country's economy, they would usually join that country's internal money supply. Under such an arrangement, argues Hume, automatic forces would guarantee that there would be neither a surplus nor a deficit in the balance of payments in the long run. Along the way to this state of affairs, the system would also automatically allocate the quantity of money in the world and dictate the "right" level of prices for all partners in trade.

Let us elaborate a little on this mechanism. The chain of causes and effects relates to several important economic processes. Let us assume that England has a surplus in the balance of trade. Precious metals will cover the gap, flowing from the Rest of the World to England. Prices in terms of gold will rise in England (and decrease in the Rest of the World). The changing relative prices will induce England to import more and export less. Hence, the surplus balance of payments will start to disappear and the process will continue until the surplus vanishes completely:

> Suppose four-fifths of all the money in GREAT BRITAIN to be annihilated in one night, and the nation reduced to the same condition, with regard to specie, as in the reigns of the HARRYS and EDWARDS, what would be the consequence? Must not the price of all labour and commodities sink in proportion, and every thing be sold as cheap as they were in those ages? What nation could then dispute with us in any foreign market, or pretend to navigate or to sell manufactures at the same price, which to us would afford sufficient profit? In how little time, therefore, must this bring back the money which we had lost, and raise us to the level of all the neighbouring nations? Where, after we have arrived, we immediately lose the advantage of the cheapness of labour and commodities; and the farther flowing in of money is stopped by our fulness and repletion. ("Of the Balance of Trade," pp. 62–63)

The argument is in favor of free trade, which leaves international trade and internal trade to regulate themselves and does not worry about the resulting quantities of money in any of the participants to trade. The assumption is that payments made across national borders – that is, for transactions between countries – use "money," which is accepted in international trade and at the same time constitutes the local medium of exchange. That money is gold and silver in Hume's analysis and, like water, can be kept only at its

our money would be spread among all our neighbours. It does not seem that money, any more than water, can be raised or lowered anywhere much beyond the level it has in places where communication is open, but that it must rise and fall in proportion to the goods and labour contained in each state" (April 10, 1749). See Rotwein (1955, p. lvi and p. 188). See also Cesarano (1998) on both the history of the debate and the role of the concept of "One-Price." However, as Humphrey (1999) correctly states, Cessarano's view is not the standard view; the latter maintains that the Price-Specie-Flow mechanism, working through changes in price levels in the partners to trade, correctly captures Hume's monetary thinking.

"proper level" everywhere. As with water, the only possibility for money to "be raised above the level of surrounding element" is "if the communication be cut off" (p. 64). That is, only by separating themselves from one another can countries avoid the forces that determine their quantities of money, price levels, and the equilibrating pressures that push toward a long-run (zero) balance of trade.

However, Hume discusses two cases where the level of money can be changed from its "natural level": One case is that of sinking its level, and the other is raising it. The former, which clarifies Hume's position on paper money and banking, is described thus:

I scarcely know any method of sinking money below its level, but those institutions of banks, funds, and paper-credit, which are so much practised in this kingdom. These render paper equivalent to money, circulate it throughout the whole state, make it supply the place of gold and silver, raise proportionably the price of labour and commodities, and by that means either banish a great part of those precious metals, or prevent their farther encrease. What can be more shortsighted than our reasonings on this head? We fancy, because an individual would be much richer, were his stock of money doubled, that the same good effect would follow were the money of every one encreased; not considering, that this would raise as much the price of every commodity, and reduce every man, in time, to the same condition as before. It is only in our public negociations and transactions with foreigners, that a greater stock of money is advantageous; and as our paper is there absolutely insignificant, we feel, by its means, all the ill effects arising from a great abundance of money, without reaping any of the advantages. ("Of the Balance of Trade", pp. 67–68)

This argument is of utmost importance. First, it is an early argument against the fallacy of composition and in favor of the need to think differently when analyzing private and general cases. Considerations that are true from an individual perspective, Hume argues, are not always true when considering society at large. Thus, the crucial differences between arguments that are true for an individual and the logic of the same argument when extended to society or the overall economy – what moderns will call "macroeconomic" considerations – are clear to Hume. The argument is also a call against interference in the working of the markets. The "paper" seems to be equivalent to "money," but it is not, certainly not from the economy's real perspective, as opposed to the nominal individual perspective. For society at large, doubling the riches in this way will result, "in time," in higher prices and a return "to the same conditions as before." Thus, more money can have advantages in our relations with other countries, but more paper, though it seems to the individual to be equivalent to having more money, cannot contribute to the country.

Suppose that there are 12 millions of paper, which circulate in the kingdom as money, (for we are not to imagine, that all our enormous funds are employed in that shape) and suppose the real cash of the kingdom to be 18 millions: Here is a state which is found by experience to be able to hold a stock of 30 millions. I say, if it be able to hold it, it must of necessity have acquired it in gold and silver, had we not obstructed the entrance of these metals by this new invention of paper. *Whence would it have acquired that sum?* From all the kingdoms of the world. *But why?* Because, if you remove these 12 millions, money in this state is below its level, compared with our neighbours; and we must immediately draw from all of them, till we be full and saturate, so to speak, and can hold no more. By our present politics, we are as careful to stuff the nation with this fine commodity of bank-bills and chequer-notes, as if we were afraid of being overburthened with the precious metals. ("Of the Balance of Trade," pp. 68–69)

Again, money's best form is in the shape of the precious metals and not notes, because the former is accepted internationally. After entering a country, the gold and silver can be used in the internal circulation or be hoarded outside the exchange process. According to Hume, the examples of France, Genoa, and the English colonies, before paper money had been introduced to them, prove the advantage of money, that is, the precious metals.[11] Hume's argument emphasizes the importance and contribution of free trade to the creation of wealth and that of money in advancing trade. Free trade is advantageous to all partners in trade: those who have higher prices as well as those who face lower prices.

Moreover, despite the Mercantilists' arguments, there is no point in trying to increase the trade balance:

But are there not frequent instances, you will say, of states and kingdoms, which were formerly rich and opulent, and are now poor and beggarly? Has not the money left them, with which they formerly abounded? I answer, If they lose their trade, industry, and people, they cannot expect to keep their gold and silver: For these precious metals will hold proportion to the former advantages. ... In short, a government has great reason to preserve with care its people and its manufactures. Its money, it may safely trust to the course of human affairs, without fear or jealousy. Or if it ever give attention to this latter circumstance, it ought only to be so far as it affects the former. (ibid., pp. 76–77)

Thus, the Mercantilist policies are doomed to fail. Both trade and the determination of the quantity of money should be left to the "course of

---

[11] "What pity LYCURGUS did not think of paper-credit, when he wanted to banish gold and silver from SPARTA! It would have served his purpose better than the lumps of iron he made use of as money; and would also have prevented more effectually all commerce with strangers, as being of so much less real and intrinsic value" ("Of the Balance of Trade," p. 70).

human affairs," to the free exchanges between traders who will thus bring riches:

From these principles we may learn what judgment we ought to form of those num-
berless bars, obstructions, and imposts, which all nations of EUROPE, and none
more than ENGLAND, have put upon trade; from an exorbitant desire of amassing
money, which never will heap up beyond its level, while it circulates; or from an
ill-grounded apprehension of losing their specie, which never will sink below it.
Could any thing scatter our riches, it would be such impolitic contrivances. But
this general ill effect, however, results from them, that they deprive neighbouring
nations of that free communication and exchange which the Author of the world
has intended, by giving them soils, climates, and geniuses, so different from each
other. (ibid., p. 75)

A Note on Noncommodity-Money

Hume's position concerning paper-credit and banking, issues on which we
will elaborate in later chapters, deserves more attention. In an important
section of "Of the Balance of Trade" that was added in 1764, twelve years
after the essay was first published, after blaming paper-credit for poten-
tially obstructing trade due to its lack of "intrinsic value" (see p. 70, note 7),
Hume admits that there are also some advantages to paper-credit and banking. Though it is true that they manage to replace "specie and bullion" and
"whoever looks no farther than this circumstance does well to condemn
them," paper-credit and banking contribute to the economy by fulfilling a
positive function in the economy:

It is well known of what advantage it is to a merchant to be able to discount his bills
upon occasion; and every thing that facilitates this species of traffic is favourable to
the general commerce of a state. But private bankers are enabled to give such credit
by the credit they receive from the depositing of money in their shops; and the bank
of ENGLAND in the same manner, from the liberty it has to issue its notes in all
payments. There was an invention of this kind, which was fallen upon some years
ago by the banks of EDINBURGH; and which, as it is one of the most ingenious
ideas that has been executed in commerce, has also been thought advantageous to
SCOTLAND. It is there called a BANK-CREDIT; and is of this nature. A man goes
to the bank and finds surety to the amount, we shall suppose, of a thousand pounds.
This money, or any part of it, he has the liberty of drawing out whenever he pleases,
and he only pays the ordinary interest for it, while it is in his hands. He may, when
he pleases, repay any sum so small as twenty pounds, and the interest is discounted
from the very day of the repayment. The advantages, resulting from this contrivance,
are manifold. As a man may find surety nearly to the amount of his substance, and his
bank-credit is equivalent to ready money, a merchant does hereby in a manner coin

his houses, his household furniture, the goods in his warehouse, the foreign debts due
to him, his ships at sea; and can, upon occasion, employ them in all payments, as if
they were the current money of the country. If a man borrow a thousand pounds from
a private hand, besides that it is not always to be found when required, he pays interest
for it, whether he be using it or not: His bank-credit costs him nothing except during
the very moment, in which it is of service to him: And this circumstance is of equal
advantage as if he had borrowed money at much lower interest. Merchants, likewise,
from this invention, acquire a great facility in supporting each other's credit, which
is a considerable security against bankruptcies. A man, when his own bank-credit is
exhausted, goes to any of his neighbours who is not in the same condition; and he gets
the money, which he replaces at his convenience. (ibid., 70–71)[12]

These arguments that focus on some of the advantages brought by the use
of paper-credit and banking address some of the important debates in monetary theory that we will survey. Hume hints first, briefly, at the role banks
play in *intermediation*: in transferring sums of money from those interested
in using them only in the future to those who desire to use them now. The
ability of merchants to discount bills and receive credit in the form of money
and Bank of England notes facilitates commerce. This advantage is derived
from the banks' role in receiving and allocating credit. The banks carry out
intermediation in a more efficient manner than do private loans between the
interested individuals. In this way, banks also create liquidity in the economy because the individual can, in Hume's language, "coin his house," thus
enabling individuals to monetize their various assets. Moreover, the banks
can create new, flexible liabilities, "bank-credit," that are equivalent to "ready
money" and cost less than other methods for raising funds. The social network that banks create and the role that confidence among merchants can
play in preventing bankruptcies, as outlined earlier, present a different attitude toward the banking system than that ascribed to Hume in some of the
secondary texts, which emphasize his negative view of banking and credit.
Thus, Hume observed, "these questions of trade and money are extremely
complicated," and because banks may also contribute to the economy, it is
possible to "represent the advantages of paper-credit and banks to be superior to their disadvantages" (p. 70).

Hume concludes that institutions such as banks that create new assets and
liabilities, including paper-credit, do contribute to the economy; however, it
is important to remember that he maintains a metallist position throughout
the different discussions, arguing that money would do better to take the
form of the precious metals. In his assessment of the banks, one can see that

---

[12] The paragraph had been added to the 1764 edition. See Rotwein's (1955) note on p. 70 and
a "Note on the Text," p. 218.

an important criterion for good money is that it is made of metals, although in this context, one can accept that Hume is a moderate metallist:

That they [banks] banish specie and bullion from a state is undoubtedly true; and whoever looks no farther than this circumstance does well to condemn them; but specie and bullion are not of so great consequence as not to admit of a compensation, and even an overbalance from the encrease of industry and of credit, which may be promoted by the right use of paper-money. (ibid., p. 70)

Thus, the adherence to metal as the preferred form of money lies in its being accepted internally and internationally; that is, the belief that the receiver will be able to pass it in due course without its losing value.[13] Both forms of money, metallic and nonmetallic, reflect conventions, but the metallic one is significantly less exposed to debasements in value. In a letter to Morellet, Hume writes: "It is true, money must always be made of some materials, which have intrinsic value, otherwise it would be multiplied without end, and would sink to nothing" (Hume to Morellet, July 10,1769, Rotwein [1955, p. 214]). Had the issuers been clever and perceptive about avoiding such multiplications, there is no reason to assume that nonmetallic money would not become the "base coin, called billon, in France." However, this is not the case; the issuers issue paper "without end, and thereby discredited the currency" (Rotwein, p. 215).

On the Rate of Interest

The importance of intermediation in the economy and its relation to money is further explained in Hume's "Of Interest." The main point of this text is to lay out the causes that determine the rate of interest, and especially to clarify that the quantity of money was *not* one of these causes. More money, whether silver or gold, would change the prices of commodities and labor but not the rate of interest. The rate of interest is determined by the demand and supply for loans and is related to the rate of profit. Although Hume is very careful to emphasize the rate of profit as a complex relation with both directions of influence possible, the interest rate is determined by more than the rate of profit:

High interest arises from *three* circumstances: A great demand for borrowing; little riches to supply that demand; and great profits arising from commerce: And these circumstances are a clear proof of the small advance of commerce and industry, not of the scarcity of gold and silver. Low interest, on the other hand, proceeds from the three opposite circumstances: A small demand for borrowing; great riches to supply

---

[13] See Paganelli (2009).

that demand; and small profits arising from commerce: And these circumstances are all connected together, and proceed from the encrease of industry and commerce, not of gold and silver. ("Of Interest," p.49)

Thus, the demand and supply for loans, not the exchange process of commodities or the quantity of money, is responsible for the determination of the rate of interest. Rising economic activity in society, more commerce, is associated with lower interest rates and lower profits, these "two events, that mutually forward each other, and are both originally derived from that extensive commerce."

Those who have asserted, that the plenty of money was the cause of low interest, seem to have taken a collateral effect for a cause; since the same industry, which sinks the interest, commonly acquires great abundance of the precious metals. A variety of fine manufactures, with vigilant enterprising merchants, will soon draw money to a state, if it be any where to be found in the world. The same cause, by multiplying the conveniencies of life, and encreasing industry, collects great riches into the hands of persons, who are not proprietors of land, and produces, by that means, a lowness of interest. But though both these effects, plenty of money and low interest, naturally arise from commerce and industry, they are altogether independent of each other. ("Of Interest," p. 56)

The dynamics of the changes – the multiple interactions over time between demand and supply for loans, the rate of profit, and the rate of interest – are here analyzed carefully. Hume's analysis of these issues sheds light on his methodological position concerning causality.

Summary

To summarize, Hume's analysis assumes that money functions both in the internal- and international-payments systems. Thus, its ideal form is that of the precious metals; one could think, like Hume, of coins as money. This argument is based on the Quantity Theory of money, wherein the more abstract formulations of the quantity of coins circulating internally in the economy "causes" the price level, measured in these same coins. The price level, for its part, causes changes in the balance of payments through its effect on both exports and imports, thus linking the internal monetary circulation with the balance of international payments. Hence, Hume formulates what came to be known as the famous Price-Specie-Flow mechanism which clearly reappeared years later as the modern monetary approach to the balance of payments. We will return to this issue in Chapter 3 on Smith.

In the various texts Hume wrote, his analysis goes beyond the simplified chain of causalities just described to include more sophisticated arguments. Thus, for example, the neutrality of money – the idea that money has no real effects on the real economy – was modified to include some short-term non-neutralities. Similarly, the perfect links between international and internal monetary aggregates are more complex, with hoards of other factors intervening in the process. Hume also addressed nonbasic forms of money like the bank notes and bank credit discussed earlier. However, the analytical framework that abstracted from these complications continued to be the basic message of Hume's monetary theory. The discussions emphasized the analysis of payments in the economy internally and internationally. The references to intermediation, as we have seen, brought some interesting observations, but they were neither fully developed nor integrated with the Quantity Theory Price-Specie-Flow mechanism.

According to Hume, monetary affairs can be left in the hands of markets. As the last sentence in "Of the Balance of Trade" states, the government "may safely trust [money] to the course of human affairs …." Thus, both the right quantity of money in each trading country and the price level will be determined by international markets. Automatic forces will take care of any changes, and the equilibrating mechanisms need not be the object of any policies. This conclusion that precluded any need to worry about monetary policy, which in fact made the concept of monetary policy void, was a Humean message that shaped monetary thinking in the second half of the eighteenth century.

Thus, monetary theory in the mid-eighteenth century evolved mainly as a critique of Mercantilist ideas. The Mercantilist analytical arguments focused on the links between wealth, international trade, and the precious metals. As Fetter remarked, "Apparently writers with mercantilist leanings were so concerned with the narrower problem of securing gold and silver from other nations that they rarely asked the more fundamental question of the world-wide adequacy of gold and silver to serve as a monetary standard" (1965, p 3). That the anti-Mercantilists, among them the "philosophers, like Hume and Smith, with their emphasis on economic growth," did not worry as well about the "world supply of gold and silver" and believed that "supply needed for monetary purposes would come in the ordinary course of trade" marked, according to Fetter, the new consensus. In Chapter 2 we will present the financial system of Britain in the second half of the eighteenth century. In Chapter 3 we will see how Hume's close friend, Adam Smith, who knew him well and appreciated his views, related to these issues.

TWO

Mid-Eighteenth-Century British Financial System

David Hume's monetary analysis described in Chapter 1 relates to the British financial system, but is of a general and abstract nature. In this chapter, we will present a brief overview of the British financial system in the mid-eighteenth century that will prepare the ground for the discussion of Adam Smith's monetary thinking in Chapter 3. The financial system in the United Kingdom was an important and intriguing feature of the fascinating British economic story known throughout the world in later years as the Industrial Revolution. One cannot fully understand the Industrial Revolution without considering its links with British finance.[1] More important in the present context, it will be impossible to assess Smith without first describing the financial system.

The British financial system was unique in performing two functions: providing payments services that facilitated a relatively efficient exchange process and contributing to an impressive rise of social intermediation. Hume and, as we shall see, Smith well understood the importance of transforming a barter economy into a monetary one as well as the role of payments services in this process. Intermediation, a more advanced function of the financial system that is not necessarily related to payments services, makes it possible not only to match buyers and sellers with ease, but also to bring surplus economic units together with those who are currently short of funds. In other words, the financial system enables transactions in which financial assets rather than commodities are exchanged (we will elaborate further on these two functions in Chapters 4 and 9).

---

[1] For a comprehensive overview of the role of finance in the Industrial Revolution, see Neal (1990) and Cameron (1967); for more general views on the Industrial Revolution see Mokyr (1985, 1993) and references therein.

As exchange became more complex in the industrial world, the means of exchange gradually changed. The use of commodities such as salt, gold, or silver as a means of payment gave way to an exchange technology where both commodities and means of payment that were not commodities were used. The latter had value only in hoarding or as a medium of exchange, but they did not in themselves have "use-value." Initially, people were tempted to use these noncommodity means of payment because interest on them was paid to the holder. This was important because their convenience and security in comparison, for example, with gold were not in themselves sufficient to induce their usage. The process of developing alternative means of payment can be illustrated by the following example: During the seventeenth century, there was a growing use of Tallies. Tallies were sealed logs of wood that were used as receipts for tax payments. They were cut into two pieces, one of which was given to the taxpayer while the other remained in the vaults of the Exchequer. When the king needed a loan, he gave Tallies, which were then used instead of commodity-money like gold for paying taxes. Meanwhile, people began to use the Tallies as means of payment both to the king (who "printed" them) and to members of the public, by endorsement on the wood. Thus, wooden logs, not "convertible" to money and which at first were good only for paying taxes, came to function as money.[2]

In 1667, Parliament decided to help the king by issuing paper receipts, known as Exchequer orders, instead of the original wooden ones. These receipts were the first government-issued papers to be used as a means of payment. Confidence in them was based on the government's promise to repay them with interest in their order of issue. It is interesting to find an early hint of the Restriction Period – begun in 1797 with a decision not to pay bank notes in gold – in the 1672 government decision to postpone payments of Exchequer orders for twelve months because of the war.[3] This act was known as the "stoppage of the Exchequer." The result of this stoppage was not just a monetary crisis, but a real crisis. A run on the banks caused them to close down and trade came to a standstill. After the crisis, there was a growing tendency to return to the wooden Tallies, as if they were closer to hard cash, a reaction that was to repeat itself in subsequent crises, but not, as we shall see, in 1797. The Tallies and their descendants, the Exchequer bills, the Goldsmiths' receipts, and the Running Cash, were

---

[2] For a comprehensive review of the rise of English money, see Feavearyear (1931), especially chapter 7.
[3] More on the Restriction in Part II of the book.

all interest-bearing securities. However, with time, means of payment no longer bore interest. The convenience in using them was sufficient to attract people to use them.[4]

The banking system was at the core of British finance, though one should also mention the insurance industry, the stock exchange, and many private, noninstitutional arrangements that created a rich financial network.[5] The various elements in the system grew out of the unique British legal structure that ranged between strictly private, individualistic property rights, and a set of more complicated joint ownerships, including joint stocks. Although full treatment of this important legal background is beyond the scope of the present book, we will review briefly some of the basic legal characteristics of the financial institutions.

There were three different types of banks active in England in the mid-eighteenth century, each characterized by different legal arrangements. The *Bank of England* (known in short as "the Bank," as many commentators addressed it) was a joint-stock bank based in London, where it enjoyed by charter a monopoly over issuing bank notes. All the other London banks were privately owned, had no more than six partners, and had no right to issue bank notes. The *country banks* on the other hand, which were those banks located outside a sixty-five-mile range from London (where the Bank of England enjoyed a monopoly), were also privately owned and had no more than six partners, but they could issue notes. While similar in many other respects – for example, in that they all accepted deposits and gave loans – each of these types of bank played different roles in the financial system, which can best be explained by their different histories.[6]

---

[4]   Feavearyear (1931), still one of the best studies of British banking, describes this process as follows: "The convenience of paper money began to be a sufficient inducement for people to use it. The adjustments necessary to allow for accrued interest and the inevitable fluctuations of value discouraged the use of securities as currency. The issue of Bank of England notes bearing interest was a retrogressive measure which was soon abandoned. The use of Exchequer bills as currency and the issue of interest-bearing notes by some private banks lingered on to the end of the 18th Century and then died out." See Chapter 4 for more on Private Debt Certificates (PDCs).

[5]   On the financial system and the Industrial Revolution, see Neal (1990); Atack and Neal (2009); On the Stock Exchange, see Morgan and Thomas (1962).

[6]   On the Bank of England, see Clapham (1944), Sayers (1976), and Roberts and Kynaston (1995), where one can find the bank in appendix 1: "Chronology" and in appendix 2: "Governors, Directors, and Serving Officials." On the banking system more generally, see Feavearyear (1931), Fetter (1965), and Wood (2005); on country banking, see Pressnell (1956); on Scottish banking, see Checkland (1975), Munn (1981), and Saville (1996); on Irish banking, see Fetter (1955).

The Bank of England was founded in 1694 in order to raise a loan for the king. It started with capital of 1.2 million pounds, 720,000 of which were raised in cash by the merchants. The rest were in Sealed Bills: one-thousand-pound paper notes stamped with the Bank's corporate seal, which were used by the government to pay for its expenditure. Soon after its establishment, the Bank of England began to buy short-term securities and received permission to print notes that were not sealed, but were endorsed by the cashier as confirmation of a deposit in the bank. These notes were equivalent to what were known as the Goldsmiths' receipts: proofs of deposits given by the gold merchants to customers who deposited gold with them. Examination of the Bank's methods reveals that these endorsed notes were also used to finance the government by inflating the currency; Bank notes were primarily suited for large transactions. In small transactions, it was still common to use gold, silver, or copper coins.

It is important to remember that in the eighteenth century, the Bank of England was the only bank that was a joint-stock company; all other banks were limited by law to a maximum of six partners. In London, the Bank of England was the only bank to issue notes, which were issued against gold or against securities. In 1775, the issuing of notes under one pound was forbidden; in 1777, it was forbidden to issue notes under five pounds. This was done to "defend the poor" (see Chapter 3 in which we discuss Smith's thinking on low-denomination notes); the effect was an almost total stoppage of the use of notes of low denominations until 1797, while the Bank of England continued to redeem its notes in specie. One should note that the arrangements were different in the Bank of Amsterdam.[7] There, when one was given a receipt against a deposit in gold, it was impossible to withdraw the gold from the Bank. In other words, the Bank of Amsterdam's notes were really substitutes for gold because it kept a 100 percent reserve ratio. The ratios of banks of issue like the Bank of England were different, and thus the confusion between money and credit in England was greater than on the Continent.

London's private banks were primarily concerned with managing deposits and arranging discounts both for London's merchants and for the country banks. The private banks' assets consisted of public and private securities, Bank of England notes, specie, and gold. Their liabilities were the deposits

---

[7] See Atack (2009) pp. 11–17 on the Bank of Amsterdam and its possible effect on the Bank of England; and Quinn and Roberds (2009) on the Bank of Amsterdam as the first central bank.

of country banks and of businessmen in London. Since 1708, the issuing of notes or receipts due to payment on demand was forbidden for companies that had more than six partners, with the exception of the Bank of England. This obstacle to the development of joint-stock banks was removed only in 1826.

London's private banks grew out of the Goldsmiths. These merchants, who dealt with precious metals, developed security arrangements that attracted people who wanted to deposit their hoards with them. During the seventeenth century, the practice of keeping deposits with the Goldsmiths spread. Since the Goldsmiths' coffers were thus generally full, they extended the scope of their activities to include loans, especially to the government.

The origin of the country banks was different from that of the private banks in London. The country banks developed not from the Goldsmiths, but largely from merchants and industrialists outside London. The country banks had agents in London and kept accounts with the London private banks. Their assets consisted of Bank of England notes, specie, and gold. Against these assets they managed deposits and issued their own country bank notes, which were the notes usually used in the counties. Thus, the major difference between the private banks in London and the country banks concerns the latter's note-issuing, whereas the former were forbidden to issue notes.

Deposits with the Goldsmiths, and later with the various banks, were of two kinds. The first took the form of lump sums against which receipts were given stating the rate of interest and the advance notice required before withdrawal. It was possible to withdraw part of the deposit by endorsing the back of the receipt. During the seventeenth century, such endorsed receipts were used in payment. Even though the Goldsmiths should legally have paid the depositors themselves, the custom of paying the bearer of the receipt – the one who signed it, rather than the depositor – grew. At the end of the eighteenth century, this led to the use of receipts not bearing the name of the payee. In 1758, after a court hearing that ruled that banks were responsible for receipts even if they were stolen, the account of the depositor was debited when he received the receipt rather than when the receipt arrived at the bank. Thus, receipts became the closest substitute for gold and the forerunner of bank notes. However, it took the onset of the Restriction Period for actual bank notes for payment to the bearer to become common practice.

The second kind of deposit was known as Running Cash. Instead of receiving a receipt, the depositor had the right to draw a "depositor draft" on the bank. In this case, the sum was transferred directly to the payee or to his account. The larger Goldsmiths had accounts with one another, and the smaller ones had accounts with one of the largest. The various accounts were settled by Exchequer bills and Bank of England notes. We can see in this practice the origin of what we know today as checks.

The difference between depositor receipts and depositor drafts is not large, as Feavearyear (1931) explains:

There was no important difference between the note signed by Francis Child, the banker, which said: "I promise to pay to Mr. John Smith or order, on demand, the sum of 186. pound.14s.2," and the draft signed by John Smith and addressed to Francis Child which said: "Pay to Robert Brown or order the sum of 186 pound.14s.2d." No one regarded the former as in any way more entitled to be considered money than the latter. (pp. 258–259)

Although early writers such as David Hume, James Steuart, and Adam Smith grouped all forms of mediums of circulation that were not metallic under the umbrella of paper-credit, they still tended to maintain – incorrectly according to modern views – that the second type could be used to create money, that is, to create means of payment out of nothing, whereas the first could only replace gold. Thus, they expanded the definition of money to include both coin and convertible bank notes. Thornton, as we shall see, was the first to try to resolve this confusion by showing that bank notes and deposits have more in common than most of his contemporaries thought. However, deposits were not considered part of the money stock by most economists at the turn of the nineteenth century.

It is important to be aware of some additional limitations on the currency during the period under discussion. Since 1663, under the influence of Mercantile principles, it was forbidden to export specie or bullion which had been melted out of coins. To this limitation on gold movements one should add the rule of maximum rate of interest. Mainly because of moral reservations, the maximum rate of interest from 1713 was only 5 percent. This was modified in 1716 so as to apply only to lending and discounting, but not borrowing from abroad. In 1773, the Bank of England rate was fixed at 5 percent and remained so until 1822. In 1795, the Bank decided to discount at this rate only that proportion upon which the Bank itself decided. This enabled the Bank to act according to its discretion in issuing notes.

As is clear from the schematic description presented in Figure 2.1, the system before the Restriction was based on the precious metals (gold and silver). To simplify, we shall use "gold" to represent the precious metals used

The Bank of England

Assets	Liabilities
Gold	Bank Notes
Public Securities	Private Deposits
Private Securities	London Banks' Deposits
	[small amount]

London's Private Banks

Assets	Liabilities
Gold	Private Deposits
Bank of England Notes	Country Banks'
Country Banks' Notes	Deposits
(small amount)	
Deposits with BoE	
Public Securities	
Private Securities	

Country Banks

Assets	Liabilities
Gold	Country Banks' Notes
Bank of England Notes	Private Deposits
Public Securities	
Private Securities	
Deposits with London's Banks	
(Deposits with the Bank	
of England from 1825)	

Figure 2.1. A schematic structure of the banking system in the mid-eighteenth century.

in circulation. Thus, as we saw in Hume and shall see in Smith in the next chapter, the system tried to imitate a circulation of only gold, which was sometimes called "the perfect circulation." As we shall see, the belief that this pure-gold circulation should be the prototype for the English system was behind many of the monetary theories of the time.

THREE

Adam Smith

The Case for Laissez-Faire in Money and Banking

Introduction

Adam Smith's (1723–1790) contributions to the rise of classical economics are well known. Many consider the publication of *The Wealth of Nations* in 1776 to have established Smith as the founding father of the hegemonic analytical approach to the study of political economy for many years. Smith knew David Hume, who was twelve years younger than Smith; the two Scottish philosophers exchanged views on various subjects, including money, banking, and credit. Hume's and Smith's philosophical agreements and differences, including their mutual debts and association with Francis Hutcheson, the great Scottish enlightenment philosopher, are well recorded.[1] As we shall see, the monetary theories of Smith and Hume, though similar in some respects, are not identical; there is enough room for interpretation to allow the secondary literature to debate their actual positions on important aspects of their theories to this day.

In the famous discussion of the "division of labor" in Book I of *Inquiry into the Nature and Causes of the Wealth of Nations* (as the full title runs), Adam Smith addressed money for the first time. The division of labor was at the heart of the theoretical conceptualization that Smith used in the book to explain the real growth phenomena that we know by now had changed the world. The inquiry into the theory of growth, as moderns would have called it, led Smith to conclude that "[t]he division of labour, however, so far as it

---

[1] For a review of Hume, Smith, and the Scottish "natural law" philosophy, see Taylor (1965), Campbell and Skinner (1982), Hont and Ignatieff (1983), Pocock (1985), and Hutchison (1988). For a review of the economic aspects in Smith, see Skinner and Wilson (1975). The monetary and banking theories of Smith are reviewed in Hollander J. (1911); Viner (1937); Mints (1945); Vickers (1959, 1975); Hollander S. (1973); Laidler (1981); Humphrey (1981); and Gherity (1994). On more detailed points see notes 14, 16, and 18.

can be introduced, occasions, in every art, a proportionable increase of the productive powers of labour" (p. 9).

The extent of the division of labor, as Smith explains, depends on many circumstances, and a well-developed exchange mechanism is certainly one of the most important.[2] Thus, after the three opening conceptual chapters of Book I in which Smith focuses on the division of labor, the fourth chapter, entitled "The Origins and Use of Money," opens with the following statement:

> When the division of labour has been once thoroughly established, it is but a very small part of a man's wants which the produce of his own labour can supply. He supplies the far greater part of them by exchanging that surplus part of the produce of his own labour, which is over and above his own consumption, for such parts of the produce of other men's labour as he has occasion for. Every man thus lives by exchanging, or becomes in some measure a merchant, and the society itself grows to be what is properly a commercial society. (Book I, chapter 4, p. 26)

Money and the Division of Labor

The concept "division of labor" used by Smith and even the language reminded many later scholars of Hume.[3] Smith considered the use of money in exchange to be a necessary condition for the proper development of the division of labor and thus for the creation of new wealth. Whole passages of his book discuss the actual evolution of money, justifying the use of money and praising its efficiency in comparison with a barter system of exchange. Like Hume, Smith elaborated the now famous argument concerning the advantages of a monetary economy over a barter economy where, by definition, no money exists. The argument focuses on how to avoid what became known in later literature as "coincidence of wants," in which a buyer and a seller have to want exactly what the other has a surplus of. Coincidence of wants is a necessary condition for exchange in barter and one which constitutes a barrier to exchange that is avoided in a monetary economy.[4] The

---

[2] "This division of labour, from which so many advantages are derived, is not originally the effect of any human wisdom, which foresees and intends that general opulence to which it gives occasion. It is the necessary, though very slow and gradual consequence of a certain propensity in human nature which has in view no such extensive utility; the propensity to truck, barter, and exchange one thing for another" (Book I, chapter 2, p. 17).

[3] See Taylor (1965).

[4] "But when the division of labour first began to take place, this power of exchanging must frequently have been very much clogged and embarrassed in its operations. One man, we shall suppose, has more of a certain commodity than he himself has occasion for, while another

use of money separates the acts of buying and selling, thus eliminating the coincidence-of-wants problem. Like Hume, Smith turned to reason and history to explain the advantages of the precious metals and their actual rise as the dominant form of commodity-money used in most countries.[5] He also argued for how beneficial coining the precious metals to standardized and well-recognized weights, qualities, and hence values was to exchange:

The use of metals in this rude state was attended with two very considerable inconveniencies; first, with the trouble of weighing; and, secondly, with that of assaying them. ... Before the institution of coined money, however, unless they went through this tedious and difficult operation, people must always have been liable to the grossest frauds and impositions, and instead of a pound weight of pure silver, or pure copper, might receive in exchange for their goods an adulterated composition of the coarsest and cheapest materials, which had, however, in their outward appearance, been made to resemble those metals. To prevent such abuses, to facilitate exchanges, and thereby to encourage all sorts of industry and commerce, it has been found necessary, in all countries that have made any considerable advances towards improvement, to affix a public stamp upon certain quantities of such particular metals as were in those countries commonly made use of to purchase goods. Hence the origin of coined money, and of those public offices called mints; institutions exactly of the same nature with those of the aulnagers and stamp-masters of woolen and linen cloth. All of them are equally meant to ascertain, by means of a public stamp, the quantity and uniform goodness of those different commodities when brought to market. (ibid., pp. 28–29)

A comprehensive discussion of Smith's analysis of the value of commodities – their use value and especially their exchange value – is beyond the scope of this study.[6] For present purposes, it is sufficient to note that Smith explained the exchange value of commodities as determined by labor to be their "real" or natural price, whereas their nominal price is that measured by money: "Labour alone, therefore, never varying in its own value, is alone the ultimate and real standard by which the value of all commodities can at all times and places be estimated and compared. It is their real price; money

has less. The former consequently would be glad to dispose of, and the latter to purchase, a part of this superfluity. But if this latter should chance to have nothing that the former stands in need of, no exchange can be made between them" (Book I, chapter 4, p. 26).

[5] "In all countries, however, men seem at last to have been determined by irresistible reasons to give the preference, for this employment, to metals above every other commodity. Metals can not only be kept with as little loss as any other commodity, scarce anything being less perishable than they are, but they can likewise, without any loss, be divided into any number of parts, as by fusion those parts can easily be reunited again; a quality which no other equally durable commodities possess, and which more than any other quality renders them fit to be the instruments of commerce and circulation" (ibid.).

[6] See Hollander (1973, 1987), O'Brien (2004), and references therein for a fuller discussion.

is their nominal price only" (p. 37). However, as we have just argued, Smith believed that money itself arises from a commodity. Thus, in Smith's analysis, the exchange relations hide the obvious fact that what people exchange, whether in barter or in a monetary economy, are "values" that represent labor. Labor itself could be measured in either goods or money, complicating the assessment of its cost: "In this popular sense, therefore, labour, like commodities, may be said to have a real and a nominal price. Its real price may be said to consist in the quantity of the necessaries and conveniences of life which are given for it; its nominal price, in the quantity of money" (p. 38). Moreover, money serves as the "standard," or measure, of value.[7] Precious metals are best suited to serve as such a standard, and in Smith's monetary discussions, as in Hume's monetary theory, commodity-money remains the basic form of money.[8] Up to this point in *The Wealth of Nations*, Smith's discussion of a monetary economy abstracts from paper money, whose use, as we saw in Chapter 2, was common at the time. But in Book II, entitled "Of the Nature, Accumulation, And Employment of Stock," which was devoted to the analysis of capital, Smith extends the discussion to cover noncommodity-money mediums as well.

Money, Banking, and the "Invisible Hand"

Concerning the "real," nonmonetary analysis, one should note Smith's famous, still-debated conclusion that the "natural" mechanism for regulating the economy is to leave it in the hands of the many competing individuals: In other words, not to regulate it. The famous "invisible hand" metaphor appeared once in *The Wealth of Nations*, late in the treatise in Book 4, chapter 2, entitled "Of Restraints upon the Importation from Foreign Countries of such Goods as can be produced at Home":

> But the annual revenue of every society is always precisely equal to the exchangeable value of the whole annual produce of its industry, or rather is precisely the same thing with that exchangeable value. As every individual, therefore, endeavours as much as he can both to employ his capital in the support of domestic industry, and so to direct

[7] "Originally, in all countries, I believe, a legal tender of payment could be made only in the coin of that metal, which was peculiarly considered as the standard or measure of value." (Book I, Chapter 5, p. 44)

[8] Smith understood well, as the following passage indicates, that in the practical working of commodity money, i.e. coins, there are difficulties that might make them imperfect: "The money of any particular country is, at any particular time and place, more or less an accurate measure of value according as the current coin is more or less exactly agreeable to its standard, or contains more or less exactly the precise quantity of pure gold or pure silver which it ought to contain" (Book II, chapter 5, p. 52).

that industry that its produce may be of the greatest value; every individual necessarily labours to render the annual revenue of the society as great as he can. He generally, indeed, neither intends to promote the public interest, nor knows how much he is promoting it. By preferring the support of domestic to that of foreign industry, he intends only his own security; and by directing that industry in such a manner as its produce may be of the greatest value, he intends only his own gain, and he is in this, as in many other cases, led by an *invisible hand* to promote an end which was no part of his intention. Nor is it always the worse for the society that it was no part of it. By pursuing his own interest he frequently promotes that of the society more effectually than when he really intends to promote it. I have never known much good done by those who affected to trade for the public good. (Book IV, pp. 477–478; emphasis added)

This famous argument – that society is best served by a regime where individuals make decisions with an eye focused only on their own self-interest, calculating their own good, and thus serving the public interest unintentionally – is extended to both internal and external economic spheres. Smith argued that with the exception of some well-specified cases (such as defense spending, administration of legal issues, public infrastructure, and education) no statesman or institution should interfere in these decisions, and the economy should generally regulate itself.[9]

Did Smith carry the invisible hand argument to the spheres of money and banking? The answer to this intriguing question can be found in chapter 2 of Book II, entitled "Of Money Considered as a Particular Branch of the General Stock of the Society, or Of the Expence of Maintaining the National Capital" ("Of Money"). In the first chapter of Book II, Smith analyzes the "Division of Stock." He distinguishes among three types of stocks: that intended for consumption, fixed capital, and circulating capital. The stock of money is part of the third type of capital.[10] Smith further distinguishes between gross revenue and net revenue:

The gross revenue of all the inhabitants of a great country comprehends the whole annual produce of their land and labour; the neat revenue, what remains free to them after deducting the expence of maintaining; first, their fixed, and, secondly,

---

[9] "The statesman who should attempt to direct private people in what manner they ought to employ their capitals would not only load himself with a most unnecessary attention, but assume an authority which could safely be trusted, not only to no single person, but to no council or senate whatever, and which would nowhere be so dangerous as in the hands of a man who had folly and presumption enough to fancy himself fit to exercise it" (Book IV, chapter 2, p. 478).

[10] "The third and last of the three portions into which the general stock of the society naturally divides itself, is the circulating capital; of which the characteristic is, that it affords a revenue only by circulating or changing masters. It is composed likewise of four parts: First, of the money by means of which all the other three are circulated and distributed to their proper consumers" (Book II, chapter 1, p. 298).

their circulating capital; or what, without encroaching upon their capital, they can place in their stock reserved for immediate consumption, or spend upon their subsistence, conveniences, and amusements. Their real wealth, too, is in proportion, not to their gross, but to their neat revenue. (p. 311)

Thus, maintaining fixed capital is a cost that should be deducted from gross revenue. However, maintaining circulating capital is different. Smith discusses four components that make up circulating capital: "money, provisions, materials and finished work" (p. 313). He then draws a distinction between money and the other three components, explaining that "[t]he maintenance of those three parts of the circulating capital ... withdraw no portion of the annual produce from the neat revenue of the society, besides what is necessary for maintaining the fixed capital" (p. 313). However, money is different from the other three parts. The analysis of money reveals that its maintenance cost reduces gross revenue:

Money, therefore, is the only part of the circulating capital of a society, of which the maintenance can occasion any diminution in their neat revenue.
The fixed capital, and that part of the circulating capital which consists in money, so far as they affect the revenue of the society, bear a very great resemblance to one another. (pp. 313–314)

Thus, from the point of view of society at large, money functions like fixed capital. That capital in the form of "machines, and instruments of trade, &c. require certain expence first to erect them, and afterwards to support them," which is deducted from gross revenue.[11] Hence, Smith claims that by reducing the quantity of commodity-money in circulation and using paper mediums, the economy will improve production. Reducing the stock of commodity-money in circulation that is part of the circulating capital – and, in fact, quasi-fixed capital – will extend production possibilities. In this fashion "dead stock," as Smith describes the unnecessary stock of commodity-money on which society could save, will be transformed into "productive capital." This process represents the (positive) function that banks fulfill:

The substitution of paper in the room of gold and silver money, replaces a very expensive instrument of commerce with one much less costly, and sometimes equally convenient. Circulation comes to be carried on by a new wheel, which it

---

[11] "Money, therefore, the great wheel of circulation, the great instrument of commerce, like all other instruments of trade, though it makes a part and a very valuable part of the capital, makes no part of the revenue of the society to which it belongs; and though the metal pieces of which it is composed, in the course of their annual circulation, distribute to every man the revenue which properly belongs to him, they make themselves no part of that revenue" (ibid., p. 317).

costs less both to erect and to maintain than the old one. But in what manner this operation is performed, and in what manner it tends to increase either the gross or the net revenue of the society, is not altogether so obvious, and may therefore require some further explication. (ibid., pp. 317–318)

In "Of Money," Smith describes the well-known process that led to a banking system based on fractional reserves, a process created by issuing convertible bank notes that were not fully backed by gold in the banks' coffers and that substituted coins in circulation with paper notes. As a result, coins became redundant in the internal circulation, although they could still continue to function as international money. Smith insists that this process, wherein the banks extend credit to their customers, compete with each other, and seek profits, will result in the right amount of money in circulation. The following well-known example is worth quoting in full:

Let us suppose, for example, that the whole circulating money of some particular country amounted, at a particular time, to one million sterling, that sum being then sufficient for circulating the whole annual produce of their land and labour. Let us suppose, too, that some time thereafter, different banks and bankers issued promissory notes, payable to the bearer, to the extent of one million, reserving in their different coffers two hundred thousand pounds for answering occasional demands. There would remain, therefore, in circulation, eight hundred thousand pounds in gold and silver, and a million of bank notes or eighteen hundred thousand pounds of paper and money together. But the annual produce of the land and labour of the country had before required only one million to circulate and distribute it to its proper consumers, and that annual produce cannot be immediately augmented by those operations of banking. One million, therefore, will be sufficient to circulate it after them. The goods to be bought and sold being precisely the same as before, the same quantity of money will be sufficient for buying and selling them. *The channel of circulation, if I may be allowed such an expression, will remain precisely the same as before.* One million we have supposed sufficient to fill that channel. Whatever, therefore, is poured into it beyond this sum cannot run in it, but must overflow. One million eight hundred thousand pounds are poured into it. *Eight hundred thousand pounds, therefore, must overflow, that sum being over and above what can be employed in the circulation of the country. But though this sum cannot be employed at home, it is too valuable to be allowed to lie idle. It will, therefore, be sent abroad, in order to seek that profitable employment which it cannot find at home.* But the paper cannot go abroad; because at a distance from the banks which issue it, and from the country in which payment of it can be exacted by law, it will not be received in common payments. Gold and silver, therefore, to the amount of eight hundred thousand pounds will be sent abroad, and the channel of home circulation will remain filled with a million of paper, instead of the million of those metals which filled it before. (ibid., pp. 318–319; my emphasis)

Thus, the "right" quantity is that which would have circulated were coins the only medium of circulation. Moreover, as long as coins continue to circulate alongside the convertible notes issued by the various banks, even under the fractional-reserves system, there will be no danger of surplus or deficiency in the internal circulation, because the surplus will be exported or, in the case of a deficiency, imported.

Smith further argues that even if the entire circulation of money was composed of convertible bank notes that cannot function as international money, the right quantity could still be maintained as long as the banks act in line with what we could describe as "responsible behavior," whose specifics will be discussed later. According to Smith, the banks' own self-interest will direct them to behave responsibly, and as an unintentional result – as in the working of the invisible-hand mechanism in the real economy – the quantity of money in circulation will be the proper one.

The Real Bills Doctrine

The proof of this theory comes during Smith's examination of the banking system, which we described in the previous chapter. Smith discusses how convertible notes enter circulation, not just through the exchange of deposited coins, but through bank loans and "cash accounts." He argues that as long as the quantity of notes in circulation corresponds to the needs of entrepreneurs for money to answer "occasional demand," there is no surplus in circulation. Such correspondence between the desire for and supply of money was achieved by the simultaneous use of several methods by the banks. First, banks made loans for which they received "sureties," that is, assets that were supposed to guarantee repayment. The loans were advanced to customers to answer their demand for ready money and were given in the form of notes. The second method allowed customers who had "cash accounts" with the banks – basically a credit line – to withdraw notes up to a certain amount.

For the first method, Smith argues that as long as the loans are given against "real bills," the banks should discount them. Real bills are defined as bills which represent a debt born from a real transaction, that is, as a result of the actual sale of a commodity, where the partners to the transaction are two respected dealers who agree to a sale on credit. The certificate of the debt, known as the "bill of exchange," is a contract between the sides on the terms of settling the debt, always within a short period:

When a bank discounts to a merchant a real bill of exchange drawn by a real debtor, and which, as soon as it becomes due, is really paid by that debtor; it only advances to him a part of the value which he would otherwise be obliged to keep by him unemployed and in ready money for answering occasional demands ... The coffers of the bank, so far as its dealings are confined to such customers, resemble a water pond, from which, though a stream is continually running out, yet another is continually running in, fully equal to that which runs out; so that the pond keeps always equally, or nearly equally full. Little or no expence can ever be necessary for replenishing the coffers of such a bank. (p. 331)

This is the essence of Smith's well-known Real Bills Doctrine. Banks behave responsibly as long as they provide the liquidity demanded by the borrowers, where the latter exchange "good" short-term commercial debts for cash.

The second method used to introduce notes to circulation beyond issuing them against coins was using what were known as "cash accounts." These accounts were popular in Scotland and, in Smith's view, had contributed to the development of the Scottish economy in the previous twenty-five years. In modern terms, this method involves the opening of a credit line by the bank to "any individual" able to provide "two persons of undoubted credit and good landed estate to become surety for him" (p. 324). The bank then allows the individual to withdraw any sum up to the limit of the surety whenever he supplies the bank with an authorized overdraft. As long as the banks take care that these withdrawals are returned on schedule, no problems should ensue.

Thus, in Smith's opinion, as long as the banks follow these methods, discounting only real bills and opening such cash accounts, the "right" quantity of notes in circulation will be maintained.[12] However, Smith does not clarify why the quantity of notes so issued will correspond to the quantity needed in the economy. He simply assumes that what the individual asks for – "ready money ... for answering occasional demand" – will aggregate to the right supply. Moreover, he notes but does not fully explain that these two methods will be implemented because they are exactly those which follow from the banks' self-interest. The argument hangs on the fact that the banks would have to maintain greater reserves if they did not stick to these principles, exposing them to high costs resulting from the need to increase and renew their reserves.[13]

---

[12] "The whole paper money of every kind which can easily circulate in any country never can exceed the value of the gold and silver, of which it supplies the place, or which (the commerce being supposed the same) would circulate there, if there was no paper money" (ibid., p. 327).

[13] "A banking company, which issues more paper than can be employed in the circulation of the country, and of which the excess is continually returning upon them for payment, ought to increase the quantity of gold and silver, which they keep at all times in their coffers, not only in proportion to this excessive increase of their circulation, but in a much greater proportion; their notes returning upon them much faster than in proportion to the excess of their quantity. Such a company, therefore, ought to increase the first article of their expense, not only in proportion to this forced increase of their business, but in a much greater proportion." (ibid., pp. 327–328)

At the heart of Smith's arguments one can find an implicit model of competitive banking regulated by gold. The convertibility of all the (many) competing bank notes and an automatic mechanism that directs excesses or shortages to the international gold markets – a system that is very similar in its spirit, although not identical, to that of Hume, as we shall see – guarantees the right quantity of money. However, Smith's discussion is related to the payments system, leaving the analysis of intermediation not fully developed. He analyzes money in the payments system; when he discusses loans, it is in the framework of short-term liquidity shortages. Thus, the loan market that he has analyzed up to this point does not represent the transfer of resources from units that have a surplus to units that have a shortage, as in intermediation, but rather represents the transfer of resources only to solve a cash shortage. Part of the confusion among scholars on this issue concerns the role of convertible bank notes. Coins are "money;" convertible bank notes are called "paper money." The latter have a dual function. On the one hand, they are substitutes for coins and thus function as money; on the otherhand, they are issued by the banks as loans and thus can function in intermediation. However, it is clear that for Smith, their function as money is primary. We will return to this point in the next chapter.

Although some banks may err at times by failing to understand their "own particular interest," the right quantity of commodity-money will be ultimately determined by the distribution of precious metals in the world. The right quantity of convertible bank notes is determined to be that which, when combined with the quantity of coins in circulation, equals the right quantity of commodity-money, were commodity-money to consist only of coins. The banks, under weak limitations, can be left to compete both in discounting real bills and in opening credit lines. In other words, Smith accepts competition in money and banking and thus sees no need for the intervention of any central body in determining the right quantity of money – assuming convertibility. This assumption explains the advantages society finds in banking; under convertibility, the resources saved in the form of a smaller quantity of precious metals to support the monetary system are turned into productive capital by sending the saved gold to the world markets.

The Bank of England was a private bank and thus should in theory be subject to the same principles of competition that apply to any other bank. However, Smith recognized that the Bank of England was not just another private bank but also an "engine of state," which dealt with state debts and taxes, and whose actions sometimes resulted in an overstock of bank notes in circulation through no fault of its managers. The Bank of England also assumed responsibility for the miscalculations of other banks because it had to convert their notes into gold when they over-issued (pp. 328–329). Thus, Smith realized that the Bank of England played a unique role in the system. That Smith is not explicit about the application of the Real Bills Doctrine to the Bank of England does not change his general support for free trade and clear opposition to what we now know as central banking. In fact, his opposition to central banking is not directly and explicitly addressed, because for Smith, such an active role is not an acceptable function of any agent in the economy; hence, it seems unthinkable for him. In principle, the banking system could be left to regulate itself, a conclusion that came to be synonymous in later years with Smith's Real Bills Doctrine.[14] An increase in the number of banks and in the competition among them would contribute to greater caution on the part of the bankers, to less danger of "malicious runs," and to greater protection for the public:

What a bank can with propriety advance to a merchant or undertaker of any kind, is not either the whole capital with which he trades, or even any considerable part of that capital; but that part of it only, which he would otherwise be obliged to keep by him unemployed, and in ready money for answering occasional demands. If the paper money which the bank advances never exceeds this value, it can never exceed the value of the gold and silver which would necessarily circulate in the country if there was no paper money; it can never exceed the quantity which the circulation of the country can easily absorb and employ. (pp. 330–331)

Smith's opposition to notes of low denomination was the only limitation he imposed upon the principle of free trade among banks, subject to con-vertibility and loan policy described earlier. His main justification for this limitation was to protect the weaker segments in society. Consumers cannot be expected to distinguish between "responsible" and "mean" bankers; they should therefore be protected against bankruptcies by provisions that

---

[14] See for example Mints' (1945) analysis of the history of banking in which he emphasizes the unfortunate place of the Real Bills Doctrine and hence the negative role of Smith in the development of banking theories. A contrarian view on Smith's position concerning the Doctrine, arguing that he did not adopt it and should have no paternity claim, can be found in Perlman (1989). He argues that all Smith assumes is convertibility of notes which suffice to make the case for unregulated banking with no need for the extreme – and fallacious – Doctrine. The true paternity of this dubious theory is handed over to James Mill, J. S. Mill's father. Gherity (1994), on the other hand – on the basis of Smith (1763), an unknown text that was discovered and published in the *History of Political Economy* in 1993 – concludes that Smith adopted the Real Bills Doctrine in the early 1760s, probably in 1763.

ensure that transactions between consumers and dealers that involve small sums be conducted in coins alone. Smith was aware that this limits free trade and "may, no doubt, be considered as in some respect a violation of natural liberty." However, he justifies it thus:

> But those exertions of natural liberty of a few individuals, which might endanger the security of the whole society, are, and ought to be, restrained by the laws of all governments; of the most free, as well as of the most despotical. The obligation of building party walls, in order to prevent the communication of fire, is a violation of natural liberty, exactly of the same kind with the regulations of the banking trade which are here proposed. (p. 353)

Smith's conclusion is clear: Subject to convertibility and limitations on low-denomination notes, banking is a trade like any other and should be subject to competition. Bankers should issue paper notes to be used in trading between "dealers and dealers" and not between "dealers and consumers," thus leaving the risks outside the domain of those who cannot be expected to properly defend themselves. However, the general argument on money and banking is that of laissez-faire. Smith's theory argues that a mixed convertible circulation, based on notes that are convertible to commodity-money, needs no regulation or control.

> This free competition too obliges all bankers to be more liberal in their dealings with their customers, lest their rivals should carry them away. In general, if any branch of trade, or any division of labor, be advantageous to the public, the freer and more general the competition, it will always be the more so. (p. 359)

Laidler (1981) regards both the constraint on low-denomination notes and convertibility to be part of Smith's recommended regulations in banking. However, the just-quoted passage, quoted also by Laidler, relates only to low-denomination notes. Convertibility should not be regarded as a (justified) violation of "natural liberty," but as arising from the need for a natural circulation based on commodity-money. Laidler (1984, pp. 152–153) argues that restricting discounting to certain assets is against free trade in banking. However, it is clear that Smith himself thought this behavior to be in the banks' self-interest.

The quantity of the circulating money will always tend to be the right one, and if at some point the quantity is not right, the system will correct itself. The quantity of money is determined by demand, that is, it is endogenous, whereas the quality (or value) of money is not related to the quantity in the long run. At the root of this approach, one will find the argument that the long-term purchasing power of commodity-money (its value) is determined by conditions in the markets for goods. Therefore, the value of the circulating medium will always be what it is supposed to be, regardless of the bankers' actions. This is not a short-run analysis. In the short run, additional money will overflow the channels of circulation and, under Smith's assumptions (full employment, open economy, and fixed exchange rate), will spill over and cause gold to outflow.

Smith and Hume

This argument is different from but – as I will argue – consistent with the Price-Specie-Flow mechanism, or what is known as Hume's mechanism, although not with either Hume's Quantity Theory or his specific equilibrating mechanism. The fact that Smith makes no direct reference in *The Wealth of Nations* to Hume's mechanism constitutes, according to Viner (1937), "[o]ne of the mysteries of the history of economic thought." The mystery is further deepened by the fact that in an earlier text, *Lectures on Jurisprudence* (1766/1982), Smith quoted Hume's analysis "approvingly" (Viner 1937, p. 87).[15] This issue has been addressed in the secondary literature by Taylor (1965), Petrella (1968), and Eagly (1970), among others, who reach somewhat different conclusions. Petrella concludes that Smith rejected Hume's monetary theory, including both the Quantity Theory of money and the Price-Specie-Flow mechanism. Petrella explains the rejection as motivated by contradictions that Smith discovered after 1766 between Hume's monetary formulations and Smith's own "real" side analysis. Thus, if money aggregates play a role in directing the real economy, Smith's "neutral" monetary analysis, fundamentally anti-Mercantilist, is weakened.[16]

Taylor and Eagly present a different interpretation. Taylor's detailed scholarly study of "the Trio" of Hutcheson, Hume, and Smith led him to conclude that Smith was heavily influenced by both Hutcheson's and Hume's

---

[15] The mystery is that "Adam Smith, although he was intimately acquainted with Hume and with his writings," did not make any "reference in the *Wealth of Nations* to the self-regulating mechanism in terms of the price levels and trade balances" (Viner, p. 87).

[16] Petrella (1968) concluded his argument by stating that the mystery would be resolved if we understand Smith as a polemicist rather than a theorist; then one can understand why "Smith … ignored the brilliance of Hume's analysis and developed his own monetary theory in order to preserve his central theme that capital and labor, not money, are the important things for the capitalist economy aspiring to economic progress and increased welfare" (p. 374).

views.[17] Taylor does not appreciate Smith's own contributions to the field of monetary theory: "Adam Smith added nothing of significance to these expositions of David Hume and Francis Hutcheson. In fact, his analysis and discussion of money is much inferior to Hume's. … Smith's original contributions to the development of monetary theory were practically nil. Much more serious, however, was Smith's failure to appreciate the value of Hume's work in the field" (Taylor, pp. 82–84). However, Taylor thinks Hume's short-term analysis is unappreciated, not the Price-Specie-Flow mechanism. On that subject, for "inexplicable reason, [Smith] omitted Hume's lucid observations [from *The Wealth of Nations*]" (ibid., p. 132).

Ten years earlier (in 1766), however, Smith summarized Hume's mechanism in this way:

> Mr. Hume published some essays shewing the absurdity of these and other such doctrines [mercantilists]. He proves very ingeniously that money must always bear[s] a certain proportion to the quantity of commodities in every country, that wherever money is accumulated beyond the proportion of commodities in any country the price of goods will necessarily rise, that this country will be undersold at the forreign market and consequently the money must depart into other nations; but on the contrary whenever the quantity of money falls below the proportion of goods the price of goods diminishes, the country undersells others in forreign marketts and consequently money returns in great plenty. Thus money and goods will keep near about a certain level in every country. Mr. Hume's reasoning is exceedingly ingenious. (Smith 1766/1978, p. 507)

Thus, the argument runs as follows: As long as the money used in the countries involved in trade is accepted in international payments, then price changes, trade imbalances, and money flows will act as equilibrating forces. In the international system, there is a built-in, automatic tendency that equates imports and exports through price changes in the countries involved in trade. If, for example, exports exceed imports, excluding gold,

---

[17] See Taylor (1965, pp. 27–51). "There can be little doubt that Smith's close intimacy with Hume and Hutcheson, and, to a lesser extent, with Oswald, exercised a powerful influence on his economic philosophy" (p. 51). Wennerlind (2000) claims that Taylor did not think that Smith's theory of money was close to that of Hume, arguing that "Smith's discussion of money only 'shows faint traces of Hume'" is misleading. The full quote from Taylor reads: "Hume's theory of money is far more elegant, consistent, and refined than Hutcheson's: and while Smith's fairly commonplace discussion is superior to his teacher's in that it shows faint traces of Hume's more perceptive notions – and, to this extent benefited from Hume's work – his rather sketchy monetary analysis is characterized by a somewhat uncritical adoption of the current orthodoxy as exemplified by Hutcheson's thought on the subject" (p. 84). Taylor, in fact like Wennerlind himself, think that "there is strong Humean paternity to Smith's theory of money" (p. 78).

then gold will flow into England. This will cause prices to rise in England (and possibly to fall in the Rest of the World); the consequences will be a decrease in exports from England and an increase in imports.

Smith's analysis in 1776 ignored the Price-Specie-Flow mechanism and, in particular, its dependence on changes in relative price levels; it favored an explanation based on a more direct effect. Some scholars, in seeking to explain why Smith chose not to quote Hume in this regard and to distance his monetary theory from that of Hume, have relied on the sentence that follows the passage quoted. Smith writes, "[Hume] seems however to have gone a little into the notion that public opulence consists in money, which was considered above" (Smith 1766/1982, p. 507). Based on this sentence, these scholars have argued that Smith had already in 1766 some reservations about Hume's theory, feeling that it hinted at a too-compromising attitude to the Mercantilists. Eagly (1970) and Wennerlind (2000) support a different reading of Smith, arguing that one can find evidence of Smith relying on Hume's mechanism. However, as Laidler (1981) argues, Hume's mechanism "could easily have been incorporated" into Smith's treatment without Smith having relied upon it explicitly to formulate his theory. As we shall see when we discuss Ricardo's monetary thought, such an inclusion of Hume's mechanism would not change Smith's basic conclusions.

What is unique and innovative in Smith's monetary analysis relates to the recent developments in the financial system and, in particular, to the rise of banking discussed in the previous chapter. Theoreticians in the eighteenth and nineteenth centuries disagreed as to whether the quantity of money in circulation was best determined by competition, that is, by the invisible hand. Smith was one of the most notable advocates of competition, and he specifically maintained that under competition, bankers should be allowed to behave freely according to their own best interests, as long as they discount only against "good bills." This famous formulation came to be known as the Real Bills Doctrine. Because later positions either accepted or rejected both competition in general and the Real Bills Doctrine in particular, the term Real Bills Doctrine has often been treated as synonymous with competition, a development that has caused no little confusion in the literature.

Smith and the Classical School in general saw money in its pure form as commodity-money that fulfilled all the functions of money: unit of account, medium of exchange, and store of value. When commodity-money alone circulates in what can be called a pure circulation, determination of the correct quantity of money in circulation seems relatively simple. In this case, the mechanism is governed by market forces in both the commodity-money market and other markets, and is unaffected by individual economic agents such as banks. The pure circulation is governed either by Hume's Price-Specie-Flow mechanism or by Smith's version of an automatic mechanism. The monetary regime of the pure circulation provided the model that most of the classicals sought to emulate.

However, it was already clear in Smith's day that commodity-money was not the only form of money in circulation. Both the privately owned Bank of England and the country banks issued convertible bank notes. Determination of quantity in such a mixed circulation, where both coins and convertible bank notes circulate, is more complicated. In this case, quantity is determined not only by market forces, but also by individual agents outside the precious-metals markets, and in particular by bankers. Despite this, Smith thought that under convertibility, determination of the correct quantity in a mixed circulation could be left to market forces as in a pure circulation. Thus, banks acting in competition could issue notes at their own discretion, on the condition that this be done only against real bills of exchange representing real transactions among respectable agents, and for a limited period of time.

Thus, although these two Scottish philosophers – Hume, discussed in Chapter 1, and Smith, discussed here – both assumed convertibility and can be described as "metallists," their analytical apparatus led to somewhat different conclusions.[18] For Hume, the mechanism that took care of the monetary system – and annulled a monetary policy and hence an institution that implements it – was dependent on the Quantity Theory of money internally in combination with changes in relative price levels internationally. For Smith, the mechanism was different; he knew Hume's monetary theory and chose not to build his argument in the *Wealth of Nations* on it. Smith also was a "metallist," but he relied on a different anchor. He analyzed a mixed monetary circulation as if it imitates a pure one, with the price level determined by "real" forces in the commodity-money market and in the other markets for the various commodities. The quantity of money is demand-determined and does not "cause" the price level in the different countries. Instead, the endogenous money supply follows the dictates of the balance of payments, price levels, and so forth; as long as convertibility prevails and the Real Bills Doctrine rules, internal monetary forces will not change the basic laws that characterize a pure circulation.

---

[18] On Hume and Smith monetary theories see Humphrey (1981) and Santiago-Valiente (1988).

Hume provided an analytical framework upon which many of the classicals relied. Hume's ideas influenced the work of some Bullionists (among them Ricardo) as well as the writings of the Currency School. And they appear in the secondary literature in many moderns' accounts of classical monetary thought. Smith, on the other hand, provided a framework that had less impact, primarily influencing the work of some anti-Bullionists, some aspects of the Banking School, and, more generally, critiques of the Quantity Theory and supporters of endogenous money. We will return to the distinctions between Hume's and Smith's theories in the coming chapters.

FOUR

"Monetary Theories of Credit" in Exchange

Introduction

This chapter and Chapter 9 present an analytical framework for understanding both the previously discussed monetary theories of Hume and Smith and the theories developed over the course of the nineteenth century, which we will cover in the coming chapters. The framework seeks to explain the roles played by monetary instruments in two separate processes: exchange and intermediation. Money, "near-monies," and various credit instruments that will be defined later facilitate these two key processes in a monetary economy. However, because the same mediums are used in the two processes, understanding the roles played by the various mediums in each process and their interdependencies is one of the more difficult problems in any monetary theory. We will start first from the roles played by these mediums in the exchange of commodities and services.

Most theories concerning money and banking within the exchange process fall into one of two categories that we will label, after Schumpeter, "monetary theories of credit" and "credit theories of money." The former have a common logical structure that typically starts with an analysis of a basic form of money. The focus of the inquiry is the process of exchange in the economy; the relationship between the flow of commodities and the flow of money becomes the pivot around which the monetary theory is built. Other means of payment are then discussed, beginning with those considered to be near-monies in some sense and continuing with those which are less near-monies. Finally, some distinction, which is not always explicitly defined, is usually drawn between "money," "near-monies," and "credit." In such an approach, the concept of credit can only be defined and given meaning in terms of the definition and analysis of money.

Adoption of a logical structure that proceeds from money to credit is hardly surprising. Classical as well as pre-classical economists began the analysis of money with a model of exchange in the economy in which payments were carried out by transferring commodity-money, typically in the form of gold or silver coins. Commodity-money was viewed not only as the historical ancestor of other types of money, but also as a natural departure point for analyzing more complex systems. Each development in the payments system, such as the rise of deposits or the introduction of convertible notes at first fully and then partially backed by commodity-money, typically resulted in great confusion in monetary theory. Such theoretical "crises" were characteristically resolved, as we shall see throughout the book, by redefining the dividing lines between money, near-monies, and credit, but the theory was still based on commodity-money as the ideal type and the role of commodity-money in exchange. These demarcations were very significant, primarily because the money aggregate was considered to be crucial in determining absolute prices, but also because of its important place in the functioning of the economy and, in particular, its international linkages. Even when this basic form of money was no longer dominant in the *actual* payments system, its role as the cornerstone on which *both theories* of money and credit rested usually remained intact. This might seem an inconsistent or sloppy theoretical foundation, but in due course we will explain and rationalize this basic characteristic of the history of monetary theory.

The most influential framework for monetary theory in the period under analysis was embedded in Hume's celebrated Price-Specie-Flow mechanism. Its logic rests, as we saw in Chapter 1, on a chain of theoretical links between internal money stocks, price levels, and trade. The allocation of the international stock of commodity-money among the economies of the world was automatically determined by trade. Hume's formulation describes the tendency to reach a steady-state condition that maintains the allocation of commodity-money between the trading countries so that commodity-money will not flow between them. The level of prices in the various countries will ensure a balanced trade. The equilibrating force working in cases of disequilibrium would be the price level that will change due to corrective flows of money and will affect trade flows. Thus, in the long run, steady-state equilibrium, the quantity of money in each country will be the "right" one, and a Quantity Theory is assumed.

Most modern theorists who have studied the evolution of exchange and the payments system have concluded that, historically, money existed before credit. However, this is by no means a unanimous view. Sir Hicks, for example, came to the conclusion that credit preceded money; merchants only began using a generally accepted medium of exchange after they discovered the convenience of a universal measure of value. In the following discussion, we will focus mainly on the logical structure of the theories of money and credit within the exchange process, rather than on the arguments about their actual histories; therefore, we will not argue with the conventional view or about the "true" relationship between the logical structure of monetary theory and the historical course of development. Rather, we will explore the implications of the conventional approach for monetary and credit theories and assess the advantages of a nonconventional theory.

The definitions of money and credit are, of course, crucial to our discussion. The 1933 *Encyclopedia of the Social Sciences* includes entries for both money and credit that defined the mainstream views. Theodore E. Gregory, an expert on the development of monetary theory in the nineteenth century, wrote the entry on money:

The accepted British-American tradition defines money functionally, assigning to it two primary and two subsidiary functions: to act as a medium of exchange and common denominator of value and to perform the functions of a store of value and standard of deferred payments.

Ralph Hawtrey, another well-known scholar of classical monetary theory, wrote the entry on credit and clearly found it necessary to rely on Gregory:

Etymologically, the word credit means belief or trust; in its technical usage it has come to be confined to the trust placed in a debtor. Credit, in fact, is best understood as simply another name for debt. ... A debt is a pecuniary obligation; it is expressed as a number in terms of a unit which is called a 'money of account.' The debt may be discharged immediately by the buyer's delivery of the agreed price in money, or it may be left outstanding. ... Debts are legally payable in money.

Thus, debts are discharged through money transfers, and credit is defined by means of the money in the system. However, a few lines later, Hawtrey almost destroys his own definition with the following statement: "Debts cannot be defined in terms of money because money must be defined in terms of debts." Hawtrey resolves this circular reasoning by invoking the State or the Law. Money is given a legal definition; credit is then defined in terms of this legal money.

Hawtrey was neither the first nor the last to be puzzled by the relationship between money and credit. His solution did not satisfy many later economists, including Schumpeter, who remarked in his important 1954 text: "[P]ractically and analytically, a credit theory of money is possibly preferable to a monetary theory of credit" (p. 717). Although attempts have been made to suggest alternative structures for monetary theory – we will review some in the spirit of Wicksell (1898 and 1906), later endorsed by Hicks (1982 and 1989) – most nineteenth-century political economists relied on the conventional approach. Although we will identify some early thinkers who thought along somewhat unconventional lines, in particular Thornton, their approaches had little effect during the nineteenth century.

In the following section we will describe the complicated theoretical (not necessarily actual) relationships between money and credit in the process of exchange. This will help to explain the source of some of the puzzlement and confusion in the history of monetary theory that we will encounter. In Section 2, we will describe and analyze a pure commodity-money exchange system, that is, a system of exchange based on the transfer of a tangible medium. We will then discuss the implications of the use in exchange of other forms of payments, from near-monies to credit. Near-monies and credit will be defined in terms of money, and a monetary theory of credit limited to the exchange process will be developed. The main advantage of such an approach is that it takes a pure-payments system, and not necessarily a real one, as its departure point. This will enable us to compare the real, historical systems of payments as they developed over the years with the pure, commodity-money-based system; the latter will serve as our benchmark model for analyzing the financial system in its role as a payments system.

One important lacuna in the early stages of the development of monetary theory was the incomplete treatment of intermediation, that is, the transfer of funds from savers to investors. The monetary aspects that received most attention were the internal and international exchange of commodities and services, with a focus on the roles money and banking played in this process. Intermediation's place in monetary theory and policy was usually restricted to the question of interest rates. Over time, the rising importance of intermediation in the economy turned this gap into a major reason for some of the weaknesses in monetary theory.

In Section 3, we describe the common monetary theories of credit in the exchange process. In Chapter 9, after reviewing some scholars like Thornton, whose ideas did not start from money, but from debts and credits, we will discuss the less conventional and more abstract credit theories of money within the exchange process. We will also elaborate on the complex relations between the different mediums used in intermediation and their respective roles. This will provide a framework for understanding the views of Thornton, and later, Wicksell.

A Pure Commodity-Money System of Exchange

Let us assume an economy in which the exchange of commodities and services (excluding financial assets, which will be defined and analyzed later) is carried out through a pure commodity-money system of exchange (CoMSE). In this system, each economic agent has a stock of commodity-money measured in units of account (UOAs) and sums are transferred from one agent to another. To simplify, the medium of exchange used for payments will be measured by the UOAs; the value of one unit of medium of exchange will be one UOA. A payment will be defined as a transfer from a buyer to a seller of the agreed number of UOAs. To further simplify, we will use "coins" and "UOAs" interchangeably. At this stage, we will assume that this is the CoMSEs only function and that there are no other means, barter or other, to facilitate exchange. Moreover, UOAs will be transferred at the same time that the goods change hands, reflecting the price agreed upon between the buyer and the seller. Thus, the act of exchange will be completed at once and no credits or debits will exist in the system.

The flow of circulating coins in the system during each interval of time is identical to the volume of transactions carried out in the economy, evaluated at accounting prices. In addition to flows, we can also define and analyze stocks in the system. Let us define, as economists traditionally did, the stock of coins in the hands of all economic units as the quantity of money in the system $\bar{M}(t)$ and its velocity as $V(t)$. The basic analysis in monetary theory seeks to relate the quantity of money to the prices of goods, and traditionally distinguishes between short-run and long-run relationships. The short-run relationship, the well-known Quantity Theory of Money (QT), assumes that $\bar{M}(t)$ "causes" or "explains" the price level. We will return to the Quantity Theory later. The long-run perspective focuses on the commodity aspects of commodity-money and compares money to the other commodities in the economy; the theory holds that, in the long run, there should be no discrepancy between the costs of producing more commodity-money and its purchasing power. In the long run, the costs of producing commodity-money and the benefits from exchanging it should be the same. These somewhat contradictory approaches to determining the value of UOAs (coins) played an important role in the debates to come.

From Money to Credit in Exchange

Each transaction will be reflected in the CoMSE in the form of more UOAs in the seller's hands and less in the buyer's, while the commodity or service moves in the other direction. Can the buyer buy through the use of some other method? Yes, if the seller agrees. Usually in such cases, the buyer issues a paper to the seller specifying the amount of the debt, including the (late) payment conditions and in particular the date of maturity. Such private-credit instruments will be called Private-Debt Certificates (PDCs). Until the buyer pays his debt to the seller, he will be considered a debtor and the transaction will thus be a sale on credit. However, it is not necessary for the buyer to issue his own PDC. Subject to the agreement of the seller, the buyer can use a third party's PDC as a medium of exchange. For example, a debt certificate granted to the current buyer by a past buyer of his products can be used by him as payment, assuming that the issuer of the original PDC will continue to respect his debt to another party. To prove consent on the part of the current debt holder (the buyer in this transaction), the custom was and remains to endorse such a PDC as a proof of its genuine transfer, thus creating a complex legal relationship between the three parties.

To complicate matters even more, and to bring them closer to reality, we will add the usage of private-debt certificates of a particular nature. Historically, not all PDCs were perceived by the public as having the same value, even when their nominal values were the same. Their perceived value depended to some extent on the credibility and expected behavior of the original PDC's issuer. If the issuer was a well-known wealthy person in the region who promised to pay his privately issued debt certificates in commodity-money immediately when they were brought to him, then the trust in those debt certificates would be high. Convertible bank notes were a unique type of PDC issued by a distinguished group of issuers and payable to the bearer on demand.[1] Thus, upon the agreement of the seller and buyer of the commodity, an exchange could be arranged wherein the payment was either deferred or made in convertible bank notes. In many cases, these notes were perceived as almost as good as commodity-money; thus, we will term them "near-commodity-money." Other PDCs were further away from commodity-money; they were circulating credit instruments, known to contemporaries as bills of exchange. They were not legally convertible on demand to the basic form of money, and they represented a mere future promise to pay.

There are several different methods used to create PDCs, and each implies different economic consequences. However, because we have so far restricted ourselves to the exchange of goods and services and have not allowed intermediation, whether private or through institutions, the menu of possible mediums is relatively small. One method available to us is the

---

[1] We elaborated on their history in Chapter 2. See also Feavearyear (1931).

sale on credit, in which a private individual or economic organization issues a PDC against the purchase of a good. A second method to create a PDC of a specific nature is the issuance of convertible notes against coins, or UOAs. This act is not part of the exchange process itself but creates a medium that can serve exchange in the same way as does the PDC. At its inception, the new medium was based on a very primitive form of financial institution in which notes were issued against deposits of coins. It is important to emphasize that these institutions are not yet involved in any other kind of transaction and, in particular, not in intermediation. Thus, we are not yet dealing with channeling funds from one unit to another. The issuing institutions specifically do not issue against PDCs, and hence the notes are 100 percent covered with coins. Thus, payments can be made in such a system through the transfer of coins, the transfer of notes, or with the aid of credit (debt) instruments. This last method can take one of two forms: either the creation of a new PDC for a specific exchange transaction or the transfer of a PDC that existed before this specific transaction.

Now that we have briefly described the modus operandi of this ideal type of exchange based on commodity-money, it is time to elaborate on the nature of the mediums that in fact circulate goods. Let us return to Hawtrey's definition. Clearly, coins/UOAs function both as a measure of value and as a medium of exchange; according to Hawtrey, they are candidates for consideration as money because they seem to function like money. However, can they also meet his criterion of discharging debts? The answer is certainly yes for coins/UOAs, but what should we think of the other mediums? Remember that convertible notes and all other debt certificates are privately issued. Can one discharge a debt through the transfer of another debt? Yes, if the debtor agrees; but what if he does not? What if the two parties did not discuss the matter before the exchange and then, after the "payment" has been made in PDCs, the original issuer goes bankrupt? Who is responsible for the debt – the buyer or the third party? Even more disturbing are questions related to convertible notes. Who is responsible for those peculiar PDCs in the not-so-rare cases in which the issuer fails to pay in commodity-money when asked to do so by the bearer of the notes? As people of the period slowly learned, those mediums which circulated side-by-side with commodity-money were in some respects money, capable of discharging a debt, but in some respects they were not.

The legal question, though important, was not the only one to attract attention. The status and role of the PDCs in the economy was also puzzling. Was the famous Quantity Theory of Money, on which more will be said later, relevant for just the basic form of money, or should the money aggregate be redefined so as to include the near-commodity-money and/ or other credit instruments as well? As we have seen, the first extension of the definition of money was straightforward. Common wisdom held that the relevant quantity for the short-run theory of money, represented by Hume, should include convertible bank notes in addition to coins. That conclusion stemmed from the perceived history of these unique PDCs – convertible bank notes – that were first introduced to the system in the form of written evidence that commodity-money was deposited in the hands of their issuers. Those issuers, known first as Goldsmiths and later as the issuing banks, kept the coins in their coffers against the notes issued. Thus, common wisdom looked upon the notes as very close substitutes for coins that for obvious reasons people preferred to hold and use in exchange. The assumption was that coins and convertible notes function in the economy exactly as coins alone would have, had coins been the only medium of exchange. This assumption, in turn, was rooted in the supposedly perfect interchangeability between convertible notes and commodity-money. Of course, this was true when the issuing bodies held a 100 percent reserve ratio against the issued debt certificates and hence were always ready, with no delays, to exchange them back as long as they were acting in good faith. Under these conditions it was simply a matter of the public using commodity-money or something representing it to facilitate exchange; the only difference was the convenience for the parties involved.

In terms of quantity, instead of only counting the coins in the hands of the public, now both coins and their representatives, the convertible notes, were counted. The presupposition was the unobstructed, smooth exchange of notes and coins by the issuers of notes, who would always have ready coins. However, as discussed in the chapter on Smith, one should remember that the assumption of 100 percent cash reserves against notes did not reflect the real institutional arrangements. As we shall see, the assumption excludes credit creation to serve exchange and intermediation on the part of the issuing bodies, both of which led to less than 100 percent reserves. Because convertibility was not always secured, due in part to the fractional reserve system that was common among the issuers of notes, the legal and theoretical status of convertible notes hung in the air, especially when crises erupted in the system. The status of other heavily used mediums used in the exchange process was even more difficult to resolve.

Implications for the Quantity Theory

Monetary theory that dealt with the long run – that which argued that the cost of producing the commodity serving as a unit of account could not deviate from its purchasing power – was, in fact, an implementation of the law of one price to money. If a unit of commodity-money could buy a certain amount of goods through exchange, and the value of those goods was different from what one had to spend in order to produce a new unit, then naturally, someone would exploit this difference. In such situations, a long-term process of arbitrage took place. The cost of producing such a unit was determined by real forces and will not be discussed here, because it is outside the scope of our discussion. The value of the unit of account in exchange, that is, its purchasing power, was determined in the short run via the Quantity Theory. In cases of a gap between the cost of production and the purchasing power, forces worked to exploit the situation. When either changed for any reason, the long-run equilibrating forces started to work. One should note that introducing inconvertibility – fiat money or inconvertible paper money – destroys the links between the long-run and short-run attractors just described, that is, between the long-term cost and short-run conditions assumed by the Quantity Theory.

Some of the major difficulties concerning monetary theory during the Classical School years resulted from the need to adapt the Quantity Theory to systems of exchange that departed from the CoMSE and were thus less than pure. More coins (*ceteris paribus*) lead to higher prices: This was the basic statement of the Quantity Theory. It was rooted in the so-called natural order of things. In a world where only pure exchange took place everywhere, there was a natural allocation of gold over the entire world. If this natural allocation of gold was disturbed due to more gold in one part of the world or a flow of gold from one country to another, the return to the natural allocation was to be reestablished through the influence of gold on prices. This led to the famous Price-Specie-Flow mechanism as it was perceived for the pure system of exchange.

The Quantity Theory is probably the oldest theory in political economy and one of the better known among noneconomists. Analytically, it is based on confronting the quantity of the simplest form of money, coins, which functioned both as unit of account and medium of exchange with commodities that had been exchanged. The prices of those commodities, measured in coins, must bear a direct relation to their quantity. The proposition was not conceived as just measuring an accounting identity of exchange – what flows in one direction should be exactly equal to what flows in the opposite direction – but as holding a description of behavior as well. Without entering into this old distinction between the Quantity Theory as identity that just measures but does not explain, and the Quantity Theory as an equation that relates some variables to each other and does explain, it will be assumed from this point on that the scholars who made up the Classical School, and those who wrote before, all addressed an equation version of the Quantity Theory, whether they accepted or rejected it. When a scholar had in mind an identity rather than equation version, we will explicitly refer to the identity version of the Quantity Theory.

The attitude toward the Quantity Theory was deeply rooted in common historical experience and in a very simple argument made about a pure system of commodity-money exchange: The more coins people had, the higher the prices of goods. The theoretical argument depended upon the effective quantity of circulating coins, thus on the velocity as well as the stock of money; but this became clear relatively early on, as we shall see. However, the exact channel through which the influence of more (or less) coins in the hands of people was transmitted was far from clear. Indeed, there is still widespread disagreement over the famous "transmission mechanism." We will examine this debate in due course; in the meantime, and for the purposes of our discussion, the statement that the quantity of coins in the economy determines (coin) prices remains the Quantity Theory's clearest expression, certainly for pure exchange systems. The historical experiences of early times and certainly that of the sixteenth century pointed in the same direction: The more commodity-money an economy had, the higher the prices, measured in commodity-money in that economy. Thus, the Quantity Theory for a pure exchange economy was the conventional wisdom.

However, the Quantity Theory traveled a much longer theoretical distance and was accepted for more sophisticated exchange systems. The Quantity Theory was extended from the simplest exchange technology to more complex ones. It was adopted with almost no debate; but contrary to Smith's position, the theory was applied to a mixed circulation where convertible notes, covered 100 percent with coins, were used. With little to no notice, it was then applied to a mixed circulation where the notes were convertible, but the reserve ratio against them was less then 100 percent. Does it matter? We will try to answer this question in the coming chapters.

So far in our discussion, we have followed the common structure that starts from commodity-money and then moves to near-monies and credit. As previously discussed, this is not the only logical possibility for analyzing systems of exchange. Maybe, then, the historical path was also different. In principle, people can exchange and use a promise as payment. As long as the partners to trade have trust in the buyer's commitment, debts can act as mediums of exchange. The debts themselves can be, and usually were, private debts, but in principle, social institutions could also step in and supply such instruments.

The understanding that exchange can be executed by debts and credits, PDCs in the just-described formulations, would wait historically for Thornton, and later on for Wicksell. Analytically, this unconventional approach came into some conflict with the Quantity Theory. The quantities of the mediums used in payments were demand-determined. Thus, in this later approach, one faced the endogenous determination of credit in its role in the exchange process. The role of money in a pure credit economy will be discussed in the chapter on Wicksell. We will continue the discussion of "credit theories of money" in Chapter 9, after we encounter Thornton's monetary theory.

PART TWO

DEBATING MONETARY THEORY UNDER
INCONVERTIBILITY

FIVE

New Reality

The Restriction Period, 1797–1821

The Restriction: An Inconvertible Monetary System

The structure of the British banking system as we described it in Chapter 2 did not change significantly until the end of the eighteenth century. The three types of banks – the Bank of England; the private, non-issuing banks in London; and the many issuing ones in the rest of the country – continued their activities. The number of private banks in London barely changed during this time; there were some fifty to sixty at the midpoint of the eighteenth century and around the same number toward the end of the century, although on average, they grew in size. The number of country banks, on the other hand, increased dramatically, doubling between 1783 and 1793 and continuing to grow until 1813 (Pressnell 1956, p. 11).[1] The banking system faced several financial crises, for example in 1783 and 1793, but managed to deal with each of them so that the system returned to function afterward as it had before. However, one major crisis at the end of the century caused a significant rift in the British banking system.

Although it is often difficult to determine the starting point of a historical process or debate, this is not the case with what is known as the Restriction Period. The Restriction started abruptly with a decision taken by the sovereign on Sunday, February 26, 1797, before the opening of the banks the following day. This decision marked a crucial turning point for money and credit in both theory and practice. The crisis that forced the decision had started a few days earlier on February 18, when, apparently due to rumors of an invasion, people in Newcastle rushed to the banks and converted notes to coins. Some banks in the region suspended payments, and a run on banks

---

[1] Since mid-eighteenth century, as we discussed in Chapter 2, country banks were active outside London. Feavearyear (1931) tells us that by 1793, there were around 400 country banks in England (162–164).

in various parts of the country spread quickly. A report that the French had landed in Wales contributed to the pressure in London at the Bank of England, where bullion reserves fell dramatically. The decision made on February 26, taken as an Order in Council, initiated the Restriction. Specifically, it forbade the Bank of England to pay its notes in specie. The suspension of cash payments, as it is also known, remained in effect until 1821.[2] Thus, these early years of the nineteenth century, the Napoleonic war years, saw a period of intense economic debate about the functioning of the new inconvertible monetary system and how a convertible one would work. This debate has since become known as the Bullion Debate.

This was not the first time that the Bank reserves had declined. In later years, information concerning the balance sheet of the Bank – information not known to contemporaries – was revealed. As Clapham (1940) observes, at the time there was a "complete statistical black-out." Before 1832, even official parliamentary committees of inquiry were not "allowed to know the amount of the Bank's cash holdings" (p. 161). The information used by scholars in later years was mostly that gathered and published by the 1832 Committee.[3] This data source reveals some of the story, which might also have been at least partially known to some contemporary observers through secret, unofficial channels.

The bullion reserves of the Bank of England were both a secret and an important element in the story of the British financial system. If one looks at the bullion reserves of the Bank of England since 1778, for which the 1832 Committee provided two quotations per year (see Table 5.1), one can see a clear pattern: Years known as "difficult" years, the years of financial crisis, usually saw declines in the reserves of the Bank's bullion. Of course, even though the data only became available to the public at a later stage, they were known at the Bank and probably also guessed by some others. In Table 5.1, one can clearly see the crises years of 1783 and 1793 as well as the decline in reserves after the mid-1790s. Looking at the biannual data points after the mid-1790s, the picture becomes even more dramatic.

Bullion reserves dropped from February 1792 to February 1793 (from around 6.5 million pounds to 4 million), climbed again to 7 million pounds in February 1794, and declined steadily to a little over 2 million pounds in August 1796. In February 1797, the bullion at the Bank dropped to just around 1 million pounds (see also Fetter 1965, p. 18). The reserves fell partly

---

[2] See PP (1797); Clapham (1944); Fetter (1965).
[3] See Clapham (1944) for description of the data and Mitchell (1988) for a summary of the period statistics.

Table 5.1. *Bullion at the Bank of England, its note circulation and deposits,*
1778 to 1797 (in thousand pounds)

	Bullion	Note circulation	Deposits
1778 Feb.	2,011	7,440	4,662
Aug.	3,128	6,758	4,716
1779 Feb.	3,711	9,013	4,358
Aug.	3,983	7,277	5,201
1780 Feb.	3,581	8,411	4,724
Aug.	4,179	6,342	6,656
1781 Feb.	3,280	7,092	5,797
Aug.	2,863	6,309	5,922
1782 Feb.	2,158	8,029	6,130
Aug.	1,957	6,759	6,759
1783 Feb.	1,321	7,675	4,465
Aug.	590	6,307	6,106
1784 Feb.	656	6,203	3,904
Aug.	1,540	5,593	6,267
1785 Feb.	2,741	5,923	6,669
Aug.	5,487	6,571	6,252
1786 Feb.	5,979	7,582	6,152
Aug.	6,311	8,184	5,867
1787 Feb.	5,627	8,330	5,902
Aug.	6,293	9,686	5,632
1788 Feb.	5,743	9,561	5,177
Aug.	6,899	10,003	5,529
1789 Feb.	7,229	9,807	5,537
Aug.	8,646	11,122	6,402
1790 Feb.	8,633	10,041	6,223
Aug.	8,386	11,433	6,199
1791 Feb.	7,869	11,440	6,365
Aug.	8,056	11,672	6,438
1792 Feb.	6,468	11,307	5,523
Aug.	5,357	11,006	5,526
1793 Feb.	4,011	11,889	5,346
Aug.	5,322	10,865	6,443
1794 Feb.	6,987	10,744	7,892
Aug.	6,770	10,287	5,936
1795 Feb.	6,128	14,018	5,973
Aug.	5,136	10,862	8,155

(*continued*)

Table 5.1 (*continued*)

	Bullion	Note circulation	Deposits
1796 Feb.	2,540	10,730	5,702
Aug.	2,123	9,247	6,656
1797 Feb.	1,086	9,675	4,892
Aug.	4,090	11,114	7,765

Source: Parliamentary Papers (1832) appendix 5; see also Clapham (1944) appendix C for explanations.

because some of the bullion was transferred to France, where the Assignat system had collapsed, and gold was used as the medium of circulation; and partly because of the demand for bullion within England, known as internal drain. Thus, the rumors of a French invasion could be seen as a trigger for the run on the banks – a kind of last straw that forced the Bank of England to suspend specie payments.

For the first few days, many expected the worst, even to the point of a return to barter, the abandonment of all monetary arrangements, and total chaos. In reality, the first three years of the Restriction were relatively tranquil and stable. People continued to use Bank notes even though they could not exchange them for gold and, more surprisingly, they continued using country banks' notes. The data concerning the Bank, not regularly published as we saw (and will see again in Chapter 6), reveal an interesting pattern. In two periods, 1800–1801 and 1809–1810, the bullion reserves at the Bank declined; as in similar circumstances in the past, this was a clear sign of trouble in the financial system. However, this time, of course, the crises were different; they were characterized not by an outflow of gold but by price changes. In fact, public alarm during these two periods was caused by price changes and negative exchanges.[4]

It is important to be aware of some additional limitations on the currency during the period under discussion as a result of past decisions. Since 1663, the sovereign, under the influence of Mercantile principles, banned the export of specie or bullion that had been melted out of coins. To this limitation on gold movements one should add the rule of maximum rate of interest. Mainly because of moral reservations, the maximum rate of interest was set in 1713 at only 5 percent. This was modified in 1716 so as to apply only to lending and discounting, and not to borrowing from abroad.

---

[4] See Viner (1937) and Fetter (1965).

In 1773, the Bank of England rate was fixed at 5 percent and remained so until 1822. In 1795, the Bank decided to discount at this rate only that proportion that the Bank itself decided. This enabled the Bank to act according to its discretion in issuing notes.

Data on prices, like those on the banking sector, were not officially gathered and published, but traders, banking officials, and the press reported on various indicators. Thus, in 1800–1801 and again in 1809–1810, the public "knew" that prices had risen; they sensed it in the markets and saw it most clearly in two prices: the price of gold and the price of wheat. Gold was a commodity that was not traded in England during the Restriction; its price has been assessed indirectly by transactions in various financial centers where people traded in bills of exchange nominated in pounds and sold for equivalents of gold. The price of wheat was clear to consumers as well as traders. In Table 5.2, we present six measures for price changes; changes whose exact amount was unknown by contemporaries, but which they probably sensed. They substantiate the famous conclusion that the debate during the Restriction, the Bullion debate, was closely linked in intensity to price changes; the debate began and was very intense in 1801–1802 with the first burst of inflation, and was intensively renewed in 1809–1810 when there was even higher inflation (see Viner 1937, Fetter 1965). Hence, in the coming chapters we will refer both to the early round of the bullion debate and to the second, more famous round that culminated in the committee nominated to inquire into the "High Price of Bullion."

Table 5.2 shows changes in prices, including in particular the price of wheat and changes in the price of gold, which together with the exchanges provided the focus of many of the arguments. Column 1 records Gayer's et al. famous price index, constructed and published in 1953, many years after the events took place. Column 2 records a simple price index constructed by Jevons earlier, in 1865, which was based on the most comprehensive data set on prices, a data set that was collected and published by Tooke in 1823–1824. Column 3 presents an index based directly on Tooke's data as he could have constructed; column 4 presents the index when it does not include wheat; column 5 is just the price of wheat; and column 6 is the price of gold. Although the early-nineteenth-century economists did not use price indexes, they did seem to have some intuitive knowledge of price trends. They realized early on that prices were moving both in 1800–1801 and in 1809–1810. All the indexes in Table 5.2, of course, confirm their intuitions. For today's reader, we include a graph (Figure 5.1) that captures the general price trends as well as those of the price of wheat and the price of gold. Those periods marked by inflation, illustrated by Figure 5.1, were also periods of crisis.

Table 5.2. *Prices during the Restriction, 1797 to 1821*

	(1)	(2)	(3)	(4)	(5)	(6)
	Price Index 1 Gayer et al	Price Index 2 Jevons	Price Index 3 Tooke-A	Price Index 4 Tooke-B [no wheat]	Price Of Wheat	Price Of Gold
1797	106.2	110	118.92	128.14	47.42	100
1798	107.9	118	113.58	132.17	37.00	100
1799	124.6	130	133.38	130.60	64.75	100
1800	151.0	141	149.20	132.17	96.50	100
1801	155.7	140	150.92	136.74	94.42	109
1802	122.2	110	121.88	126.39	55.88	108
1803	123.6	125	123.06	139.67	49.42	103
1804	124.3	119	133.53	134.25	68.38	103
1805	136.2	132	132.76	132.85	67.21	103
1806	134.5	130	129.10	129.33	65.88	103
1807	131.2	129	127.30	129.06	63.83	103
1808	144.5	145	150.68	151.80	78.08	103
1809	155.0	157	162.49	170.84	85.75	103
1810	153.4	152	157.65	155.65	88.33	116
1811	145.4	136	151.96	152.25	92.63	109
1812	163.7	121	167.93	156.85	119.92	123
1813	168.9	115	168.45	169.99	92.25	130
1814	153.7	114	162.10	174.10	71.08	134
1815	129.9	109	139.97	148.24	61.00	120
1816	118.6	91	131.07	117.01	83.50	120
1817	131.9	117	140.48	127.25	90.07	103
1818	138.7	132	140.85	138.61	76.38	103
1819	128.1	112	128.87	121.05	65.63	105
1820	115.4	103	114.46	110.72	62.47	103
1821	99.7	w94	102.16	100.58	54.50	100

Sources: Column (1) Mitchell 1962, p. 470; base year 1782=100. Column (2) Jevons 1884, pp. 144–145. Column (3) The Author's calculations; for detailed explanations, see Arnon 1991, chapter 10. The price data is from Tooke's 1823 publication using Gayer's weights. Column (4) As in column (3) excluding wheat. Column (5) Computed from Tooke's 1823 quotations for the price of wheat. Column (6) From Tooke 1824, appendix 1; used also by Jevons 1884, p. 139.

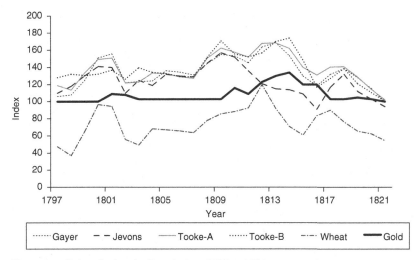

Figure 5.1. Prices during the Restriction, 1797 to 1821.

Economic crisis, as we shall see, played an important role in shaping theory and practices regarding money and banking in the eighteenth and nineteenth centuries, as they do today. Before the Restriction, the state of gold reserves, that is, the solvency of the banks, was the most important single aspect of a crisis: In 1783, there was a drain of gold that, according to Feavearyear, prompted the Bank of England to attempt to make policy for the first time (1931, pp. 176–179); and in 1793, the war with France caused a crisis followed by a run on the banks and their eventual collapse. However, with the start of the Restriction, the state of gold reserves was less crucial; inflation and stability took center stage instead, as we shall see.

During the Restriction, coins stayed mostly outside active circulation and were almost not in use in transactions; the economy relied more on bank notes as the medium of exchange. Bank of England notes used in circulation increased from around ten million pounds at the beginning of the Restriction to close to twenty million by 1809 (see Table 5.3). Notes in circulation of all the other issuing banks – the country banks – rose from five and a half million in 1796 to twenty-five million in 1809; at the same time, deposits in Great Britain, exclusive of the Bank of England, increased from eight million pounds to fifteen million pounds. Although one should notice that in the few years just before the Restriction, these two last aggregates declined, their sharp increase after the start of the Restriction was dramatic. The total money supply, using modern conventions – Bank of England's notes in circulation, other issuing banks' notes in circulation, and

Table 5.3. *Bullion at the Bank of England, its note circulation and deposits, 1797 to 1821 (in thousand pounds)*

	Bullion	Note circulation	Deposits
1797 Feb.	1,086	9,675	4,892
Aug.	4,090	11,114	7,765
1798 Feb.	5,829	13,096	6,149
Aug.	6,546	12,181	8,301
1799 Feb.	7,564	12,960	8,132
Aug.	7,001	13,389	7,642
1800 Feb.	6,144	16,844	7,063
Aug.	5,150	15,047	8,335
1801 Feb.	4,640	16,213	10,746
Aug.	4,335	14,556	8,134
1802 Feb.	4,152	15,187	6,858
Aug.	3,892	17,098	9,739
1803 Feb.	3,777	15,320	8,050
Aug.	3,593	15,983	9,817
1804 Feb.	3,372	17,078	8,677
Aug.	5,879	17,154	9,716
1805 Feb.	5,884	17,871	12,084
Aug.	7,625	16,388	14,048
1806 Feb.	5,987	17,730	9,981
Aug.	6,215	21,027	9,636
1807 Feb.	6,143	16,951	11,829
Aug.	6,484	19,678	11,789
1808 Feb.	7,855	18,189	11,962
Aug.	6,016	17,111	13,013
1809 Feb.	4,489	18,543	9,983
Aug.	3,652	19,574	12,257
1810 Feb.	3,501	21,020	12,457
Aug.	3,192	24,794	13,618
1811 Feb.	3,351	23,360	11,446
Aug.	3,243	23,287	11,076
1812 Feb.	2,983	23,408	11,595
Aug.	3,099	23,027	11,849
1813 Feb.	2,885	23,211	11,268
Aug.	2,712	24,828	11,160
1814 Feb.	2,204	24,801	12,455
Aug.	2,098	28,368	14,850

Table 5.3 *(continued)*

	Bullion	Note circulation	Deposits
1815 Feb.	2,037	27,262	11,702
Aug.	3,409	27,249	12,696
1816 Feb.	4,641	27,014	12,389
Aug.	7,563	26,759	11,856
1817 Feb.	9,681	27,398	10,826
Aug.	11,668	29,544	9,085
1818 Feb.	10,055	27,771	7,998
Aug.	6,363	26,202	7,928
1819 Feb.	4,185	25,127	6,413
Aug.	3,595	25,253	6,304
1820 Feb.	4,911	23,484	4,094
Aug.	8,211	24,299	4,421
1821 Feb.	11,870	23,885	5,623
Aug.	11,234	20,295	5,818

Source: Parliamentary Papers (1832) appendix 5; see also Clapham (1944) appendix C for explanations.

Table 5.4. *Assets and liabilities in Great Britain, 1792 to 1824 (thousand pounds in the money columns)*

	1	2	3	4	5	6	7
	Bank of England Note Circulation	Note circulation of other banks	Total bank deposits in Great Britain exclusive of Bank of England	Total of columns 1, 2, & 3	Approx. total number of banks	Total deposits of Bank of England	Total coin & bullion in the Bank of England
1792	11,000	12,000	10,000	33,000	300	6,000	7,000
1796	11,000	5,500	8,000	24,500	250	5,000	6,000
1809	20,000	25,000	15,000	60,000	750	12,000	4,500
1819	24,000	20,000	12,000	56,000	550	4,000	4,500
1824	20,500	20,000	20,000	60,500	600	10,000	9,000

Source: Feavearyear (1931) 304–305 [in the second edition].

total deposits (excluding those at the Bank of England) – increased from twenty-four and half million pounds in 1796 to sixty million pounds in 1809. Again, the decline in the years before the Restriction – from thirty-three million pounds in 1792 to twenty-four and half in 1796 – was more than compensated in the years up to 1809 (see Table 5.4).

From 1809, a crises year and an outstanding year for the development of monetary theory as we shall see, the money supply aggregate shows relative stability; it was around the sixty million pounds mark up to 1824. The note circulation of the Bank of England was stable as well; it increased a little by 1819, but then returned to be around twenty million pounds after the end of the Restriction in 1821 and, what is more surprising, for the next fifty years (see Table 10.2). The major changes in the banking system occurred in the various banks' deposits, an issue that the debates during the Restriction did not address and which came to the forefront only after the Resumption of cash payments. In the coming chapters, we will focus on those who discussed the implications, if any, of the disappearance of bullion payments from the system.

SIX

The Early Round of the Bullion Debate
1800–1802

Boyd versus Baring

Introduction

As we saw in Chapter 5, the Restriction Period began in England in February 1797 when, under the shadow of a run on the banking system, the sovereign suspended the specie convertibility of Bank of England notes. The suspension of cash payments remained in effect until 1821 and marked a crucial turning point for both banking theory and monetary policy.

The Bank of England, as we recall from Chapters 2 and 5, was a private institution with privileges; it was the only bank in London whose charter permitted it to issue notes within the city and its vicinity. The London private banks did not issue notes but dealt with all other aspects of banking; the country banks outside London faced almost no legal restrictions concerning note-issuing. The heavily capitalized Bank of England, which financed public expenditure and held reserves for the other banks, thus became the pivot of the British banking system. In hindsight, it was the Bank's powerful position, particularly concerning reserves, its monopoly in note-issuing in London, and its lack of understanding of its consequent responsibilities that made it the focal point of a controversy within the British economic system that lasted over seventy years.

The French War years around the turn of the nineteenth century witnessed a period of intense economic debate in England. The debates during the Restriction about the complicated relationship between inflation, the exchanges, and monetary control came to be known as the Bullion Debate, referring to a prevalent Restriction-era conversation about the reasons for the fluctuating market price of gold and the advisability of a return to specie convertibility. The Bullionists were critical of the Bank of England and supported an early return to convertibility; the anti-Bullionists defended the Bank and inconvertibility. Debate about the reasons for the discrepancy between the fixed pre-Restriction Mint price of gold and its market price continued into the nineteenth century, fluctuating in intensity with gold's market price, as Jacob Viner (1937) and Frank W. Fetter (1965) point out.[1] The controversy intensified when the price of gold in terms of inconvertible notes was high and the exchanges were bad (as in 1800–1801 and 1809), and when the exchange of the Irish pound was not on a par with the English pound (as in 1803–1804). These debates proved fruitful insofar as they culminated in attempts to formulate theories tenable in situations of inconvertibility. The debates extended to the relationship between internal circulation and international movements of gold and commodities, the influence credit and banking had on the economy as a whole, and a new assessment of the Bank of England's role in the monetary system.

The first round in the debate occurred in 1801–1804 with the publications of the Bullionists Walter Boyd (1801), John Wheatley (1803), and Peter King (1804) and their opponents Francis Baring (1801) (an anti-Bullionist) and Henry Thornton (1802) (more on Thornton in Chapter 7). Many others participated in forums where the public debate took place: in Parliament, parliamentarian committees of inquiry, the press, and pamphlets exchanges. The Bank of England's advocates were particularly well represented. David Ricardo entered the scene of political economy via the second round of the debate in 1809–1811. He has since been strongly associated with the Bullionist position, although he presented an extreme version of Bullionism that was very similar to Wheatley's (more on Ricardo in Chapter 8). That second round of debate also brought us the famous Bullion Committee whose report was written by Francis Horner, William Huskisson, and Thornton. The third round of the Bullionist debate was mostly concerned with the practicalities of a return to cash payments and the phenomenon of falling prices; it was mainly publicized not through pamphlets, but through the press and the 1819 parliamentary committees on the return to cash payments.

Many modern scholars have tended to present the Bullionists' position as more reasonable and well argued than that of their opposition; they lean toward the view that the anti-Bullionists, who represented the interests of the Bank and the government, were wrong. Viner (1937), Fetter (1965), Denis O'Brien (2004), and Friedrich von Hayek (1929/1991), among others, present Boyd, King, Horner, and Thornton as the main contributors to the debate from the Bullionist side.[2] This latter group of writers is often referred

---

[1] See Viner's definition of Bullionists and anti-Bullionists (1937, p. 120).
[2] See Viner (1937, chapter 3, especially pp. 119–122); Fetter (1965 chapter 2); O'Brien (2004 chapter. 6, pp. 175–181); and Hayek (1929, p. 197).

to in the secondary literature as the "moderate Bullionists," to be distinguished from the "extreme Bullionists" such as Wheatley (1803) and, later on, Ricardo (1809–1811). Baring is usually described as the only serious anti-Bullionist, a defender of the Bank of England and the Restriction.[3]

Boyd initiated the debate four years after the unexpected start of the Restriction. Boyd was a controversial figure, a financier who had some interests that put him in a very dubious position. The relatively late start of the debate well suits the argument that economists, like the general public, tend to address theoretical issues only when a practical problem is pressing. The sudden crisis in 1800 concerning several important aspects of the economy, particularly related to what modern economists would term "the nominal dimensions of the economy," triggered intense interest in the implications of the three-year-old inconvertible regime. The sovereign's unexpected decision in February 1797 to suspend cash payments should have started the discussions, but apart from some superficial exchanges and Baring's famous *Observations* (1797), to which we will turn later, the serious discussions had to wait for a real, not theoretical, crisis.

Although the dramatic events of 1800–1801 attracted much interest, accurate data was not readily available; "facts" such as prices, the exchanges, and monetary aggregates were contested by the participants, which partially explains the very different attitudes evident among the debaters. Boyd's pamphlet, written in late 1800 and published in early 1801, is a strong statement of the early Bullionist position. He put the blame for the rising price of bullion and the deteriorating exchanges on the Bank of England, which he claimed had expanded its note-issuing. Boyd argued that the country banks are blameless because they could not expand their note-issuing unless the Bank of England did so first. He emphasized the damage that the deteriorating exchanges did to the domestic prices of basic provisions; he blamed the Bank of England not just for the high price of bullion and the poor performance of the exchanges, neither of which directly affected too many people, but for the high price of wheat as well. In response to this early publication, and apparently due to its success, Baring (1801), an early anti-Bullionist, came to the Bank's and the government's defense. He emphasized the incomplete and unsatisfactory nature of Boyd's arguments, particularly concerning the supposed link between note expansion and the rising prices of foodstuffs.

That early round of the Bullionist debate (1801–1802), particularly Thornton's seminal treatise and the exchanges between Boyd and Baring,

---

[3] O'Brien adds Henry Boase (1804) to the "serious" anti-Bullionist pamphleteers.

represented the first serious attempt to deal with the Restriction. This new regime had not even been seriously discussed before the British sovereign suddenly adopted it as a rescue measure after a run on the banks in February 1797 nearly destroyed the financial system. Thus, one can look upon the Restriction as an unplanned experiment without a sound theoretical basis. Expectations of disaster were running high. When, to the surprise of many, the system continued almost uninterrupted for a couple of years, interest in understanding the foundations of the new regime subsided and was only renewed by the sudden rise in prices in 1800–1801. This rise in the prices of gold, wheat, and other commodities, not properly recorded at the time, provided the incentive for debate, as did the somewhat better-recorded phenomena concerning the "bad exchanges."

Boyd's Letter to Pitt (1800): A Critique of the Bank of England

Boyd was born in 1753 in Scotland. His career brought him to the Continent, where he was active in banking and finance; in 1785, he became a partner in a private bank in Paris. The revolutionary changes in France sent him back to London in 1792, where he was active in the exchanges markets and in making large loans to Austria, a British ally, to finance Austrian war expenditures. The huge deals he helped broker brought criticism and even led to the establishment of a committee of inquiry. By the late 1790s, his financial standing had deteriorated; by March of 1800, Boyd was bankrupt. When he traveled again to France, he regained some of his fortune, though he lost his freedom. He returned to England in 1814.[4] Boyd was a Member of Parliament in 1796, and from 1823 to 1830. He had close links to policy makers, particularly Prime Minister William Pitt (the younger) in the 1790s, though at the time he also had strained relations with the Bank of England.

Boyd's best-known text, *A Letter to the Right Honourable William Pitt on the Influence of the Stoppage of Issues in Specie at the Bank of England on the Prices of Provisions and Other Commodities* [*A Letter to Pitt*], was written in late 1800. It was sent a few weeks later and published in early 1801.[5] The

---

[4] See Daunton (2004).

[5] See the preface to the first edition. Boyd mentioned the date of writing the letter as November 11, 1800. In the weeks that elapsed before he actually sent it to the publisher, new facts became available in response to a request made by Parliament to the Bank of England concerning the amount of Bank of England notes in circulation which, along with the price of gold, strengthened his arguments. Later, we will designate the publication as Boyd (1801a).

pamphlet provoked many reactions, the most influential from the famous Sir Francis Baring. Boyd then published a second edition, *With additional Notes; and a Preface Containing Remarks on the Publication of Sir Francis Baring* (1801b).

The pamphlet's first edition analyzed the new inconvertible regime and its economic consequences and proposed some reforms. Boyd's analysis of note-issuing under inconvertibility was straightforward: Because there were no restrictions on the Bank of England as an issuing body, that body, acting under the rules prevailing since February 1797 and in line with its own best interests as a private company, was responsible for the monetary expansion and price rises. For over one hundred years, the Bank of England had observed the obligation to pay on demand in specie, which

indeed formed the fundamental condition of its institution ...; but, from the moment this condition was dispensed with, the danger of excessive issues became apparent. Indeed it is not to be supposed, that a corporation, whose profits chiefly arise from the circulation of its Notes, and which is exclusively directed by persons participating in those profits, has been, or could possibly be, proof against the temptation, which the license they have enjoyed since February 1797 has afforded. (1801a, p. 4)

The crucial conflict between public and private interests changed radically with the legal change concerning the convertibility of the Bank's notes. Although neither the general public nor Boyd himself knew the size of the "increase in paper" that occurred after February 1797, Boyd based his critique on the assumption, sometimes described by him as a "feeling," that there was too much paper money in circulation:

I am aware that it may be said, that there exists no *proof* of the increase of paper to which I attribute the increase of price. It is precisely because no *positive proof* does, or can, publicly exist, of a fact necessarily secret in itself, that I shall endeavour, by reasoning from effect to cause, to establish the existence of the fact, or at least to render the probability of its existence so great, as to warrant my assuming it in the observations I have to submit to your consideration. (1801a, p. 4–5)

Whether this fact should remain a secret was another subject of debate. Was this information internal business data to which only the Bank should be privy, or was it general knowledge to which every well-informed person should have access? Before this question received sufficient attention, the Bank answered an order of the House of Commons and supplied information concerning its note circulation. The Bank stated that the amount in circulation on December 6, 1800 – just after Boyd's *Letter* had been sent to Pitt, but not yet to the publisher – was close to 15.5 million pounds, compared to around 8.5 million pounds on February 26, 1797, and to 12 million pounds, the average circulation in the three years ending in December 1795.[6] The new data was insufficient for Boyd's case; he wanted to know the "balances on the books, for which the Bank is likewise liable," because otherwise, "... no accurate estimate can be formed of the positive difference between the present and the former circulation" (1801a, p. iv; from the preface to the first edition). Boyd also understood the impossibility of obtaining specific sums concerning the specie in the Bank coffers, but he wanted to know the proportional changes over the relevant dates and felt the Bank should have no objections about publishing the information.

The new data referred to in the preface of Boyd's second edition made him conclude that the increase in the average circulation was 30 percent.[7] This new solid data greatly strengthened Boyd's case, but the reader of the first edition has to remember that the argument is presented there without the new dramatic figures. Still, Boyd was confident that the *a priori* principles hold: "That the augmentation of the quantity of money, or paper performing the functions of money, in a country, has a tendency to depreciate that money or paper, is a principle universally recognized. It is invariable in its operation, as the law of gravitation..." (p. 7). The additional money, called by Boyd the "multiplication of the representative signs of money" to distinguish it from what it represents, caused prices to rise. Boyd described the rise in prices – caused by misguided "principles of public economy" – as "evil," on account of its proportion and timing. In a convertible system, the surplus would have been exported to other countries; under inconvertibility, it stayed in England where it had an enormous effect:

Under such circumstance, ought we to be surprised, that the effects of an increase of the circulating medium of the metropolis (thus operating as the elementary means of circulation and communicating its influence to the whole Paper Circulation of the country which turns, if I may so express myself, round it as it's common center) are felt in all articles of domestic consumption and expence, and they are felt the most in those articles which form the nourishment of the great body of the people? (1801a, p. 9–10)

In a very interesting statement that attracted the attention of later commentators, Boyd explained that:

---

[6] See preface to the first edition written on December 31, 1800. The exact figures were for December 6, 1800: 15,450,970; for February 26, 1797: 8,640,250; and for the average three years ending on December 1795: 11,975, 573.

[7] See preface to the second edition, p. xiii.

By the words "Means of Circulation," "Circulating Medium" and "Currency," which are used almost as synonymous terms in this letter, I understand always *ready money*, whether consisting of Bank Notes or Specie, in contradistinction to Bills of Exchange, Navy Bills, Exchequer Bills, or any other *negotiable* paper, which form no part of the circulating medium, as I have always understood the term. The latter is the *Circulator*; the former are merely *objects of circulation*. (1801a, pp. 1–2, note)

What constitutes the circulating medium, how its quantity is determined, and what should be its right proportion relative to the value of the annual produce were questions that fueled much of the debate. What was clear to Boyd while writing the *Letter to Pitt*, before the data from the Bank became public, was that a sharp increase in that quantity during a short time interval could produce a significant effect on prices.

Not only was the amount in circulation unknown, but the proper proportion of the circulating money to the "annual produce of the land and labour of the country," argued Boyd, "will probably for ever elude the researches of human ingenuity." The point Boyd tried to emphasize, however, was quantitative: Taking into account the small amount of money in relation to produce, minor changes in the quantity of money can create enormous effects. If this is correct, it "may fairly be inferred that an addition of 1–6th, 1–8th, 1–10th, or even 1–14th, in the short period of three years, to the amount of notes and credits" will have significant results, especially because it is now inconvertible.[8] Boyd estimated the additional quantity of money at the end of 1800 to be 10 percent higher than that of February 1797, a significant increase in less than three years.[9] As for the crucial information on the Bank balance sheet, "[t]here ought not to exist any reason for withholding this information, as long as the Bank avails itself of the licence for refusing to pay its notes on demand" (p. 17). Thus, the choice is between convertibility as a disciplinary device or public scrutiny based on the available data.

[8]   A note attached to the calculations revealed the lack of agreed information. In it Boyd mentioned a discussion in Parliament that he himself had missed, where the governor of the Bank "acknowledged in the House of Commons, on Thursday the 27th of November, that the circulation of Bank Notes had been increased one-sixth or one-seventh since the stoppage of issues in specie, in February 1797." Boyd was naturally satisfied with this confirmation of his assumptions.

[9]   The computation is based on the statements made to Parliament in February 1797. The Bank then owed 13,770,390 £ out of which 8,640,250 £ in notes and the rest (5,130,770,390 £) in "Credits in the books of the Bank." These "may be considered as Bank Notes, *virtually*, though not *really* in circulation, seeing all those credits might have been converted into Bank Notes, at the pleasure of the persons so credited in the books of the Bank." Thus, Bank accounts, although not really part of the circulation are measured as "circulating money of the country." As we have seen, the new data, published after the volume went to press, put the estimated increase at 30 percent.

The subject of the circulation is "peculiarly complex and obscure," wrote Boyd. The "human mind" tends to "confound causes with effects" and to "ascribe to one object the qualities which belong to another" (p. 17). According to Boyd, though some writers argue that "the encrease of the public debt, as forming an addition to the circulating medium of the country," is responsible for the rise in prices, "… the fact is, that the public debt and the currency of the country are 'Distinct, as is the swimmer from the flood'" (pp. 17–18).

Another area of confusion at the heart of the debate was the role of country banks vis-à-vis the circulation. Blaming the country banks for the great rise in prices "is clearly mistaking a secondary cause for a primary one," commented Boyd. The country banks must either pay their notes in gold or with Bank of England notes.[10] The same mechanism which kept the Bank of England from increasing its issues under convertibility now prohibited the country banks from increasing theirs. Thus, the Bank of England carried the blame:

> The circulation of these notes of Country-Banks is under a controul equally salutary as that which restrained the issues of Bank of England notes, while that corporation was bound to pay, and did pay, every demand upon it, in specie … [these notes] must necessarily be proportioned to the sums, in specie or Bank of England notes, requisite to discharge such of them as may be presented for payment; *but the paper of the Bank of England has no such limitation. It is itself now become (what coin of the country only ought to be) the ultimate element into which the whole paper circulation of the country resolves itself.* (1801a, p. 20; emphasis added).

The Bank of England, Boyd argued, is the regulator of the circulation during the Restriction, as gold had been before. Bank of England notes are the standard of the circulation. Both the country banks and the London banks follow the rules set up by the Bank of England. Both types of banking institutions,

> … like all human institutions, may have been frequently turned to improper purposes. The balances due on the books of a London Banker to his customers, and the notes in circulation of a Country-Bank, equally constitute the amount of the demands, which the public has a right to make. … The effect on the general powers of the circulating medium of the country is, in both cases, to augment those powers; … The effect of each, to the Banker in Lombard-street, as to the Country

---

[10] "Every note which the Country Banker issues is payable on demand, either in specie, or in notes of the Bank of England. It may therefore be inferred, that no part of these issues can possibly remain in circulation, beyond what the encreasing prosperity and industry of the country where they circulate, can fairly absorb or digest" (Boyd 1801a, p. 19).

Banker, is to afford a revenue, which, but for their intervention, would have been lost to the community. The circulation of Country Bank-notes may be defined *Active Circulation*, as proceeding from the proper Act of the Bank which issues them: that of a London Banker may be called *Passive Circulation*, as proceeding from the operations of others, who have the power of issuing their Orders upon him. (1801a, pp. 21–22)

The size of the total circulation depends on the Bank of England; both active and passive parts "must be greater or smaller, in proportion to the abundance or scarcity of Bank of England notes or specie, at any particular time" (ibid.). The quantity of the medium in circulation is determined by the complicated relationships between the public, the banks acting in their own self-interest, and the Bank of England. The determination of the quantity results from the confidence the public has in the various institutions, and in particular, the trust it has in the institutions' ability to repay their obligations in specie and Bank of England notes. The primary force driving the changes of the previous three years, argued Boyd, was the changing behavior of the Bank of England; other banks were secondary.

It is important to note that Boyd treated both the country banks' notes and the London bankers' deposits as part of the circulating medium. Both had an impact on prices and the exchanges. This modern approach to deposits, identifying them as similar in function to notes, was mostly lost in later years until the Banking School.

Price changes are proof of the changes in quantity, argued Boyd, although measuring both of them was uncommon and difficult at the time. The proof, Boyd argued somewhat unconvincingly, was in the feeling: "Every man feels, in his abridged comforts, or in his increased expences, the existence of this melancholy truth" (p. 25). What many called an increase in prices in "vulgar language" is properly called the "Depreciation of Paper." Boyd's calculations also resulted in an estimated 8 3/8 percent depreciation of Portugal Gold. Turning to English currency, Boyd remarked wittily that "[i]f the idea of a discount upon our currency is unpleasant, we may say, that Gold bears a premium in the market." He calculated this premium to be 9 1/8 percent. Comparisons with other currencies resulted in a difference of 9 percent, based on evidence he delivered to the Lords Committee of 1797.

Boyd was careful to distinguish between the state of the exchanges and depreciation of the currency (price rises). The exchanges had experienced unfavorable conditions under convertibility as well, but only for a short time. Boyd took care to distance himself from the familiar "one and only one reason" explanation, and argued that the state of the exchanges can be the result of various causes, real as well as monetary. Boyd argued that, under the circumstances, it was most probably the excess of the circulation that contributed to the deterioration of the exchanges.

Boyd developed a unique and sophisticated position on this crucial point. Under convertibility, if the exchanges were bad and an external drain of gold took place, the Bank's reaction could not provide

of itself, a powerful antidote to the very evil of an unfavourable exchange, but it naturally led the Bank to take defensive measures against the effects of this drain, and these measures, in their turn, tended to restore the exchanges to its natural level. In the present case, ... that establishment is not compelled to any exertions to remedy the evil of an unfavourable exchange, or to restore the equilibrium between coin and bullion. (1801a, p. 33)

Again, a clear conflict existed between the Bank as a profit maker and the desire to achieve price stability, because the Bank would not risk short-term profits for the sake of long-term stability. There were two sides to the unfavorable exchanges: the negative side related to imports, whether by government or private, which became expensive; and the positive side – the "pleasing task" – which was related to exports. The positive effect would come "[i]f the increase of prices in the home-market should fortunately not keep pace with the depreciation of the exchanges" (p. 37). Boyd avoided an assessment of the net effect, mentioning more complications due to expected changes in wages.

Boyd understood the importance of the changes introduced by the restriction of cash payments. The public had high "confidence" in notes because for over one hundred years the public knew that notes could be exchanged at will for specie. Bank of England inconvertible notes enjoyed the backing of Parliament, which made those notes a medium where "[t]he whole revenue of the state was receivable in it" and made "[t]he annuities on the public debt paid in it." Yet the question of confidence remained open, and the public debate over "legal tender" status continued. As to whether individuals were forced to use the paper or were using it willingly, Boyd wrote:

The true test ... [t]hat the circulation Bank-notes is *free*, not *forced*, would be to withdraw the authority over which the Bank refuses to pay them in specie. If, in that case, public confidence continued to repose as securely as it is now supposed to do, then indeed might their circulation be justly said to rest on *confidence;* but the very circumstance of continuing the power of refusing the payment proves incontestably that *authority* or *necessity*, not pure, unmixed *confidence*, forms the basis of the circulation of Bank-notes, in their present state. (p. 48)

Boyd concluded that the Bank mismanaged the circulation when left with no obligation to pay its notes in cash, and "the issues are under no other controul than that of the corporation whose profits depend upon them"

(p. 49). Hence, "it is impossible to stifle the suspicion, that these issues may have been extended much beyond the limits by which they would have been bounded, had the Bank continued to be subjected to the salutary obligation of paying its notes on demand" (ibid.).

Pre-Restriction confidence in Bank notes had been the result of Bank notes representing gold and silver in the convertible system, making inquiries about the Bank's procedures – particularly concerning the quantity of its notes in circulation – unnecessary. But when Bank notes do not represent gold and silver, and the rise in prices of "all necessaries and conveniencies of life, as well as of every species of exchangeable value" points to some general failure, confidence disappeared. Sir William Pitt was asked to "look down, with scorn, upon the … causes" (p. 51) that revealed the misbehavior and responsibility of the Bank of England's directors. They created "an increase of the representative signs of money … [resulting from] the rash attempt to extend the empire of credit beyond those limits which the eternal laws of nature had marked out for it" (pp. 51–52).

The phenomena of rising wheat and bread prices naturally attracted much attention. Whether the cause was a real scarcity in grain or pure speculation, Boyd argued that the roots of the problems were to be found in the inconvertible regime. Let gold and silver return as the "axis," and the difficulties will be cured without intervention in the businesses of traders, whether in banking or wheat: "To bring back the circulation of Bank-notes to the original condition of their circulation, is merely to correct an abuse which never ought to have existed" (p. 56).

Boyd clearly (and correctly, as we shall see) felt that his criticism might "embarrass the Administration." He reacted to the criticisms leveled at him with a fierce attack on inconvertibility combined with an appeal to the best interests of the government, the public and the Bank. England did not need a "forced paper-money, that dangerous quack-medicine, which, far from restoring vigour, gives only temporary artificial health, while it secretly undermines the vital powers of the country that has recourse to it" (see note 57).

Like almost every other participant in the debate, Boyd relied on the authority of Adam Smith. Boyd argued that had Smith been alive and been asked about the so-called price revolution, he would not have supported the arguments promoted by the defenders of the Restriction. Neither the war, nor the seasons, nor population changes would have satisfied Smith as convincing explanations:

[Smith] would find none of the assigned causes, which are *partial*, equal to the effects, which are *general*. He would naturally proceed to enquire, Whether some important cause might not have diminished the Value of Gold and Silver. He would begin to suspect some astonishing increase of the *quantity* of those metals, or of their *powers*. (1801a, p. 65)

Although possible in principle, argued Boyd, the dramatic increase in prices in such a short time period could not be accounted for. But had Smith been told that a Stoppage had been declared since February 1797 on payments of Bank notes, and that the Bank could issue *"… ad libitum …* Would he not say that this cause is, of itself, adequate to all the extraordinary rise which had taken place?" (p. 64). Boyd's answer was straightforward:

He [Smith] would say, that not only the currency of the country had been changed from a *certain* to an *uncertain* standard, but that the *quantity* of it, in all probability, had been greatly augmented … and that thus the prices of all objects of exchangeable value necessarily feel the influence of a *positive* degradation of the standard, and of a *probable* augmentation of the *quantity* of money in the country. … He would recommend to those who are entrusted with the great interests of the country, to examine, without delay, whether or not the Directors of the Bank of England had yielded to the almost irresistible temptation to which they had been exposed; for he would consider, that, in all probability, those Gentlemen, far from thinking it their duty to *with-hold* the advances solicited from them, may have thought they were rendering a meritorious service to the country, by *lending liberally*, on good security, the paper-money which Parliament had invested them with the power of coining. (1801a, pp. 64–65)

Indeed, the Bank's directors answered the demand for credit coming from private interests and from government requests for huge loans (three million pounds in just eight months). To act differently was "utterly incompatible with the ideas which led to the system of issuing paper not payable on demand." Parliament set the rules that created the inconvertible regime, Boyd argued, and was therefore responsible. Furthermore, the decision to extend the Bank's charter for an additional twenty-one years – a decision Boyd described as reward for a six-year interest-free loan to the government – sent the wrong signal: "If they had justly estimated the tendency of such a system; if they had thought, as it became the *acting guardian of public credit to think*, on that subject, they would have spurned the boon which they accepted" (1801a, p. 67; emphasis added).

Probably the most sensitive line of criticism was to question the authority's motives. Was Sir Pitt acting as a statesman in February 1797 when he supported the new regime, or was he managing the support of "the Monied Interest?" Boyd sarcastically added, "I wish you could answer in the negative" (p. 69). Boyd also suspected that the suspension had been prepared in advance; looking back in 1801, he believed the policies implemented during the months before the Restriction were calculated to create a shortage in the circulation so that the public, suffering from this scarcity, would be ready to accept new measures. The idea that such a conspiracy took place may explain Boyd's decision to quote an interesting initiative by a group he led in April 1796, which had proposed a reform that would have created a rival institution to the Bank in London.[11]

Boyd responded to criticism that his position was an "*ex post* observation" with a detailed account of his position on the day the measures were taken. He was working in Paris at the time, and he knew of the alarm caused by the run on the banks; ideas about how to counter it were debated in the City circles. The night before the Restriction, he had sent a letter to a "Friend" (apparently Mr. John Fordyce) describing in very negative terms the outcome of inconvertibility.[12] The addressee was someone who "on many occasions, conveyed my ideas to you [Pitt] ." He was a well-known expert, supportive of the letter's contents, and "you yourself, in common with the rest of the world, knew him to be distinguished" (p. 72). The letter was then apparently carried to the speaker of the house.[13]

Boyd's letter proposes an alternative solution to the difficulties facing England's monetary system in February 1797. Instead of Pitt's dangerous innovation, Boyd recommended "the operation of *well-founded confidence alone* upon the public mind, of which so unequivocal a proof was given by the Meeting at the Mansion House, which immediately followed the stoppage" (p. 75). Boyd referred here to a well-known meeting that took place immediately after the decision of the Stoppage was taken, wherein policy makers convinced the City community to remain loyal to the pound. The results of that meeting help explain the continued usage of paper notes after the Stoppage, at least for a while. Boyd argued that this confidence-building policy should have been implemented under convertibility; it could have prevented the distress of 1796, as shown by the evidence given by Thornton to the Lords Committee that inquired into the causes of those events. Though Thornton and Boyd did not know each other, they gave very similar evidence according to Boyd.[14]

---

[11] See appendix B in Boyd (1801a, pp. 86–102).
[12] See Boyd (1801a, pp. 72–75) and appendix C: (Boyd 1801a, pp. 103–107).
[13] Somewhat apologetically, Boyd then vaguely described the circumstances that prevented him from being on record before the writing of the letter: "you collect the cruel circumstances in which I was then placed, and those, still more dreadful, which have since occurred to annihilate my commercial existence in this country" (1801a, p. 73).
[14] See 1801a, p. 7, note.

The postscript to the first edition of Boyd's pamphlet is in fact the public cover letter attached to it; the real purpose of the postscript was to convey the author's reaction to Sir Pitt's speech in the House of Commons on November 27, 1800, concerning Mr. Tierney's proposal.[15] According to press reports, Sir Pitt had argued that there was no "redundancy of the circulating medium;" Boyd had "great difficulty" believing he had ever said this. Pitt's proof was "that Exchequer Bills bore a premium, instead of being at a discount" (p. 81). Boyd, who was not present in Parliament, was eager to report that since he had sent the *Letter,* new evidence had come in. He "little dreamt so early and striking a proof would be afforded of the truth ..." Contrary to Pitt's arguments, the fact that Exchequer bills not belonging to the circulating medium were bearing a premium when exchanged for "ready money ... indicate[s] a great abundance of the money." Likewise, "the high price of grain" was never considered proof that there was "no superabundance of money." Thus, Boyd supposed that "your argument has been misstated; for it would be a supposition altogether unworthy of the Finance-Minister of this country" to use such an argument in Parliament when it contradicted the conclusion (pp. 81–84).

Boyd's 1796 Proposals

The proposals that both Boyd and others referred to from time to time were made by "a Select Meeting of Gentlemen" gathered in the London Tavern on Saturday, April 2, 1796. The meeting attempted to address the difficulties in the circulation that were apparent even before the Restriction, namely "an alarming scarcity of money in the City of London" (p. 87). As a result of the scarcity, trade could no longer depend on discounting bills of exchange; the Bank directors had cut lending and discounting. The participants did not believe they could influence the directors, thus they selected an unofficial committee to formulate their proposals.[16]

They met again on April 5, 1796 and argued for a huge investment in bringing more specie; gold and silver alone, they claimed, could not supply the rising demands of circulation and supply the needs of "national industry and commerce in their present extended state" (p. 91). Meanwhile, the

---

[15] The letter was written on November 29, 1800. The pamphlet had been sent to Sir Pitt six weeks before publication of the first edition in February 1801.

[16] The committee included the following members, Boyd tells us: Chairman Walter Boyd Esq; Sir James Sanderson, Bart; Mr. Alderman Anderson; Mr. Alderman, Lushington (Sir Stefphen Lusgington who chaired the first meeting); John Inglis, Esq.; J. J. Angerstein, Esq.

"wise introduction of a paper currency, *constantly convertible into* Gold and Silver" would help to solve the scarcity because the partial reserve kept in the Bank against its note circulation gave more "powers" to the circulation.[17] That power is the result of "Confidence and Capital." But the other bankers also added to the power of the circulation because so many people in society deposited their cash balances with the banks:

The sum of money which every Merchant, Trader, or Manufacturer, and indeed almost every man of whatever description, finds it necessary to keep altogether unemployed to answer the various calls of business and expense, is generally deposited, not in his own strong box, but in the hands of his Banker; and this Banker, from being the depositary of a great number of such sums, finds, from experience, that the whole of these sums cannot, according to the general course of things, be all wanted at once; but, on the contrary, while he possesses good credit, that a part of these deposits will fully answer all the calls that can be made upon him. He therefore employs a part of these deposits in discounting Bills of Exchange, by which means he draws a revenue from what, in the hands of his customers, would have been a dead unproductive fund. The sum he thus employs is another clear addition to the powers of the money of the country" (Boyd 1801a, p. 93).

These deposits are made chiefly in Bank of England notes. Because the Bankers will also keep fractional reserves, the pyramid of the circulating medium will have an even stronger effect. The committee presented the following example: Assume the outstanding quantity of Bank of England notes to be forty-five million whereas the Bank keeps just fifteen million in coins. The bankers receive deposits of twenty-one million out of those notes, but keep just seven million in notes while advancing the rest. Thus, the system behaves as if the reserve kept is just one million, argued Boyd:[18]

No Bank could ever be so imprudent as to keep so small a balance with so large a circulation, and yet by the combined effects of Confidence and Capital, and the intervention of the Bank, and a number of private Bankers, not only the same effects are produced to the country, but they are produced without any risk or imprudence. (Boyd, 1801a, pp. 94–95)

The advantages to be gained from the joint operation of the Bank of England and private banks led the committee to propose the creation of another institution. With due respect for Parliament and "your instructions" (appendix B, p. 95), the "researches [propose] neither to infringe the

---

[17] "The difference between the amount of the notes in circulation and the specie, kept for paying them, is a clear addition to the powers of the money of the country" (Boyd, 1801a, p. 92).

[18] Boyd (1801a, p. 94).

privilege of exclusive Banking granted to the Bank of England, nor vio-
late any principle of public faith or confidence." The committee detailed the
functions of the Bank, namely discounting, bullion dealings, and Exchequer
Bills purchases, and concluded that they were not exclusive to the Bank. Its
only exclusive business was

> the power of borrowing, owing, or taking up money on their bills or notes pay-
> able on demand; no other body politick or corporate, nor any persons united in
> covenants of partnership, exceeding the number of six, being permitted to borrow,
> owe, or take up money on their Bills or Notes payable on demand, *or at any less time
> than six months from the borrowing thereof.* (ibid., pp. 96–97; emphasis added)

Thus, the committee concluded that introduction of a new paper, payable
only after six months, could relieve the shortage as long as the new paper
acquired "all the qualities of ready money." With such aims in mind, they
proposed a new institution with twenty-five board members "to act without
fee or reward." The board was to issue promissory notes payable with small
interest, calculated as less than 2 percent and supported with a "ready-
money-fund." Thus, the notes would become ready money and carry some
interest. The fund itself should consist of Bank of England notes, and not
specie, thus maintaining the place for the other mediums in circulation.
The new board would not be created for the "benefit of individuals" like the
Bank of England, but to serve the interests of trade, "furnishing to trade, a
temporary assistance which the Bank of England do not find it convenient,
or perhaps do not think themselves sufficiently authorised, under their present powers, to give" (pp. 98–99).

The conclusions were presented to the chancellor of the Exchequer. Boyd
reported that he apparently preferred to try another measure, proposed by the
Bank directors, first: "that the floating debt should be funded." If this worked,
"the establishment of a Board for the support of credit would be unnecessary,"
they concluded (p. 101). In a note added to the second edition of the *Letter*, to
which we will turn next, Boyd commented: "Sir Francis Baring has not hesi-
tated to say, that the principles of this plan were refuted at the time!!!"[19]

Sir Francis Baring, 1801: A Defense of the Bank

Boyd's pamphlet had an impact on the public and naturally irritated many
in the government and in the Bank. One famous reaction came from the
respectable Sir Francis Baring (1740–1810), who in 1797 had published

---

[19] See Boyd (1801b, appendix B p. 17).

two pamphlets considered an early defense of the Restriction. Baring was a merchant and banker who created the well-known House of Barings and was close to Lord Shelburne (later Lord Lansdowne) and the Whigs.

The first of Baring's 1797 pamphlets was *Observations on the Establishment of the Bank of England and on Paper circulation of the Country*; it was followed by *Further Observations*. In these pamphlets, one can find one of the earlier responses to the new measures and, as Fetter wrote, the only one that displays "any economic statesmanship or independence of view."[20] Baring expressed views close to those of Thornton; he understood well the pivotal place of the Bank of England and explained that in times of crisis the Bank should aid the system. In *Observations*, he used the expression, "*dernier resort*," lender of last resort, the first time that expression is on record.

Baring argued that the Bank of England was run by responsible and clever directors who

[f]rom long experience ... must understand correctly the amount to which their Notes can circulate without depreciation or discount; and although they acted very wisely at the awful moment to issue a larger sum than usual, yet the event has proved, that they have conducted themselves with equal judgment, by not extending their issues beyond what the currency of the country requires, and can support." (1797a, p. 12)

The banking system in England in the late 1790s was very different from the one Smith knew. Banks had been established "in almost every town, and even in villages" (p. 15). The competitive system that evolved was a source of obvious benefit to the economy but also of some dangers: "if Country Banks ... should fail, the contagion will immediately spread, and the consequences are incalculable" (p. 17). Under such circumstances, "the Bank are not an intermediate body, or power; there is no resource on their refusal, for they are the *dernier resort*" (p. 22). This is the French term that is the forerunner to the Lender of Last Resort.[21]

Baring tried to explain the directors' conduct to the public based on principles to which the directors would not object. However, even the loyal and cautious Baring expressed worry in a second publication a few months later. In *Further Observations*, a publication apparently intended only for private circulation to those he trusted, he was not satisfied with decisions made by

---

[20] See Fetter (1965, pp. 22–30).
[21] The term *dernier resort* appears again in Baring (1797a): "the merchants, manufacturers, etc. can pay no more than 5 per cent. Per annum, and as money was not to be obtained at that rate in the market, they were driven once more to the Bank as a *dernier resort*" (p. 47). The term probably comes from the French legal structure, referring to the concept of no further appeals. See Capie (2007, p. 311).

the government after the Restriction that threatened the "tranquility of the country." He wanted Bank notes to be "general legal tender," the country banks to be regulated, the Bank to be independent of the government, and the amount of the Bank notes issued to be limited. Baring kept these critical comments almost secret, sharing them only with those "who ... may be disposed to consider the question in private and deliberate manner" (1797b, p. 2). Baring continued to trust the directors and defend the Bank, but as Bank notes were not made legal tender, he criticized the Restriction as an unregulated banking system. In remarks atypical for an anti-Bullionist, he wrote, "I must express my regret that the Bank are *not* limited with regard to the amount of their Notes, so long as they enjoy any legal protection to screen them from payment" (1797b, p. 13).

Early in 1801, after being provoked by Boyd, Baring published *Observations on the Publication of Walter Boyd*. He explained that he decided to react because in "some circles [Boyd's] work had made an impression and contributed to raise an alarm" (p. 5). Baring accused Boyd of contributing to "lessen that confidence" in the Bank circulation, thus causing the "Public to believe that the excessive dearness of provisions arises from the circulation of Bank Notes." As a result, the "ignorant" and "half informed" might be influenced by "a name," especially because Boyd argued for some sound principles. Sir Baring felt it was his duty to defend the Bank of England: "I hope to prove that the paper issued by the Bank has never exceeded wants, and even the convenience of the Public, still less that it has operated to produce any advance in the price provisions" (p. 9). Baring placed the blame for the difficulties on the war. Accusing the Bullionists of eroding public confidence was calculated to reduce their effectiveness; Boyd, who had some conflicting material interests, was a particularly easy target.

The quality of Baring's and the anti-Bullionists' arguments was another matter. Baring, like the Bank directors and government policy makers, relied on Smith's Real Bills Doctrine, which Smith argued for under convertibility. Baring and the Bank, however, made it the basis of their monetary theory under inconvertibility. As early as 1797, Baring argued that even when "gold was refused on the presentation of the Notes," the "Directors of the Bank must understand correctly the amount to which their Notes can circulate without depreciation or discount; their Notes continued to circulate at par."[22] The discussions in the secret committees of 1797 and in parliamentary debates made clear how widespread that doctrine had become.

---

[22] See Baring (1797b, pp. 10–13). Baring trusted the directors' skills as is clear from his discussion of their role as a lender of last resort in 1797a (see note 20).

Boyd's Rebuttal: The Second Edition (1801b)

Boyd's pamphlet may well have contributed to the country's economic instability by eroding public confidence in the Bank. In any event, the pamphlet became the focus of heated debate and attracted much criticism immediately after publication, some of it in the form of personal attacks. Two such pamphlets, which have been ascribed to Baring in the Goldsmith Library catalogue, were especially tough.[23] Boyd reacted strongly to these criticisms, adding many notes to his pamphlet's second edition as well as a more than fifty-page preface. He also "endeavoured to obviate" with some success the "personal abuse" directed at him, especially in some of the anonymous tracts.

The reaction to Sir Baring was of an altogether different attitude. Boyd believed that their differences were rooted in the days immediately after the Stoppage, when their first discussions occurred. Boyd argued then that the augmentation of the circulation was significant; it was the *circulator* which increased by more than three million, to be distinguished carefully from the *objects of circulation*. This distinction escaped Baring. But because the two seemed to agree in theory, it came down to definitions and measurements to try and settle their differences. Thus, Boyd's new preface included some revealing definitions while also elaborating on theory, so far only partially addressed.

I have laid it down, as a principle, that there is but one criterion by which the issues of paper can safely be regulated, *the condition of its immediate conversion into specie*. All attempts to ascertain, by any other standard, the quantity of paper which the circulation of a country may require, or can bear, without inconvenience, must necessarily partake of an uncertainty and a danger similar to those which would attend the voyage of the mariner who should venture to sea, without chart or compass. (Boyd [1801b], second edition, p. x)

[23] Baring [?] (1801b) "A Twelve-Penny Answer to a Three Shillings and Six-Penny Pamphlet, Intitled A Letter on the Influence of the Stoppage of the Issue in Specie at the Bank of England, on the Prices of Provisions and other Commodities" to be followed by Baring [?] (1801c) "A Second Twelve-Penny Answer to a New (and Five Shillings) Edition of Three Shillings and Six-Penny Pamphlet, Intitled "A Letter on the Influence of the Stoppage of the Issue in Specie at the Bank of England, on the Prices of Provisions and other Commodities; with additional Notes and a Preface." The advertisement page in the First Twelve-Penny mentioned Baring's Observation as appearing too late for the author to take notice. If so, the attribution of those two pamphlets to Baring in the Goldsmith Library catalogue, although uncertain because square brackets appear around the name, may be wrong unless it was intended to hide the author. The author's agreement with Baring is almost complete, and he had used many similar arguments that might have convinced some that it was another pamphlet by him. The date for the advertisement was February 3, 1801, whose date points to Boyd's earlier publication.

Although Baring argued that the rise in quantity was small relative to the supposed consequences, it was in fact high relative to the quantity then existing, and it was increasing fast. According to Boyd, the disproportional increase and its speed contributed to the significant impact on prices.

What is striking in the debate between Baring and Boyd is that both argued that confidence in the Bank and its notes had not declined, because there was no difference in prices quoted in Bank notes or in coins and "[t]he *current* value of Bank-notes and of gold is the same" (Boyd 1801b, pp. xxxix-xl). That was also Baring's view. The depreciation in value affected both mediums and occurred as a result of the Stoppage of cash payments and the disappearance of a mechanism capable of restricting the circulation of money. True, the increase was only three and a half million pounds, but Boyd insisted it was enough to cause the effects. Furthermore, confirmation from official sources that this increase actually took place came late, between the writing and the publication of the *Letter*'s first edition.

Boyd thought that Baring had changed his position concerning the suspension of cash payments without appropriate explanation. In 1797, Baring described the Bank as having "failed," claiming it "had passed the line of bankruptcy" (Boyd 1801b, p. lv). Now, four years later, the events which Baring then described as a "bitter pill which the Public had been forced to swallow" were "passed over in perfect silence." In closing, Boyd complained: "Sir Francis has taken some pains to represent me as at variance with myself. It would have been fully as proper to have reconciled his printed opinion of 1797, with that of 1801" (Boyd 1801b, p. lvi).

Baring (1801a) accepted Boyd's calculation that put the increase in the amount of Bank notes since the beginning of the Restriction at 3.5 million pounds, compared to an average of 12 million pounds in circulation before. However, Baring's interpretation of the facts was completely different: "This sum alone is a complete answer, in my humble opinion, to every argument of Mr. Boyd, in consequence of its comparative insignificance," (p. 10) because it could not have produced the effects it supposedly had. Arguing with Boyd's 1796 proposals, which had appeared as an appendix to the *Letter to Pitt*, Baring called attention to an apparent inconsistency: Boyd proposed then to increase the too-tight circulation, but as its level was 12 million pounds, what was the complaint? Was 12 million too little and 15 million too much? If the circulation was considered too large, it can easily be reduced by increasing the annual loan by 5 million.

Baring ridiculed the supposed impact that a 3 million increase in Bank notes supposedly had:

> [They] produce a difference in the Exchange on Hamburgh ... of 14 per cent ... [O]ccasioned a very considerable advance in the price of provisions and other commodities. ... attribute to the advance in the price of Stocks. ... I cannot understand how it is possible for the sum of three million and a half to produce any one of the three effects. (Baring [1801a], pp. 23–24; Baring relates to Boyd [1801a], pp. 40 and 45)

On another crucial point, Baring's position completely opposed Boyd's. Baring rejected a theoretical link between the exchanges and prices of locally-produced goods, arguing that the price of wheat produced by Essex and Kent farmers had nothing to do with the exchanges in Hamburgh. "If he [Boyd] cannot prove this, he must admit that the foreign Exchanges have no influence or effect upon the price of corn grown in this country" (ibid. p. 20).[24]

But the argument was really about control over the circulation: Boyd did not trust the Bank and its directors and Baring did, although Baring also worried about leaving them in full control.[25] Baring commented that if Boyd thought that the sum in circulation was even larger than "what has been stated in the return from the Bank to the House of Commons, [Boyd] ought to speak out" (Baring [1801a], pp. 23–24). Boyd's reaction was forceful: "I am sure the Honourable Baronet is incapable of intentionally insinuating any thing which might injure me with the public. ... I have not feared to tax the Bank Directors with *error* – I never thought

---

[24] Baring tried to present the absurdity of the argument by asking Boyd whether changes in the exchanges that occurred just after his *Letter* went to print, 7 percent in just three days from December 31, 1800, when the introduction was written, should have resulted in price changes of "commodities grown and consumed in Great Britain." No, answered Baring.

[25] Though Baring trusted the directors of the Bank, in one place, he seemed to be worried about their relations with the ministers:

> "If he imputes to them a disposition to yield too easily to the wishes of the Minister, there can be no doubt on that head, as the fact has been proved. And for that reason I humbly conceive that, so long as the Bank shall not pay their Notes in money, either the extent to which those Notes shall issue, ought to be limited by Act of Parliament, or there should be an annual return of the highest amount of their Notes in circulation the preceding twelve months, to be laid upon the table of the House of Commons." These limitations will not restrict the government in its war efforts, wrote Baring. However, they will reduce the alarm created, also "from discussions like the present." Their advantage will be in forcing ministers to reveal the "total amount of taxes necessary to cover the real expenditure of the year" (Baring 1801a, pp. 16–18).

them capable of *intentional delinquency*" (Boyd [1801b] p. xliv). This unworthy insinuation, Boyd added, was the result of his attempt to figure out the real size of the circulation in 1800 for comparison with that of 1797. Boyd needed to know the quantity of outstanding Bank notes ("active circulation") and balances on its books, that is, deposits ("passive circulation"), as well as specie in its coffers (ibid. p. xlv-l). Only the first had been reported by the directors; Boyd's comment that he was unable to estimate accurately referred to the information that was missing, not that which was provided.

Baring emphasized the possibility that different prices might be quoted for the same goods depending on whether the medium of payments was coins or Bank notes. However, in reality, prices paid in notes and in gold are the same; thus, he argued, full confidence in Bank notes prevailed. Bank notes, he stressed, circulate at par:

> If they were below par, and circulating at a discount, it is evident that the price of every thing must be higher for paper than for gold, even more than in the proportion of the discount. But we have no such instance; the confidence in the Bank is perfect and entire. (Baring [1801a], pp. 21–22)

This is indeed a crucial point, and most later commentators argue that gold coins stopped circulating early on during the Restriction. Baring concluded by stating that on November 11, 1800,

> ... when Mr. Boyd's Letter was written, no cause existed which could possibly shake the confidence which had been reposed in the Bank; that none has appeared since; and that neither the quantity of Bank paper in circulation, nor the course of Exchanges with Hamburgh, could contribute towards raising the price of such articles of provisions as are grown and consumed in this country. (ibid., p. 25)

Boyd rejected and ridiculed Baring's assertion that Boyd's well-known name caused the first edition of Boyd's pamphlet to have an undesirable impact on the public. I am "misfortune" and the Bank is strong, Boyd declared; but more significantly, Boyd argued that his argument was based on good reason. In a dramatic and personal point in the reasoning Boyd suddenly referred to "that 'inevitable hour' which equally awaits us all." Then "I shall have the satisfaction ... of reflecting that in the work which has drawn upon me so much obloquy and misrepresentation, there is '*No line which, dying, I would wish to blot*'" (Boyd [1801b], p. xx [quoting Dr. Johnson]).

Conclusion

The Restriction was one of those sudden events that changes the way things are done and forces people to rethink the obvious. For most mainstream monetary theorists in the eighteenth century, certainly those who remembered Law and concluded that the precious metals provided the only solid basis for the monetary system, convertibility was a presupposition. Suddenly this was not the case; the monetary system lost its anchor, and it did so under the order of the sovereign. There was no theory to assess the implications of the sudden change; some, as we know, expected the worse.

However, for three years the inconvertible system functioned, and functioned relatively well. There was no inflation, no loss of trust in the (inconvertible) bank notes and in the financial system in general, and no decline to barter as some feared. The first serious attempt to analyze the new arrangements, to come up with a theory that would address the new conditions, was that of Boyd. Beyond explaining how an inconvertible system can and should work, he criticized it and proposed a return to convertibility. Thus, Boyd and the other Bullionists, as we shall see in Chapter 8, in fact avoided the challenge by bringing back the old system and adopting a basically Humean or Smithian point of view.

On the other hand, the defenders of inconvertibility did a poor job. They used political arguments, like claiming that the Restriction was an emergency measure that fit the needs of financing the war efforts. They did not provide a persuasive framework that could justify and explain the working of an inconvertible system. The most serious attempt to rise to this challenge had to wait another year, for the publication of the seminal treatise of Henry Thornton in 1802.

SEVEN

Thornton on Inconvertibility and Central Banking

Ahead of His Time[1]

Introduction

Henry Thornton (1760–1815) was born in London to an Evangelical family and became one of the leaders of what has been known as the "Clapham Sect," probably named after his house in Clapham, which was the group's headquarters. One of the group's better-known leaders was his close friend and second cousin, William Wilberforce, remembered mainly for his work in the antislavery abolitionist movement, for promoting literacy in Britain, and for his missionary activities throughout the Empire. The family was engaged in trade with Russia, but Thornton left the family business against his father's advice and made a successful living as a banker in London. His deep religious belief guided him in life; he contributed six-sevenths of his income to charity before his marriage in 1796, and one-quarter after.[2] Thornton was a Member of Parliament from 1782 until his death in 1815. He wrote many works on religious matters and one seminal treatise on money and banking, *An Enquiry into the Nature and Effects of the Paper Credit of Great Britain* (1802) (*Paper Credit*) that we will discuss in this chapter.

As we argued in the previous chapter, Jacob Viner (1937), Frank Fetter (1965), Denis O'Brien (2004), and Friedrich von Hayek (1929a/1991),

---

[1] This chapter draws on my paper in the *History of Political Economy* (2009) entitled, "Reexamination of Thornton's Innovative Monetary Analysis: The Bullion Debate during the Restriction Once Again." An earlier draft of the paper was presented at the 34th Annual Meeting of the History of Economics Society, June, 2007 at George Mason University in Fairfax, Virginia. I would like to thank David Levy for his discussion and Neil Skaggs and other participants for their helpful comments; two referees provided very helpful and constructive criticisms. The usual caveat holds. The paper was written while I was visiting IRLE at UC Berkeley. I thank the Institute and its director Michael Reich for their hospitality and intellectual environment.

[2] On Henry Thornton's life see Hayek (1939), Tolley in DNB (2004), and Skaggs (2008).

among others, present Walter Boyd, Peter King, Francis Horner, and Henry Thornton as the main Bullionist contributors to the Bullion debate.[3] This latter group of writers is often referred to by scholars as the "moderate Bullionists," as opposed to the "extreme Bullionists" such as John Wheatley (1803) and David Ricardo. In the earlier secondary literature, one can find a different categorization. Jacob Hollander (1911) associates Thornton with the anti-Bullionists. However, he does not think highly of him as do later scholars, and in fact argues that Thornton's stance on inconvertibility is untenable. Thornton was in his view "handicapped by his partisan espousal of the cause of the Bank" (pp. 450–451). He confuses Henry Thornton with his brother Samuel, who was a Bank director, which may explain his partisanship claim. James Angell's (1926) account of Thornton's writings is similar to that of Hollander: He also confuses Thornton with his brother and erroneously describes him as "a Director of the Bank of England, and hence a staunch defender of its policy" (p. 46).

Historians of economic thought have debated the reasons for Thornton's prolonged disappearance from the canon of monetary theory. An emerging consensus contends that Thornton's views, although often not attributed to him, remained influential by virtue of their impact on other major thinkers, especially those from the Banking School (for example, Tooke, see Skaggs 1995, 2003).[4] Thanks to the efforts of Friedrich von Hayek, Thornton's pathbreaking book, *Paper Credit* (1802) – considered by Hayek to be a response to Boyd – was republished in 1939

Hayek's celebrated introduction secured Thornton's place in the history of monetary theory by overturning previous scholarship[5] and recognizing Thornton's momentous achievements. Hayek addresses the issue of consistency in the views Thornton advocates in *Paper Credit*, and emphasizes the differences between the first part of the book – "devoted to pointing out the

---

[3] See Viner (1937, chapter 3, especially pp. 119–122); Fetter (1965, chapter 2); O'Brien (2004, chapter 6, pp. 175–181); and Hayek (1929, p. 197). Although, Hayek's (1929) paper was not published until 1991, Thornton's ideas were important to Hayek's intellectual development. (See editors' comments in Hayek ([1929] 1991, 127). Hayek's deep appreciation of Thornton may explain his decision to republish Thornton's *Paper Credit* ten years later, in 1939, and to write the famous introduction to the republication. However, in 1939, unlike his colleagues Viner and Fetter and his own 1929 text, Hayek did not repeat the association of Thornton's theoretical stance with that of the moderate Bullionists. We will return to this point later.

[4] See also Arnon (1991, pp. 28, 48–49, and 76). But Arnon as well erroneously identified Thornton as a moderate Bullionist. See also Peake (1978, 1982, 1995), Beaugrand (1982), and Arnon (1987).

[5] "Although Thornton's merits have long been overshadowed by the greater fame of Ricardo, it has now come to be recognized that in the field of money the main achievement of the classical period is due to Thornton ..." (Hayek 1939, p. 36).

dangers of an excessive contraction of the issue of paper" (labeled "deflation-ary" in the secondary literature) – and the later sections, where Thornton primarily addresses "the effects of an absolute increase of the circulation" ("inflationary"). Hayek argues that it is in the latter parts of the book, where Thornton discusses inflation and foreign exchanges, that his "best-known achievement" appears (see Hayek's introduction [1939, pp. 45–48]).

Like Hayek, many observers agree that there are at least two Thorntons in that great work. John Hicks (1967), in "Thornton's Paper Credit (1802)," emphasizes the "change in the character of the historical situation that is being considered" (p. 181) while insisting on the conformity of Thornton's "Keynesian" positions.[6] However, Hicks also argues that in the second part of the book, Thornton shows "the other side of the medal; the danger of maintaining inconvertibility when it was not necessary" (p. 181). Moreover, Hicks claims that "Thornton always believed in the Gold Standard," while adding, "[t]hat looks a surprising statement, in view of his support of the 1797 Restriction."[7] By establishing Thornton's principled support for a non–gold standard, we expect that surprise will fade.

In a recent exchange, Antoine E. Murphy (2003, 2005) and Neil T. Skaggs (2005) returned to these issues. Murphy argues that there were not two, but three Thorntons. The first two, as suggested by Hayek and Hicks, criti-cize deflation in the early parts of the work and inflation in the latter parts. Murphy adds a third Thornton: a supporter of nonmetallic money (Murphy 2003, pp. 447–451). Skaggs' *Comment* on Murphy agrees with Murphy's description of the first Thornton, the antideflationist, while disagreeing with him on the second and third. In Skaggs's view, there is only one per-sona – no schizophrenia and no internal contradictions – that adheres to stability and to gold as the preferred standard.

The present chapter proposes a different reading: Thornton disagreed with Boyd and the Bullionists and developed an innovative anti-Bullionist position very different from Baring's.[8] In particular, Thornton rejected the Smithian approach. While Baring and the Bank advocated Smith's Real Bills

[6] "If we look at these introductory chapters alone … we must, I think, be of opinion that Thornton has started off on what we should consider a remarkably Keynesian tack. And it is not in this section alone that he exhibits 'Keynesianism;' it persists, as we shall see, into the next round" (Hicks 1967, p. 177).
[7] The proof comes in the form of a quote from a speech in 1811, on which Hicks com-mented: "This, to be sure, is 1811, not 1802; but it is incredible that the man who believed this, with such conviction, in 1811 could ever have believed anything else" (1967, p. 184). We will return to this issue later.
[8] See Baring's famous tracts at the start of the Restriction (1797a, 1797b) and Baring (1801a) to which we will return later.

Doctrine under inconvertibility, Thornton rejected it together with other Smithian monetary ideas. Thus, maybe he can best be described as a moderate anti-Bullionist: one who supported the Restriction but rejected the Real Bills Doctrine. Thornton's association with the Bullionists in the secondary literature is due to his public activities and positions on policy after 1802, his participation in the 1804 Irish Currency Committee, and, most significantly, his participation in the Bullion Committee of 1810. If Thornton can be said to have changed his views after 1802, he did so on a pragmatic level for political reasons; his theories remained unchanged. Thus, although Thornton joined the Bullionists in 1810 to recommend an early return to cash payments, his alliance with them did not signal a change in theory, but rather his disappointment at the Bank's failure to understand its role. He still believed during the years of the second round of the Bullion debate that, had the Bank's directors understood the monetary system, inconvertibility could have been maintained.

Thornton constructed the most important monetary theory of his era in defense of an inconvertible system based on discretionary policy. Unlike the Bullionists, Thornton did not reject inconvertibility; at times he seemed to refer to it as the superior system: "... gold is by no means that kind of circulating medium which is the most desirable" (Thornton [1802/1939], p. 276).[9] As with any financial system, though, whether convertible or inconvertible, Thornton insisted on the need to implement discretion, that is, monetary policy. In Great Britain, monetary policy had to be implemented by the Bank of England. Thus, in our view, the "real" Thornton was the third one, and the apparent differences in analyses in the first and second parts of the book are simply the implementation of one framework under two different circumstances. The one consistent Thornton was the innovative monetary theorist whose analysis favored a nonmetallic, managed monetary system.[10] To fully appreciate the power of Thornton's thinking, one has to recall that two hundred years ago, what twenty-first century economists think of as a natural and obvious theoretical position on inconvertibility was considered by many to be extraordinarily innovative and unconventional.

[9] This quotation is taken from the closing paragraphs of *Paper Credit*. We will return to the full statement later. In the following references to Thornton's *Paper Credit*, only page numbers will be used.

[10] David Laidler (2000) comes closer to this chapter's interpretation by arguing that "[Thornton's 1802] position in that debate is hard to classify, because though its analytic content places it firmly in the Bullionist camp, it nevertheless defends the policies pursued by the Bank of England after 1797" (p. 8). However, we will argue that Thornton in 1802 provided an anti-Bullionist analysis.

The Bank of England under the Restriction was a private institution, profit-seeking and free from supervisory authority. The Bank was legally free to act only in its own self-interest. Its directors displayed a profound ignorance of the Bank's pivotal role in the system and how the Bank's policies impacted public interests; perhaps they were under the influence of the need to finance the war efforts. What changed for Thornton between 1802 and 1811 was based on his new assessment that the Bank directors failed to apprehend that they had a responsibility to implement proper policies.

Although both Reisman (1971) and David Laidler (2000) describe Thornton as a moderate Bullionist in 1802 as well as in 1810–1811, they are aware of the changes in his position concerning the Bank's policy. Reisman writes: "By 1810, [Thornton] may simply have altered his position on events in the real world as he learned the Bank was not exercising what he felt to be adequate discretion" (p. 73). Laidler's claim is stronger: "By 1810, [Thornton] and his colleagues could have no such confidence in the Bank, given its directors' enthusiastic embrace of the Real Bills Doctrine: hence the *Bullion Report*'s emphasis on the urgent need to reimpose convertibility as constraint on their activities" (p. 16). However, even in 1810–1811, Thornton would not have rejected the feasibility of inconvertibility as a matter of principle had the Bank understood its discretionary role.

In the introduction to *Paper Credit*, Thornton states that the "general treatise" consists of two parts: The early chapters address "the evil of a too great and sudden diminution of our circulating medium," and the "latter … are employed in pointing out the consequences of a too great augmentation of it" (p. 68). As we will see, both parts contain penetrating and innovative ideas, some of which disappeared for a long time from more conventional monetary thought. We will argue that in the two parts of *Paper Credit*, Thornton writes as an anti-Bullionist within one consistent conceptual framework that allows him to explain the causes for changes in various monetary aggregates, linking them to both nonmonetary internal economic developments and to international trade.

Thornton gives sophisticated explanations for both the deflation years before 1797 and the inflation after 1800, when the increase in circulation became the focus of discussion. His convincing theoretical defense of the Restriction and the Bank directors' policies leaves no doubt that his position puts him in the anti-Bullionist camp that supported inconvertibility. Thus, *Paper Credit* can be read as an early exploration of the possibility of having a stable monetary system that is not based on convertibility to a commodity-money. Moreover, Thornton's inquiry led him to develop an early innovative formulation concerning monetary policy and to elaborate on how a national bank can manage the monetary system.

In sections 2 and 3 of this chapter, we elaborate on Thornton's 1802 analysis of the deflationary and inflationary phases, and establish the consistency of his positions in the two parts of the book where he defends the Restriction and the Bank's directors and advocates the possibility and advantages of having an inconvertible monetary system. Section 4 presents his insights about central banking, and section 5 reviews Thornton's positions after 1802, up to and after the 1810 Bullion Committee.

Paper Credit on the Contraction of the Circulation

Thornton begins his book with some general observations about money, credit, and transactions. He defines commercial credit as the "confidence which subsists among commercial men" and argues that confidence does not depend on the existence of money: Commercial credit can be used even before "bills [and] money are as yet known" and "is the foundation of *paper credit,*" which helps to "enlarge, confirm and diffuse confidence among traders" (pp. 75–76). Thornton then describes the transformation of exchange in society from barter to the convenient use of gold as money. But the focus of the analysis is on understanding the workings of the exchange of goods using credit instruments like bills of exchange. The book offers a critique of Adam Smith's monetary theory, written in a modest and reserved tone.

A Critique of Smithian Monetary Theory

Smith's monetary analysis assumes both convertibility and that the banks discount only so-called real bills, thus guaranteeing the proper working of the banking system.[11] His underlying assumptions are that real bills are well-defined, their quantity is restricted, and, most significantly, the banks' self-interest would force them to discount only such bills.

Thornton argues that banks can't differentiate between "real" and "fictitious" bills. The former supposedly derive from the genuine sale of a commodity, where the buyer receives credit from the seller, and in exchange, provides a bill stating the terms of his debt; the fictitious bill originates in the coordinated actions of merchants who want a medium that can be discounted. Thornton describes the fictitious bill as a "note of accommodation." He disagrees with

---

[11] See Smith (1776, Book 2, chapter 2); Laidler (1981); Santiago-Valiente (1988); and Gherity (1994). For a review of the Bank's policy and the Real Bills Doctrine see Smith V. C. (1936), Hetzel (1987), Humphrey (1988), O'Brien (2003), and Laidler (2004).

Smith that the use of fictitious bills will prove "ruinous" to those who, acting in their self-interest, discount them. Moreover, he thinks it improbable that the bankers or any of the merchants could distinguish between the two types of bills: The merchant either doesn't know or doesn't care, and the banker is only interested in "the credit of the bills ... in judging whether he ought to discount them" (p. 89).[12] Thus, Thornton also rejects Smith's Real Bills Doctrine and the application of the "invisible hand" argument to banking.

Thornton's analysis of bills (debts) was the foundation for his analysis of circulating paper. In *Paper Credit*, he discusses the rise of bank notes "payable to Bearer on Demand," where the issuing body keeps only fractional reserves in money. He argues that a "powerful and well accredited company will probably be the first issuer" of such paper. The tendency to see a great public bank at the pivot of the system makes this body a source for a "reservoir of gold to which private banks may resort with little difficulty, expence, or delay, for the supply of their several necessities" (p. 90). Thornton here explicitly criticizes Smith and the Bullionist Boyd, whom he believed did not fully appreciate either the complex links between bills, bank notes, and gold, or that bills and bank notes are both money. The somewhat mechanical treatment of note-issuing by Smith, argues Thornton, misses some important distinctions. Smith argues that the rise of fractional reserves frees resources by supplying the circulation with a cheap medium (notes) while keeping less gold in reserve than had to be kept without the service of banks. But Thornton argues that gold and notes are not perfect substitutes because they have different effects in their performance of payments; for example, gold's velocity of circulation is higher than that of notes. Moreover, bills are part of the circulating medium and perform better than notes in that capacity. The major advantage of bills is that their value rises over time when they are held as a means of payment that carries interest. This sophisticated and modern discussion concerning costs and benefits of the various means of payments covers both the individual agents in the exchange process and the macroeconomic implications.

Thornton's discussion of the macroimplications caused him to criticize Smith once again. This time, he directs his critique at the nature and role of debts and credits. Thornton quotes from Smith's chapter on banking: "The

---

[12] "To determine what bills are fictitious, or bills of accommodation, and what are real, is often a point of difficulty. Even the drawers and remitters themselves frequently either do not know, or do not take the trouble to reflect, whether the bills ought more properly to be considered as of one class or the other; and the private discounter, or banker, to whom they are offered, still more frequently finds the credit of the bills to be the only rule which it is possible to follow in judging whether he ought to discount them" (p. 89).

whole paper money of *every kind* which can *easily* circulate in any country, never can exceed the value of the gold and silver of which it supplies the place, or which (the commerce being supposed the same) would circulate there, if there was no paper money" (Thornton 1802, p. 95, quoted from Smith's Book 2, chapter 2; Thornton's emphasis). This formulation enabled Smith to argue that if the banks followed his Real Bills Doctrine, which they would out of self-interest, the quantity in circulation would be the right one.

Thornton focuses on the term "*of every kind*": What was included in paper money according to Smith? Are bills of all kinds included, as Thornton thought they should be? If so, were Smith's criteria valid for determining whether the circulation was "right" when he compared the total sum of all the mediums in circulation with the quantity of gold that was supposed to circulate if only coins existed? "[W]e feel surprised that the erroneousness of the position did not strike Dr. Smith himself" (p. 95).

The error seems to be technical at first. According to Thornton, it is the effect of gold coins and notes on the economy – not their quantity – at which one should look. Their effect depends on their velocities, the speed at which mediums change hands, which are not identical for each medium. Neither are velocities constant over time, because they depend on many economic circumstances. Hence, Smith's simplistic comparison of paper money and gold is misleading.[13]

Thornton takes his criticism of Smith further. In the act of circulation, when payments are made, mediums other than gold and notes can be used. These credit and debt mediums, based, as we have seen before, on confidence, can perform the role of making payments. Thus, both bills of exchange and bank deposits should be considered part of the mediums in circulation.

[I]t appears, that the sentiment which Dr. Smith leads his readers to entertain, namely, that there is in every country a certain fixed quantity of paper, supplying the place of gold, which is all that "can easily circulate" (or circulate without being forced into circulation), and which is all (for such, likewise, seems to be the intended inference) that should ever be allowed to be sent into circulation, is, in a variety of respects, incorrect. ... [T]he same remark ... would lead an uninformed person to conceive, that the trade of a country ... might be carried on altogether by guineas, if bank notes of all kinds were by any means annihilated. It may already have occurred,

---

[13] "The error of Dr. Smith, then, is this: – he represents the whole paper, which can easily circulate when there are no guineas, to be the same in quantity with the guineas which would circulate if there were no paper; whereas, it is the quantity not of 'the thing which circulates,' that is, of the thing which is *capable* of circulation, but of the actual circulation which should rather be spoken of as the same in both cases" (p. 96).

that if bank paper were abolished, a substitute for it would likely to be found, to a certain degree, in bills of exchange; ... But further; if bills and bank notes were extinguished, other substitutes than gold would unquestionably be found. ... Merely by the transfer of the debts of one merchant to another, in the books of the banker, a large portion of what are termed cash payments is effected at this time without the use of any bank paper, and a much larger sum would be thus transferred, if guineas were the only circulating medium of the country. (pp. 100–101)

Thornton recognized that many different assets and debts can be used in payments and exchange.[14] His criticism of Smith led him to break from conventional "monetary theories of credit" and is an early expression of what Schumpeter called "credit theories of money."[15]

The Role of the Bank of England

The Bank of England stood at the core of the English financial system. Thornton investigates the Bank's modus operandi by again critically reevaluating Smith's positions. The outcome is an innovative, revisionist monetary theory in which Thornton criticizes Smith's empirical observation that the quantity of notes in circulation, particularly those issued by the Bank of England, was too high.[16] This was a point of great importance in the debate, and Thornton returns to it repeatedly:

[H]owever just may be the principle of Dr. Smith when properly limited and explained, the reduction of the quantity of Bank of England paper is by no means a measure which ought to be resorted to on the occasion of every demand upon the bank for guineas arising from high price of bullion, and that such reduction may even aggravate that sort of rise which is caused by an alarm in the country. (p. 104)

This critique of Smith's policy conclusion – which hints at the necessity to determine first what kind of demand the Bank faces, and only then to act, acknowledging that contraction may lead sometimes to more damages – calls for special attention. From its inception, Thornton writes, what was unique about the Bank of England was its independence vis-à-vis the government: The Bank did not raise funds for the government by relying on its ability to issue notes; the government did not really need the Bank to finance itself; and the Bank's directors would not even allow such an

---

[14] The criticisms also remind one of Wicksell's "pure credit" frameworks, although this approach was not developed consistently until more than one hundred years later.

[15] See Schumpeter (1954, pp. 722–728).

[16] "Dr. Smith probably could not be acquainted with the secret of the actual quantity of those bank notes, of the number of which he complains; he must, therefore, have taken it for granted, that they were what he terms excessive, on the ground of the price of gold being high, and the coinage great" (p. 103).

operation unless they were convinced it was in the Bank's best interest. The role of the Bank's owners was crucial in achieving the proper balance between private and public interests: "the numerous proprietors who chuse the directors, and have the power of controlling them ... are men whose general stake in the country far exceeds that particular one which they have in the stock of the company" (p. 109)[17].

Thornton supports this somewhat naïve claim with the more realistic argument that for most proprietors, the "dividend" from excessive issue would not be worth the damage to the "commercial credit of the country" and would have a negative impact on price levels (p. 110). Moreover, it is not the quantities of either paper in circulation or gold reserves that constitute the appropriate measure for judging the circulation. The only measure that Thornton and "commercial men" knew was that "all bills and paper money should have their value regulated as exactly as possible" by gold coin: "This is the great maxim to be laid down on the subject of paper-credit. Let it, then, be next considered what is necessary, in order to secure sufficiently that, whatever the circulating paper may be, gold shall be the standard to which the value of that paper shall conform itself" (p. 111).

Thornton's description of a crisis is illuminating, and should prevent one from concluding that his desire that paper be as valued as gold supports convertibility. Convertibility will not suffice to maintain the value of notes and is not necessary.[18] The only security that could be found in a convertible system was in a "considerable fund of gold" at the Bank of England, which could answer both common fluctuations in the demand for coins and the less common demands arising from either an "unfavourable balance of trade" or "any extraordinary demand at home" (pp. 111–112). But that security could never be perfect. The analysis led to Thornton's well-known discussion of external and internal drains. The two are not symmetrical, he argues, and there is no way to guarantee that the reserve will always suffice to cover an internal drain. Hence, there are imperfections in any monetary system, whether convertible or inconvertible. It is necessary to manage risks and maintain discretion to guarantee that the value of paper will conform to gold.

As an example, Thornton analyzes the period just before the suspension. The demand for gold coins in the counties outside London and the demand for Bank notes in London caused interest rates to rise. The Bank pursued a

---

[17] As one of the referees pointed out, it is possible that the independence of the Bank from the "executive government" declined in later years.

[18] See also in the second part of the book, p. 248: "... banks, if they pay in gold, or if, while not paying in gold, they maintain the value of their notes, must observe some limit in respect to their emission of them."

contractionary policy – a policy that Smith's readers would consider appropriate – that would lessen the number of its notes (p. 113). Thus, such a
policy could aggravate the economic conditions and, in fact, the contraction policy failed.

The supporters of the contraction policy assumed that gold would be
brought in as a result of their actions. Thornton analyzes and rejects the
various channels for such a causal link. While discussing the contraction
policy's failure, Thornton explains the differences in principles between a
"national bank" and "private houses," which, he argues, must be judged by
different criteria. The Bank was a "national bank" that should not "pur-
sue its own particular interest" but should take "upon itself the superin-
tendance of general credit, and seeking its own safety through the medium
of the safety of the public." Although the Bank was very different from any
"private house," the Bank's directors had not understood this fact, and had
behaved as if the Bank was still in its "infancy" when the "country was less
dependent upon it for the means of effecting its payments" (pp. 126–127).
However, the Bank became responsible for the country's financial health,
concludes Thornton, and ought to evaluate the macro conditions and
then determine and implement the appropriate discretionary policy. Thus,
Thornton rejects automatic contractions, which were in line with Smithian
ideas as well as with the Bank's profit-seeking motive.

The suspension of cash payments was, in Thornton's view, an expression
of "the general wish of the nation" to substitute payments in money with
payments in "money's worth" (p. 139). It is clear that Thornton supported
the decision to suspend cash payments in 1797,[19] a position that he continued to defend, as we shall see.

Paper Credit on the Expansion of the Circulation

The second part of Thornton's book addresses the Restriction years, in particular, the "unfavourable state of the exchange between this country and Europe"
(p. 141). This part of his book, from at least chapter 5 on, was likely written or completed after 1800–1801.[20] Thornton's general theoretical argument
concerning trade imbalances is clear: A discrepancy between commercial

---

[19] "The parliament, then, were led by the practical view which they took of the subject, to dis-
regard theory, as well as some popular prejudice, for the sake of more effectually guarding
the public safety, and promoting real justice" (p. 139).
[20] Hayek thought that *Paper Credit* had been written over a long time. But see Murphy (2003)
for another assessment concerning the dates.

imports and exports has a tendency to disappear. Assuming otherwise would mean that either we accumulate debt infinitely or that we hoard more and more bullion.[21] The mechanism described is not the Humean one based on relative price changes, but one based on the equalization of incomes and expenditures by individuals who will react to a possible gap between imports and exports by either economizing on expenditure or creating more income. However, summarizes Thornton, "[o]ur mercantile exports and imports, nevertheless, by whatever means they may be rendered disproportionate, necessarily become, in the long run, tolerably equal" (p. 145). Thornton thus articulates another long-term equalization mechanism, similar in essence, but not identical to the famous Humean mechanism.

Gold is not only an "article by which a balance of trade is discharged," but also a commodity; as such, its movements are determined by its profitability. Thornton discusses a well-known example concerning the financing of large importations of corn to England, in which it was assumed that the Bank of England still paid its notes in cash. These importations caused unfavorable exchanges.[22] The price of bullion in Hamburg, reflected in the price of bills of exchange traded there, would then be higher than the mint price of gold. If the difference between the market and mint prices of gold were large enough, gold coins would be bought from the Bank in exchange for bills of all kinds. The Bank would then have to buy bullion dear and sell it cheap, in the process "waging a very unequal war; and even though it should not be tired early, it will likely be tired sooner than its adversaries" (p. 147).

Through this example, Thornton primarily seeks to clear the Bank of England of any wrongdoing: The high price of bullion was not the responsibility of the Bank. This was neither the common doctrine nor Smith's position. Thornton writes:

There seems … to be much of inaccuracy and error in the doctrine of Dr. Smith on this subject. He begins by representing the quantity of paper which may properly circulate, as to be measured by that of gold which would circulate if there were no paper. The reader is, therefore led to believe, that the difference between the mint price and the market price of gold arises from an issue of a greater quantity … At the time of a very unfavourable balance of trade (an event which Dr. Smith leaves totally out of his consideration), it is very possible … that the excess of paper, if such it is to be called, is merely an excess above that very low and reduced quantity to

---

[21] "The equalization of the commercial exports and imports is promoted not only by the unwillingness of the richer state to lend to an unlimited extent, but also by the disinclination to borrow in the poorer" (Thornton 1802, p. 142).

[22] See the example discussed in pp. 145–153. "It is assumed, for the present, that the bank is paying in guineas" (p. 147).

which it is necessary that it should be brought down, in order to prevent the existence of an excess of the market price above the mint price of gold. (pp. 150–151)

Thornton argues that in a case of unfavorable balance of trade, it makes sense that some of the payment for a commodity's excess importation would necessarily be in gold. Changes in the level of prices brought about by a contraction of the circulation might be costly and could take some time. Again, he criticizes Smith, who

leaves totally out of his consideration … whether the bank, in the attempt to produce this very low price, may not, in a country circumstanced as Great Britain is, so exceedingly distress trade and discourage manufactures as to impair … those sources of our returning wealth to which we must chiefly trust for the restoration of our balance of trade, and for bringing back the tide of gold into Great Britain … It is also necessary to notice in this place, that the favourable effect which a limitation of bank paper produces on the exchanges is certainly not instantaneous. (p. 152)

Country Banks and the Bank of England in Exchange and Intermediation

Thornton's analysis of the role of the country banks within the banking system shows his most innovative arguments. His biggest achievement, as we noted earlier, was his description and analysis of the complicated British financial system, namely the relationship between the country banks, the London private banks, and the Bank of England. The advantages in having hundreds of competing country banks are clear, but Thornton also addresses the disadvantages. Moreover, Thornton is clear about an issue that was only vaguely understood for many years: that the monetary system is involved in both payments and intermediation. The country banks, he says, supply payments services, namely "receipts and the payments of money," which reflect further division of labor. As is usually the case with further division of labor, the specialization provides payments services more efficiently, cutting the costs dramatically. However, country banks do not only fulfill the function of payments services. *They are also involved in intermediation*:

Country banks are also useful by furnishing to many persons the means of laying out at interest, and in a safe manner, such money as they may have to spare. … All who have money to spare know where they can place it, without expence or loss of time, not only in security, but often with pecuniary advantage: and all commercial persons of credit understand in what quarter they can obtain such sums, in the way of loan, as their circumstances will fairly warrant them in borrowing. (p. 175)

Thus, Thornton understands and addresses the dual role of banking in both providing payments services, which facilitate exchange, and in linking economic agents who have surpluses with those who face shortages of resources. Hence, Thornton argues that country banks play an important role in the "flourishing state of our internal commerce."

A banker accumulates information about customers through "[the] bill transactions of the neighbourhood [that] pass under his view: the knowledge, thus obtained, aids his judgment." As a result, the country bankers who "view" the credit given to "surrounding traders" manage to contribute to society by increasing the confidence in the system. As the country banks direct credit in their areas, the London banks similarly supervise the country banks and the Bank of England oversees the London banks:

> While the transactions of the surrounding traders are thus subject to the view of the country banks, those of the country banks themselves come under the eye of their respective correspondents, the London bankers; and, in some measure, likewise, of the Bank of England. The Bank of England restricts, according to its *discretion*, the credit given to the London banker. Thus a system of checks is established, which, though certainly imperfect, answers many important purposes, and, in particular, opposes many impediments to wild speculation. (p. 176; my emphasis)

Thornton argues that the banking industry plays a positive role in the economy through its dual functions of payments and intermediation, and not, as Smith had argued, only through its role in increasing the "productive capital of the country" by issuing paper and so replacing gold, an expensive medium, with paper, a cheap one. By overseeing intermediation, Thornton explains, the Bank of England implements its discretion and can restrict credit expansions that too often lead to dangerous speculations.

Thornton is at his best in his analysis of the country banks, which emerged when merchants entered the business of turning bills of all sorts into money and vice-versa. His discussion of tradeoffs between liquidity and income of the different kinds of paper, represented by their time to maturity and interest rates, is innovative. His analysis of the important role of probability in banking and his justification of less than 100 percent reserves on the part of the banks are evidence of a complex mind seeking to understand the big picture. But Thornton's greatest achievement is his understanding of the complicated relationship between the country banks, the London private banks, and the Bank of England. His analysis of the outcome of these interdependencies, their advantages and disadvantages, and their effects on the British monetary system is probably the best in the literature.

Altogether, banking plays a positive role in the economy on account of its cautious practices and disciplinary actions, both of which restrict credit expansions and speculations. By issuing paper, banks increase the "productive capital of the country." Here, Thornton explicitly follows Smith's celebrated arguments and provides additional ones to counter the claim that more paper was the cause of the high price of corn in 1800. According to Thornton, this claim was rooted in a misunderstanding:

> [A] paper medium ... has been ... quite as convenient an instrument in settling accounts as the gold which it has displaced ... To reproach it with being a merely fictitious thing, because it possesses not the intrinsic value of gold, is to quarrel with it on account of that quality which is the very ground of its merit. Its merit consists in the circumstance of its costing almost nothing. (pp. 178–179)

The substitution of expensive gold with cheap paper leads to the employment of more productive capital. Nevertheless, there are, argues Thornton, some "solid objections" to this system of banking, notably "the tendency of country banks to produce, occasionally, that general failure of paper-credit," which could cause a crisis in commerce and manufacturing. This could be the result of a single bank failure, but the chain of links and dependencies that constitute the banking system may very well have transferred the crisis to other banks, including the Bank of England. Naturally, the Bank of England would have to be prepared for such occurrences. Thus, in weighing the advantages of having the country banks' note circulation, one would have to deduct not only the gold kept as reserve in the country banks' coffers, but also the costs incurred to the Bank of England for having to hold additional gold (pp. 180–182).

Thornton's analysis of a typical financial crisis, starting at the peripheral counties and ending at the metropolis in "a general failure of commercial credit," is illuminating. Thornton hypothesizes a situation to illustrate such a crisis and concludes: "The observations which have now been made sufficiently shew what is the nature of that evil of which we are speaking. It is an evil which aught to be charged not to any fault in the mercantile body, but to the defects of the banking system" (p. 186).

According to Thornton, the risk of such a crisis would diminish as three corrective counter-forces were strengthened. First, the Bank of England would learn to be more generous towards the country banks and navigate between leaving the country banks to face their responsibilities and saving the credit system.[23] Second, and most important, the country banks would

---

[23] "It is by no means intended to imply, that it would become the Bank of England to relieve every distress which the rashness of country banks may bring upon them: the bank, by

learn to accumulate enough liquid assets. This would increase the stability of both the country banks and the Bank of England, making the entire system safer. Third, those among the public using notes of different houses would learn to distinguish between them and to place confidence in those notes issued by the most prudent banks.

Thornton criticizes the common allegation that country banks tended to expand their note-issuing, which caused prices to rise. The system, he writes, prevents such occurrences. Thornton ascribes the formation of prices to two factors working together: the relative state of supply and demand – a general process that reflects the circulation of money – and the bargaining process, which is specific to the commodity and which utilizes power relations (p. 194). How can an increase in paper "lift up the price of articles"? When more paper circulates, traders' behaviors change, prompting the bargaining positions of buyers and sellers to change in opposite directions and prices to rise. As events in the 1795 corn market had shown, the same force will also work in the other direction: A "sudden scarcity of cash, not any new plenty of corn … caused the price of corn to drop" (p. 196).

The same process can influence trade in financial instruments, as happened in 1797 in the government securities market. Just days before the suspension, a shortage of Bank of England notes drove securities prices down, and a few days later, when the quantity rose, their prices went up again. The truth, wrote Thornton, is "that paper fluctuates in price on the same principles as any other article, its value rising as its quantity sinks, and *vice versa*," although "an exact correspondence between the quantity of paper and the price of commodities can by no means be expected always to subsist" (p. 197).

This issue of the causal link between the quantity of money and prices attracts Thornton's attention throughout *Paper Credit*. He writes:

> The reader possibly may think that, in treating of this subject, I have been mistaking the effect for the cause, an encreased issue of paper being, in his estimation, merely a consequence which follows a rise in the price of goods, and not the circumstance which produces it. That an enlarged emission of paper may often fairly be considered as only, or chiefly, an effect of high prices, is not meant to be denied. It is, however, intended to insist, that, unquestionably, in some cases at least, the greater quantity of paper is, more properly speaking, the cause. (pp. 197–198)

> doing this, might encourage their improvidence. There seems to be a medium at which a public bank should aim in granting aid to inferior establishments, and which it must often find very difficult to be observed. The relief should neither be so prompt and liberal as to exempt those who misconduct their business from all the natural consequences of their fault, nor so scanty and slow as deeply to involve the general interests" (p. 188, note).

Thornton on Discretionary Policy

Thornton's next argument links the changes in the prices of commodities to the market price of gold, causing the latter to differ from the mint price of gold and from the exchanges. When prices rise, exports decline and imports rise, assuming that the exchanges are not moving. However, because the exchanges will move, they will compensate and "in a great degree, prevent the high price of goods in Great Britain from producing that unfavourable balance of trade, which, for the sake of illustrating the subject was supposed to exist" (p. 199). At this point in the argument, Thornton distinguishes between the value of the circulation, including notes and coins, and that of bullion. Bullion, like all commodities, rises in price, creating an incentive to turn coins to bullion, and drawing coins out of the Bank of England. Smith's treatment of this "important subject… is particularly defective and unsatisfactory," according to Thornton.

Smith does not explain that gold will be exported or imported as a consequence of changes in prices, but only "in consequence of our circulation at home being over full." Contrary to this explanation, Thornton insists that the "circulation can never be said to be over full," and that the increase in paper pushes prices up, thus creating a reduction in the price of coin. "The coin, therefore, in consequence of its reduced price, is carried out of the country for the sake of obtaining for it a better market." The difference in analysis is important:

One of the consequences of Dr. Smith's mode of treating the subject, is, that the reader is led into the error of thinking, that when, through an excessive issue of paper, gold has been made to flow away from us, the expense of restoring it consists merely in the charge of collecting it and transporting it. … It follows, on the contrary, from the principles which I have laid down, that, in order to bring back gold, the expence not only of importing it may be to be incurred, but that also of purchasing it at a loss, and at a loss which may be either more or less considerable: a circumstance of great importance in the question. If this loss should ever become extremely great, the difficulties of restoring the value of our paper might easily be surmounted, and a current discount or difference between the coin and paper of the country would scarcely be avoidable. (p. 205)

Furthermore, Smith was "inaccurate" when explaining the process whereby an individual bank "persists in the false policy of issuing more paper than is sufficient to fill the circulation of the neighbouring district." The mechanism which will discipline the banks, argues Thornton, is the need to keep funds in London to cover excessive circulation. Thus, if country bankers understood their own best interests, they would be "limiting their issues" in the face of the Bank of England's "disciplinary" power. This is of "particular importance" under the conditions since 1797:

For, if the usual means of preventing an excess of country banks notes were nothing else than the liability of the issuer to be called upon for a money payment for them, it might fairly be assumed, that, at a time when the money payments of them has been suspended, we must necessarily have been exposed to the greatest inundation of country paper, and to a proportionate depreciation of it. The unbounded issue of country bank notes has been restrained by the obligation under which country bankers have considered themselves to be of granting bills on London; that is to say, orders to receive in London Bank of England paper in exchange for their notes, if required to do so: and it is certain that they would be required to so whenever the quantity of their notes should be much greater in proportion to the occasion for them, than the quantity of the notes of the Bank of England in proportion to the occasion for those notes. (p. 208)

The competitive mechanism, where banks issue their notes to excess, is then clearly explained. If more notes are issued in one place, the prices in that area will rise and people will seek to transform those notes into more valuable ones by buying cheaper commodities.

In this manner, therefore, the exchangeableness of country paper for London paper will never fail very nearly to equalize the value of them both. It is, moreover, important clearly to point out that their value will be equalized, or nearly equalized, not by the tendency in the London paper to partake in a low value which the country paper has acquired in consequence of its not being limited by any voluntary act of the issuers; nor by a tendency in each to approximate in value to the other; but by a tendency in the country paper to take exactly the high value restricted by the issuers. (p. 210)

This, of course, depends on the directors of the Bank of England and is the "consequence of a principle of limitation which the directors of the Bank of England have prescribed to themselves." However, this conclusion depends on certain assumptions which Thornton considers carefully.

The first assumption is that only Bank of England notes circulate in the metropolis and they do not circulate outside of it. The next assumptions are that the quantity of Bank notes supplied and the payments made with them in the metropolis do not change. Then, "the Bank of England paper could not fail both to maintain its own value, and also to maintain the value as well to restrict the quantity of the general paper of the country." Thus, the competitive system is ruled by the interplay of various demands and supplies of notes, so that "the quantity of the one, in comparison with the demand for that one, is the same, or nearly the same, as the quantity of the other in proportion to the call for the other" (p. 215).

Both before and after 1797, the Bank of England was a major force in influencing the country banks' circulation. However, contrary to conventional thinking, it had exercised its influence not through the convertibility of country bank notes into gold coins but rather through their convertibility to Bank of England notes.

If, then, the directors of the bank [Bank of England] were used before the suspension of their cash payments to limit their issues through a necessity which sometimes urged them, and if thus they limited the paper of the country in the manner which has been described, it follows that, supposing them after the event to have restrained their issues in like manner, though through a somewhat less urgent motive, the general effect must have been the same. (p. 219)

And in another place, after quoting Locke approvingly:

The point which I wish here to establish may be still more clearly explained in the following manner. It has been shewn in a former Chapter, and, indeed, it is stated by Mr. Locke that the selling price of bills determines the rate of exchange. When, therefore, for example, persons abroad wishing to sell bills on England are more numerous than those who are disposed to buy them, the price of bills must drop; and it must continue to fall until it becomes so low as to tempt some individuals to become purchases of them. … The money or bank notes thus received … must be invested in British articles, and exported. … Thus, therefore, an unfavourable exchange may be considered not only as becoming, according to Mr. Hume's expression, "a new encouragement to export," but as affording all that degree of encouragement to export which is necessary to secure as much actual exportation either of gold or of goods, or both, as shall serve to equalize the exports and imports; unless, indeed, the same cause, namely, the unfavourableness of the exchange, should tempt foreigners to remit money to England, and lodge it for a time in our hands, with a view to the profit to be obtained by this species of speculation. (pp. 246–247)

Thus, Thornton's fundamental argument is not with the Quantity Theory per se, but with some inappropriate policies that led to undesired consequences. In this case, he disagrees with the anti-Bullionists' argument that monetary expansion does not raise prices.

Defending the Bank Directors

Thornton defends the Bank's directors by asserting that the pressures on the exchanges were the result of the war and bad harvests, not of an expansion in note circulation. Although a larger quantity of Bank of England notes can raise the price of goods, just as the high prices of goods can cause an increase in the quantity of Bank notes, "[t]here is considerable danger, lest … we should, in some degree … mistake the effect for the cause; and should too much incline to consider an advanced price of commodities to be both the cause of an encreased issue of paper and the justification of it" (p. 221).

Thornton's defense of the structure of British banking is firm. The Bank uses its monopoly power to guide the system between dangerous alternatives: "that of a depreciated paper currency on the one hand, and that of an interruption to our paper credit, and a consequent stagnation of our commerce and manufactures, on the other" (p. 226). Thornton rejects the too-liberal approach of Smith, based on the latter's Real Bills Doctrine, because it sees "no danger in almost any extension of its discounts ... provided only the bills discounted ... were real bills ... of sufficiently safe and responsible houses" (p. 227). But he also rejects other proposals, for example, the establishment of a "rival" institution to the Bank of England, because they may encourage "that liberality in lending, which it is the object of competition to promote, the London notes, and also the country bills and notes, would be more liable to become excessive. Our paper credit would, therefore, stand in every respect on a less safe foundation" (p. 229).

Thornton concludes that the Bank's monopoly on note-issuing in London provides "a material advantage ... To this very circumstance the bank stands indebted for its faculty of regulating all the paper of the kingdom" (p. 228). Thornton's analysis provides the basis for his unique position on the policy implemented by the Bank's directors. In *Paper Credit*, he specifically targets those who think that it is enough for the Bank's directors to follow the Real Bills Doctrine. He analyzes and rejects two possible arguments: one, that there is no such thing as too much money causing prices to rise, the exchanges to fall, and the market price of gold to be above the mint price; and two, that the possibility of too much money exists, but does not happen because "bank paper has a natural tendency sufficiently to limit itself" (p. 232).

Like Hume, whom he quotes, Thornton thinks that the impact of more money will be short-lived (p. 238). It will neither change the basic characteristics of the economy nor create more capital or trade, except perhaps for a brief period during which those who find themselves with more money will try to exchange it, causing prices to rise. Thornton explains that the expansion of Bank notes is similar in effect to mining more gold:

[T]he value of it would fall nearly in proportion to the extension of its quantity, especially if it were used for the sole purpose of a circulating medium, and were also the only kind of circulating medium. The metropolis of Great Britain is so circumstanced, that the issue of an extraordinary quantity of bank paper for the purpose of effecting the payments in London, in a considerable degree resembles the creation of an extraordinary supply of gold for the general uses of the world. (p. 242)

The same argument holds true for a pure coin circulation, a mixed coin and paper circulation, and a pure paper circulation. In all cases, goods will rise

in price and gold will be exported. Thus, concludes Thornton, gold movements depend on the balance of trade and on the quantity of the circulating
medium, because the latter influences the former.

Does the Bank "restrain" itself? To answer this question, Thornton again
rejects the "security of real bills," because they can easily be multiplied. "If
the bank directors were to measure their discounts by the amount of real
bills offered ... bankers and other discounters ... might become much more
considerable holders of mere notes of hand, or of fictitious bills; and that
an opportunity might thus be afforded of pouring a vast additional quantity of real bills into the Bank of England" (p. 253). Thornton explains that
the restriction of the quantity will not come from the borrowers, who will
compare the rate of interest at the bank with the "current rate of mercantile profit" (p. 254). As long as the former lies below the latter, there will be
demand for bank loans. The increase in note circulation may seem to provide
some relief, but this will be temporary and will translate into higher prices.
Thornton concludes that the Bank is the regulator of the monetary system
and explains why the directors limit their weekly loans to merchants:

> The preceding observations explain the reason of a determination, adopted some
> time since by the bank directors, to limit the total weekly amount of loans furnished
> by them to the merchants. The adoption of a regulation for this purpose seems to
> have been rendered necessary by that impossibility of otherwise sufficiently limit-
> ing, at all times, the Bank of England paper ... The regulation in question I consider
> as intended to confine within a specific, though in some degree fluctuating, sum,
> the loans of the bank, for the sake of restricting the paper. (p. 258)

In an oft-quoted statement, Thornton makes it clear that he has (monetary)
policy in mind while talking about the "true policy of the directors of an institution circumstanced like that of the Bank of England." He emphasizes the
"principle of restriction," but also the need to control the monetary system:

> To limit the total amount of paper issued, and to resort for this purpose, whenever
> the temptation to borrow is strong, to some effectual principle of restriction; in no
> case, however, materially to diminish the sum in circulation, but to let it vibrate
> only within certain limits; to afford a slow and cautious extension of it, as the gen-
> eral trade of the kingdom enlarges itself; to allow of some special, though tem-
> porary, encrease in the event of any extraordinary alarm or difficulty, as the best
> means of preventing a great demand at home for guineas; and to lean to the side of
> diminution, in the case of gold going abroad, and of the general exchanges continu-
> ing long unfavourable. (p. 259)

Here, Thornton states the need to act according to prevailing circumstances,
and not to leave the monetary aggregates to the determination of market

forces, the demands of borrowers, or a rule. It is the Bank directors' responsibility to assess economic conditions and decide what course to take. Thus, Thornton defines, again, in very modern terms, the conflicting targets of monetary policy.

The concluding chapter of *Paper Credit* presents, in a strong anti-Bullionist tone, Thornton's views on the core issue of prices and money. The criticisms are directed at both Montesquieu and Hume. Thornton extends the analytical approach he has used to understand how the British system disciplines itself: as the exchangeability of country paper and London paper prevents over-issuing in Britain, so it does in the world at large.[24] But one circumstance is unique to the "isle": that country bank paper is always convertible to "London paper" without any discount.

In his analysis, Thornton distinguishes between prices in terms of British paper and British coin, and prices in terms of bullion. He focuses on whether an increase in the quantity of paper can be a cause for discrepancy. He measures the first discrepancy by looking at the difference between the market and mint prices of bullion, or by examining the state of the exchanges. These differences are small, argues Thornton, and attributable to "real" factors like bad agricultural seasons. Bullion prices of commodities may have changed, he tells us, but not due to credit expansion.

Thornton then describes what is commonly known as Hume's celebrated international mechanism, or the Price-Specie-Flow argument. To make Hume's argument, Thornton first assumes an ideal type, a pure circulation, where only coins are used as means of payments. In his scenario, high prices for exports lead to a favorable trade balance and a rise in prices in Britain. The resulting importation of gold, like "an augmentation of paper," raises prices in Britain further:

[T]he bullion will continue to flow in until it shall have brought the bullion price of goods in England to a level with the bullion price of the same articles in foreign parts, allowing for charges of transportation. On the ability, therefore, of Great Britain to maintain a high bullion price for her goods abroad, would depend the bullion price of her commodities at home, in the event of her employing gold as her only circulating medium. (pp. 263–264)

---

[24] "It was observed in a former Chapter, that a very considerable advance in the price of the commodities bought and sold in one quarter of this kingdom, while there was no such rise in any other, was not supposable; because the holders of the circulating medium current in the spot in which goods were imagined to have been rendered dear, would exchange it for the circulating medium of the part in which they were assumed to be cheap, and would buy the commodities of the latter place, and transport them to the former, for the sake of the profit on the transaction" (p. 260).

Thornton then assumes that paper takes the place of coins as the circulating medium. As in the example concerning pure circulation, he assumes that Britain will face higher bullion prices abroad. The same logic and process will be at work, and Britain "will experience, exactly as if she made use only of gold, an encrease in the price of her commodities at home, as well as an enlargement of the quantity of her circulating medium." However, in this case Britain will "create," not import, "the additional circulating medium" (p. 264). This difference will have an effect on the level of exports and the exchanges.

Hume, argues Thornton, understood these considerations. However, he preferred the use of gold to that of bank paper unless the paper was fully covered by gold reserves, as it was in Amsterdam's bank. Quoting from Hume's "Of Money," Thornton argues that although Hume's argument had been made for a pure circulation, it is valid for a mixed one (p. 269, note). Criticizing Hume, Thornton explains how more money will raise prices and cause gold to "transport itself." However, a country that does not improperly expand the quantity will enjoy the advantages of substituting gold for paper, while deriving the "whole advantage of this augmentation of capital" (p. 270).

Thornton further argues that paper credit has no influence on whether or not the price of provisions rises.[25] His proof is twofold. First, there had been no increase in the total circulating medium over the last few years, when prices were high. Thornton's case is based on the size of London's circulation and the previous argument that the counties' circulation must conform to London's. Thornton then rejects a second argument, based on the supposedly negative impact of loan extensions on prices. Due to their note creation capacity, country banks extended loans and "encouraged mercantile speculation; and … we may ascribe to the spirit thus excited much of

---

[25] "In thus representing the subject, he [Hume] appears to forget, that when the total circulating medium of a country, whether consisting of gold, or of paper, or of both, is rendered excessive; when it has thus lifted up the gold price of articles above the point at which they stand in adjacent countries, the gold is obliged, by the operation of the exchange, to transport itself to these other parts; and that paper credit, therefore, enhances the prices not of that single spot in which it passes, but of the adjoining places, and of the world. The state which issues paper only in such quantity as to maintain its general exchanges, may be considered as substituting paper in the place of gold, and as gaining additional stock in return for whatever coin it may cause to be exported. It derives, therefore, from its own issue, the whole advantage of this augmentation of capital. It participates with other countries in that inconvenience of a generally increased price of commodities which its paper has contributed to produce. That the popular opinion which was lately entertained of the great influence of paper credit in raising the price not only of commodities in general, but of provisions in particular, had no just foundation, is a position which admits of easy proof" (pp. 269–270).

the late rise in the price of articles in general, and of corn in particular" (p. 271). The important factor in determining prices is "paper" – that is, notes issued – not loans, argues Thornton. He claims, moreover, that intermediation has no effect on prices. Banks extend loans either by accepting deposits and using the sums for extending loans, or by extending their own notes. These notes will substitute for gold in circulation, which will either be hoarded or exported.

Thornton's support for the Restriction is not in doubt. Britain had been saved from the violence on the Continent "through the favour of Providence."[26] The island's political strength, however, depended on prosperity, and that necessitated what Thornton calls "mercantile confidence." The enemy tried to disturb this confidence; hence, the measures taken by Britain, which Thornton defends in the last paragraphs of his treatise:

[T]he continuance of the law for suspending the cash payments of the Bank of England has been one of the steps which parliament has deemed necessary ... In a commercial country, subjected to that moderate degree of occasional alarm and danger which we have experienced, *gold is by no means that kind of circulating medium which is the most desirable.* It is apt to circulate with very different degrees of rapidity, and also to be suddenly withdrawn, in consequence of its being an article intrinsically valuable, and capable of being easily concealed. If, during the war, it had been our only medium of payment, we might sometimes have been almost totally deprived of the means of carrying on our pecuniary transactions; and much confusion in the affairs of our merchants, great interruption of manufacturing labour, and very serious evils to the state, might have been the consequences." (pp. 275–276; emphasis added).

One cannot read Thornton's *Paper Credit* but as a principled defense of inconvertibility and the Bank's directors. In defending inconvertibility, he explains how this new system can function and can provide the country with a sound monetary system.

A Brief Look Beyond 1802

Thornton's views of the Restriction, the Bank of England, and in particular, his position on an early return to cash payments changed before 1810, a year in which he became a major figure and played a central role in the

---

[26] Thornton was well known for his religious activities with the famous Clapham Sect. He was also heavily involved with the abolitionists at this same time. As David Levy suggested in his discussion of this chapter in the HES meeting, his leaning towards public policy in monetary matters may have been related to his desire to see government actions also on the side of the anti-slavery movement.

Bullion Committee on the side of the Bullionists. An interesting window into the process and scope of change can be found in Thornton's comments, written around April 1804,[27] on King (1804) as they appear in Thornton's copy of that important work, now in the Goldsmith Library.[28]

Thornton's disagreements with King focus on whether the paper circulation was excessive, and in particular, whether the Bank of England overly expanded its paper. Thus, the argument was largely about the behavior of the Bank's directors: "The chief danger of an over-issue arises from the circumstances of the Directors perhaps not sufficiently perceiving that a limitation of Paper will improve the Exchanges and that it is necessary if the Exchanges continue long unfavourable to make this reduction even against the general sense of the merchants" (Thornton 1804, p. 316).

Thus, argues Thornton, the general circumstances that put the directors in a difficult position, forcing them to work against the merchants and their own instincts, created the incentives that led to periodic increases in the circulation. However, by 1804, the directors had learned their lesson. King argued that in 1799–1802, the exchanges were "against England … probably occasioned by the increase of the paper currency of the Bank" (King 1804, p. 37). Thornton has some reservations concerning the criteria King used to assess the circulation and the exchanges, but he agrees "that it is probable there may have been about this time a somewhat too great issue of Bank of England Notes" (Thornton 1804, p. 317). Throughout his commentary on King, however, Thornton continues to express support for the Restriction and for the feasibility of a well-functioning inconvertible system. Thus, he writes: "A non-convertible Paper *which is limited* and is in full credit may maintain its price just as if it were convertible" (Thornton 1804, p. 317; emphasis in the original).

Thornton feels that as long as the war lasts, the Bank of England has to be "protected from the danger of having Gold demanded in indefinite quantities." However, he is careful to add that the Bank should not be protected when the demand rises due to "long continuance of an unfavourable Exchange" (p. 321). Thus, a major question for him is whether the Bank is responsible for such a long-term situation. In 1804, Thornton clearly still considered the answer to be negative:

---

[27] See Thornton ([1802] 1939, p. 321).
[28] See Hayek's introductory note in Thornton's *Paper Credit* (1939, p. 312). In the copy of King (1804) at the Goldsmith Library, the following statement appears: "The Manuscript Notes in this copy are by Henry Thornton Esq. M. P." Hayek noted that "there seems to be no reason to doubt the correctness of the ascription." The comments are on King's "second enlarged edition" of the original work that had been originally published in 1803.

The Directors of the Bank of England if they have erred at all, have erred but a little and their Error has resulted from the circumstance of their not sufficiently perceiving the great and important principle which Lord King has so well laid down, namely that an Excess of Paper is the great radical cause of a long continued unfavourable Exchange. (Thornton 1804, pp. 321–322)

Thus, it was not "expedient now to determine the period when the Bank Restriction Bill shall cease, except indeed that it ought to be made to cease in a moderate time after the termination of the War." This was indeed the anti-Bullionists' position.

King (1804, p. 32) argued that "the Proof of a degraded currency founded upon the two tests of the price of bullion and the rate of exchange was strongly and successfully urged by Mr. Boyd in his Letter to Mr. Pitt, published in December 1800." In response, Thornton comments:

Mr. Boyd in his letter to Mr. Pitt insisted that the Nonconvertibility of Paper into Gold was the cause of a depreciation of it which he assumed to be so great as to account "more than any other cause" for the high price of Bread. He did not measure the degree of the Rise which an Excess of paper occasioned by the variation in the Exchange as he ought to have done and he did not seem to consider that this Nonconvertibility of Paper into Gold does not necessarily produce a depreciation of paper, but produces only when it serves to encourage the Issues [sic. Should have been Issuers] of Paper to issue it to excess. A non-convertible Paper *which is limited* and is in full credit may maintain its price just as if it were convertible ([1804/1939], pp. 316–317; emphasis in the original).

Thus, Thornton again defends an anti-Bullionist position. One can see here the seeds of modern monetary thinking on inconvertibility. Thornton founds his explanation for preserving the inconvertible monetary system – in spite of the obvious incentives of private interested parties like the banks to expand it – on a concept of the Bank of England's "responsibility." Thornton asks why the Bank's directors, the ultimate regulators of the English monetary system, should be motivated by public interest rather than by the Bank's private interests. Thornton's comments on King's discussion of Irish banking are revealing in this context.

King addressed the crucial tension between private and public interests under inconvertibility. At the time of his writing, the Irish currency had depreciated; King argued that the depreciation was due to an excess quantity of notes. Thornton points out that the Irish and English systems are quite different: The Bank of Ireland does not have a monopoly over the supply of paper currency in Dublin and does not have the same power as the Bank of England over the circulation in the country. "[T]he limitation of the Bank of Ireland paper ... might possibly have little other effect than that of leaving to the other private Banks (which are completely rival Establishments) those profits which the Bank of Ireland should relinquish" (Thornton 1804, p. 319). Thus, the structure of the English system made the difference.

Thornton was already deeply involved with the Irish currency question when he read and responded to King. This familiarity resulted first in some speeches in Parliament, and then in his role in the important but sometimes neglected Irish Committee of 1804. Fetter, in his 1955 introduction to *The Irish Pound 1797–1826*, credits Thornton with "major responsibility for the work of the Committee."[29] Moreover, the issues concerning the Irish banking structure became the subject for many of the questions the committee put before those who gave evidence, which Fetter thought "suggest[ed] the hand of Henry Thornton."

Thornton's position as expressed to the Irish Committee is that of an anti-Bullionist who supports the suspension and defends the Bank's directors. Although the committee concluded that the 1797 Restriction had permitted a monetary expansion, it did not recommend a repeal of the act. Rather, its recommendations were directed at the Irish banks, calling for their notes to be redeemed in Bank of England notes or in "London funds," and for a more restrained credit policy.[30] The latter recommendation was valid, in Thornton's view, for the Bank of England as well, though the Bank of England was a powerful monopoly that was fulfilling its duties. By 1810, Thornton's positive assessment of the Bank's directors and their credit policy would change.

The Bullion Committee

In 1809–1810, attention had moved again to the monetary disparities concerning the English currency, which showed clear signs of declining in value, as both the price of gold and the Hamburg exchanges depreciated. Thornton's colleague and admirer, Francis Horner, founder of the *Edinburgh Review* and a Member of Parliament, was an important figure in that debate.[31] As a result of

29 Beyond Fetter's important introduction, the volume includes a reprint of the 1804 Report and a selection from the Minutes of Evidence from the House of Commons Committee On the Circulating Paper, the Specie, and the Current Coin of Ireland.
30 See Fetter (1955, pp. 44–48). In a debate in Parliament in March 1805, Thornton stated that he "was surprised" that the Bank of Ireland "had not taken the hint given in the report of the committee."
31 In his famous *Review* of *Paper Credit*, Horner (1957, pp. 28–56) summarized the foundations of Thornton's monetary theory, clarified his main arguments and contributed to his reputation.

Horner's proposal, the Bullion Committee was established in 1810 with Horner as its chair.[32] This committee was the best known and most heavily quoted monetary committee among the many British parliamentary committees. The Bullion Committee's work showed clear links to the Irish Committee in terms of both membership and content.[33] Horner, Thornton, and William Huskisson drafted its report, which has long been considered a Bullionist manifesto.[34] Two speeches made by Thornton after Parliament rejected the report in 1811 will help establish the nature of the modifications in Thornton's position.

According to the preface to the pamphlet in which Thornton's speeches appear,[35] the first speech addressed "the practical measure of limiting the Bank paper." The Bullion Report, the subject of the debate, focused on a difficult point of principle that Thornton tried at length to clarify: whether it was "expedient that the Bank should regulate the issues of its paper with a reference to the price of Bullion, and the state of the Exchanges. ... The Committee affirmed that the quantity of paper had an influence on the price of Bullion, and the state of the Exchanges; all the Directors of the Bank who had been examined, affirmed that it had not" (Thornton 1811, p. 327).

Thornton now found himself with the Bullionists in criticizing the Bank and its directors. However, he did not accept the Bullionists' doctrines and should not be identified as a Bullionist, but rather as an anti-Bullionist who entered an alliance for exclusively political or pragmatic reasons. In failing to convince the directors to act in accordance with his thinking, Thornton joined forces with their critics.

In his speech, Thornton analyzes the effect of changes in the quantity of money in two instances: first, in its influence over the price of commodities, and then in its impact on the price of gold and the exchanges. By way of illustration, he methodically describes three hypothetical cases, one of which was the case of inconvertibility as it existed after 1797 and up to the time of his speech. Analyzing this case, Thornton expresses his reservations with the Bank directors' decisions:

The Bank, since they became protected against the necessity of making cash payments, not unnaturally thought that they might use more liberality than they would have ventured to exercise under the same circumstances of our trade, if they had been subject to a drain for cash. They, perhaps, were not much to be blamed on this account. Indeed, they appear not to have believed that a reduction of their paper

---

[32] See Horner (1957, 1994) and Cannan (1919).
[33] See Fetter (1955) and Fetter (1965).
[34] Full coverage of the report is outside the scope of this discussion.
[35] The first speech was made on May 7, 1811, the second on May 13, 1811. The two were issued together with a short preface. See in Thornton (1802/1939, pp. 325–361).

would mend the Exchange, for they had not examined very deeply or philosophically into the subject. (p. 333)

Here one can find a hint as to the probable causes for Thornton's changing attitude towards the Bank's directors:

It was, however, important not to mistake leading principles, and not to fancy that an exchange running against us with all countries for two or three years, and reaching the height of 25 and 30 per cent., accompanied with a corresponding high price of gold, *ought at no time and in no degree to be checked by that limitation of the currency to which nature, as it were, as well as our own practice before 1797, taught us in such cases to resort.* (p. 333; emphasis added)

In other words, the Bank's directors, freed from the dictates of gold, stopped listening to the signals that should have led them to implement better policy. Surveying other banking systems, Thornton shows that the same principles apply and summarizes his disagreement with the anti-Bullionists:

[T]he Bank of France, the Bank of Sweden, and the Banks of America, were establishments more or less independent of the government: they all emitted their paper in the way of loan, furnished at a moderate or low interest; and they had all issued it to excess. The adversaries of the Bullion Committee had grounded a great part of their argument on the following distinction between the Bank of England and all those Banks of which the paper had been depreciated: – The Bank of England, they said, issues nothing, except in return for something valuable: they receive a bill, representing real property, for every note which they emit; and therefore they cannot issue to excess ... But it was of the utmost consequence to understand, that, even when a supposed equivalent is received in return for the paper issued, excess might arise; and the excess, as he had already said, was likely to be great in proportion as the rate of interest was low. (p. 341)[36]

Thornton maintained a consistent position that was critical of other anti-Bullionists like Baring. In particular, he rejected their support of the Real Bills Doctrine. However, he disagreed on a theoretical level with the Bullionists' reliance on gold as an automatic device that leaves the system free to regulate itself.

Surprising as it may seem to those who remember Thornton mainly from the Bullion Committee, his views of 1802 put him in the anti-Bullionist camp, defending both the Bank of England and the Stoppage of cash payments. Thornton's published comments on King's book, as well as his involvement

---

[36] And again: "The Bank Directors should not continue to act on the principle that a limitation of paper had no influence whatever on the exchange. This was the point on which they were at issue with the Bullion Committee ... The Parliament had now to decide on this point of difference between the Committee and the Bank" (p. 343).

in the Irish currency debates and the Irish Committee of 1804, paved the way for his important role in the celebrated Bullion Committee. In the end, however, his role in the committee was restricted to expressing his dissatisfaction with the Bank's directors concerning their misunderstanding of the Bank's public role. Thus, in 1810 Thornton gave reserved support to a return to cash payments, but did not accept Horner's and Huskisson's metallic approach. On the Bullion Committee he was and remained the third Thornton.

Thornton's Pioneering Monetary Ideas

Thornton's monetary thinking as it appears in *Paper Credit* deserves the many compliments it has received over the years. Although it is not the most eloquently written book, it contains fascinating ideas and reflects some of the modern tenets of monetary theory. In it, Thornton addresses a system on the brink of collapse; under the pressure of war and bank runs, the decision to stop cash payments caused much suspicion about the system and made it fragile. Contrary to the Bullionists, Thornton did not think that an inconvertible system could not work; in fact, he argues that the necessary condition for the proper functioning of the financial system was to direct various aggregates in the monetary system, the same condition that is necessary under convertibility.

Crises are possible under both convertibility and inconvertibility. Crises are in the nature of the real economy and the financial system; the need to react to recurring crises with the proper policies should be clear to those who have control of the system. Thus, those who run the monetary system have responsibility to implement proper policies to ensure that the system functions. The advantages of a monetary system over a barter system are clear and justify the implementation of discretionary policy. But the discretionary policy should aim at directing the economy, not just saving it from the danger of collapsing into barter.

Thornton concludes that there is a need for a body that would direct the financial system, and that this body should focus on the public good, rather than adopt profit motives as its only considerations. This modern conclusion, derived by Thornton from his analysis of exchange and intermediation, is ahead of its time. It returned to conventional mainstream thinking only in the twentieth century.

EIGHT

Ricardo versus Bosanquet

The Famous Round of the Bullion Debate

Even during his relatively brief lifetime, David Ricardo (1772–1823) came to provide a special point of reference for his fellow political economists. Since 1776, almost every work of criticism on political economy had taken Adam Smithas its starting point. With the publication of Ricardo's works, he came to share Smith's status as a founding father of political economy. Ricardo wrote for only fourteen years, from the age of thirty-seven until his death at the age of fifty-one.[1] He had become very wealthy as a broker in the London Stock Exchange and then devoted his time to studying economic issues of public importance. His first publication, for example, reflected his concern with monetary theory through one of the troubling practical issues of the time: the high price of bullion in 1809, during the Restriction, when the price of gold rose even more than it had in 1800–1801. The implications of the high price of bullion reverberated throughout contemporary society.

Ricardian Monetary Theory: 1809–1811

Ricardo's contribution to monetary theory began in 1809 with three letters to the *Morning Chronicle* newspaper. The letters were followed by a pamphlet

---

[1] Ricardo's writings, speeches, letters, etc. appear in the definitive *Collected Works and Correspondence* edited by P. Sraffa in collaboration with M. Dobb, in eleven volumes (1951–1973). References to this edition use the following notations: Roman numbers for the volume followed by the page number. The editors' excellent introductions to the various publications are an important secondary source. There is a vast secondary literature on Ricardo's works, though less on its monetary aspects. The main works used, apart from the editor's "Introductions to the Collected Works," are: Hollander (1911), Bonar (1923), Sayers (1953), Blaug (1958), Hollander (1979), Peach (2004), and Davis (2005), and many references therein. The more recent work by Davis proposes a complete revision of Ricardo's monetary thought with which the present author does not agree.

in 1810 entitled *The High Price of Bullion, A Proof of the Depreciation of Bank Notes*, known in short as *The High Price of Bullion*.[2] It is interesting to note that, although the ideas expressed in Ricardo's celebrated first pamphlet were not original, they won him a name as a distinguished thinker on questions of political economy.[3] From that point until his early death, he analyzed the core, real, and monetary issues in the economy in pamphlets and in the book *Principles of Political Economy* (1817),[4] and he became a highly acclaimed authority on political economy.

In the *High Price of Bullion*, Ricardo argues that rises in the price of gold and depreciation of the pound in the foreign exchanges stem from one, and only one, cause: a monetary expansion. The reason for the expansion was an over-issue of Bank notes by the Bank of England; a return to convertibility could solve the problem. The opposing, anti-Bullionist position, discussed in previous chapters, attributed the same phenomena to several different causes rooted in real, rather than monetary, factors, such as disturbances in trade caused by war expenditures and bad harvests. In between these two positions, one can find the moderate Bullionists like Boyd, who acknowledged the influence of real factors without completely discounting the influence of over-issue.

In the introduction to *The High Price of Bullion*, Ricardo argues, in what became typical of his approach, that it is necessary to know the cause of the evil before attempting to remedy it. Sayers (1953, p. 77) summarizes Ricardo's interpretation of the disturbing economic phenomena of his time as follows: "The high price of bullion was the sign and measure of depreciation"; gold was "the principal measure of value"; and there was "one, sole" reason for the high price of gold: its price in terms of paper. It rose because the Bank of England issued too many notes.

---

[2] Over the years, there was much confusion on the exact relation between the letters and the pamphlet. As the editors of Ricardo's *Collected Works* concluded, the pamphlet "was almost entirely written afresh," though the main points discussed in the pamphlet were outlined in the letters. See III, pp. 3–6. The pamphlet went into four editions, the fourth published in 1811, and which contained a new appendix under the title, "Suggestions for Securing to the Public a Currency as Invariable as Gold, with a Very Moderate Supply of that Metal." The appendix also appeared under a separate cover; see III, p. 99. The appendix was in fact Ricardo's reaction to an article in the *Edinburgh Review*, written by Malthus, which reviewed both the *High Price of Bullion* and other pamphlets written during the intense debate, among them those of Bosanquet and Ricardo's answer to him (*Reply to Bosanquet*, to which we will turn later), Mushet's (1810) pamphlet, and others.

[3] Hollander (1911) writes: "What are commonly regarded as Ricardo's important contributions were neither new, independent, analyses of contemporary monetary events, nor fresh deductions from general economic principles" (p. 469). See also Rist (1940), p. 140. On the question of metal distribution over the world, he returned to Locke and Hume, and on inconvertible paper money, to Wheatley and King.

[4] A revised second edition appeared in 1819, and a further revised third edition in 1821.

The point of departure for Ricardo's analysis is that there is a certain quantity of gold in the world that functions as the medium of exchange in internal trade; gold is also the means for settling debts in international trade. Thus, it functions as currency in the trading countries and as means of payment in international trade. The distribution of the given quantity of gold over the world satisfies the "law" of equal values of gold everywhere. As Ricardo makes clear, "value" in this early text means purchasing power: The value of gold is its price in other commodities. However, gold is itself a commodity, and thus gold and commodities follow the same laws and have the same value in all places, subject to the costs of transferring them from one place to the other.

Following Smith and Lord King, whom he quotes approvingly, Ricardo emphasizes the commodity aspects of money. Central to his argument is the claim that the balance of payments between trading countries tends to balance itself without gold flowing between them, even when conditions change:

> While the relative situation of countries continued unaltered, they might have abundant commerce with each other, but their exports and imports would on the whole be equal. England might possibly import more goods from, than she would export to, France, but she would in consequence export more to some other country, and France would import more from that country; so that the exports and imports of all countries would balance each other. (III, pp. 53–54)

A famous example of a change concerns the effects of a new stock of gold. Assuming the discovery of a new gold mine in a country, the value of gold will fall and gold will temporarily be redistributed throughout the trading countries until a new uniform value for it is reached. The gold flows that take place under this scenario should not inspire worry. Under a regime of convertibility, an increase of notes in circulation will have the same effect, and "[t]he circulating medium would be lowered in value and goods would experience a proportionate rise. The equilibrium between that and other nations would only be restored by the exportation of part of the coin" (III, p. 55). Ricardo is guided by the concept of a "pure circulation," that is, a circulation in which gold coins are the only money and their value is determined by the same laws governing any other commodity. As long as convertibility prevailed, issuing more bank notes would just push gold outside the country, because its value was higher abroad.[5]

---

5   "If in France an ounce of gold were more valuable than in England, and could therefore in France purchase more of any commodity common to both countries, gold would immediately quit England ... because it would be the cheapest exchangeable commodity in the English market." (III, p. 57)

In Ricardo's analysis, the advantages of banking are those already described by Hume and Smith. Under convertibility, the quantity of money would still be the right one, that which would have circulated in a pure circulation:

The Bank might continue to issue their notes, and the specie be exported with advantage to the country, while their notes were payable in specie on demand, because they could never issue more notes than the value of the coin which would have circulated had there been no bank ...[6]

If they attempted to exceed this amount, the excess would be immediately returned to them for specie; because our currency, being thereby diminished in value, could be advantageously exported, and could not be retained in our circulation. These are the means, as I have already explained, by which our currency endeavours to equalize itself with the currencies of other countries. (III, p. 57)

Ricardo argues that, as both Smith and Thornton explained, if the Bank continued issuing notes beyond the right quantity, it would bring losses upon itself because it would have to buy gold high and sell it low. Thus, under convertibility, the Bank would not misbehave:

The Bank would be obliged therefore ultimately to adopt the only remedy in their power to put a stop to the demand for guineas. They would withdraw part of their notes from circulation, till they should have increased the value of the remainder to that of gold bullion, and consequently to the value of the currencies of other countries. All advantage from the exportation of gold bullion would then cease, and there would be no temptation to exchange bank-notes for guineas. (p. 59)

During the war years, there were two much-discussed, significant changes in the relationship between the sum of transactions and the amount of currency. One was the foreign allowances awarded to finance war expenses; the other, which was not new, was a series of bad harvests. Ricardo's argument concerning the effects of these factors on gold movement was unique even among the Bullionists. Common wisdom held that these factors changed the value of gold in different countries, resulting in immediate gold movements to restore a new uniform value for gold. For example, bad harvests in England would lead to a decrease in the value of gold in England, and gold would flow out of the country (reflux). At the same time, corn would flow into England until a balance between corn and gold was restored. This argument, as we have seen, had already been formulated by Hume and others,

---

[6] [Ricardo's note] "They might, strictly speaking, rather exceed that quantity, because as the Bank would add to the currency of the world, England would retain its share of the increase."

and more recently had been restated in the most important work on monetary thought to date, that of Thornton. Ricardo, on the other hand, argued that the value of gold in the different countries would not change because of bad harvests in England. If unfavorable exchanges did exist, England would export more goods. Gold has no preferential status in this context; although conventional thought assumed that gold would move to restore balance, the movement would in fact be of other commodities, especially those whose value was relatively low in England. In Ricardo's words, directed specifically against Thornton:

> If we consent to give coin in exchange for goods, it must be from choice, not necessity. We should not import more goods than we export, unless we had a redundancy of currency, which it therefore suits us to make a part of our exports. *The exportation of the coin is caused by its cheapness, and is not the effect, but the cause of an unfavourable balance*: we should not export it, if we did not send it to a better market, or if we had any commodity which we could export more profitably. It is a salutary remedy for a redundant currency. (III, p. 61; my emphasis)

This led Ricardo to a crucial conclusion: if gold does flow out of England, it is only because gold's value in England is lower than in other places. Such lower value can again have only one cause, which is an abundance of the currency. The balance of trade is not the cause of gold movements, because other commodities will help to close the gap without the aid of gold. Because England has no gold mines, only the Bank of England and its excessive note-issuing could be responsible for the outflow of gold. The country banks, commonly suspected of over-issuing notes, could not and should not be held responsible. In Ricardo's view, the principle regulating the distribution of precious metals in the world also operated within the country. The circulation of each local bank's notes had the same purchasing power as those of banks in other areas. Only the Bank of England could expand the amount of currency, because local banks could not do so without immediate local price rises that would encourage people to exchange the local notes for Bank of England notes, thus reducing the amount of currency.

Ricardo's reasoning on this point is so peculiar that several different interpretations have been tried to help explain it. Viner (1924) argues that this "erroneous" conclusion derived from the fact that "Ricardo denied that gold would be exported if it were soon to be reimported" (p. 198). Viner bases this statement on the appendix to the fourth edition of the *High Price of Bullion* (April 1811), in which Ricardo claims that because the original cause of this kind of gold movement was transitory (bad harvests one year which could be followed by good harvests the next), there was no point in exporting gold one year simply to reimport it the next. In Ricardo's words: "Is it conceivable that money should be sent abroad for the purpose merely of rendering it dear in this country and cheap in another, and by such means to ensure its return to us?" (III, p. 103; appendix to the fourth edition, April 1811).

On the basis of the same text, Sayers (1953) suggests that Ricardo thought that if a little gold were to flow out of the country, the immediate result would be cheaper exports, and hence a reflow of gold into the country. Sayers argues that Ricardo assumed that

the slightest fall in our export prices – the fall implied by the movement to gold export point – will sufficiently stimulate the export of commodities, just as it stimulates the export of gold. Instead of this happening, the development of exports to fill the gap was being prevented by the rise in home prices consequent upon the increase in the supply of money. (Sayers 1953, p. 34)

Sayers thus interprets Ricardo as adopting Thornton's belief that changes in the value of gold are the means to achieving a new equilibrium. In Viner's interpretation, Ricardo still thinks that changes in the value of gold do not occur. As Viner puts it: "[Ricardo maintained that] ... a shift in relative prices in subsidy granting and subsidy receiving countries, respectively, was not the mechanism of adjustment of the commodity balance to the subsidy" (Viner 1924, p. 201). Both Sayers and Viner agree that according to Ricardo, bad harvests will not result in a movement of gold; however, they differ in their interpretations of the mechanism by which balance is restored.

Although this mechanism remains disputed,[7] Ricardo's conclusion is decisive. Gold flowing out of the country is a clear sign of surplus currency. The remedy for such outflows of gold is to decrease the amount of notes in circulation. In the final analysis, Ricardo believes that this mechanism for restoring balance would work "naturally" if people were left alone to carry on their business. Thus, it is unnecessary to limit the export of gold and coins. Indeed, the trouble in the system only occurs because of the Bank's power to increase the medium in circulation. In convertible regimes, the Bank can only cause disturbances in the movement of gold and slight variations in its value. However, in inconvertible situations, as had been the case since 1797, the Bank could cause almost infinitely large changes in value.

Such an analysis reflects Ricardo's view that, in contrast to the injurious meddling of the Bank, a system that enables individuals to act according to

---

[7] On the dispute, see Grubel (1961), Humphrey (1990), and de Boyer des Roches (2007).

their private best interests cannot be harmful. In dealing with gold, private interests "are never in variance" with community interests, like in "most other commerce where there is free competition" (III, p. 56). Ricardo, one of the founders of the liberal free trade movement, believed its principles to be general enough to be applicable to the banking system, as long as convertibility was retained. Thus, at this point, his position was not different from that of Smith.

In this first pamphlet, Ricardo draws an analogy between clipped coins and inconvertible paper money. In certain circumstances, both can act as the standard of value, that is, the unit of value with which all things are compared. The value of the standard itself under such circumstances was determined by its quantity. This caused Rist (1940) to argue that Ricardo was "obsessed by the idea of quantity" (p. 140). Rist also claims that Ricardo thought that the standard during the Restriction was paper money. In fact, Ricardo thought that all values were still compared with gold, as we see in the following example of clipped coins, which have the same effect as depreciated paper. Gold was considered suitable for providing a measure of purchasing power ("value") across commodities because of its "utility, beauty and scarcity" (these are Smith's words, which Ricardo repeats). In other words, gold is first a commodity and then currency, and because it follows the laws concerning commodities, the international mechanism applies.

When Ricardo explained his controversial argument about the "international mechanism" in the *High Price of Bullion*, he remarked that the error of those who followed Thornton – and so would oppose Ricardo – was that they failed to "distinguish … between an increase in the value of gold, and an increase in its money price" (III, p. 60). By the value of gold, Ricardo meant the purchasing power of gold (coins or bullion) measured against other commodities. By its money price, he meant this weight measured in (fine) gold coins. The value of gold and its money price will not differ from one another except in the case of clipped coins, which can retain the purchasing power of nonclipped coins while changing the money price of bullion. Thus, the similarity between clipped coins and bank notes, when the latter were overissued, was clear. This idea is found in a letter to Horner written on February 5, 1810 (VI, pp. 1–7). Ricardo wrote this letter after Horner first proposed the creation of a committee of inquiry in Parliament that led to the establishment of the Bullion Committee; Ricardo tries to convince Horner that his "observation, in the House of Commons" was wrong. That observation reflected the moderate Bullionist position and did not explain the high price of bullion as "wholly, and solely" caused by a superabundance of paper circulation, as Ricardo thought it was. Ricardo explained that if gold was exchanged for imported commodities, this would not change the money price of bullion: "[Gold bullion's] *value* would no doubt be increased, and it is from not distinguishing between an increase in the *value* of gold, and an increase in its *money price*, that much of the error of our reasoning is derived" (VI, p. 5). This fundamental disagreement marked the divisions in the Bullion Committee chaired by Horner, as we shall see.

Even assuming that resumption was to take place and convertibility to prevail, questions arise about the limitations, if any, on the application of free trade principles in banking. Ricardo and the Bullionists in general assumed the Humeian and Smithian positions to hold, and believed that as long as convertible money was issued, there could be no such thing as an over-issue of convertible paper money. Thus, Ricardo's position on free trade in banking under convertibility was similar to the views held before the Restriction by the major authorities on the subject. Ricardo did not doubt this approach until his posthumous pamphlet of 1824, which, as we shall see, contains new principles.

The Bullion Committee

The Bullion Committee was appointed in February 1810 amid the controversy surrounding the high price of gold, the exchanges, and inflation. The motion to appoint a committee of inquiry came from Horner, who chaired the committee and most probably wrote the committee's report together with Huskisson and Thornton.[8] The basic position of the Bullion Committee was similar to that of the Irish Committee of 1804. The authors of the report argue in favor of the theory that the monetary system controls the exchanges. On policy issues, they recommend a return to convertibility within two years, regardless of whether or not the war would end. This recommendation was in clear contrast with the 1797 law that spelled out that the Resumption should take place only after the war. The report was published in August 1810, but the full debate in Parliament had to wait until April 1811. A month later, Parliament, in a famous vote, rejected the Bullion Committee's theory as well as its practical recommendations.

---

[8] Fetter (1942) showed that Ricardo's influence on the committee, which for some time has been described in the literature as decisive, was in fact fairly limited. See also Fetter (1959, 1965).

Fetter speculates that the Bullion report's criticism of the Real Bills Doctrine was "probably written by Henry Thornton."[9] Clearly, the committee had been worried about the Bank directors' rejection of the possibility that the Bank may have contributed to inflation or to the deteriorating exchanges. Thus, the committee opted to support a return to pre-1797 convertibility, rather than support the continuation of inconvertibility, acknowledging the dangers of internal drain with which the Bank could not deal. Thus, the Bullion Committee wrote:

> Your Committee therefore, having very anxiously and deliberately considered this subject, report it to the House, as their Opinion, That the system of the circulating medium of this Country ought to be brought back, with as much speed as is compatible with a wise and necessary caution, to the original principle of Cash payments at the option of the holder of Bank paper. (Cannan, p. 68)

Parliament's rejection in May 1811 of both the theory behind this conclusion and the practical steps recommended by the committee reflected – and has since been understood as – tacit acceptance by Parliament of the anti-Bullionist position. As we shall see, most anti-Bullionists extended the Real Bills Doctrine – which maintained that the banks could lend as long as they lent against good securities – to hold under inconvertibility. This theory implies that the banks need do nothing beyond ensuring that their securities are good.

Over the next ten years, however, Parliament completely reversed its position on monetary policy, as the influence of the Bullionist position and that of its famous advocate, Ricardo, grew. Critiques of the Bullion Committee's report claimed that its recommendations were an impediment to the war effort. The critics included bankers and officials who proposed to continue the Restriction and discuss a possible resumption only after the end of the war. One of their more able exponents was Charles Bosanquet.

Charles Bosanquet (1810): The Anti-Bullionist Position

Charles Bosanquet (1769–1850) was a merchant and financier. He was a member of Lloyds, a subgovernor of the South Sea Company from 1808 and its governor from 1838 to 1850, and a director at the West India Company. His 1810 text *Practical Observations on the Report of the Bullion-Committee*

---

9 "That this doctrine [of the Bank directors] is a very fallacious one, Your Committee cannot entertain a doubt. The fallacy, upon which it is founded, lies in not distinguishing between an advance of capital to Merchants, and an additional supply of currency to the general mass of circulating medium." Fetter (1965, p. 43) quoted from Cannan (1919, p. 50).

(second edition), was "regarded at the time as the most effective of the criticisms published on the Bullion Report," as Sraffa notes,[10] although it is probably remembered today because of the rebuttal written by Ricardo (to which we will turn later). "Abstract reasoning is foreign to my purpose," Bosanquet declares in the opening paragraph of his pamphlet, quoting Sir Davenant on the importance of data for reaching a conclusion. He argues that the data included in the appendix to the Bullion Report proves that the Report's conclusions are wrong. The depression of the foreign exchanges and the rising price of gold bullion moved together, changing by around 20 percent by November 1809. Ricardo drew the public's attention to these facts, but Bosanquet argues that Ricardo's pamphlet "is wholly theoretical, and so far unsatisfactory; – because the theories are not brought to the test of experiment" (ibid., p. 2). Bosanquet focuses on Ricardo because he initiated the debate and his work has become "a syllabus" to the Report. Bosanquet also briefly addresses the *Inquiry*[11] of Mushet, another Bullionist who came from the mint – an important and respected official establishment – and who published valuable data in an appendix to that pamphlet.

Thus, in 1810, after the publications of both Ricardo's *High Price* and the *Bullion Report*, Bosanquet wrote *Practical Observations*. The pamphlet is primarily directed, as the title states, against the arguments contained in the Report but also specifically against Ricardo's *High Price*. The two publications were perceived as very close to one another, and together with the pamphlet produced by Mushet, they were regarded as the "Trio." According to Bosanquet, all three works – not just Ricardo's pamphlet – fail to appropriately test their theories and suffer from a lack of supportive data (p. 2).

The committee was appointed to explain the cause of the high price of bullion, but in Bosanquet's view, it failed to do so. Instead, it provided "a variety of opinions, and laid down several axioms. … from which they deduce the inference, that the high price of bullion and low rates of exchange are caused by an excess in the amount, and consequent depreciation of value, of banknotes" (p. 4). The major arguments in the "three Treatises" – the Report, Ricardo's *High Price*, and Mushet's *Inquiry* – are so similar "even in expression" that to Bosanquet it is clear that the Bullion Committee accepted the view that paper currency was excessive (p. 7). This view of the committee was "at variance with those of the persons selected for examination" – people

---

[10] See editors' "Note on the Bullion Essays," *Ricardo's Collected Works* vol. III, p. 10.
[11] Mushet, R. (1811), An Inquiry into the Effects Produced on the National Currency and Rates of Exchange by the Bank Restriction Bill; Explaining the Cause of the High Price of Bullion; With Plans for Maintaining the National Coins in a State of Uniformity and Perfection, third edition, London: Robert Baldwin.

mainly from the banking sector. Thus, he argues, the professionals' view was rejected by the committee, who "called for opinions, and, where these have proved adverse to the theory which it was intended to establish, has been more occupied in refuting them, and proving their absurdity, than in ascertaining on what they were founded" (p. 50). Thus, Bosanquet accuses the Bullionists, the Bullion Committee, Ricardo, and Mushet of being unprofessional and reaching conclusions far from the truth.

Bosanquet distinguishes between theories and their application, and claims that sometimes even true abstract theories, when applied improperly, lead to disastrous results. He presents the professional party to the debate, the anti-Bullionists, as representing the view of the practical bankers who concentrate more on facts and less on abstract theories, especially when these theories are not applicable. To convince readers, Bosanquet recounts a historical experience when well-known theoreticians applied wrong theories, leading to negative and costly results:

> A theory brought forward by Mr. Locke, as counsel to the chancellor of the exchequer, and acted upon by Sir Issac Newton, as warden of the mint, might challenge the world for higher sanction. – Yet the recoinage of silver, in the reign of King William, directed by these great men, was made on erroneous principles and failed in its object. ... It will probably therefore be admitted as possible, that an incontrovertible theory may, even in the hands of the ablest men, be erroneously applied. (pp. 36–38)

This same erroneous theory appears in the three treatises. For example, in the Bullion Report:

> The basis of the argument of the Committee, ... "that the difference of exchange, resulting from the state of trade and payments between two countries is limited by the expense of conveying and insuring the precious metals from one country to the other; at least, that it cannot, for any considerable time, exceed that limit:" (Rep. p. 11) therefore, all excess of depression on the exchange, beyond the expense of conveyance, is to be attributed to depreciation of our currency. ... but, boldly as the principle is asserted, and strongly as reason appears to sanction it, I insist that it is not generally true, and that it is at variance with fact. (pp. 15–16)

Bosanquet first relates what he describes as the three "negative" propositions assumed in the Report, which are proven wrong by the facts that he surveys. He then discusses two additional "positive" propositions that are also wrong. The first of the three "negatives" is that "variations of the exchange with foreign countries can never, for any considerable time, exceed the expense of transportation and insuring the precious metals." The second is that "the price of Gold Bullion can never exceed the mint-price, unless the currency, in which it is paid, is depreciated below the value of gold"; and the third is that based on customs reports, the "state of the exchanges ought to be peculiarly favourable" (p. 8).

Bosanquet describes these propositions as "negative arguments" because the Report – and Ricardo's pamphlet, which also contains these claims – hoped to "induce the admission of the depreciation of the paper currency of this country as the necessary consequence of the impossibility of accounting for the depression of the exchanges and the increased price of bullion in any other way" (p. 48). Thus, these arguments served the Trio like a proof by negation. The proof that they are in fact incorrect, claims Bosanquet, lies in data that were available to the committee had it seriously wanted to establish the truth and not to argue for opinions. The method used to prove that the three propositions are incorrect and should not apply to the real world was to check whether they prevailed under convertibility. The data were there, provided to the committee by the Bank representatives and others, mainly merchants and other bankers. Bosanquet used the data to refute the validity of the abstract propositions.

The first point, that "variations of the exchange with foreign countries can never, for any considerable time, exceed the expense of transportation and insuring the precious metals," was crucial. Bosanquet reports in detail on many occasions where the gap between the prices of gold in different locations was higher than the costs for "conveyance" of gold, transportation, and insurance. The first example, strangely enough, relates to the first two years of the Restriction and is followed by a long list of cases before the Restriction, where the gaps were large (pp. 15–22). "In every case here cited the fluctuations of the exchanges greatly exceeded the expense of conveying gold from one country to the other, and to a much greater degree in most of them than the present instance" (p. 18). A possible explanation for the examples provided by Bosanquet was a high price of gold in the place where the exchanges had been unfavorable. However, even in such a case, it is not just the price gap that matters, but also the absolute price of gold, which again contradicts the theory. Thus, argues Bosanquet:

[But] if the price of gold abroad enters into the calculation of the "natural limit" of depression of the exchange, then the course of foreign exchanges, rectified by the expense of sending gold abroad, does not form a just criterion of the adequacy or excess of our circulating medium. (p. 19)

This last criterion was at the heart of the debate. Some scholars, like Viner, make it the dividing line in the debate between the Bullionists and anti-Bullionists.

Using the same method, Bosanquet goes on to refute the second of the negative arguments: that "the price of Gold Bullion can never exceed the mint-price, unless the currency, in which it is paid, is depreciated below the value of gold." He surveyed many instances of a significant gap between the price of gold in the markets and its mint price. These cases cover different dates in English history; the data came from the report and its appendices and should have been noticed by the committee. The conclusion of the historical survey was that a gap of 12–13 percent between the exchanges, the price of gold, and the mint price had appeared repeatedly.

Ricardo, who had brought the issue to the forefront and was responsible for many of the Report's incorrect ideas, also championed this wrong concept. Bosanquet accused Ricardo (this was not the last time such an accusation was directed at him) of being too much of a theorist and of not understanding reality, certainly not the reality of the war:

> At a moment when we were compelled to receive corn, even from our enemy, without the slightest stipulation in favour of our own manufactures, and to pay neutrals for bringing it, Mr. Ricardo tells us, that the export of bullion and merchandise, in payment of the corn we may import, resolves itself entirely into a question of interest, and that, if we give coin in exchange for goods, it must be from choice, not necessity. Whilst providing against famine, he tells us, that we should not import more goods than export, unless we had a redundancy of currency: writing in the end of 1809, Mr. Ricardo thinks it necessary for Mr. Thornton to shew (in support of his opinion, that the demand for bullion and an increased price, might be occasioned by an importation of corn,) "Why an unwillingness should exist in the foreign country to receive our goods in exchange for their corn; and that if such unwillingness did exist, we should consent to indulge it."[12] – This *equalizing system* is a very just one, where it meets with no external impediments; but when applied to practice, it appears to me like the experiment in vacou, where all friction, all obstruction, being removed, and the power of gravitation alone allowed to operate, the guinea and the feather descend with equal velocities. The fact is undeniably true under the circumstances of the experiment, but it is true only within the limits of an exhausted receiver, and is, therefore, wholly inapplicable to any of the common purposes of life. (pp. 47–48)

The equalizing system or mechanism was based on the model that was behind Ricardo's arguments, and which Bosanquet summarized in the three "negative" propositions. Of course, as we discussed earlier, it had its roots in the Price-Specie-Flow mechanism as formulated by Gravise, Hume, and others.

---

[12] This is an inaccurate quote. The full sentence read: "that if such an unwillingness were to exist, we should agree to indulge it so far as to consent to part with our coin." From Ricardo, III, p. 61.

Bosanquet now turns to the remaining two "positive arguments" concerning the supposed reasons for the excess currency. Both of these arguments address the mechanisms in the banking industry that determine the quantity of money. First is the claim that the Bank had the "power" to add its notes to the circulation "beyond the absolute demand for paper, as a circulating medium." Second is that the Bank notes' circulation "regulate those of the country banks, which are dependent upon and proportionate thereto." Data was the key to refuting these two "positive" arguments as well.

When the committee asked the directors about the power of the Bank to increase the circulation of their notes, it received repeatedly negative answers from the directors. "The answer is this;" summarized Bosanquet, "1st. The paper would revert to us [the Bank], if there were a redundancy in circulation; 2dly. By discounting only solid paper given; as far as we can judge, for real transactions" (pp. 50–51). That is a brief summary of the Real Bills Doctrine as advocated by the anti-Bullionists. That line of defense concerning the sensitive question of "responsibility" was crucial in understanding the collapse of the anti-Bullionist school. The theory behind the mechanism that supposedly guaranteed the right quantity in circulation had been inherited from Adam Smith, on whose authority Bosanquet happily relied more than once, as we will see.

Ricardo and the Bullion Committee were wrong in their assumption that the Bank of England during the Restriction was similar to the famous case made in Ricardo's *High Price of Bullion* of a gold mine within a country. In the latter, oft-quoted case, additional production in the mine caused the circulation to be in excess and to depreciate. However, Bosanquet argues that understanding the mechanism at work when this takes place is very important and clearly shows the differences between a gold mine and the Bank of England. The gold mine

... would produce it [the price rises], because the proprietors would issue it [gold], for whatever services, without any engagements, to give an equal value for it again to the holders, or any wish, or any means, of calling back and annihilating that which they have issued. By degrees, as the issues increase they exceed the wants of circulation; gold produces no benefit to the holder as gold; he cannot eat it, nor clothe himself with it; to render it useful, he must exchange it either for such things as are immediately useful, or for such as produce revenue. The demand and consequently the prices of commodities and real properties, measured in gold, increases; and will continue to increase so long as the mine continues to produce. And this effect will equally follow whether, under the circumstances I have supposed, the issue be gold from a mine or paper from a government-bank. (p. 52)

Bosanquet puts the blame for this confusion on Ricardo, who "assimilated the Bank of England, during the Restriction, so far as relates to the effects of its issues, to a gold-mine" (p. 51). However, the Bank of England is not a government bank: "The principle on which the Bank issues its notes is that of loan." Hence, the party who is receiving the notes becomes indebted to the Bank. "No note is issued in payment of any service, moral or physical, constituting the consideration for it, and there is therefore no analogy between the circumstances of the issues from a gold mine and those from the Bank of England" (pp. 52–53).

In the case of the mine, the excess has an effect on prices; in the case of the Bank, Bosanquet quotes the governor of the Bank as saying that the "surplus would revert to us by a diminished application for discounts and advances on government-securities" (p. 53). This point, argues Bosanquet, was not properly understood by the Bullion Committee.

The argument that under the modus operandi of the Bank of England no excess is possible rests on the complicated market mechanism whereby the needs and demands of those who apply for loans from the Bank, for various genuine reasons, should be answered, but will not result in excess. It is exactly the same logic that Adam Smith used to rationalize competition as a proper mechanism in banking, given the genuine motives of the demand for loans; but in Smith's case, of course, the logic applied to convertibility. The Real Bills Doctrine provided the answer, assuming the loans granted were "genuine." Both Bosanquet and the Bank accepted this logic under inconvertibility as well. Thus, if the demand for loans was genuine – again, the check for that was to have proper securities against the loans – the quantity in circulation could not be too high. Even when there were many "applications for discounts, which may be as unlimited as the spirit of adventure, [and] bank-notes be multiplied ad infinitum, at the will of the Directors," the quantity would not be excessive. Why? Because as the Bank directors explained to the committee, "[if] we issue too many notes, the excess will return upon us" (pp. 56–57). Later authors referred to this mechanism as the Law of Reflux.[13]

Thus, in representing and defending the Bank's position, Bosanquet in fact argued for an "impossibility proposition": the impossibility of excess Bank notes in circulation. The quantity is determined by demand, and the flexibility in the system provides that the supply will meet the demand through discounting. Bosanquet gives many examples of the efficient and speedy changes in the amount in circulation and the flexibility of the system

---

[13] We will return to the Law of Reflux in Chapter 12, while discussing the Banking School.

as it reacts to shocks in the amount resulting from extraordinary payments (pp. 58–62). The doctrine that the Bank and Bosanquet presented and that met with contempt from the Bullion Committee was "founded on the authority of Dr. Adam Smith. ... That the Committee may be right and Dr. Smith wrong is very possible," added Bosanquet; "I am not a theorist enough to decide between them" (pp. 63–64).

The links and interdependencies between the Bank in London and issuing country banks was the fifth and last point of disagreement. Bosanquet thought that the mechanism linking them and that resulted in the assumed control over the country banks by the Bank of England – control that the Bullion Report accepted as real – was "metaphysical." Ricardo and the Bullion Report had in mind a mechanism that gave control to the Bank; they claimed that through price changes in the various regions, the Bank in fact regulated the circulation in the country. The signal – and medium – that activated the transmission of changes from London to the rest of the country and back was that of excess notes. Excess notes in any district, they argued, would lead to higher prices there; customers would then prefer to buy in London rather than in the more expensive district and would return the local notes, whose quantity would then diminish. As a result, "the excess of paper being returned upon the issuers for the Bank-of-England paper, the quantity of the latter necessarily and effectually limits the quantity of the former" (p. 74). If the Bank is the expanding side, the country banks will follow its lead.

Bosanquet did not accept this theoretical framework; he did not believe that differences in prices between the regions could cause the country banks to expand and cause prices in the districts to be higher than in London. Neither did he think that an expansion caused by the Bank's excess would translate into an expansion of the country banks' notes. In presenting his disagreement with Ricardo and the Report, Bosanquet introduced a slight change in language, inserting "country" instead of "town" in the Report's conclusions: "If an excess of paper be issued in the London district, while country circulation does not exceed its due proportion, there will be a local rise in prices in the London district" (p. 77). It is interesting to note that Bosanquet adopts Smith's definition of the right quantity. The right quantity according to Ricardo, argues Bosanquet (though "Mr. Ricardo's language is not quite so clear"), is that quantity that will be in the right proportion to the value of commodities. That makes it a nonoperational definition, and "we must be content to admit proof of [the excess] existence from its effects, and our attention must be directed to ascertain depreciation, or an increased price of commodities, solely arising out of, and occasioned by, the increased amount of the *circulating medium*" (p. 86). Smith's authority is brought to bear again:

A prince who should enact that a certain proportion of his taxes should be paid in a paper money of a certain kind might thereby give a certain value to this paper money, even though the term of its final discharge and redemption should depend altogether upon the will of the prince. If the bank which issued this paper was careful to keep the quantity of it always somewhat below what could easily be employed in this manner, the demand for it might be such as to make it even bear a premium, or sell for somewhat more in the market than the quantity of gold or silver currency for which it was issued. (Bosanquet [p. 86] from Smith's *Wealth of Nations*, Book 2, chapter 2 [p. 358])

Thus, the value of the notes can be high or low depending on their usage. If, for example, they are to be used to pay taxes, at certain periods and under specific circumstances their value may be higher than that of gold. There are reasons other than money that explain price changes; in any case, the Quantity Theory of Money was rejected (pp. 118–119).

Bosanquet concludes by stating that he believes that he has proved three things: "1st . That the propositions stated by the Committee ... are not generally true ... 2d. That the facts, where any are brought forward. ... are erroneously stated; and, when corrected, lead to opposite conclusions: 3d. That the effects we witness are sufficiently accounted for, by obvious and ordinary causes ..." (pp. 107–108). Moreover, the committee came into this inquiry with "a judgement very early formed," embraced only those points that supported the prejudgment, and ignored those that contradicted it. Thus, it was not really an inquiry in the right sense of the word, but rather a "Report ... from the school of those economists" described by Playfair as those "who, not very attentive to facts, have established ingenious theories and attempted to reduce every thing to a system, on which they reasoned till they became enthusiasts, incapable of appreciating any thing that did not conform to the theories they had laid down" (p. 108).[14]

Bosanquet added a supplement to his work's second edition in which he describes his "battle" with Huskisson (p. 116) and adds an interesting discussion of the standard. The Bank's notes had been the standard measure of value since 1797; "[if] gold be not the standard of value, its increased price, beyond the standard or mint-price, does not necessarily prove depreciation in that which forms the currency" (p. 122). This very negative verdict

---

[14]   Bosanquet quotes from William Playfair's introduction to the twelve edition of the *Wealth of Nations*.

against the Trio of the Bullion Committee, Ricardo, and Mushet caused Ricardo and Mushet to respond quickly.

Ricardo's Reply to Mr. Bosanquet

In January 1811, Ricardo's *Reply to Mr. Bosanquet's Practical Observations on the Bullion Report* was published.[15] In the *Reply*, Ricardo makes it clear that he defends the Report and agrees with most of its arguments, though not with all. Ricardo believes that Bosanquet has his facts wrong, because Bosanquet relied on data from Mushet, which Mushet had later corrected. Ricardo attempts to refute all of Bosanquet's five points one by one.

Ricardo and Bosanquet disagree on the possible causes for the balance of payments being against Britain. Ricardo quotes Bosanquet:

At a moment when we were *compelled* to receive corn, even from our enemy, without the slightest stipulation in favour of our own manufacturer, and to pay neutrals for bringing it, Mr. Ricardo tells us, that the export of bullion and merchandize, in payment of the corn we may import, resolves itself entirely into a question of interest, and that, if we give corn in exchange for goods, it must be from choice, not necessity. Whilst providing against famine, he tells us, that we should not import more goods than we export, unless we had a redundancy of currency. (III, p. 207; Ricardo's added emphasis)

To which Ricardo replies:

Mr. Bosanquet speaks as if the nation collectively, as one body, imported corn and exported gold, and that it was compelled by hunger so to do, not reflecting that the importation of corn, even under the case supposed, is the act of individuals, and governed by the same motives as all other branches of trade. What is the degree of *compulsion* which is employed to make us receive corn from our enemy? I suppose no other than the want of that commodity which makes it an advantageous article of import; but if it be a voluntary, as it most certainly is, and not a compulsory bargain between the two nations, I do still maintain that gold would not, even if famine raged amongst us, be given to France in exchange for corn, unless the exportation of gold was attended with advantage to the exporter, unless he could sell corn in England for more gold than he was obliged to give for the purchase of it. ...

Seeing nothing in Mr. Bosanquet's statement to induce me to change my opinion, I must continue to think that it is interest, and interest alone, which determines the exportation of gold, in the same manner as it regulates the exportation of all other commodities. Mr. Bosanquet would have done well, before he had deemed this opinion so extravagant, to have used something like argument to prove it so;

---

[15] For a detailed history of this pamphlet and Ricardo's refusal to review the Bullion Report in the *Edinburgh Review*, see editors' "Note on the Bullion Essays," vol. III, pp. 3–12.

and he would not have hurt his cause, if, even in the year 1810, he had explained his reason for supporting a principle advanced by Mr. Thornton in 1802, the correctness of which was questioned in 1809. (III, pp. 207–208)

Thus, Ricardo's position on this crucial issue differs from that of Bosanquet, but also from that of Thornton, though the latter was one of the drafters of the Bullion Report.

The role of the Bank of England and its ability to increase the circulation is another contentious point. Ricardo argues that under the Restriction, the Bank could increase the circulation beyond that which would have circulated without that measure. This is, in fact, a debate about the Real Bills Doctrine, and Bosanquet indeed quoted Smith. Ricardo's polemical response is to quote Smith's other approach, that the quantity can never exceed that which would have circulated in a pure commodity-money circulation. That this is not the case in England under the Restriction is clear in Ricardo's mind.

The Ingot Plan

After establishing the theoretical basis for his views in the *High Price of Bullion*, and after publishing the *Reply to Bosanquet*, Ricardo proposes a monetary reform that goes beyond convertibility of notes to coins. The policy reform was first presented, albeit very briefly, in 1811 in an appendix to the fourth edition of *The High Price of Bullion* (III, pp. 123–127). The plan, known as the Ingot Plan, "showed him at his best as an economist," according to Fetter (1965, p. 91). Other writers considered this plan to be Ricardo's most original and brilliant contribution to political economy. Ricardo himself had a similar evaluation. In contrast to his modest view of *High Price of Bullion*, which he considered as merely a reformulation of known principles, Ricardo considered this plan to "unite all the advantages of every system of banking which has been hitherto adopted in Europe" (III, p. 126). Even though Ricardo's influence on the Bullion Committee was not as great as had been claimed by some of the secondary literature,[16] the committee's final proposals were in line with the practical proposals of the Ingot Plan.

The Ingot Plan itself was based on simple principles. First, a country needs money. Second, cheap money like paper money is not necessarily worse than expensive money like gold. The problems arising from using paper money, such as the absence of a principle of limitation, could be avoided by linking the paper to gold. Third, to avoid the actual use of gold coins, the Bank should buy

---

[16] See Fetter on the secondary literature on the Bullion Report (1942, 1959, 1965).

and sell gold in bars, and not in coins, making these transactions more costly and complicated. On the basis of these principles, Ricardo arrived at a scheme for providing the country with paper circulation based on a gold standard that would not use gold itself in circulation. The Bank would exchange Bank notes against gold bars rather than gold coins. Thus, gold would be kept mostly out of circulation but would continue to determine the value of the notes. This system retains the advantages of gold – relatively stable value, clear principle of limitation – without its disadvantages – waste of productive opportunities, waste of wealth because of the need to transfer heavy metals, the cost of preventing clipping, and so on. "The perfection of banking is to enable a country by means of a paper currency (always retaining its standard value) to carry on its circulation with the least possible quantity of coin or bullion" (III, pp. 126–127).

Five years later, this plan was the theme of the pamphlet, *Proposals for an Economical and Secure Currency* (1816, IV, pp. 43–141). The 1816 pamphlet was written during the controversy over the Corn Laws, when Ricardo's attention had moved on to nonmonetary debates and to the famous argument about the determinant of the rate of profit and the relationship between the price of wheat and other commodities. The direct push to write this pamphlet came from M.P. Pascue Grenfel, who was active at this time in fighting to reduce the profit of the Bank of England. Like the *High Price of Bullion*, it was written to be used as a weapon in certain political arguments. Like Grenfel, Ricardo did not like the Bank and was consistently skeptical of its governors. In 1819, as we shall see, a parliamentary committee decided to implement the spirit of Ricardo's plan.

In 1816, in *Proposals for an Economic and Secure Currency*, Ricardo explained that metals are of comparatively stable value and are therefore good for measuring the value of other things (IV, p. 55). The perfect money is uniform, cheap, and its standard is stable. As a standard, he advocated gold, whose value is determined by "its quantity relatively to the payments which it has to accomplish" (IV, p. 56).

In this pamphlet, Ricardo expresses an interesting Popperian view of those who support abstract currency, or a currency not based on a specific commodity. He argues that they treat bank notes as invariable "things," "which were, therefore, eminently well calculated to measure the value of all other things" (IV, p. 61). In Ricardo's view, "[the] argument is certainly a safe one because it cannot be disproved. … The depreciation [of a 'currency without standard'] could not admit of proof, as it might always be affirmed that commodities had risen in value, and that money had not fallen" (IV, 62).

When we use a standard, there is no remedy for fluctuation in its value. However, it is clear that if the market price of gold is higher than its mint price, the currency is depreciated. This depreciation is unfair toward the "class of persons possessed of one out of the thousands of commodities," as they will suffer when the value of money falls and derive no benefits when its value rises. Ricardo's plan for paper based on gold bars solves this problem by managing to keep the price of gold constant regardless of the amount of paper. This still leaves Ricardo with the problem of panics, for which he has no remedy: "Against such panics, Banks have no security, *on any system*" (p. 68; emphasis in the original). In this pamphlet, Ricardo appraises free trade and expresses his belief that England should "set an example to the world in liberal politics and free trade" (p. 71) with the exception of certain cases in which the government should interfere, namely to avoid fraud or to certify a fact. Contrary to Davis's (2005) claims, Ricardo does not make a case for discretion at this stage.[17]

In 1819, the Ingot Plan became the focus of much discussion when it was circulated in the Parliamentary Committee in the form of the following six points:

1. That the Bank should be subjected to the Delivery of uncoined Gold or Silver at the Mint Standard and Price, in Exchange for their Notes, instead of the Delivery of Coin.
2. That the Bank should also be obliged to give their Paper in Exchange for Standard Gold or Silver, at fixed Prices, taken somewhat below the Mint Price.
3. That the Quantity of Gold or Silver to be so demanded in Exchange for Paper at the Bank, and the Quantity to be so sold to the Bank, should be limited, not to go below a fixed amount.
4. That the Mint should continue open to the Public for the Coinage of gold money.
5. That the most perfect Liberty should be given at the same time to export and import every Description of Bullion.
6. That the same Privilege of paying Notes in Bullion should either be extended to the Country Banks, or that the Bank of England Notes (their value being thus secured) should be legal Tender. (Bonar [1923], p. 287)

---

[17] Davis argues that Ricardo advocated discretionary monetary policy already in 1816. He quotes Ricardo arguing that "additional quantity [of money] can be presently…" supplied, as a proof of "a clear case for discretion." It is not a clear case for discretion; the banks are passive, accommodating the demand of the public; that is not discretionary monetary policy that assumes the initiative to come from the monetary authorities, based on their considerations, and not from the public. See Davis (2005, p. 198).

Ricardo's evidence is a commentary on this text, writes Bonar. Its influence was decisive. "Ricardo has converted the committee, their second report proposed his plan with very few changes" (ibid., p. 291). These changes and the Bank of England's hostile attitude toward the plan were later held by Ricardo to be responsible for the unfortunate phenomena that occurred after its implementation.

The Resumption

After 1816, steps toward a return to convertibility became more acceptable. First, a decision to formally demonetize silver prepared the ground for a pure-gold-standard regime. Then, a deflationist trend made the return to cash payments at the old par seem reasonable. The 1819 committees appointed to inquire into the return to cash payments recommended a resumption at the pre-Restriction par in two years. By 1821, the Restriction was over, and for the next few years, the most disturbing phenomenon was of falling prices, particularly in agriculture, which were blamed partly on the Resumption of cash payments. Thus, debates on proper monetary arrangements continued to occupy political economists, though now in the context of the deflationary process.

The return of the monetary question to the forefront in 1819 was prompted by the end of the war and the need for a rapid decision about the Resumption of cash payments. Two committees, one in each house of Parliament, were formed to discuss this issue. Not only was Ricardo a member of the Commons' Committee, but by this time, his status as an economist was so high that he was given special permission to give evidence before the Lords' Committee. Parliament's final conclusions were very close to Ricardo's recommendations. As a result, the famous bullion ingots, "the Ricardoes," were cast for the first time. One should note that implementation of this specific recommendation was short lived. After a few months, it was decided to return to the old coin payments. Thus, only a few Ricardoes were actually issued and used. However, this did not affect the return to gold payments and convertibility.

In his last years, Ricardo was troubled by two main issues. First of all, the dramatic fall in prices – a decrease of over 50 percent, when Ricardo had predicted a fall of about 5 percent – roused public ire against him and forced him to defend himself both in Parliament and in writing. In these years, he found a valuable ally in Tooke, a point to which we shall return later. Second, his realization that his previous treatments were incomplete forced him to return to the complicated question of values. In the last weeks of his life, he was busy writing an article on each of these issues: *The Plan for the Establishment of a National Bank* and *Absolute Value and Exchangeable Value*. After his sudden death, both of these articles were sent to James Mill, who decided to publish the former. This pamphlet contains a radical change in Ricardo's monetary thought, a departure from what was considered to be his basic position on monetary policy. However, this break was ignored by his contemporaries as well as by later commentators, who continued to describe Ricardo as an opponent of active monetary policy. On the other hand, his proposals for reform in the banking structure were to influence later monetary theorists, in particular the Currency School.

Ricardo's Break from the Smithian Theory of Money – 1824

The final version of the Ingot Plan can be found in the *Plan for the Establishment of a National Bank* (*Plan for a National Bank*) (1824); it was published six months after Ricardo's death[18] and contains significant changes from the previous versions.[19] One important point in the new pamphlet is the distinction between issuing paper money as a substitute for gold and issuing it as the result of loans to merchants and others (IV, p. 276). Ricardo argues that these two different functions should be the responsibilities of two different bodies. A monopoly, not competitive banks, should carry out the former function; the second function is part of regular banking activity.[20] Ricardo recommended that commissioners be responsible for the exchange of gold for notes and vice versa (IV, p. 282) because he considers them to be more trustworthy than the government. The second function, the business of loans, should be divorced from issuing altogether and be left to the competitive banks. The government should finance itself by taxes, Exchequer bills, and loans, but not by loans from those who have the power to issue notes, that is, to create money. Thus, the 1824 *Plan* was in fact a rejection of free trade in the business of issuing notes by competitive banks and a milestone in the monopolization of the money-supply process. The issuing of notes was supposed to be the result of actions on the part of those holding gold. Thus, the monopolistic bank responsible for that activity should remain passive.

---

[18] James Mill was the literary executor of Ricardo's works. Tooke was slightly involved in this decision. See a letter from Tooke to John Murray, Tooke's publisher, on January 8, 1824 (XI p. XXVI).

[19] See Arnon (1987) on the supposed break in Ricardo's monetary thought.

[20] That these two operations of banking have no necessary connection will appear obvious from the fact "that they might be carried on by two separate bodies, without the slightest loss of advantage, either to the country, or to the merchants who receive accommodation from such loans" (IV, p. 276).

In Ricardo's opinion, this separation would not change the system apart from transferring profits from the banks to the public. There would be no shortage of loans for discounting bills for the same reason given in 1816 (IV, pp. 280–281). The amount of notes would be the correct one, because these would be given only "in exchange for gold at the price of 3 17s 10 1/2d per ox.," and "not against discounts". Thus, "regulating their issues by the price of gold, the commissioners would never err" (IV, p. 293). The commissioners do not have to lend to the government, which should finance itself. In addition, at this point Ricardo demanded that "country bank notes be withdrawn from circulation" (IV, p. 287, the seventh proposition). Thus, for the first time, Ricardo clearly rejected competition in issuing notes.

Moreover, in this last text, Ricardo allowed the Bank certain discretionary activities with its securities, in contrast with his so-called followers in the Currency School, whom we will discuss in Chapter 11.

If the circulation of London should be redundant, it will show itself by the increased price of bullion, and the fall in the foreign exchanges, precisely as a redundancy is now shown; and the remedy is also the same as that now in operation; viz. a reduction of circulation, which is brought about by a reduction of the paper circulation. That reduction may take place two ways; either by the sale of Exchequer bills in the market, and the cancelling of the paper money which is obtained for them, or by giving gold in exchange for the paper, cancelling the paper as before, and exporting the gold. (IV, pp. 296–297)

The first way, in the form of "open market operations," is now a well-known method for applying central banking, and is clearly incompatible with competition in banking in general, and with the Real Bills Doctrine in particular. All the restrictions on banking that Ricardo had proposed up to this point were insignificant in that they were designed to protect the weak or to transfer profits to the public, and did not touch on the question of control of the quantity. Only here, perhaps after examining the practical working of the resumed convertible system, did Ricardo arrive at conclusions quite contrary to those of the spirit of the Real Bills Doctrine, arguing that the quantity of notes should not be determined by competition between issuers. Because he did not suggest a rule as the Currency School did, but rather advocated discretion, even those who draw a distinction between a rule and discretion should agree that Ricardo's position should have logically developed into a comprehensive theory of central banking.

It could be argued that such open market operations do not necessarily imply discretionary control of the monetary system, because their only aim is to defend convertibility by ensuring sufficient reserves of gold. In our

view, such operations do include all the elements of discretionary control;
the Bank's managers respond to developments in the gold market or the
exchanges and exercise their discretion in determining policy. Moreover,
they will not just respond mechanically to supply and demand for gold,
but will have to decide about intervention in the Exchequer bills' market
in order to influence the quantity in circulation according to macroeconomic data. As is clear from Ricardo's own discussion, he recommended
not merely a defense of convertibility, but an attempt to control the quantity
in circulation.

> It would be only when, from the increasing wealth and prosperity of the coun-
> try, the country required a permanently increased amount of circulation, that it
> would be expedient to invest money in the purchase of securities paying interest,
> and only in a contrary case, that a part of such securities would be required to be
> sold. ... [T]wenty five millions of paper money will be issued; that sum will not be
> too large for the circulation of the whole country, but if it should be, the excess
> may be exchanged for gold coin, or the commissioners may sell a portion of their
> exchequer bills, and thus diminish the amount in the paper circulation. (IV, p. 284;
> p. 290)

In these passages, Ricardo is discussing both the means by which the
quantity should be determined in the transition from the previous to the
reformed system, as formulated in the *Plan*, and also how the quantity in
the reformed system should be adjusted over time according to changes
in wealth and prosperity (see also Ricardo, pp. 290–297). This "just level"
of circulation would be determined by the Bank's commissioners, who are
thus would be given a critically different role from the commissioners of the
1816 plan; the latter were really given no discretionary powers and were thus
automatists. Moreover, a careful reading of the different texts reveals that
Ricardo was still discovering the possibilities of open market operations,
a discovery process interrupted by his death. *The Plan for a National Bank*
went through at least two drafts. The last one was published by James Mill
in 1824, whearas the earlier one had to wait more than one hundred years
for publication. The differences between them are all in the direction of
expanding the discretionary powers of the Bank.[21]

---

[21]   We now know of different drafts in which Ricardo formulated his *Plan for the Establishment
of a National Bank*: an earlier draft described by Sraffa as the MS and the final paper as we
know it (see Sraffa's introduction to the *Plan for a National Bank*, IV, pp. 272–274). It is significant that the crucial reference to the sale of Exchequer bills as an instrument of policy
aimed at controlling the quantity in circulation did not appear in the equivalent sentence
in the MS, although a similar idea can be found in its last paragraph.

Summary

Although Ricardo's position on the determinants of the quantity of credit is less clear, he did argue that for a given quantity of money, the amount of advances (credit) "must essentially depend upon the amount of money in circulation" (IV, p. 277). Thus, the foregoing discussion reveals that the tendency to see Ricardo as an obstacle to the development of central banking (Sayers 1953, pp. 46–49) is due to the over- identification of his position with that of the later Currency School, and of his 1824 *Plan* with the 1844 Bank Act. As we shall see, it is true that Ricardo's clear distinction between the two functions of the Bank, together with his proposal of a monopoly in issuing notes, formed the basis of the Bank Act. However, Ricardo's position in this last text differed significantly both from his own earlier views and from those of the Currency School. Not only did he explicitly reject competition for notes, but his system is closer to what we would call central banking than it is to the automatic-mechanism characteristic of the Currency School's proposals, which left almost no place for discretion in either money or credit. Thus, Ricardo was moving toward a consistent integration of views on both the rejection of the application of the invisible-hand mechanism to money and the adoption of what was basically a central-banking theory. If this is the case, the failure of the Classical School to develop a theory of central banking should be attributed less to the influence of Ricardo than to that of the two main schools which followed him.

NINE

"Credit Theories of Money" in Exchange and Intermediation

Introduction

In Chapter 4, we presented a framework for analysis that falls within what we have called, after Schumpeter, "monetary theories of credit"; we addressed these theories mainly to the exchange process. In this chapter, we present an extension of the framework that moves beyond just "monetary theories of credit" to present "credit theories of money," again after Schumpeter. We will present these theories in the contexts of both the exchange process and intermediation.

The understanding that exchange can be executed by debts and credits in the formulations defined in Chapter 4 – Private Debt Certificates (PDCs) – had to wait for Henry Thornton, and then one hundred years later, for Knut Wicksell. Analytically, this unconventional approach came into some conflict with the Quantity Theory. The quantities of the mediums used in payments were demand-determined. Thus, in this later approach, one faced the endogenous determination of credit in its role in the exchange process. The role of money in a pure credit economy will be discussed in the chapter on Wicksell.

The following discussion represents an attempt to invert the customary logical order of analysis that we covered in Chapter 4, and which was used by almost all scholars. We will describe and analyze a pure Accounting System of Exchange (ASE): a system of exchange based on the transfer of abstract social units of purchasing power, known also as a pure credit system in Wicksell's terminology (see Chapter 17). We will first discuss the possible existence and meaning of other forms of payments, from "near-credits" to "money," in an economy with such a pure credit system. Thus, money will be defined in terms of credit, and a credit theory of money will be developed. The main drawback of this approach, which may also be its main advantage, is that it takes as its departure point not a real-payments system, but an abstract, ideal one. Thus, real, actual systems of payments will be compared to the pure system and will be treated as deviations from it. However, developments in the financial system are today rapidly approaching the conditions postulated by the pure credit system. Thus, in contrast to monetary theories of credit wherein such developments entail changes in theory, in this framework, the theoretical structure can remain intact while the imperfections introduced to explain discrepancies between the real and ideal systems will gradually diminish.

An Accounting System of Exchange (ASE)

We shall assume an economy in which the exchange of commodities (goods, services, and financial assets) is carried out through an Accounting System of Exchange (ASE). In this system, each economic unit (*i*) has an account (A_i), and sums are transferred from one account to another. A payment is an order from a buyer to transfer a number of units of account, or "accountees," to the seller. This is the ASE's only function; the system will not manage asset portfolios for its clients, nor will it hold any reserves against its liabilities, whatever they may be. A price agreed upon between a buyer and a seller will take the form of a sum of accountees from *i* to *j*. The transfer of accountees will be executed immediately with the buyer's order or, more realistically, at the next discrete exchange time (for example, every hour, ten minutes, and so on).

We shall assume that balances in each account at time zero, when the system is initiated, are zero: If we denote account *i* at time *t* as $A_i(t)$, then $A_i(0)=0$ for each *i* (*i* = 1, ..., *n*). Because we are not discussing barter, but rather a monetary or, preferably, a credit economy, it is clear that some accounts in the ASE will show a negative balance. It is further clear that at each point in time, the sum of balances in all accounts will be zero; thus:

$$\sum_{i=1}^{n} A_i(t) = 0 \quad \forall t$$

where *t* = 1, 2... are the discrete exchange times. Furthermore, because each transaction takes the form of a sum of accountees from *i* to *j*, the sum of changes in the balances of all accounts at each discrete period (or momentarily if the system operates continuously) will also be zero. Thus, for the discrete time framework:

$$\sum_{i=1}^{n} \Delta A_i(t) = 0 \quad \forall t$$

where

$$\Delta A_i(t) = A_i(t) - A_i(t-1)$$

The quantity of accountees circulating in the system at each discrete time period t will be denoted by $\tilde{\bar{A}}(t)$ where

$$\bar{\bar{A}}\left(t\right)= \frac{1}{2} \sum_{i=1}^{n}\left|\Delta A_i\left(t\right)\right|$$

This quantity is identical to the volume of transactions carried out in the economy (T) evaluated at accounting prices (Pacc). Thus:

$$\bar{\bar{A}}\left(t\right)= T(t)\times \mathrm{Pacc}(t) \quad \forall t$$

Similarly, the flow of accountees in the system from time t_0 to t_1

$$\bar{\bar{A}}\left(t_0,t_1\right)= \sum_{t=t_0}^{t=t_1} \bar{\bar{A}}(t)$$

and is always exactly equal to the opposite flow of goods, services, and financial assets.

In addition to flows, we can define and analyze stocks in the system. For example, let us define the outstanding debt in the ASE as the sum of the total debts of customers to the system. This will also be equal to the sum of all accounts showing a positive balance and will be denoted by $\bar{\bar{A}}(t)$. However, one should not be surprised if no relationship between $\bar{\bar{A}}(t)$ and $\tilde{\bar{A}}(t)$ will be found, because $\bar{\bar{A}}(t)$ changes only as a result of transactions between economic units where one holds a negative and the other a positive balance. $\bar{\bar{A}}(t)$ will not change when the transactions are between units which both hold positive balances or both hold negative balances. It should be emphasized that $\bar{\bar{A}}(t)$ is not private credit because it is not a debt which i owes to j. Thus, inside money does not exist in the pure ASE. Neither is $\bar{\bar{A}}(t)$ a form of outside money, because it does not represent wealth for all economic agents (see Gurley and Shaw [1960] and Patinkin [1961]).

Each transaction will be reflected in the ASE in the form of more accountees in the seller's account and less in the buyer's. Until the buyer repays his debt to the system, he will be, in fact, a debtor and the transaction will thus be a sale on credit. However, this credit takes a peculiar form: It is not the seller, but the ASE that credited the buyer; thus, it is a transaction against social rather than private credit. This means that the relationship between two units terminates as soon as accountees are transferred.

Thus, exchange is executed through a medium that does not exist except in a social and abstract form. The medium can only be held as an entry in an ASE account and cannot be transferred outside the system, as can checks, for example. Accountees cannot be produced, as can commodity-money.

Most significantly, so far, there is no way of changing their quantity in the ASE either as a flow $\tilde{A}(t)$ or as a stock $\bar{A}(t)$, except through exchange as defined earlier. We shall elaborate on this last characteristic when discussing possible government roles in such a system.

We have not yet discussed the nature of restrictions on account holders. Several possibilities come to mind, all of which would attempt to ensure that buyers will also sell. We shall assume a simple credibility rule according to which account holders will be required to show a positive balance in their accounts after each arbitrarily determined time interval. Thus. the credibility of i at "credibility time" t will be affirmed if, for example,

$$A_i(t) \geq 0 \quad \forall t = k\alpha, \quad \forall k = 1, 2, 3,\ldots$$

where α is the arbitrary time interval (α integer, $\alpha > 1$)[1] and $k\alpha$ are the credibility dates.

This restriction will force account holders to change their behavior before credibility dates, introducing arbitrarily determined cycles into the economy. A smoother approach might have been to choose different credibility dates for different individual account holders, or to formulate a credibility rule that is not related to a specific date. The former, however, has the disadvantage of making it worthwhile for individuals to have at least two accounts with different credibility dates, because this would facilitate the transfer of infinite quantities of accountees from account to account before credibility dates. The latter approach will not be explored here.

Accounts showing a negative balance at the credibility time will be closed and their holders expelled from the system.[2] Because this will be very damaging, account holders will make every effort to ensure that they attract accountees to their accounts in time. The simplest way to do this will be to sell goods, services, or financial assets, although they could also take a loan from accounts showing a positive balance. One can predict that new private debts will be created, which may even begin to circulate in transactions carried out outside the ASE, thus introducing "near-credits" into the economy. The expulsion of account holders and the existence of transactions which individuals prefer to carry out outside the ASE will contribute to the rise of "money." The following section will be devoted to a discussion of near-credits and money.

---

[1] No exchange will take place in the ASE if $\alpha = 1$ because, by definition, the sellers will have positive balances whereas the buyers will have negative balances and will not pass the credibility rule.
[2] To eliminate the temptation to create huge debts to the system before a "planned" expulsion, we will assume that each account holder will repay his debts, even in case of expulsion through a collateral system, limits on debt quantities, and legal unlimited responsibility.

Credit, Near-Credits, and Money

Now that the modus operandi of this ideal type of exchange in its purest form has been described, it is time to elaborate on the nature of the medium that in fact circulates goods. Are the accountees money or credit? Are they a circulating stock or a flow? Let us return to Hawtrey's definition: Clearly the accountees function both as a measure of value and as a medium of exchange. Thus, according to Hawtrey they are candidates for consideration as money because they seem to function like money. However, can they also meet his criterion of discharging debts? The answer is that in addition to being a very peculiar medium, accountees are incapable of discharging a debt when transferred to a seller. They do not complete the exchange either from the buyer's point or socially.

A seller of a commodity who receives accountees from a buyer is not a creditor; his relationship with the buyer vis-à-vis this particular transaction is over. What about the buyer? In a transaction where a commodity was exchanged for money, the buyer's debt to the seller was discharged by transferring the agreed-upon price in the form of money. It may seem that transactions in the ASE are similar to those carried out with money in a monetary economy. However, this is true only for the seller; his part in the deal is completed in both cases. The buyer, by receiving the commodity in exchange for his accountees, has in fact become a debtor – not a private debtor, as in a monetary economy, but a social debtor. Thus, for the buyer, the transaction has not yet been completed. From the point of view of society, if he had no positive balance before this transaction, he will remain in debt until a future sale will cancel the debt. Only if his account showed a positive balance from previous sales would he avoid becoming a debtor; but then someone else in the ASE must be in debt. In other words, a sale is completed (the buyer's debt is discharged), either when past "credit" is canceled (if $A_i(t)$ was positive) or when accountees are paid to the buyer's account at some point in the future. One buys either by creating a new debt or by canceling a previous credit. Thus, the medium in circulation is social debt.

The Rise of Near-Credits

In some transactions, the buyer will transfer accountees to the seller, not against a commodity, but against a commitment that the debt will be returned in the future. Such a private market for loans will be most active immediately prior to credibility dates, when those whose accounts show a negative balance will try to meet the credibility rule. We will assume, for the sake of simplicity, that loans are standardized and are given for the period between credibility dates (α). If the cost for being expelled from the ASE is high, this means that the demand for such loans is almost perfectly inelastic at $\overline{\overline{A}}(t)$, whereas the supply is positively sloped starting from r, the rate of interest in the ASE. Thus, Private Debt Certificates (PDCs) will earn higher interest than that paid in the ASE. Furthermore, one can assume the rise of agents who will specialize in transferring accountees from those who have them to those who do not. Such Intermediaries will reduce both the risks for those giving loans and the price of loans for those in need.

Intermediation is based on two main activities. One is the acceptance of surplus accountees from account holders against which the Intermediaries will issue Intermediaries' Debt Certificates (IDCs), or promises to repay the loans given to them. IDCs may take two main forms: Intermediary Notes (INs), which are tangible promises to pay accountees to note holders on demand, and Intermediary Deposits (IDs), which are promises that can either be withdrawn on demand or transferred with a check. Some INs might not carry interest and would circulate under conditions of anonymity of the transferee, like bank notes in a monetary economy. The second intermediation activity occurs when the Intermediaries use the accountees they receive to give loans to those in need. In exchange for the accountees, the parties who borrow them will provide the Intermediaries with promises to repay the loans. These debts are equivalent in essence to the PDCs described earlier. Clearly, this second activity will be possible only if we assume, as we shall, that Intermediaries hold only fractional reserves; in other words, their liabilities (IDCs) are higher than the quantity of liquid assets (accountees). We can summarize the Intermediaries' activities so far by looking at the following schematic balance sheets:

Liabilities	Assets		Liabilities	Assets		Liabilities	Assets
+ IDC	+ Accountees			− Accountees		+ IDC	+ PDC
				+ PDC			
=	=		=	=		=	=
(a)			(b)			(c) = (a) + (b)	

Balance sheet (a) describes a 100 percent reserve ratio (R = Accountees \ IDC), which reflects the fact that IDCs are covered in full by accountees held in the Intermediary's own account. In such a case the Intermediary is not, in fact, functioning as an Intermediary, but as an agency providing depository services; this is an unnecessary and redundant function in the ASE. Usually, the reserve ratio R will be lower than 1. R will approach zero if the IDCs specify a certain date before which no withdrawals are allowed; R will increase if the IDC's can be withdrawn on demand. If R is strictly positive, the Intermediary's intermediation activities use only some of the funds he raises. Thus, a "pure" Intermediary will have a zero reserve ratio.

The situation is more complex because some economic units might approach the Intermediary and ask for a loan in the form of IDCs rather than accountees. Against these IDCs, which are commonly in use as means of payments in various transactions, the borrowers will give the Intermediary a PDC. Thus, the transaction will be registered on the Intermediary balance sheet as:

Liabilities	Assets
Δ IDC	Δ PDC

It is very difficult, and sometimes even impossible, to distinguish between the two types of PDCs – those given against accountees and those given against IDCs – because there is no reason to assume that the Intermediary will mark them differently and keep separate accounts for each. However, the complete balance sheet of the typical Intermediary can be broken down, in principle at least, into the following two balance sheets:

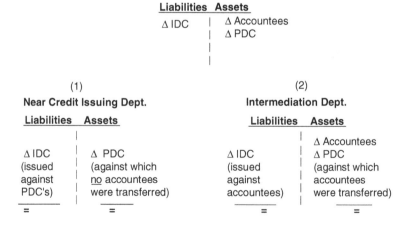

Intermediary Balance Sheet

Liabilities	Assets
Δ IDC	Δ Accountees
	Δ PDC

(1)	(2)
Near Credit Issuing Dept.	**Intermediation Dept.**

Liabilities	Assets	Liabilities	Assets
			Δ Accountees
Δ IDC (issued against PDC's)	Δ PDC (against which <u>no</u> accountees were transferred)	Δ IDC (issued against accountees)	Δ PDC (against which accountees were transferred)
=	=	=	=

For reasons that will become clear in the discussion of the implications of this approach for the history of monetary theory, we will denote the first department as the "Near-Credits Issuing Department," and the second as the "Intermediation Department." This description captures the important additional functions of the typical Intermediary: Not only is it involved in intermediation, transferring accountees from those who have a surplus to those who have a deficit, but at the same time, it also creates near-credits. This highlights one of the most difficult points in analyzing any financial system. IDCs are created in one of two ways: first, as a result of excess liquidity in the form of excess accountees held by individuals who deposit them with an Intermediary in exchange for IDCs; and second, as a result of a shortage in liquidity, this time in the form of demand for IDCs. The former type will tend to be less active and will probably act as a relatively idle stock, whereas the latter will function as a quickly circulating stock. However, in order to distinguish between these two types, one has to inquire into their roots and determine their history.

One should note an interesting and sometimes confusing point regarding the system just described: There are financial assets, not just liabilities, used as means of payment. This is the result of the fact that some of the PDCs are accepted in exchange for goods, services, or other financial assets. An example of the importance of this property of acceptance is the widespread use of bills of exchange as a means of payment in the nineteenth century. Thus, both IDCs and PDCs can circulate among agents outside the ASE. It is reasonable to assume that in many cases, the rate of interest earned on both will be higher than r, the rate of interest in the ASE; thus, in many cases, people will prefer not to use them as a medium of exchange. The liquidity of both PDCs and IDCs will also depend on the issuer's wealth and reputation. In the ASE itself, all forms of debt certificates will function as "near-accountees", that is, as near-credits. They will facilitate exchange but, in contrast with accountees, the transaction will not be completed for either buyer *or* seller. The seller has not really been paid, nor has the buyer's debt really been discharged, until the paper used in the transaction has proved to be genuine. Clearly, the responsibility of the various issuers is a complex matter that raises several very interesting questions, such as the degree of legal responsibility associated with the transfer of each kind of these near-credits. Although discussion of these issues is not essential to developing or understanding the basic model, one should note that PDCs and IDCs are not the only possible types of near-credit. One can expect account holders to issue stocks and bonds that will represent ownership and/or claims on future incomes. These too can circulate, thus extending the range of near-credits to include not only debt certificates, but also all kinds of financial assets. However, their liquidity will be limited and will depend both on their expected values and on the existence of developed markets for them.

Except in times of crisis, people will usually not hesitate to accept near-credits, just as they willingly accept near-monies in a monetary economy. However, it is important to remember that all transactions made with near-credits are executed outside the ASE.

The Rise of Money

At the extreme end of near-credits, money will appear. Whereas, as previously discussed, near-credits can be used to carry out transactions outside the ASE, this will not be possible in every case. Money will arise to meet the needs of economic agents who have been expelled from the ASE or who prefer for some reason to keep a particular transaction hidden. Expelled agents can only use commodities or near-credits bought with commodities as a medium of exchange. They do not have the option of using accountees. The usual description of the rise of commodity-money in a barter economy fits this case as well. First, one commodity will begin to function as commodity-money. Then Intermediaries that accept deposits in the form of commodity-money and generate deposit rights against them will develop. These Intermediaries dealing with Money (IM) will issue Intermediary Notes (IMN) and create new deposits against private debts (IMD).

We have described the pure form of credit as that which enables the seller to conclude his relationship with the buyer at the moment of transfer but may leave the buyer in debt. Following this description, we can define near-credits and money. Near-credits are those debts that can be transformed either directly or indirectly into accountees but which do not enable either the seller or the buyer to complete the transaction and finalize their relationship. The reason for this is that they both depend on the issuers of near-credits to stand behind their obligations. Money is a form of medium of exchange that one cannot always convert into credit; it can only be converted when the money holder is an ASE member and there are other members who are willing to exchange accountees with the money holder in return for his money. Paradoxically, whereas the transfer of money in its basic form as commodity-money will complete the transaction for both seller and buyer, as in a barter economy, with the more developed forms of money (IMNs and IMDs), the transaction will not be completed for either.

To summarize the exchange process, accountees will be used in the ASE in transactions between members of the ASE. ASE members will also be able to exchange commodities outside the ASE using near-credits or money. If they prefer anonymity, they will use INs or IMNs or commodity-money, which do not bear individual fingerprints. If they are not concerned with keeping their transactions hidden, they will probably use accountees, IDs, IMDs, or even PDCs. However, in transactions in which at least one of the partners has been expelled from the ASE, only near-credits or money can be used.

Money and Credit in Intermediation

An economic unit may decide at some point that it prefers at the moment not to use its resources for buying goods – either consumption goods or investment goods. His savings can be hoarded in the form of additional stocks of money, near-money, or other (private and/or government) debt certificates. The saver can implement his decision unilaterally by hoarding existing instruments or by contracting an agreement with another party. In the former case, the abstention from spending leaves resources idle, with no specific compensation to the absentee and no clear mechanism for putting the unused resources to use. In the latter case, the saver, in fact, decides to transfer the surplus funds he does not currently want to use to an interested party in exchange for an asset that will specify the terms for future repayment. This will enable the surplus unit to have a higher income in the future, whereas the shortage unit will become able to extend its consumption or investment today. This is the essence of intermediation: channeling funds between economic units in the present – not within the process of exchange, but in a framework of financial transactions performed over time.

Historically, intermediation not only became more sophisticated over time, but its importance within the economy reached a point where it overshadowed the importance of making payments. Intermediation during the Classical School days was much more restricted than in the twentieth century, but it was always there. Intermediation activities are in some respects similar to what happens within the exchange process, that is, in the payments system; thus, many observers confused the two processes. However, intermediation is of a fundamentally different nature than exchange, and the economic laws which prevail in the two processes are different.

Although we have already encountered the time factor in exchange in the form of delayed payments, and interest has been mentioned as compensation for the delay in payment, in intermediation, the transaction does not involve either buying a commodity or spending on consumption or investment. The essence of intermediation is the transfer of funds to be used by an economic unit other than the one who currently owns them. Intermediation does not belong to the process of exchange characterized by passing equal values in the transactions, whether in a barter or a monetary economy, and whether using cash or debts. The decision of the surplus unit not to use his wealth now can be implemented (unilaterally) by putting her funds to rest. However, to be compensated fully for this decision, someone in the economy has to have a desire for funds he does not control and for which he is ready to pay. Intermediation is the process of matchmaking, bringing the savers to the investors, whether these investors are institutionalized or not. The bargaining between the two sides reflects their future plans and expectations: The recipient, for example, hopes to make more funds out of the funds he will receive. His desire for funds also reflects the nonzero-sum aspect of the process, where the expectation for more funds in the future is the major difference from what we know occurs in exchange. Thus, the source for interest payments in the intermediation process is quite different from that which we described in the exchange process.

Private intermediation, or intermediation directly between two economic units with no help from a third party, can take different forms. The simplest is the transfer of coins from unit i to j, whereas in the other direction, *not* a commodity, but rather what we will label a financial asset, is transferred. The latter usually takes the same form as a PDC: It specifies the conditions of the obligations taken by the recipient of the coins. Thus, it is important to note that the distinction between a PDC that emerged from the exchange process and the PDC created in intermediation cannot be determined just by looking at one moment of the economic process. The two instruments seem to be identical: They look the same, and one cannot distinguish between them without knowing their histories. This, of course, might lead to analytical confusion. In order to distinguish between them, we will designate, when possible, the PDCs born from exchange as "exchange credit," whereas the same instruments that emerged from intermediation will be named "intermediation credit." This distinction, though important analytically, will be very difficult to apply practically, because the same instrument can serve different purposes throughout its life.

There are other methods for transferring funds privately from surplus units to shortage ones. For example, one can transfer notes or other existing

PDCs that had been hoarded. In order to be used in intermediation, PDCs need to have a long "life expectancy," usually longer than the terms to maturity of PDCs created in exchange. Otherwise, they would expire too early and would not be able to serve the purposes of intermediation. The most important point in intermediation from the receiver's point of view is that it should enable him to buy goods, something he cannot achieve without it. The implication is that funds transferred, whatever their form, could be turned into "purchasing power" with no difficulties. Thus, if intermediation is not carried out with a liquid form of currency, it should be very easy to transform its proceeds to such a form. We can summarize private intermediation in coins, 100-percent convertible notes, and PDCs using the following balance sheets:

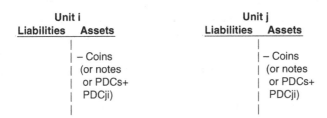

Unit i		Unit j	
Liabilities	Assets	Liabilities	Assets
	– Coins		– Coins
	(or notes		(or notes
	or PDCs+		or PDCs+
	PDCji)		PDCji)

Unit i gives up on coins (or notes or PDCs), and instead gets a private debt certificate from unit j. This certificate will be described as PDCji – the debt of j to i. The cases of coins and notes are self-explanatory; less so is the case where PDCs are the instrument used for private intermediation. In such cases, unit i transfers a debt to unit j; this debt is made by a third party who was capable of buying goods now. Such mediums were able to exist historically because some of the debtors were known to stand behind their obligations and their debts were circulating; in particular, one should mention such circulating debt certificates as the famous private bills of exchange and publicly issued Tallies (see Feavearyear 1931, chapters 5 and 6).

Historically, noninstitutional private intermediation between individuals was not the most popular form of intermediation; thinking logically, this should hold no surprise. For reasons that can be explained by the efficient allocation of risks, the more common process of intermediation involved the help of institutions that specialized in risk sharing. These institutions developed expertise in evaluating borrowers' risks, which made them efficient mediators between borrowers and lenders and turned them into Intermediaries, that is, economic units that sold the service of intermediation. With the rise of these institutions, our story changes completely.

Institutionalized intermediation is based on two main activities. The first is the acceptance of surplus funds from economic units against which the Intermediaries issue their PDCs. We will term these PDCs Intermediaries' Debt Certificates (IDCs) – promises to repay the loans given to them.[3] In the second activity, the Intermediaries use the funds they have received to give loans to those in need, whose willingness to pay interest has proven their ability to use the loan efficiently. The parties who borrow the funds provide the Intermediaries with promises to repay the loans. These debts are equivalent in essence to the PDCs described earlier, although they are not necessarily issued in the exchange process. The IDCs are similar to PDCs but for the fact that the issuer specializes in the specific trade of intermediation.

We have already encountered IDCs: In the exchange process, when individuals deposited coins with the Goldsmiths, they received convertible notes in exchange. These were promises to repay coins on demand to the bearer of the notes. With the introduction of intermediation, the Goldsmiths could issue convertible notes not only against the commodity-money deposited with them, but against promises made by individuals to repay their debts to them. These promises could have been issued by the party receiving the notes or against existing third-party PDCs held by the receiver of the notes. The exchange of bank notes for self-issued surety was just a loan; the exchange of bank notes for others promises was the well-known procedure of discounting bills of exchange at the banks, a famous method used to monetize debts. Clearly, both methods arose from the second activity of the Intermediary – functioning as a lender – which was possible only if we assume, as we shall, that Intermediaries held only fractional reserves, that is, if they had more outstanding liabilities (IDCs) of a certain type than the quantity of assets for which they were promised to be exchanged.

Let us summarize the nonprivate, institutionalized intermediation process through the use of a three-party balance sheet: the lender (i), the borrower (j), and the Intermediary (I):

---

[3]   IDCs may take two main forms: Intermediary Notes (INs), which are "tangible" promises to pay "accountees" to note holders on demand, and Intermediary Deposits (IDs), which are promises that can either be withdrawn on demand or transferred with a check. Some INs might not carry interest and would circulate under conditions of anonymity, without the transferrer being identified, like bank notes in a monetary economy.

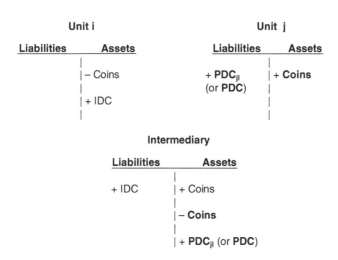

Unit i transfers coins to the Intermediary and receives an IDC. The Intermediary takes the coins and lends them to unit j; in exchange, he receives a PDC that carried a higher rate of interest than the rate of interest he paid to i (all transactions between I and j are in bold type; the ones between I and i are not in bold). At the end of the day, the intermediary has no additional coins, even though he promised that his notes (IDC) were convertible, and both the lender and borrower got what they wanted. The same scheme can be drawn for a lender who pays in notes and receives as IDC a certificate of debt promising to pay the notes on demand (deposits). In this case, the receiver gets

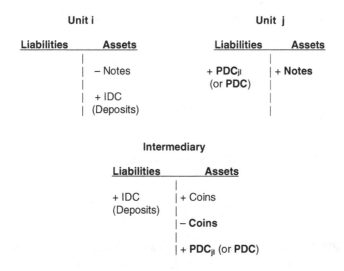

notes and enters in a PDC. The process would not have been started had the Intermediary just exchanged coins for *i*'s notes or given him notes for notes. The Intermediary has to create a new type of debt that promises to pay notes to the depositor – in other words, he creates deposits. The receiver of the funds could have passed an asset held by him to the Intermediary, for example, a PDC issued by a third party or his own debt [**PDC$_{jl}$**].

Thus, for the note-issuer to function as an Intermediary, he has to change his rules of conduct; he has to stop behaving as an automatic machine that exchanges coins for convertible notes and vice versa, and become a lender who assesses risks and takes some. He can only become an Intermediary through the creation of convertible notes not covered 100 percent by coins; however, after leaving the issuer, the convertible notes cannot be distinguished from those issued against coins. Again, the same medium is involved in two different processes wherein different types of transactions take place and different theories hold.

The intermediation process could be carried out without the use of coins or notes. The lender could deposit a third party's PDC, but not his own, with the Intermediary, and receive in exchange a "better" IDC (deposits). The borrower would then receive the same third-party PDC, assuming of course that this would serve his purposes, in exchange for a different third party's debt or even his own. The debt certificates transferred from the borrower to the Intermediary has to carry higher rates in order to ensure that the Intermediary would benefit. This process can be summarized in the following scheme:

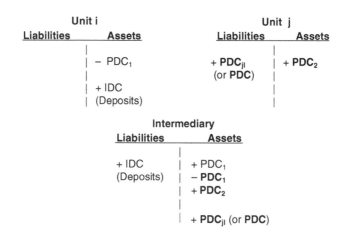

where PDC$_1$ represents the debt certificate deposited by the lender (unit i), and PDC$_2$ represents a different debt certificate, apparently less liquid, which the borrower gives to the Intermediary. Alternatively, as before, the borrower could have given the Intermediary PDC_{ji}, a self-made debt certificate issued by unit j to I. This complicated scheme proves again that, historically, when the intermediation process was not carried out privately, new mediums located in layers lying further and further away from the basic forms of money were created. Their relationship to the pure exchange systems described earlier was difficult to analyze and provided the major focus of debate in monetary theory of the time. It is important to note the distinction between loans against future sales versus loans against future production; in other words, credit in exchange is different from credit in intermediation.

Some Implications for the History of Monetary Theory

The implications of the scheme detailed in the previous section and in Chapter 4 are far reaching. Money is the outcome of imperfections in the payments system and plays a less important role than is usually attributed to it. The quantity of money is endogenously determined and is not relevant to the determination of the price level. More generally, the other quantities of the different mediums used to carry out payments are determined endogenously as well. The "needs of trade," to use the classical expression, determines the quantities of money and credit. The financial system is passive: It reacts to the public desires and does not require regulation. These conclusions are, of course, very different from those of the classical Quantity Theory.

Most modern supporters of the Quantity Theory share three basic arguments. They argue that there exists a monetary aggregate whose quantity determines prices because (a) there is a relatively stable demand function for this aggregate, which includes the price level as one of its parameters; (b) the supply function of this monetary aggregate is not identically equal to the demand; and (c) they usually claim that the quantity supplied of this monetary aggregate can be controlled at the discretion of policy makers.

This third component of the Quantity Theory is supported by most modern quantity theorists but was not accepted by many of the classicals who mainly analyzed the gold-standard system. They adopted only the first two propositions, namely, the existence of demand and supply for a monetary aggregate that together determine the price level. Many of the classicals thought the supply was endogenous to the economic processes, and thus was uncontrollable. More specifically, they thought that, in line with the famous Price-Specie-Flow mechanism, the supply of the monetary aggregate and the price level are determined in such a way that, in the long run, the value of money is determined by the value of the commodity-money.

With the development of the payments system, especially the issuing of convertible bank notes by many competing banks and the rise of fractional reserves as in England at the height of the Classical Period, the monetary aggregate was redefined by quantity theorists to include notes in addition to specie. However, the mixed quantity of notes and gold coins in circulation was not equal to the quantity of gold coins that would have circulated were notes not in use. In an attempt to solve this apparent complication, some of the reformers of the Classical School proposed steps toward monopolization of note-issuing. This was supposed to guarantee the imitation of the "pure" circulation. Thus, what is commonly described as the mainstream classical theory of money (see for example Wicksell [1898, 1906] and O'Brien [2004]) holds to the first two propositions of the Quantity Theory, but rejects discretionary control of the monetary aggregate, which was now to be defined as commodity-money and convertible Bank of England notes.

Deposits, which were already in use in the first half of the nineteenth century, were included in the relevant aggregate only years later, under the pressure of the Banking School critics. However, these critics did not direct their objections specifically at the Quantity theorists' definition of the relevant aggregate, but against the Quantity Theory itself. This anti-Quantity tradition had its roots in the positions of the Banking School and the anti-Bullionists as well as that of Adam Smith.

The implications for monetary issues that Smith drew from his celebrated Real Bills Doctrine are very similar to those we have reached from the ASE. Smith argued that the demand for means of payments (money) creates its own supply, so that demand and supply are always equal. Furthermore, without discussing the Price-Specie-Flow mechanism, Smith maintains that the price level is not determined by the quantity of money. Most important, there is no support for monetary control or regulation whatsoever beyond the need to retain convertibility of notes. How can we explain why Smith's position on monetary policy was so similar to that which we reached from developing the ASE?

Clearly, never in the history of payments systems has there been a pure ASE. However, certain institutional arrangements function just like the ASE with regard to the Quantity Theory and the determination of the price level. One example is a decentralized, or what Hicks (1982) describes as "polycentric," payments system, where individuals have accounts in various institutions, each of which uses "his" accountees. Together, these institutions will have the same properties as the ASE, as long as transactions between them are executed by transferring funds from one institution to another. The necessary condition for this arrangement is the ability to transform funds measured in one unit of account into funds measured in another. The existence of a clearing house and a known conversion rate are sufficient.

The payments system of the Classical Period usually used commodity-money as a common measure. Thus, Adam Smith's analysis of a system that worked according to the conditions outlined here reached the same conclusions as those that hold for the ASE. Some of the later monetary theorists, such as David Ricardo as we have seen, did not accept Smith's conclusions under inconvertibility, but accepted them for convertibility, whereas the Currency School theorists rejected Smith's conclusions for inconvertibility and convertibility. However, under unusual circumstances, confidence in the agreed-upon measure and the functioning of the clearing-house mechanism collapsed. Then the system moved back to what can be called a Quantity Theory regime. Thus, the Quantity Theory approach that could function well during stable periods, when confidence flourished, failed when instability occurred. In such circumstances, the Quantity Theory, after defining the "right" monetary aggregate, can provide a powerful conceptual framework. Thus, changing circumstances should have led to different approaches. Instead, theorists tended to either accept or reject the Quantity Theory approach without sufficient regard for the historical circumstances.

The implications for monetary theory are clear. Institutional arrangements concerning money and credit depend on complex considerations involving many agents, from individuals to government. These considerations seem to suggest that an anti–Quantity Theory approach may be most relevant in the decentralized, deregulated modern environment. However, in a crisis, we should not forget the lessons of the Quantity Theory.

PART THREE

DEBATING: LAISSEZ-FAIRE, RULES, AND
DISCRETION

TEN

From the Resumption to 1837

More Crises

Introduction

The debate over the monetary system and a possible return to gold that took place during the Restriction changed course after 1816, when the war ended with Napoleon's defeat at Waterloo. The Resumption of cash payments proved to be a slow process; questions about both the appropriate standard – gold or silver or none – and the health of the issuing country banks received much attention during the following years.[1] The period after the war was characterized by deflation and a relatively bad economic performance that particularly affected agriculture. The decline in the volume of credit extended by both the Bank of England and the country banks and the sharp fall in their note circulations contributed, apparently, to the difficulties. It took the work of two additional committees of inquiry in 1819 – one of the Commons, one of the Lords – debating the *Expediency of the Resumption of Cash Payments*, and three more years of debate before Parliament accepted an end to the Restriction and agreed on the details of resuming cash payments. The committees' recommendations were enacted into a law that implemented the reform in May 1821.[2] The financial system was now back to where it had been in 1797: The Bank and the country banks had to pay their notes in cash on demand in the old gold parity. At first, they had to do this in bullion,

---

[1] See chapter 3 of Fetter (1965) for a comprehensive and detailed account of the period leading to the Resumption.

[2] The Commons Committee was under the chairmanship of Robert Peel (the younger); the two committees each examined more than twenty witnesses between February and May 1819. As Fetter explains, a clear majority of the witnesses favored a return to cash payments, though some were worried about the return to the old gold parity of 3l 17s 10.5d. The legislation was approved on July 2, 1819; Fetter (1965, pp. 85–94).

as Ricardo's Ingot Plan proposed; two years later, from 1823, they had to do it in coin.[3]

The discussions from 1816 on, in the two committees of inquiry in particular, addressed the difficult question of the possible negative consequences of a return to the old parity. Would a return enhance deflation? Was there an alternative that was less risky for the economy? One has to recall that the price of gold in 1817 and 1818 was higher than the pre-Restriction price; the attempts to bring down the price of gold constituted a difficult task in itself and also had some unpleasant consequences that were not always well understood. Ricardo's ideas, discussed in Chapter 8, had a very strong influence on the thinking of the two committees; the practical plan to resume cash payments was very much in line with his ideas. However, when the Resumption was at long last a fact, the disappointing recession known to contemporaries as the agricultural distress placed Ricardo at the center of the debate; he was responsible, in the eyes of some, for the unfolding events. This was probably one of the strongest reasons behind Ricardo's reengagement with monetary questions and his rethinking of the ideal monetary system.

As a result of the disappointing performance and fragility of the monetary system, the voices critical of the Resumption as a matter of principle, as well as those who supported the idea but did not like the return to convertibility at the old par, became louder and stronger. The opposition to the Resumption concentrated around the Birmingham School; its better-known writers, the two Attwood brothers, were very influential. The questions they raised concerned the possible impact of the Resumption on the disturbing deflation and the agricultural distress. Put squarely, they asked: "Has the Resumption any responsibility?" They certainly thought it did and answered in the affirmative (see Checkland [1948]).

The fall in prices from 1819 to 1822, especially of agricultural goods, and the crisis in that important section of the economy troubled Parliament and resulted in the creation of several committees of inquiry which naturally also discussed the monetary system: the Committee on Agricultural Distress (1820) and the Committees on Agriculture (1821, 1822). Ricardo was a member of the first of these committees. Some observers – like, as we have just noted, Thomas Attwood – put the blame on the Resumption. As we shall see, Thomas Tooke joined forces with Ricardo at this point to argue, based on the facts he had collected, that the Resumption was not entirely to blame (see Chapter 12 and Fetter [1965], chapter 4).

---

[3] During the two years that notes were redeemed in gold bullion (Ingots, known also as Ricardoes) apparently only very few were actually exchanged for notes. Fetter (1965, pp. 96–97)

Other topics arose during these discussions of the link between the monetary system, the return to gold, and the recession. One of these topics was the role of the country banks in the monetary system, these banks' poor reputation, and the mistrust of the public towards them. In this context, the right of country banks to issue notes of less than five pounds came to the forefront, and a decision to ban this right was taken in May 1821. More generally, along with growing criticism of the issuing banks, a demand to allow joint-stock banking, as a measure that would strengthen them, came up. The more basic question of who should issue notes did not yet capture center stage in the debate and had to wait for a few more years. After the actual Resumption, in spite of the difficulties just discussed (mainly in agriculture), there were a few years of relative stability of the financial system (from 1821 to 1825); as a result, the debates concerning the reformed monetary system subsided during this short period. But then the serious crises of 1825 restarted the monetary debates.

The 1825 Crisis

In late 1824, unfavorable exchanges and an external gold drain were the first signs of one of the more serious financial crises in the history of Britain. In February 1825, the Bank's bullion reserves were lower than at any point since 1820 (see Table 9.1). Over the following months, an internal drain developed; people demanded gold from the various banks, which could not always pay. The Bank was at first unwilling and then slow to react. By December 12, 1825, "the storm began," as John B. Richards, the deputy governor of the Bank, later told a committee of inquiry.[4] The Bank clearly changed its policy at this point, probably at the request of the government; it now extended credit in the hope of saving the collapsing financial system. The data show how aggressive the Bank now became in its efforts. The crisis continued, and the Bank decided to issue low-denomination notes, less than five pounds, for the first time since the Resumption. The circulation of such notes rose from less than 400,000 pounds on December 17th to 1.25 million pounds by December 31st. A famous story contends that officials at the Bank accidentally found a box of unissued notes that they then used to save the nation.[5] Be that as it may, the Bank's notes continued to circulate and were considered almost as good as gold. The system was saved. As we shall see, the lesson was not forgotten in the coming years.

[4]   See the Bank Charter Committee of 1832, Q. 5056; also in Fetter (1965, p. 113).
[5]   See Fetter (1965, 114) and the sources quoted there. Fetter does not think that the story can be confirmed. Feavearyear tells us: "Beds were installed in the Bank and the whole staff slept there over Christmas. Gradually, by measures such as these, confidence was restored" (1931, p. 238).

It is no wonder that many claimed the credit for the (belated) policy change that rescued the economy. One of the first to urge the Bank to change its policy was Thomas Attwood who, after some meetings with the Bank directors, wrote to Robert Peel (the younger) on December 16, 1825 about the Bank's power, public and private interests, and the need for the government to intervene:

> As respects the objection to interfering with the Bank on the ground of its being a private & not a public body … the Bank has been placed … to perform … functions of a Public Nature. … It cannot therefore for a moment be held that so long as the Bank is entrusted with Powers as great as they ought not to be held subject to such control & Interference on the part of Government as may be necessary to prevent any great public calamity from the mismanagement of this great public power.[6]

Thomas Joplin also repeatedly claimed credit for changing the Bank's policy. However, Fetter writes: "Whether the Bank, the Government, Attwood, Joplin, or Stuckey deserves the credit is a detail compared with the fact that action was taken by the Bank in 1825 on a scale far beyond anything that it had done before" (1965, p. 116).

This time, the government refused to start a new Restriction, although this was the Bank's preferred strategy. The crisis ended in late December, probably due to the actions taken by the Bank; but when a new, less severe but still significant round of instability started in February 1826, the Bank refused to step in. As will become evident in Chapters 11–13, when we discuss the theoretical debate concerning the 1844 Bank Act, the Bank's role as a lender of last resort was not accepted by the directors before 1844, and also not after. The right policy was debated in Parliament; as Fetter comments, the opposition convinced the government not to issue Exchequer bills, leading to a situation in which "probably for the only time in British history a Government staked its life on an issue of central banking" (p. 119). The opposition wanted the Bank, not the government, to lead the action, arguing that it was in the Bank's power and duty to act. This disagreement was clearly hiding a theoretical debate about the principles and tools of monetary policy – a debate to which we will return – but it was also an early example of the power struggle between the government and the Bank so typical of the relations between the two ever since.

The 1825 crisis shattered the British economy and its financial structure. It occurred exactly when the Resumption seemed to so many to provide stability and create conditions supporting growth. Instead, the banking

---

[6]   Quoted in Fetter (1965, pp. 115–116) from Peel's papers in the British Museum Add. MS. 40, p. 384.

system proved a source of instability and danger. The 1825 crisis was one of those major events that shape debates on money and banking, similar to and maybe even surpassing the impact of 1797. The 1797 crisis led to inconvertibility; the reform debated was along a clear and simplistic dividing line – yes or no to convertibility – that ended in the Resumption and brought the system back to convertibility. The question now was more complicated: After the return to convertibility, how to reform the banking system? How could the banking system be improved so that it could provide the stability and flexibility so necessary for the performance of the economy? These questions stayed on the agenda of both reformers and supporters of the status quo for many years to come after 1825.

The focus of the discussions after the 1825 crisis moved from whether the standard should be gold at the old par to the broader issues related to the desired structure of banking. Many did not trust the note issues of the country banks, which continued to fail too often. The country banks' governance seemed to others to be the major problem; making them stronger and increasing their reputation was an urgent task. One feasible strategy was to allow joint-stock banking, which had been forbidden in England, but was now thought to answer concerns about the country banks. The proposals did not go as far as to suggest joint-stock banking in London, where the Bank continued to enjoy a monopoly on note-issuing and was the only joint-stock bank. The question of whether or not to allow joint-stock banking outside of London was debated in Parliament in February 1826 and was the subject of two committees of inquiry. The Bank, which took much of the blame for the 1825 crisis, was now too weak to resist the reform in joint-stock banking. Two acts, restricting small notes and permitting joint-stock banking, were passed in 1826.

The March 1826 Act did not allow issuing banks in England and Wales to issue small-denomination notes. Practically, although it is not clear whether legally, this restriction was extended to Bank of England notes. In both Scotland and Ireland, the traditional small-denomination notes were already issued by joint-stock banks; in Scotland, banking was also done with joint-stock banks. Another act passed in May 1826 allowed the creation of note-issuing joint-stock banks on the condition that these have no branches within sixty-five miles of the Bank of England in London, where the Bank continued to have monopoly power.[7]

The debates on money and banking continued over the next few years but with less urgency. The agricultural distress continued, and many people continued to put at least some of the blame on the errors of the Resumption.

[7]   The same law allowed the Bank to open branches and issue notes there as well.

Convertibility was apparently not – and certainly not by itself – the good policy rule that the Bullionists expected it to be. There is a debate as to who initiated the currency principle, to which we will return in Chapter 11. One early expression – Fetter argues that it is the first – came in 1827 from Pennington. He proposed that the Bank be required to issue notes (or withdraw notes) only against its bullion reserve.[8] We will explore these ideas further when we discuss the Currency School.

Meanwhile, some Bank directors, led by Palmer, worked on a rule of action, or policy rule, that linked the liabilities of the Bank to its reserves in bullion (Fetter 1965, pp. 132–133). The idea was very simple: When the circulation was "full," the Bank had to maintain a third of its liabilities, meaning its notes in circulation and deposits, in bullion. From then on, the combined liabilities should move with bullion. If there were more bullion in the Bank's coffers than the reserve in the "full" situation, the Bank's liabilities should be higher by exactly the same increase and vice versa. The rule was not discussed in public and was first explained in the Committee on the Bank Charter in 1832.

The 1832 Committee and Palmer's Rule

The Bank's charter was to expire in 1833; in 1832, an extensive inquiry into the principles that should direct note-issuing evolved, this time not under the shadow of a financial crisis. The *Committee of Secrecy on the Expediency of renewing the Charter of the Bank of England, and on the system on which Banks of Issue in England and Wales are conducted* provided one of the more detailed accounts of the banking system. It was a very extensive undertaking that included evidence from more than twenty witnesses and a collection of data that had never previously been published; its records still serve as an important source of information. In retrospect, this committee was the venue in which ideas that were to be debated for many years were first raised. The committee was well aware of its importance; it brought to the discussions the disappointing lessons learned in 1825, and it was not satisfied with the structure of banking that was implemented in 1821. Specifically, as is clear from the opening statement of the committee's report, the inquiry focused on three topics. The first was the supply of notes in London, and specifically whether to continue the Bank's monopoly or to establish "a competition of different Banks of issue, each consisting of

---

[8] See Pennington (1827) and Sayers (1963); Pennington's view on deposits, which he considered money, can be found in an early 1826 memorandum and in an appendix published in Tooke (1829a).

an unlimited number of partners" (PP 1832, p. 3). Second, if the Bank was to remain an issuing monopoly in London, how should it carry out this function? The third question was how to protect the public vis-à-vis the other banks of issue, and more specifically, "whether it would be expedient and safe to compel them periodically to publish their accounts" (ibid.). The committee also inquired into the advantages of the Bank of England having branches and the opening of joint-stock banks of issue.

As we mentioned earlier, this committee was the forum in which the Palmer Rule was first introduced to the public and thus became known outside the Bank. Palmer was the governor of the Bank, and his evidence before the committee occupied its first four meetings (PP 1832, pp. 7–71; Questions 1–926). It was in these committee meetings that he explained the rule in detail. Before serving as governor of the Bank (1830–1833) he had served as a deputy governor (1828–1830); he was a director from 1811 until a year before his death in 1858.[9] Palmer's approach in the late 1820s recognized the importance of the Bank, and he wrote in a letter on February 9, 1829, that the Bank was "the head and pivot of the circulation of the Empire" (quoted in Horsefield [1949a], p. 145). He emphasized the need for a clear rule of action but was less supportive of publicity for the Bank's actual behavior as it appeared on its balance sheet. The link between the exchanges and the Bank's credit policy, including the credit given by the other banks, was a major issue for the committee. As we have seen, the Bank changed its position gradually, as a response to crises, and not because of Thornton's ideas. After the 1825 crisis, twenty-three years after the publication of *Paper Credit*, the Bank admitted that money supply and credit may have had an influence on the exchanges. Palmer certainly thought so; he explained to the 1832 committee how the link would work:

Q. 678 What is the process by which the Bank would calculate upon rectifying the Exchange, by means of a reduction of its issues? – The first operation is to increase the value of money; with the increased value of money there is less facility obtained by the commercial Public in discount of their paper; that naturally tends to limit transactions and to the reduction of prices; the reduction of prices will so far alter our situation with foreign countries, that it will be no longer an object to import, but the advantage will rather be upon the export, the gold and silver will then come back into the country, and rectify the contraction that previously existed. (PP 1832, p. 52)

This process, which reminds one of Hume's Price-Specie-Flow mechanism, was behind Palmer's monetary proposals. In a memorandum passed to the

[9] See Parliamentary Papers (1832) and Horsefield (1949a). Palmer served for three years as governor due to the appointment in 1832 of the Committee of Secrecy on the Bank Charter; he remained a director until 1857.

committee, Palmer put the blame for many of the past errors on the government rather than the Bank, arguing that the former forced the Bank to accept more Exchequer bills than it thought right, "in opposition to the repeated remonstrances of the Directors of the Bank" (ibid., p. 71). We will return to Palmer and his contributions in the next chapter.

The committee was very interested in the witnesses' views on the link between the banking system, its assets and liabilities aggregates, and the exchanges. Some thought, as Ricardo argued, that the flow of gold always has a monetary cause, hence it is the responsibility of the Bank to address it. More thought that gold flows are sometimes not the result of monetary causes, or at least not only due to monetary causes. Thus, the troublesome question of what the appropriate Bank policy should be in times of drains worried the committee. Palmer, in his evidence, argued not only for his rule, which had been formulated as a guide for ordinary times, but also for the appropriate Bank action in times of distress, even against its short-term interests. Asked if "under peculiar circumstances of pressure, the Bank may come forward and assist most materially by discounting private paper?" he answered:

That is precisely my view. The Bank of England is required to provide a requisite supply of paper money for the average circulation of the sphere in which it acts, and to uphold public and private credit when called upon. When commercial credit is affected, it is in such times that the credit of a great body like the Bank of England is available, and has the power to uphold the credit of the country. (PP 1832, Q. 198, p. 18)

One of the results of the committee's efforts was a decision to renew the Bank's charter in 1833. In addition, the government passed legislation in Parliament to make the Bank's notes legal tender; to repeal the Usury Laws; and to add regulations for joint-stock banks. There were also new arrangements concerning the relations between the state and the Bank. The debate in Parliament in May 1833 revealed the strong support for a single-issuer arrangement, although this had to wait for the next discussion on the renewal of the charter in the 1840s. The most important debate on the proposed reform in the banking system will be the subject of the next three chapters.

Appendix: More Data

From the reports of the 1832 committee and that of 1847, contemporaries outside the Bank's inner circles could know the basic information concerning the Bank of England. We present the data up to 1821 in Chapter 5 in Tables 5.1 and 5.3. In Table 10.1, we present the data for the years 1821–1837.

The crisis years, as before, are clearly shown; one can notice in the Table the decline in the bullion reserves in 1826 and 1837.

Table 10.2 presents the annual data for the Bank of England from 1750 to 1844. The data and Figure 10.1 clearly show the decline in the bullion reserve relative to the note circulation. What is less clear is the significant change in deposits.

In Table 10.3 we present data relating not only to the Bank of England, but to the overall banking system. Table 10.3 shows the main trends in banking between 1792 and 1865. Whereas in 1796, just before the Restriction, Bank of England notes were the dominant medium in circulation (11 million out of 24.5 million, or about 45 percent), in 1809, 1819, and 1824 they constitute only about one-third of the total. At the same time, there was a tremendous rise in the amount of notes from other banks. The next twenty years, from 1824 to 1844, saw the rise of deposits against the decline of bank notes. From constituting one-third of the circulation in 1824, deposits accounted for more than 60 percent in 1844. The same trends continued between 1844 and 1856.

Column 3 represents the total of bank deposits of Great Britain, exclusive of the Bank of England, at the end of each year. The figures down to 1865 are estimates based upon such information as is available in the reports and papers published by the various committees of inquiry. Until after 1824, the greater portion of these deposits were held by the London bankers, whereas the note issues in column 2 were entirely outside London and the surrounding counties.

The total money supply in those years increased dramatically, from around 60 million pounds at the end of the Restriction to around one 150 million in 1856, and 230 million pounds by 1865; in 1896, the figure climbed to almost 700 million pounds (see Column 4). That increase occurred almost fully due to the sharp increase in the deposits of the banks. Clearly, the role of deposits in the monetary system was the focus of the debate after the end of the Restriction, and we will address the debate on the role of deposits in the coming chapters.

Table 10.4 presents some of the reserve ratios; one should note that these were not calculated at the time and thus were not at the focus of the discussion. They are mentioned here only for those readers who would most probably look for them in the discussions that will follow. They clearly show how thin the reserves became over the years, certainly in relation to the total money supply as defined in modern terms, if not relative to the Bank's own notes. These stylized facts are at the background of the debates and drove, at least in part, our story.

Table 10.1. *Bullion at the Bank of England, its note circulation and deposits, 1821 to 1837 (in thousand pounds)*

	Bullion	Notes circulation	Deposits
1821 Feb.	11,870	23,885	5,623
Aug.	11,234	20,295	5,818
1822 Feb.	11,057	18,665	4,690
Aug.	10,098	17,465	6,399
1823 Feb.	10,384	18,392	7,181
Aug.	12,658	19,231	7,827
1824 Feb.	13,810	19,737	10,098
Aug.	11,787	20,132	9,680
1825 Feb.	8,779	20,754	10,169
Aug.	3,634	19,399	6,411
1826 Feb.	2,460	25,468	6,936
Aug.	6,754	21,564	7,200
1827 Feb.	10,159	21,891	8,802
Aug.	10,464	22,748	8,052
1828 Feb.	10,347	21,981	9,198
Aug.	10,499	21,358	10,201
1829 Feb.	6,835	19,870	9,554
Aug.	6,796	19,547	9,035
1830 Feb.	9,171	20,051	10,763
Aug.	11,150	21,465	11,621
1831 Feb.	8,217	19,600	11,214
Aug.	6,440	18,539	9,069
1832 Feb.	5,293	18,052	8,937
Aug.	7,397	17,981	10,875
1833 Feb.	9,500	19,370	12,395
Aug.	8,895	19,630	12,588
1834 Feb.	8,537	19,253	13,356
Aug.	6,521	18,840	13,793
1835 Feb.	6,259	18,329	10,823
Aug.	6,202	17,892	13,742
1836 Feb.	7,889	18,102	14,323
Aug.	5,274	18,159	12,276
1837 Feb.	4,090	18,233	10,594
Aug.	6,673	18,741	10,376

Source: Parliamentary Papers (1832) appendix 5 and Parliamentary Papers (1847), second report (p. 505) appendix 4; see also Clapham (1944) appendix C for explanations.

Table 10.2. *The Bank of England, its note circulation, deposits, and bullion, 1750 to 1844 (thousand pounds)*

Year	Cir	Dep.	Draw	Bull	Year	Cir	Dep.	Draw	Bull
1750	4318		1914	1959	1797	10394	6328	2644	2588
1751	5195		1933	2970	1798	12638	7225		6188
1752	4750		2135	2730	1799	13175	7887		7282
1753	4420		1723	2289	1800	15946	7699		5647
1754	4081		1675	2829	1801	15385	9440		4488
1755	4115		2259	3789	1802	16142	8299		4022
1756	4516		2815	4034	1803	15652	8934		3685
1757	5150		3052	3727	1804	17116	9196		4626
1758	4864		2328	2241	1805	17130	13066		6754
1759	4800		1620	2208	1806	19379	9809		6101
1760	4936		1913	2628	1807	18315	11809		6314
1761	5247		1814	2020	1808	17650	12487		6936
1762	5887		2121	3053	1809	19059	11120		4071
1763	5315		1550	367	1810	22907	13037		3347
1764	6211		1504	1873	1811	23324	11261		3297
1765					1812	23218	11722		3041
1766	5846		1497	1871	1813	24020	11214		2798
1767	5511		1568	818	1814	26585	13653		2151
1768	5779		1797	1564	1815	27255	12199		2723
1769	5707		1810	1379	1816	26886	12123		6102
1770	5237		1820	2873	1817	28471	9955		10675
1771	6823		1716	2278	1818	26987	7063		8209
1772	5962		1553	1505	1819	25190	6359		3890
1773	6037		1784	1192	1820	23892	4257		6561
1774					1821	22090	5721		11552
1775	8762		2136	6829	1822	18065	5545		10578
1776	8626		2108	5141	1823	18812	7504		11521
1777	8033		1858	3279	1824	19935	9889		12799
1778	7099	4689	2182	2570	1825	20076	8290		6207
1779	8145	4780	2241	3847	1826	23516	7068		4607
1780	7376	5690	2306	3880	1827	22319	8427		10311
1781	6701	5859	2564	3071	1828	21669	9700		10423
1782	7394	6445	2520	2057	1829	19709	9295		6815

(continued)

Table 10.2 (*continued*)

Year	Cir	Dep.	Draw	Bull	Year	Cir	Dep.	Draw	Bull
1783	6991	5285	1911	956	1830	20758	11192		10161
1784	5898	5086	1970	1098	1831	19069	10141		7328
1785	6247	6461	2250	4114	1832	18016	9906		6445
1786	7883	6009	2506	6145	1833	19500	12492		9697
1787	9008	5767	2269	5960	1834	19046	13575		7529
1788	9782	5353	2399	6321	1835	18110	12282		6231
1789	19465	5970	2815	7937	1836	18130	13299		6581
1790	10737	6211	2957	8510	1837	18487	10485		5381
1791	11556	6401	3264	7062	1838	19266	9825		10036
1792	11157	5525	2564	5913	1839	17958	7979		4618
1793	11377	5895	3010	4666	1840	16773	7058		4342
1794	10515	6914	2776	6879	1841	16971	7215		4630
1795	12440	7064	3716	5632	1842	18543	8661		8103
1796	9988	6179	2522	2331	1843	19812	11285		11722
					1844	21317	12333		15764

Source: Mitchell (1988).

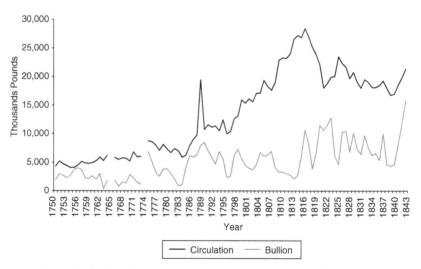

Figure 10.1. The Bank of England, note circulation and bullion, 1750 to 1844 (in thousand pounds).

Table 10.3. *Assets and liabilities in Great Britain, 1792 to 1896 (thousand pounds)*

	1	2	3	4	5	6	7	8
	Bank of England note circulation	Note circulation of other banks	Total bank deposits in Great Britain exclusive of Bank of England	Total of Columns 1,2,& 3	Approx. Total Number of banks	Total deposits of Bank of England	Total coin & bullion in the Bank of England	Banking Department reserve
1792	11,000	12,000	10,000	33,000	300	6,000	7,000	
1796	11,000	5,500	8,000	24,500	250	5,000	6,000	
1809	20,000	25,000	15,000	60,000	750	12,000	4,500	
1819	24,000	20,000	12,000	56,000	550	4,000	4,500	
1824	20,500	20,000	20,000	60,500	600	10,000	9,000	
1844	21,250	11,000	50,000	82,250	350	13,500	15,250	8,000
1846	21,250	7,750	55,000	84,000	330	18,000	14,500	9,000
1856	20,500	6,750	120,000	147,250	300	16,000	11,000	5,750
1865	21,250	5,750	200,000	227,000	250	20,000	15,000	8,000
1896	26,500	1,750	648,000	676,250	138	59,750	44,250	33,750

Source: Feavearyear (1931) pp. 304–305 [second edition].

Table 10.4. *Bank of England reserve ratios against various liabilities: Great Britain, 1792 to 1896*

	1	2	3	4	5	6
	BoE Gold Reserve **Against** "Money Supply"	BoE Gold Reserve **Against** BoE Notes	BoE Gold Reserve **Against** BoE Notes & Deposits	BoE Gold Reserve plus Banking Department Reserve **Against** "Money Supply"	BoE Gold Reserve plus Banking Department Reserve **Against** BoE Notes	BoE Gold Reserve plus Banking Department Reserve **Against** BoE Notes & Deposits
	Col. 7 to Col. 4	Col. 7 to Col. 1	Col. 7 to Col. 5	Col. 7 + Col. 8 to Col. 4	Col. 7 + Col. 8 to Col. 1	Col. 7 + Col. 8 to Col. 5
1792	21%	64%	41%			
1796	24%	55%	38%			
1809	8%	23%	14%			
1819	8%	19%	16%			
1824	15%	44%	30%			
1844	19%	72%	44%	28%	109%	67%
1846	17%	68%	37%	28%	111%	60%
1856	7%	54%	30%	11%	82%	46%
1865	7%	71%	36%	10%	108%	56%
1896	7%	167%	51%	12%	294%	90%

Source: Table 10.3 and author's calculations.

ELEVEN

The Currency School Trio

Loyd, Torrens, and Norman

The Automatism of the Currency School

As we saw in the preceding chapters, the 1821 Resumption, contrary to the expectations of the Bullionists at the time, did not bring an end to the monetary fluctuations or to the debates about the role of the monetary system and the responsibility, if any, of the Bank for these fragilities. The agricultural crises of the early 1820s, the severe crises of 1825, and then the downturn of 1836 forced the continuation of public discussions of monetary issues. As we shall see in this chapter, new proposals for reform based on Humean and Ricardian principles were again put at the center of the debate. The supporters of the new reform were known as the Currency School. This chapter will follow their major theoretical arguments and their policy proposals.

The Currency School, typically represented by Samuel Jones Loyd, Robert Torrens, and George Warde Norman, successfully promoted the 1844 Bank Act. The background to the Act was the continued instability and recurring financial crises in the British economy. The banking sector was particularly fragile, and the rise of joint-stock banking after the Resumption caused much alarm. In times of instability, the system relied on the Bank of England, as those who were well informed about the banking system recognized; although by its charter, the Bank had no legal obligation to support the financial system. The recognition that the system was not well secured led in the late 1830s to an old-new idea: Make the money supply – the quantity of coins and notes – behave as would a "pure," coins-only currency.

On matters of theory, the Currency School rejected the Real Bills Doctrine and agreed with Henry Thornton's argument that discounting "good bills" would not ensure the right quantity in circulation. They argued that bankers would find it difficult to distinguish "bona-fide" good bills from fakes, because good bills could be created by fictitious deals between merchants.

Criticism of Smith's formulation of the Real Bills Doctrine does not necessarily imply rejection of the general position that the quantity should be
determined by market forces, including competition between joint-stock
banks; however, the Currency School's position, as we shall see, led them
away from competition in note-issuing. As a result, they sought an alternative method for supplying the country with money – determining the
quantity of coins and convertible notes in circulation, which in Loyd's view
was the aggregate to watch and direct.

The Currency School's position is most clearly expressed in the 1844 Bank
Act, passing of which also marked the Currency School's victory in its debates
with the Banking School.[1] With the passage of the Act, every change in the
quantity of Bank of England notes would equal the change in the amount of
precious metals in the reserves of the Issue Department. This change would
not depend on the banking system's discretionary actions, but rather on
autonomous economic factors and the public will; it would free the bankers
from all responsibility other than obeying the Act. The Issue Department
was to be the sole issuer of new notes and would exchange gold for notes
and notes back to gold in an unchanging ratio: 3l 17s 10.5d for an ounce of
gold. The Act thus provided a clear rule of conduct that entailed no discretionary decision, making the Bank's actions in this sense "automatic," hence,
leaving the control of what the Currency School saw as the money supply –
coins plus convertible Bank notes – to market forces. The members of the
Currency School did not think it important to control aggregates other than
notes, and while they rejected the Real Bills Doctrine and competition for
notes, they accepted competition in all other aspects of banking, including
all the quantities of other assets and liabilities in the different institutions.
Two different arguments were raised to support this position.

Loyd, who is considered by many to be the leader of the Currency School
and the main influence behind the Bank Act, argued that only the money
aggregate (notes and coins) is important to the smooth and stable working
of the monetary system.[2] He derived this conclusion from his reliance on the
Price-Specie-Flow mechanism and from his belief that only money as defined
earlier affects prices; all other activities of the banks, he claimed, could be left
to the bankers. Torrens had a different argument, which was based on the view

---

[1]   For an overview of the Currency and Banking School debate, see Viner (1937, chapter 5),
    Rist (1940, chapters 4 and 5), Fetter (1965, chapters 5 and 6).
[2]   O'Brien (1971) provides comprehensive coverage of Loyd's life and thinking in his detailed
    introduction to *The Correspondence of Lord Overstone*, including the exciting story of
    the discovery of the letters. Loyd became Lord in 1850; in the text, I will refer to him as
    Loyd.

that money controls the other monetary aggregates and thus it is sufficient to control the quantity of notes.[3] In any event, they both accepted competition between all banks, including the Bank of England, in the fields of deposits and loans, but not in that of issuing notes. Their aim was to arrive at a system in which the banks would have no discretionary powers in what both Loyd and Torrens considered to be the critical aggregate: the quantity of convertible notes and coins. Loyd and Torrens believed that such a system would function best if it acted according to the rule of the Bank Act, which would answer all contingencies. The mechanism should be automatic, without any attempts to distinguish between internal or external, terminable or nonterminable drains.

Thus, those in the mainstream of the Currency School as represented by Loyd held a strange position. Their rejection of competition for issuing notes should have led them to adopt a concept of central banking. Yet their conviction that the Price-Specie-Flow mechanism would not work properly under discretion and their suspicion of bankers led them to cling to an alternative solution of "rules" even in the years following the Bank Act, when a succession of crises (1847–1848, 1857–1858, 1866) necessitated discretion. Similarly, their acceptance of competition for all banking functions other than the issuing of notes derived mainly from their insistence that the banks would not create negative risks for the real economy – an odd position in view of the growing significance and fragility of intermediation in the monetary system of the time. That these two banking operations need not be connected is obvious to those who read Ricardo's 1824 text, where he writes that the operations can be "carried on by two separate bodies, without the slightest loss of advantage, either to the country, or to the merchants who receive accommodation from such loans" (IV, p. 276). In Ricardo's opinion, this separation would change nothing in the monetary system apart from transferring profits from the banks to the public. There would be no shortage of loans for discounting bills (IV, pp. 280–281) and, in what was the most important new argument of 1824, he claimed that the amount of notes would be the correct one because they would be given only "in exchange for gold at the price of 3l 17s 10 1/2d per ounce" and "not against discounts." Thus, "regulating their issues by the price of gold, the commissioners would never err" (IV, p. 293). The commissioners do not have to lend to the government, which should finance itself. In addition, at this point Ricardo demanded that "country bank notes be withdrawn

---

[3]   See Robbins (1958) for a detailed analysis of Torrens's life and views, including in particular (chapters 4 and 5) on the subjects of money and banking. See also O'Brien (1965) and Poitras (1998).

from circulation" (IV, p. 287, the seventh proposition). Thus, for the first time, Ricardo clearly rejected competition in issuing notes. However, in this last text, in contrast with his so-called followers in the Currency School, Ricardo allowed the Bank of England certain discretionary activities with its securities.[4]

Loyd's Early Formulations

Samuel Jones Loyd (1796–1883) was born in the City of London to a banking family and, according to some sources, literally on the bank's premises.[5] He was an only child, educated at Eton and Cambridge; at the age of twenty-two, he became a young partner in his father's bank. He was a Member of Parliament from 1819 to 1826, but he was defeated in the 1832 elections, and he never tried to enter Parliament again. The family's private bank, run by his father, was very profitable in the 1830s and was later sold. Along with his years as an MP, Loyd was involved in other areas of public life from an early age: He was a member of the Political Economy Club from 1831 to 1872; had a brief appointment as an Exchequer bill commissioner in 1831–1832; and appeared before the 1832 committee on the renewal of the charter of the Bank of England. Loyd became Lord Overstone in 1850; when he died, he was one of the richest, best-known, and influential persons in England.

In his evidence before the 1832 Bank Charter Committee, Loyd argues some of the principles that will characterize him in later years, though not yet with the supportive theories that he developed later. Although the language is not as strong as that used by him in later years, Loyd already expresses his preference for a Bank of England monopoly over issuing notes and for separating the Bank's note-issuing activity from its banking (dealing with loans and deposits):

> My idea is, that the management of the issues of notes is a business entirely distinct from other banking business, and that everything connected with it ought to be kept perfectly distinct from the other affairs of the Bank; that whatever be done by the issues of notes, and whatever funds are reserved for meeting that issue, is entirely independent of the rest of the business which may be strictly called banking business (Parliamentary Papers, 1832 Committee, pp. 240–241, Q. 3380).

As O'Brien (1971) suggests, Loyd's discussions with Torrens and with Norman, a director at the Bank of England, over the few years after 1832

---

[4] See Viner and Fetter on the similarity between the Currency School and Ricardo.
[5] See Reed (2004).

probably led him to develop some of the elements that characterize his mature thought.[6] These elements appear in Loyd's first heavily quoted and influential pamphlet of 1837, *Reflections Suggested by a Perusal of Mr. J. Horsley Palmer's Pamphlet on the Causes and Consequences of the Pressure on the Money Market.*[7] Palmer, who was the direct cause for writing the *Reflections*, was a deputy governor of the Bank, and in his earlier 1837 pamphlet, the one that triggered Loyd's response, he explains the rules of conduct of the Bank of England (see our Chapter 10), which the Bank had also presented before the 1832 committee that decided to extend the Bank's charter.[8] The policy known as Palmer's Rule was clear and straightforward: The Bank should maintain proper reserves against all its liabilities, defined to include both Bank of England notes and deposits. Proper reserves were described as a third of the total liabilities when the circulation was full. When changes occurred in the amount of gold in the Bank's coffers, the responsibility of the Bank directors was to induce an equal change in its liabilities. Thus, changes in bullion reserves should have equaled changes in the total liabilities. Looking at a typical Bank balance sheet, it is clear that this rule was equivalent to maintaining a fixed, or at least very stable, amount of the Bank's securities. Hence, the stability of the quantity of the Bank's securities became the criterion for a good policy. In Loyd's words in his 1837 pamphlet:

The principle upon which the Bank professes to be guided in the regulation of the currency is this: to meet its outstanding liabilities consisting of circulation and deposits, it holds at its disposal securities and specie, and its principle of action is, to keep the amount of its securities fixed, and to leave the variation in the amount of circulation and deposits to be balanced by a corresponding variation in the amount of specie. (pp. 5–6)

But, argued Loyd, this practice was based on an incorrect understanding of the functions of banking. In terms that are remarkably similar to Ricardo's

---

[6]   O'Brien (1971) writes about the 1832 evidence: "Here, above all, there are not the two crucial features of all his later analysis, the insistence that a paper currency should fluctuate exactly as ... metallic one would have done, the inflows and outflows of metal indicating the necessary expansion and contraction and the prime insistence that above all, convertibility should be maintained" (O'Brien, 1971, p. 92).

[7]   It appeared also in Loyd's collected works that were put together by McCulloch in 1857: Loyd, S. J. [Lord Overstone] (1857) *Tracts and Other Publications on Metallic and Paper Currency*, London: Harrison. In a "Notice" introducing the volume, McCulloch describes how he approached Loyd and asked him to collect the various publications, committee appearances, and letters for "distributions among his friends," to which "he was good enough to consent."

[8]   The committee extended the charter and privileges of the Bank from 1833 for twenty-one years with an option – "break clause" – that enable a change in 1844. See Horsefield (1944).

1824 formulations (see our Chapter 8), Loyd explained that there are two "capacities" to the Bank: It is the "manager of the circulation" and a "body performing the ordinary functions of a banking concern." The Bank had not fully "attended to" the fact that these two are of a "distinct nature." Moreover, "[t]he rules applicable to its conduct as a manager of the currency are mixed with the rules applicable to its conduct as a simple banker" (pp. 6–7).

The Palmer Rule makes sense if applied only to the business of circulation, but when applied to the other business of the bank, it becomes "wholly impracticable" and was rejected by Loyd. Loyd argues that we could create a mechanism that really imitates a pure gold circulation only if we ignored deposits as if they did not exist and then fixed the amount of securities, because only then would changes in the quantity of notes in circulation always be equal to changes in gold at the Bank. Moreover, in such a case, the changes in the circulation would be caused by the public, who is the active side, whereas the Bank remains the passive partner to the transactions. Thus, "the amount of the circulation … will by this principle be made to fluctuate precisely as it would have fluctuated had the currency been purely metallic." However, this is not the case when the other businesses of the Bank are addressed in the same fashion: "when the same rule is further applied to the regulation of its conduct as a banking concern, it is necessarily found to be wholly impracticable" (p. 7).

Loyd's reasoning for what he saw as the failure of the Bank rests upon the unique position he held, even among the Currency School, concerning deposits. On the one hand, he argues, from the point of view of the Bank of England and that of any bank, deposits are liabilities to the banks and assets to the holders. Deposits create resources that can be lent and thus increase the quantity of securities (or, in our Chapter 4 terms, PDCs – Private Debt Certificates) on the banks' balance sheets. But Loyd did not think that deposits are money; on this he differed not only from the Banking School, but also from Torrens, as we shall see.

Bank of England Balance Sheet

Liabilities	Assets
Δ Bank notes	Δ Gold
Δ Deposits	Δ Securities (PDC's)
==========	========
=	=

A look at the balance sheet of the Bank of England, and in fact any bank, makes the differences between Palmer and the Currency School very clear. Maintaining unchanging quantity of securities will guarantee the close movement of gold and total liabilities, as they are the remaining items on the balance sheet and hence must move together with changes in gold (Δ Gold). The Bank faced criticism in 1835–1836 because the quantity of its securities was volatile, and Palmer's 1837 pamphlet, to which Loyd reacted, was mainly dedicated to reconciling the official stated policy of the Bank with the real outcome. Palmer thus based his argument on a new phenomenon concerning the Bank's policy; the Bank turned less secretive after 1833 and was forced under the new charter to publish data on its activities. The idea of more openness emerged from the 1832 Bank Charter Committee; the assumption was that publicizing information about the Bank aggregates would enable the public to better judge risks and thus reduce the possibility of a crisis.

In reality, the availability of data forced Palmer and the Bank to make excuses for the fact that the Bank did not succeed in keeping its securities stable, as it purported to do. The Bank was blamed, for example, for the difficulties in 1836. Palmer offered two kinds of explanations for the failure: First, he blamed a set of "other reasons," and not the misbehaving monetary aggregates, for the negative developments in the economy; second, Palmer claimed that the published aggregates were not the right ones, and that if one were to distinguish between different kinds of deposits and securities and then to construct a new definition and a better and more accurate measure of securities, one could then show the desired stability.

Loyd, however, did not accept Palmer's Rule about securities as an appropriate guideline for Bank policy. He thought that there was no point in aiming for a stable amount of securities, whatever be their exact true measure. Loyd argued that this was in fact a policy target based on a serious theoretical error:

> To those who are practically conversant with banking business, or who have reflected upon the nature of it, it can hardly be necessary to point out the simple consideration, that banking deposits are necessarily variable in their amount and duration, and that with such variations the amount of securities held by the Bank will also fluctuate. It is therefore unreasonable to talk of the invariable amount of a banker's securities and this observation is equally applicable to banking business when conducted by the Bank of England, as when it is conducted by any other body. (p. 9)

The right principle should aim to make the circulation function as if it were a pure metallic circulation:

> The rule ought to be, That the variations in the amount of circulation shall correspond to the variations in the amount of bullion … The importance of a rigid

adherence to this rule cannot be over-estimated: and if it is incompatible, as is alleged by some, with the mixed functions of the Bank of England, it seems to become a very serious question, whether it is not better to separate altogether the business of banking from that of regulating the currency... (pp. 10–11)

This was the basis for Loyd's monetary thinking and for the policy recommendations of the Currency School: The Bank has two functions that should be carried out by two separate bodies, each acting according to its own specific principles, "unencumbered by the conflicting tendencies and opposite action of its former companion" (p. 11). Loyd claimed that he did not want to be "unjust to the Bank," as the Bank accommodated demands for mercantile credit and "is a public body ... [It] must partake of the feelings, attend to the wants, and obey the expectations and demands of the community in which she exists." The problem was that the Bank had *"a power over the paper issue of the country"* and cannot perform the "opposite and inconsistent duties" that sometimes contradicted each other (pp. 34–35; emphasis in the original). This conclusion was critically important. Loyd and the Currency School believed that the Bank's failures were rooted in the inherent contradictions between the two functions; without two separate bodies acting independently from one another, the failures would repeat themselves. This was the crux of the difficulty as summarized by Loyd:

A Bank of Issue is entrusted with the *creation* of the circulating medium.
A Bank of Deposit and Discount is concerned only with the *use, distribution, or application* of that circulating medium.
The sole duty of the former is to take efficient means for issuing its paper upon good security, and regulating the amount of it by one fixed rule.
The principal object and business of the latter is to obtain the command of as large a proportion as possible of the existing circulating medium, and to distribute it in such a manner as shall combine security for repayment with the highest rate of profit. (p. 31)

Further, the monetary system should be structured so that any change in bullion reserves would be reflected in a change in the circulation; the timing of the change is also crucial. Loyd explains that Palmer's thinking leads to improper reactions for either of two reasons: First, a decision might not be taken at all due to questions raised repeatedly as to the causes behind changes in reserves; or second, an action might be delayed. On the first obstacle, Loyd comments that those who support Palmer's reasoning will in many cases not act because they will argue that

... the mere fact of a diminished amount of bullion is not necessarily a proof of an undue range of prices or of an unfavorable state of the Foreign Exchange; that it is no conclusive evidence of a state of things requiring a contraction of the circulation; that it may be caused by an internal demand, or by a peculiar, local, and transient cause ... (pp. 22–23)

On the second obstacle, that of timing, Loyd introduces a well-known and oft-quoted metaphor:

There is an old Eastern proverb which says, you may stop with a bodkin a fountain, which if suffered to flow will sweep away whole cities in its course. An early and timely contraction, upon the very first indication of excess in the circulation, is the application of the bodkin to the fountain; commercial convulsion and ruin in consequence of delay, is the stream sweeping away whole cities in its course. (p. 23)

The essence of the argument led Loyd and the Currency School to negate discretion; decisions would necessarily lead the Bank to misconduct or delays. Loyd was well aware here of the legal state of affairs by which any bank was entitled to make considerations as it found fit, serving its best private interests. But this was just another proof of "the defective state of our legislation." That logic also holds true for the Bank of England, which faced a dilemma that called for a major reform. Because it was both an issuing bank and an intermediary, the Bank performed two functions – it managed the currency and engaged in banking activities. The two functions would best be managed by two separate administrations upon different principles, especially because they carried "*conflicting* duties."

Loyd relates his critique of the flawed banking structure to the recurrent changes in the economy. Loyd's well-known description of a typical cycle goes like this: "... state of quiescence, – next improvement. – growing confidence, – prosperity, – excitement, – overtrading, – convulsion, – pressure, – stagnation, – distress, – ending again in quiescence" (p. 31). In periods of expansion, the Bank would expand loans, using its power to issue "paper-money *ad libitum*." This is where the Bank's duties as Banker of Issue and Banker of Deposit or Discount came into conflict. Based on the principles of "human conduct" as well as experience, it would be natural to expect that the bankers would act without regard for the public's real good, abusing their power by issuing notes. As a result, the banks, including the Bank of England, would "give further stimulus to the existing tendencies of the trading world, and ultimately ... aggravate the convulsion to which they must lead" (p. 33).

The proper system should create a monopoly supply of convertible notes: "[The] issue of paper-money should be confined to one body,

entrusted with full power and control over the issues, and made exclusively responsible for the due regulation of their amount" (p. 37). At this
stage, however, Loyd was not yet sure whether such a reform is practical: "[We] fear we must not now attempt altogether to eradicate" the present system (pp. 37–38). "[In] the meantime," however, Loyd recommends
a gradual separation of the accounts of the proposed two "departments"
by a number of interim steps. One is increased centralization of note-
issuing by giving more control to the "central issuer" over the other issuers. Another is "subjecting the superintendence of this Department to a
separate Committee of Currency, and of associating with this Committee
a representative of the Government, whose presence should always be
requisite to constitute this Committee efficient for business" (p. 39). This
representative was intended to provide a defense against abuse of power
by the Bank, whereas the "Bank would exercise a similar restraint over the
Government" in the best tradition of checks and balances. Loyd further
recommends the addition of "a full and intelligible publication of the
proceedings of this Committee, and the public will thus be enabled to
exercise a sufficient control over this body in any case in which it may
be conceived that the two parties united can have a common interest in
neglecting their duty to the public" (p. 39).

All the major elements of the Currency School proposals that culminated
a few years later in the 1844 Bank Act can be found in this early text. What
Loyd recommends – watching the recurrent crises (1825, 1836) and expansions, or what the literature calls sometimes "cycles" – is imposition of a
strict rule on the monetary system in order to prevent crises as much as
possible, and if were to fail, to smooth the cycles. The rule would make
the system fluctuate as if it were a pure metallic circulation; under such
an arrangement, Loyd believed, crises would disappear. Thus, when gold
outflows for any reason, the monopoly responsible for issuing notes would
reduce the quantity of notes; when gold inflows, notes would increase.
Although this proposal constituted a major change in the monetary regime,
describing these arrangements as "management of the currency" is misleading. The "manager" was supposed to follow simple rules with no discretion on his part, but this does not mean that he was conducting monetary
policy. Loyd's proposed mechanism would also help to smooth the cycles,
if one accepted that a system that was supposed to work counter-cyclically
worked procyclically. But this result would be an unintended consequence
of the reform, whose aim was to guarantee convertibility, and hence to avoid
banking panics and ensure the continued functioning of the monetary system. Thus, for Loyd, the major task was to avoid threats to convertibility;

stabilizing the economy would be a welcome side-benefit of implementing
the new strict rule.[9]

Loyd in the 1840s

Three years later, in 1840, Loyd published a second pamphlet, *Remarks on
the Management of the Circulation and the Conditions and Conduct of the
Bank of England and the Country Issuers During the Year 1839*. This text,
written after intensive discussions with those who would become members of the Currency School, explicitly locates the roots of the new views
in the Restriction-era Bullionists, on whose authority Loyd relies. During
the Restriction, the Bank of England adopted what Loyd describes in 1840
as the wrong position; the "practical people" – the Bullionists – were right.
However, argues Loyd, the Bank was in a process of change. For example,
the positions the Bank directors presented in the 1819 Committee, just
before the Resumption, showed that they did not have any well-established
principles to guide them. Loyd depicts the Bank directors' claim in 1819
that the Bank supposedly met the "wants of commerce, and … discount[ed]
all commercial bills arising out of legitimate transactions…" (1840, p. 49) as
typical of anti-Bullionists who adhere to the Real Bills Doctrine. According
to Loyd, the directors ignored any indication of the unreasonable amount
of the circulation; they did not at that time understand the link between
gold flows and the quantity of the circulation and behaved like the "man
who, because he had accumulated an unusual quantity of water, thought
that he could therefore fill with it a tub which had lost its bottom" (p. 51).
They did not understand either why they had accumulated gold or why they
had lost it.

By 1832, thirteen years later, the Bank's position in the Committee on the
Renewal of the Bank Charter had changed. In 1832, argues Loyd, they at
least advocated the right principles, if not the right policy:

The convertibility of the notes of the Bank was to be secured, by regulating the amount
of the issues with reference to the state of the Foreign Exchanges; and the increase or
diminution of gold, in the hands of the Bank, was to be taken as the only certain and
safe test of the favourable or unfavourable state of the Exchanges; consequently the

[9] O'Brien (1995, 1997) argues that Loyd's and the Currency School's policy recommendations were "anti cyclical" in the modern sense of the word. However, the aim of Loyd was
first and foremost to increase stability and avoid the inconsistencies described earlier that
led to crisis; anti-cyclical policy was a secondary effect resulting from the increased stability. As O'Brien's empirical studies show, there was in fact no increase in stability (apart
from prices) as a result of the 1844 Bank Act. See also O'Brien (2007) chapter 10.

amount of her paper issues was to vary with a direct reference to the fluctuations in the amount of bullion in the possession of the Bank. (pp. 59–60)

However, although the Bank's directors were now arguing for the right principles, Loyd argues that they still had some way to go toward the proper implementation of these principles. Palmer claims that the Bank policy is aimed at securing convertibility, but according to Loyd, Palmer and the Bank are wrong on the measures to guarantee convertibility. Loyd's detailed analysis of the Bank's actions in 1839 tries to prove this point (pp. 66–78). The Bank's stated goal was to preserve its treasure and do it in such a way that no pressure would ever spill over and ruin the money market:

The duty ... imposed upon the Bank ... [is] she is bound not only to protect her treasure from actual exhaustion by foreign drain, but also to preserve it at such an amount as shall leave her at all times prepared to bear the probable, or reasonably possible, demands of internal alarm. (pp. 74–75)

It is here that Loyd turns to Ricardo's *High Price of Bullion* as an authority on the dangers of a too-close relationship between the Bank and the government. The Bank has to be independent from government pressures as well as from the pressure of private commercial interests in conducting the management of the circulation (pp. 80–81). "[It] seems unreasonable to expect a steady and consistent course of her part, until she is released from these improper influences, and placed in such a position that she can regulate her conduct with reference to no consideration than that of maintaining the convertibility of her notes" (p. 85).

One of the most difficult and important analytical questions concerns the distinction Loyd makes in his theoretical framework between what is, and what is not money. Loyd argues that money does not include all the liabilities of the Bank of England, or for that matter, of any issuing bank. As he did in 1837, Loyd considers only coins and convertible notes to be the quantity of money in circulation. Thus, deposits were not part of the aggregate that should enter the considerations of those who would like the circulation to behave as if it were a pure circulation. The explanation for this unique position puzzled many of his contemporaries. The most elaborate answer was given by Loyd, in fact almost forced out of him, in the evidence given to the Committee on Banks of Issue of 1840.

His exchange concerning deposits, mainly with Joseph Hume, includes the following:

Deposits business is a mode of economizing the use of the circulation; ... but an economic use of the circulation is not itself circulation. When you put the question, are not the bank notes in my till, and the bank notes deposited by me in the hands of the Bank of England, equally at my disposal, it is undoubtedly true that they are; but it is true only with respect to the bank notes which I have in the Bank of England, upon the supposition that all persons, similarly circumstanced with myself, do not act simultaneously. The Bank of England, or any other banker, can clearly pay his deposits only to the extent of the banking reserve in his till. The banking reserve in his till is the money with which that business is worked, and constitutes the amount in circulation. It is to mistake the amount of business done for the instrument with which it is done, to call deposits circulation. Deposits are the business worked; the reserve in the banking till is the instrument with which they are worked; and the business by which your instrument is worked, is the circulation of money of the country. (461–462 Q. 3109, July 22, 1840)

The important distinction between the individual banker and the banking system worried the committee:

[We] are here reasoning upon a philosophical question, we must clearly understand this, that that which is true of any one individual, is not therefore necessarily true of a large aggregate of individuals, simultaneously. You may split every thing into its subordinate parts, and affirm of each part, separately, that which will not be true of the whole, simultaneously, in the aggregate" (462 Q. 3111, July 22 1840).

The problem Loyd had with deposits was that they were not as secured as notes. The Bank used the deposits for giving out loans, as every other bank would have done. Hence, although each individual could rely on his bank – and Loyd did not want to encourage suspicion against the Bank of England – the depositors, in principle, could not all rely on the Bank to get notes instantaneously if they all applied together. Deposits were only partially covered by reserves and enjoyed only restricted substitution with notes. Thus, deposits are a form of debt, argues Loyd, and enjoy a different status than that of notes, which are also debts:

Q.3121 What difference, then, is there between the bank note you hold in your hand, and the money you deposit in the Bank? – The difference is this; in one case, the debt has assumed that form which makes it the representative of metallic coin, for all purposes; in the other case, it has not assumed a form which gives it those properties. (464)

This distinction did not convince many of the committee's members or other contemporaries; neither did it convince later theorists. Even those who were close to Loyd on other issues rejected his insistence on that distinction. It was true that deposits were a form of debt, and that in looking at the aggregate macro-level, there were circumstances when they could not fulfill their role in payments; but this was also true for notes. Notes were also not covered 100 percent, and in times of crisis, they were not capable of being the perfect money that Loyd aspired for. The inquiry continued relentlessly, with the questions returning time and again to that inconsistency in an attempt to embarrass Loyd.[10] Loyd protested the repeated questions, many of which came from Hume, and concluded: "It is my opinion that deposits do not possess that property of universal exchangeability in endless succession which money does possess" (p. 477).

Loyd and Torrens became close associates during the debate in the 1840s, to the extent that one can see them as partners in the promotion of the ideas of the Currency School. John Ramsay McCulloch, the editor of the 1857 volume of Loyd's *Tracts*, writes in the preface (Notice) that one of the pieces in that collection, a running commentary on a famous petition, "was the joint production of Lord Overstone and Colonel Torrens, one of the ablest and most consistent supporters of the Act. In as much, however, as their respective contributions were so blended together as to make their separation impossible, it was thought best to reprint the entire tract with this notice of its divided paternity."[11] Torrens's contributions were significant although he held some markedly different positions that we will describe next.

Torrens's (Mature) Monetary Position

Robert Torrens (1780?–1864) was a marine colonel, an MP, and a founder, along with Tooke, Ricardo, and Malthus, among others, of the Political Economy Club. He was a prolific writer on political economy, where his contributions ranged from value and trade theories to fiscal policy. For our purposes, his contributions to money and banking theories and policies are of primary interest. Robbins's 1958 study, *Robert Torrens and the Evolution of Classical Economics*, remains the definitive evaluation of this unique scholar. Torrens's views on money and banking are particularly interesting because he changed them radically: He went from being an anti-Bullionist in his early writings during and after the Restriction to being a member of the Currency School's famous Trio.[12] Thus, as in many other cases of radical transformation,

---

[10] The committee quoted a definition of money given by him previously (Q. 2663) to question his consistency. See Q.3132.

[11] See Loyd (1857) p. iv. The jointly written tract appears as *The petition of the Merchants, Bankers, and Traders of London against the Act of 1844, with Comments on each close.* (Loyd 1857, pp. 285–309).

[12] Robbins credited Torrens with "the first published proposal for the separation of the Issue and Banking Departments of the Bank of England" (1958, p. 73). See also O'Brien (1965) and Poitras (1998).

the most promising question is: What led to the change? Robbins, however, argues convincingly that the change happened suddenly and "seems to defy explanation." This is even more disturbing because it was a "… complete *volte-face* on matters relating to the theory of money and banking" (p. 74).

In Torrens's *Essay on Money and Paper Currency* (1812), he expresses anti-Bullionist views totally opposed to Ricardo and the Bullion report. The pamphlet starts with a sympathetic description of the impact more commodity-money has on the economy as well as a negative description of the consequences of less commodity-money, close to the tradition of John Law and the other inflationists. It is along this line of thinking that Torrens presents a positive approach to inconvertibility. The advantages of having a flexible supply of money with which to accommodate the needs of the mercantile community were attractive to him. The dangers of excessive supply could be addressed via careful discounting by the banks, who would only discount solid mercantile bills. Thus, Torrens expands Smith's approach to the case of inconvertibility, arguing with the anti-Bullionists that excessive notes would return to the banks: a mechanism of reflux under inconvertibility. Torrens, at this stage, defended the Real Bills Doctrine.

Neither his meetings with Ricardo nor the friendly though complex relations between the two changed Torrens's mind.[13] He continued to hold to his anti-Bullionist position and in 1819 criticized Ricardo's Ingot plan, arguing that it would increase the fluctuations in the internal circulation. Robbins rightly remarked that "[in] view of later developments in Torrens's thought, it is worth while underlining the nature of his argument: the bullion plan is rejected *just because it would make the fluctuations of the internal circulation exactly what they would be under a purely metallic currency*" (Robbins 1958, p. 83). However, by 1819, Torrens had already moved a little; he took a more centrist position between the Bullionists and anti-Bullionists. For example, he thought the former were right in arguing that the precious metals and bullion were "the only standard of money" (1819, p. 84), and he also accepted that some expansions of the quantity of notes might be due to too-liberal discounting.

The change in Torrens' views first appeared in public[14] in a discussion in Parliament in 1833, twelve years after the Resumption and after the 1825

[13] See Robbins (1958, pp. 81–86) on the Bullion debate. On his relations with Ricardo concerning value and distribution generally see Robbins pp. 9–11.

[14] O'Brien (1965) discusses in detail the transition in Torrens's monetary thought. The paper draws on an unpublished, and up to that point, unknown paper written by Torrens in 1826. Thus, O'Brien goes some way to explain that the "*volte-face*" of 1833 was less dramatic, at least for Torrens himself. The 1826 paper, not available to Robbins, is attached as an appendix.

financial crisis that caused the monetary debate to intensify again. The parliamentary discussion occurred when Thomas Attwood proposed to set up a committee of inquiry into the monetary system. In a speech in Parliament on April 24, 1833, Torrens presented the *"volte-face"* that Robbins is unable to explain: To the surprise of many, Torrens articulated a new position based on the Currency Principle (Robbins [1958], pp. 86–90) in which he defends convertibility and recommends a remedy to the monetary system basically along the old Ricardian lines. Torrens's additional proposals for remedies explicitly mention Ricardo's celebrated Ingot Plan as well as his posthumously published *Plan for a National Bank*. Ricardo's *Plan*, writes Robbins, "anticipated the main proposals of the Currency School with regard to the Bank of England" (p. 90).[15]

In 1837, after the previous year's infamous crises brought monetary issues back to the forefront and spurred a most productive year of money and banking pamphlet-writing, Torrens wrote the famous *Letter to Lord Melbourne*. The pamphlet played an important role in the ensuing debate and is perhaps where the reform was first proposed; Robbins argues that Torrens's possible claim to priority concerning the idea of the separation of the Bank's departments is found here:

> So far as is known, this was the first occasion on which the principle of separation of the departments had been put forward in print. But Torrens, who is touchy about his own priorities, was very scrupulous about those of others, has acknowledged here an obligation to Overstone. The first suggestion, it appears, was thrown out in discussion at the Political Economy Club.[16] (Robbins, pp. 92–93).

Torrens's statement, whether original or not, was certainly one of the first formulations of the principles that later led to the 1844 Bank Act. It started with the following general description:

> That the recent disturbance in the money market was occasioned by the error committed by the directors of the Bank of England, in departing from the principle,

---

[15] Torrens's transformed attitude to monetary theory and policy and to the Bank of England in this context was further expressed in Parliament in another discussion in June 1833 on the renewal of the Bank's charter (pp. 90–92).

[16] Torrens went back to the issue of priority in his last publication on the subject, from which Robbins quotes the following: "His Lordship, in one of his lucid expositions … propounded the doctrine, that the separate functions of issue and discount should be entrusted to separate departments. The importance of such a separation flashed upon me. My mind dwelt upon it, and the further explanations and suggestions of his Lordship convinced me that the principle of the separation of departments supplied the requisite complement to the theory of currency, as established by Adam Smith and Ricardo" (Torrens [1858], pp. xii-xiii).

of leaving the currency to contract or expand under the action of the foreign exchanges: -
That this error originated in the failure of the Bank directors to distinguish between effects produced upon the general medium of exchange, by a diminution of their circulation, and by a diminution of their deposits: -
That if the Bank of England were to regulate its issues of paper by the course of the foreign exchanges, the circulation would always remain in the same state, both with respect to amount and to value, in which it would exist were it wholly metallic. (Torrens [1837], pp. 62–63)

Such policy could be achieved "if the Bank directors were to adopt a judicious division of employment, in conducting the two-fold operations of the Bank, and to establish a complete separation between its functions as a bank of issue, and its functions as a bank of discount and deposit ..." In case there is any

practical obstacle to the establishment of a complete separation between the business of issuing paper, and the business of holding deposits and making advances, it will become necessary for the Legislature to place the medium of exchange under the management of competent functionaries, qualified by the possession not of Bank stock, but economical science; appointed, not by the holders of Bank stock, but by the Government; responsible, not to their co-proprietors, but to Parliament; and having for their first object and primary duty the protection, not of their own corporate property, but of the general interest of the nation. (Torrens [1837], pp. 63–64)

The state, argues Torrens, should be responsible for issuing notes, because this is in the interest of the nation. Private interests could not be trusted to do the right thing in guaranteeing the notes that serve as money.

Torrens's views of deposits were, as we have said, different from those of Loyd. In fact, the 1837 text is important not only for suggesting the separation of the Bank's functions, but also because, relying on Pennington's explanations, it explains that deposits are money.[17] Torrens claims that controlling the notes in circulation will indirectly control deposits. Thus, although Torrens and Loyd did not agree on the appropriate definition of the money aggregate and the role of deposits in the system, which Torrens describes as performing the "function of money," they found themselves in agreement as to what has to be controlled in the banking system and how.

The Currency Principle has its roots in the "natural order" assumed by both preclassical and classical thinkers, including Hume, Smith, and Ricardo. Monetary theory was, first and foremost, a theory of the open economy. In fact,

---

[17] See Robbins (1958, pp. 105–116).

the modern distinction between the closed and open models did not exist, and the closed model certainly did not serve as the benchmark. The cornerstone for monetary theory was the "natural" mechanism that was believed to be working smoothly in the open economy at all times, with no role whatsoever for policy. This model was based on the idea that precious metals would serve as both internal and international money. Thus, in a world where all countries have a pure circulation – not a mixed circulation of precious metals and convertible notes, and certainly not one that included inconvertible notes – the invisible hand would have led always in the right direction.

The problem for monetary theory, of course, was that the mixed circulation was a reality; despite calls to amend it, it would not change. Most observers, including Torrens, accepted that the mixed circulation had some advantages and were looking for ways to improve its management, rather than change it to a pure one. The Currency School supporters, including Torrens again, argued that the Resumption of 1819 made the circulation convertible again, but did not succeed in making it behave like a pure circulation. The reason for that, mentioned by Ricardo in his posthumously published 1824 text, was the failure to properly address the two different functions of banking: money creation and intermediation. Hence, the mixed circulation departed from the Currency Principle; it did not imitate a pure circulation as it was supposed to do.[18]

The note issues of country banks became a major issue in the debate with the Banking School. Torrens's views in 1837 and later on the need to reach a monopoly in note-issuing were less strict than those of other Currency School members. He argues that if country banks issue too many notes, the price differences between the regions will force equilibrium. This is a similar argument made by Thornton in the early round of the Bullion debate; Loyd criticizes it in his *Remarks*.[19] Torrens later changed his view; in the *Inquiry* (1844), he joins forces with the other Currency School members to put some blame on the country banks for the failure to implement proper policy while they "continue to act upon their avowed principle, of uttering their paper without reference to the action of the foreign exchanges, and without regard to the principle of keeping the securities at a uniform amount" (Torrens [1844], p. 39).

The major differences between the Currency School and the Banking School concerned the Bank Reform and future policy. In 1840, the debate

---

[18]   Joplin (1823) argued for a similar arrangement. As to whether he had been plagiarized by Ricardo, see a negative view by Robbins (1958, p. 101 n1) and a positive one by O'Brien (1993), to which we will return in Chapter 13.

[19]   See Loyd (1840, pp. 100–101) in the 1857 McCulloch edition.

on the Bank Reform was on. In *A Letter to Thomas Tooke in Reply to His Objections Against the Separation of the Business of the Bank into A Department of Issue and a Department of Deposit and Discount,* Torrens lays down their major disagreement. He uses an example that the two sides later analyzed repeatedly: Torrens assumes a reformed Bank, after a "functional separation" between the departments, and explains how the reformed banking system would work as if it were a metallic one, and how it would be superior to the system proposed by Tooke. The pamphlet was directed at Tooke's criticism of Torrens's proposal as it appeared in the former's third volume of the *History of Prices* (1840). The issue Tooke and the other Banking School members raised concerned the case where depositors made sudden significant demands from the banks. Whereas in the current system the deposit department of the Bank could apply to the issue department for notes or gold, under the reformed system they "might stop payments." Torrens agrees that the "supposed case furnishes an illustration, not of the injurious, but beneficial consequences which would result from the proposed separation of the functions of the Bank" (1840, p. 7).

Tooke argues, and Torrens quotes him at length, that the 1835–1836 crisis would have been worse than it was if the reform had been enacted before. The characteristics of the crisis were a low rate of interest; speculations and overtrading; and too many advances. But, argues Torrens, the advances would have been lower had the Bank known that it could not issue more notes than gold inflows allowed it to. Thus, argues Torrens:

The difference between us is this: you contend that the proposed separation of the business of the Bank into two departments, would check overtrading in the department of issue, but would not check overtrading in the department of deposit; while I maintain, on the contrary, that the proposed separation would check overtrading in both departments. (Torrens [1840], pp. 10–11).

The adversaries returned again and again to the example Torrens analyzed; we will return to it in the next chapter on the Banking School Trio.

Torrens's unique position on deposits calls for an elaboration. He analyzes deposits in the 1837 *Letter* under the heading "Bank Deposits perform the Function of Money." Within that discussion, he explains the potential of deposit banking to create purchasing power, quoting approvingly from Pennington who was one of the first to understand this idea. He never changed his mind on this point, leaving Robbins to wonder what Torrens had in mind when he did not include deposits in his definition of money. The only answer, it appears, is his belief that the ratios between notes and deposits is stable: If one had successfully managed to regulate notes, he would have succeeded also in regulating deposits. For a man well informed about the changing role of deposits in the economy, who faced the critique of the Banking School and others on this issue, this answer is less than satisfactory. It left Torrens in the unique position of defending the Currency School, assuming that the right definition for money was coins plus notes, while admitting that deposits were very near money and important.

Norman: A Voice within the Bank

George Warde Norman (1793–1882), the third person in the Currency School Trio, was associated with the Bank of England for many years and held a unique position in the debate. He came from a family in the Baltic timber trade and studied at Eton, but then, to his frustration, had to join the family businesses instead of studying at Cambridge University as he had wished to. In his autobiography, he wrote about his depressions and breakdowns openly. He was a trader, but he was also active in banking and insurance and was an influential director at the Bank of England from 1821 to 1872.

Norman gave evidence before the 1832 Bank Charter Committee, and in 1833, he wrote *Remarks upon Some Prevalent Errors with Respect to Currency and Banking*, which was apparently circulated privately. A modified second edition of the pamphlet had been published and circulated in 1838.[20] Fetter (1965) thinks that Norman's pamphlet was a "politically, if not theoretically, important contribution" (p. 171). O'Brien (1971) seems more appreciative: "Norman had developed, with subjective originality, the principle that a paper currency should fluctuate as if metallic" (p. 92). These ideas were most probably discussed between Loyd and his "close friend," O'Brien tells us, and influenced Loyd's 1837 pamphlet. Norman's pamphlet contains what he later thought to be the first exposition of the "doctrine that a perfect paper currency, in addition to being strictly convertible and little liable to discredit, should 'at every moment be of precisely the same value as the metallic medium which might supply its place, being increased and diminished under the same circumstances, at similar periods, and to a like extent.'"[21] The idea that the money supply should imitate that which

---

[20]   In the 1838 edition, Norman wrote: "In the autumn of 1832 the Author of the following pages wrote a pamphlet containing a short exposition of what he considered the true principles of Currency, and their application to the state of our monetary system as it existed before the renewal of the Bank Charter. He was prevented from publishing it at that time by circumstances unnecessary to be detailed" (p. 6).

[21]   Norman comments in his memoir: "So far as I know, this opinion was original – and it may have had something to do, with the Act of 1844 – in which it was embodied – I

would have circulated had the circulation comprised only coins, later called "metallic fluctuations," is there: "The paper currency will be more or less perfect in proportion as its contractions and expansions resemble those which would take place in the amount of a purely metallic currency under similar circumstances" (p. 24).

In his early, privately distributed pamphlet, Norman hints at the possibility[22] "of separating completely the business of issue from all other banking transactions" (p. 22). Already in that pamphlet, Norman calls for perfecting the monetary system by creating a monopoly in issuing notes, ideally to be held by the Bank of England. The Bank is the only issuer who can "adhere to correct principles," although Norman is "frequently embarrassed by difficulties of its position in the twofold capacity of money issuer and agent for ordinary banking business!" (pp. 24–25). These two functions are at the root of the problem. They are "not merely distinguishable, but dissimilar, and, under certain circumstances, hardly reconcilable" (p. 25). They should be placed in the hands of the government directly, or delegated indirectly to a body; that body should be engaged only in issuing and be "strictly forbidden" from ordinary banking business.

The body responsible for issuing notes should be a monopoly. It should not be misled to look at the level of prices, the rate of interest, the relative amount of money in different times, or the quantity of deposits as do the issuing banks currently. These are all "fallacious criteria" (p. 24). This argument is derived from Norman's theoretical position based on gold as the ideal measure of value; the international distribution of coin and bullion; the autonomous equilibrating forces that work internationally; and the internal supply of money. Norman rejects "the principle of competition" in issuing notes as well as its advocates who called for "a free trade in banking" (p. 40). The best competing banks can do is to imitate one bank; they cannot do better than a monopoly. The defense of a monopoly is not trivial, of course. But the argument is compelling: There is no mechanism that works against overissue if the banks expand together, as so often happened. This is especially true when the banks don't exchange their notes regularly. The experiences of the United States and Scotland serve to support this argument (pp. 44–47).

---

followed it out on all subsequent occasions." See O'Brien (1971, p. 205). The quotation is from Norman (1833, p. 24); in the original "increased" not "encreased."

[22] In the 1833 text on p. 22, Norman describes the "possibility": "Under other circumstances, a question might arise as to the advisableness …" The paragraph is erased from the 1838 text, but the idea is expanded in a new section, see (1838, pp. 97–109).

The final section of the 1833 pamphlet explains why the scheme "cannot be adopted." The argument is that of a person worried about a radical change where one cannot predict the consequences, as well as the sheer volume of vested interests that will arise against the reform. Norman writes as if his is, in fact, an attempt to prepare public opinion, to test the waters: "it is best to leave the suggestion to produce its effect on the public mind … it will not, and indeed cannot, be acted on at the present conjuncture" (p. 44). Instead, he proposes measures that do not radically change the issuing structure (pp. 65–69).

Norman was instrumental in convincing the Bank to rethink its approach, consider changes, and maybe even adopt the new reform. He appeared on the 1840 Committee, chaired by the chancellor, Sir Charles Wood, to whom he addressed a *Letter on Money and the Means of Economising the Use of It* in 1841. He also appeared on the committees after the 1847 and 1857 crises and remained active in the 1860s when the debate took a new turn. However, his collaboration with Loyd in promoting the 1844 Bank Act remains Norman's most outstanding contribution to monetary thinking and policy.

The Currency School Trio was successful in promoting the reform in banking that they had advocated since 1837. It was a simple framework that they advocated, though it called for a major change in the rights of some strong players in the banking industry; for example, country banks were to lose their rights to issue convertible notes. Of course, it also had far-reaching effects on the Bank of England; the separation of the Bank into two departments took some flexibility away from the Bank's directors. They could not issue notes above a certain amount, and then only against additional gold in their possession. This was a significant restriction on their powers. The debate concerning the pros and cons of the reform was most intensive in the years 1840–1844 when a group of writers known as the Banking School rejected the rationale behind the proposed reform. That group also had three leading writers; the Banking School Trio will be our next subject.

TWELVE

The Banking School Trio

Tooke, Fullarton, and Wilson

Introduction

The Currency School, represented by Loyd, Torrens, and Norman, proposed a significant reform in the banking system, as we saw in the previous chapter. This reform called for a monopoly in note-issuing by the Issue Department of the Bank of England while making the Bank adhere to a strict rule. The Currency School advocated this reform as the only cure for the shortcomings in the monetary regime that manifested themselves in recurring instability and repeating crises. Criticism of the Currency School proposals came from various quarters representing different perspectives; some came from parties that had a clear interest in preserving the status quo, but some came from critics who genuinely challenged the Currency School's monetary theory. Those whose line of critique was most important and influential in the evolving debate soon became known as the Banking School.[1]

The basic disagreements between the two schools became clear in the early 1840s: The Currency Principle, shorthand for the theory advocated by the Currency School, was rejected by the critics. This principle provided the rationale for the Currency School's call for a major reform in the banking system, which was naturally rejected as well. In fact, recognizing those who rejected both the Currency Principle and the reform is a

---

[1] There are several general assessments of the Currency School versus Banking School debate. Hayek (1929b), published only in 1991, is in our view one of the best commentaries on the dispute. See also the seminal studies by Viner (1937, chapter 5), Mints (1945, chapter 6), and Fetter (1965, chapter 6). Schwartz's (1987) is a shorter summary that also covers the Free Banking School that we will cover in Chapter 13. Views in the secondary literature reflect in many cases contemporary conventions on monetary theory; on the different readings, and what they reveal about the readers, see Skaggs (1999) and later, here.

common way of defining the group of scholars who were later labeled the Banking School.[2] These scholars questioned the Price-Specie-Flow mechanism, the mechanism that was at the heart of the Currency Principle and that, as we have seen, was accepted with some modifications by Hume, the Bullionists, and now by the Currency School. Even Smith, in our reading of his monetary theory (though he may be closer to the monetary approach of the balance of payments), and certainly Ricardo assumed a similar link between the internal and international equilibriums. Thus, the rejection of this well-established tenet of conventional classical monetary theory by the emerging group of critics presented a major departure from accepted doctrines.

On the other hand, the Currency School itself departed from some basic received doctrines. They explicitly rejected competition in note-issuing, which was not rejected by conventional doctrine until the 1840s; the competitive view was shared by Smith, the anti-Bullionists, and the Bullionists, including Ricardo, certainly up until his second thoughts on this topic just before his early death, as presented in *A Plan for a National Bank*. This posthumously published paper should be seen as a formative text in the development of monetary theory, and it played an important role in the rise of the Currency School in the late 1830s, when this school became the mainstream.[3] The policy recommendations proposed in the 1840s by the Currency School argue, along the same lines as the 1824 *Plan*, for monopolization of note-issuing and for the separation of the Bank of England into two departments, with the establishment of a strict rule to control the note supply. We have seen that the members of the new school were well aware of their debts to Ricardo and to the Bullionists.

Like the debates between the Bullionists and anti-Bullionists during the Restriction, the debates in the 1840s were productive in terms of ideas and innovative analysis of the most basic questions in monetary theory: What is money? How does it affect the real economy? What is the best way to supply a country with the right quantity of money? And even more generally, what is the role of the financial system and credit in the real economy? The debates did not, however, culminate in final answers to important questions related to monetary policy, and they left the accepted new doctrine with a weak theory – some will say no theory – on this key issue. This lacuna is

---

[2]   The Banking School was not alone in rejecting the Currency Principle, the Bank reform, or both. Other critics dissented from both the Currency and Banking Schools; we will discuss some of these critics, like Joplin and the Free Banking School, in Chapter 13.

[3]   The question of priority is always a difficult and interesting one. In this context, the issue relates to Joplin's place; we will come back to it in the next chapter.

more surprising because Thornton was still a well-known, oft-quoted theorist, not the neglected author that he would be toward the 1870s; the participants in the debates had access to *Paper Credit* where, as we have seen in Chapter 7, monetary policy was addressed. The implicit and indirect influence of Thornton on the debate and on the development of monetary theory has received some attention in the secondary literature over the last few years.

The leaders of the Banking School knew and appreciated Thornton's views. The major members of the Banking School – Thomas Tooke, John Fullarton, and James Wilson, and to some extent John Stuart Mill – all quoted Thornton and accepted some of his doctrines. Tooke was considered by his contemporaries, and has been considered in the secondary literature, as the leader of the new school. As we shall see, he changed his views radically; he originally held views close to those of Ricardo and, in some respects, closer to those of Thornton, but ultimately he completely rejected Ricardian monetary theory as advocated by the Currency School. Tooke initially accepted both the Quantity Theory and the possibility of disequilibrium in international relations, as Thornton proposed in his innovative and critical analysis of Smithian and Humeian monetary thinking; later, he changed his views and rejected the Quantity Theory. Fullarton and Wilson, apparently independently, joined Tooke in the critique. We will emphasize Tooke's transformation and devote some attention to Fullarton and, to a lesser extent, to Wilson.

Tooke's Early and Mature Positions[4]

Thomas Tooke was born in Cronstadt in 1774 to a wealthy family that soon moved to England. Tooke himself was connected "with Business in London" beginning in his early twenties. He developed an interest in public questions relatively late in life, after many years as a successful merchant in the Russian trade.[5] It is not clear how his early reputation was formed, but by 1819, he was sufficiently respected in economic circles to

---

[4] This section draws partially on Arnon (1997) *Thomas Tooke, The Currency Principle and The 1844 Bank Act*, an introductory chapter prepared for the issue of Tooke's German edition of 1844.

[5] See Tooke's evidence before the Lord's committee of 1848. Tooke told the committee that "I ... have not been engaged in any mercantile Concern" during the twelve years before this evidence. However, he was active in economic life in his capacity as the Governor of the Royal Exchange Assurance Corporation and as Chairman of the St. Katherine Dock Company.

be invited to appear before the Parliamentary Committees that discussed the Resumption of cash (specie) payments. This taste of public life seems to have appealed to him, because he immediately became active in two important public ventures: the Merchants' Petition in favor of Free Trade, which he himself initiated and wrote, and the establishment of the Political Economy Club, which brought together the leading political economists of the day to discuss economic issues and to support free-trade principles. In the same period, Tooke was elected a Fellow of the Royal Society, even though he had not yet published anything. After his sudden appearance on the public scene, Tooke remained in the limelight on economic issues almost continuously until his death in 1858.[6]

Tooke's works cover a long period of economic change in England, but from his first publication in 1823 when he was forty-nine years old to his last in 1857, his methodology and style of writing did not change. His first book, written under the shadow of the Resumption of cash payments and the crises that followed, described the economic developments of the previous thirty years. Tooke was first and foremost a man interested in and knowledgeable about economic data. This is a reflection of his personal background as well as his methodological preferences, and made his works the richest single source for economic historians for many years to come.[7] This emphasis on data is present in Tooke's "minor" but important pamphlets (1826, 1829a, 1829b) as well as in the definitive "major" work, *A History of Prices*.[8] His attraction to collecting facts does not mean that he had no analysis to propose; it just makes uncovering it more difficult, as we shall see.

There is general agreement[9] that Tooke's early publications reflect an approach to monetary issues quite different from that which characterizes his late works. Those early publications, which appeared before and during

---

[6] For studies of Tooke's thought, see Gregory (1928) in his comprehensive *Introduction* prepared for the occasion of reissuing the *History of Prices* and also published as a separate volume; Laidler (1972), Arnon (1984, 1991), Smith (2001), and Skaggs (2003) and references therein.
[7] It is interesting to note that when Jevons constructed his price indexes in 1863, he used Tooke's raw data. The same data were still heavily used in the twentieth century by, among others, Gayer, Rostow, and Schwartz (1953). See also Mitchell and Deane (1962).
[8] The first two volumes of *A History of Prices* were published in 1838 as a continuation of the 1823 book. More volumes followed: the third volume covering only two additional years in 1840, the fourth in 1848, and the fifth and six, in collaboration with Newmarch, in 1857. The fact that they all appeared under the same title hides the dramatic change in Tooke's views that took place during those years.
[9] Gregory (1928), Laidler (1972), Arnon (1984, 1991), and Skaggs (2003); For less emphasis on the transformation in Tooke's views, see Smith (2003).

1838[10] and include the first two volumes of the *History of Prices*, were mainly concerned with price fluctuations and with a defense of convertibility based on a theoretical approach best described by O'Brien's (1975) term, "moderate bullionist."

In the early years, Tooke advocated a view that was later to characterize the Currency School: Prices are determined by the quantity of the medium in circulation, which he defined then as coins plus bank notes. He thought that this medium of circulation ought to behave as would a pure gold circulation. However, when describing the causes for difficulties in the balance of payments, his position was not that of Ricardo's "pure monetary explanation," but that of Thornton's "real as well as monetary" one (see Arnon 1984, 1989, and 1991). In Skaggs's 2003 study of Tooke and Thornton, he supports the claim that Tooke agreed with Ricardo on policy while differing from him on theory.[11] The theoretical influence that shaped Tooke's early views, before the transformation to his mature Banking School position, was that of Thornton, although the two also had some important differences.[12]

An Early Critique of Ricardo

Tooke's 1826 pamphlet is remarkable for containing both his theory of interest – which did not change and to which we will turn later – and his first explicit written criticism of Ricardo. Tooke devotes a whole chapter to Ricardo's Ingot Plan as it was presented in his pamphlet *Proposals for an Economic and Secure Currency* (1816). Tooke's main criticism concerned what he saw as the lack of stability in Ricardo's proposals. In Tooke's view, the currency would be more stable (its value would be more uniform), were it to consist mainly of metal, with only a small amount of paper. Tooke

---

[10] The publications that were written during this early period include: Tooke, T. (1823), *Thoughts and Details on the High and Low Prices of the Last Thirty Years*, (two volumes); (1824), *Thoughts and Details on the High and Low Prices of the Last Thirty Years*, (second edition, in one volume); (1826), *Considerations on the State of the Currency*; (1829a), *A Letter to Lord Grenville on the Effects Ascribed to the Resumption of Cash Payments on the Value of the Currency*; (1829b), *On the Currency in Connection with the Corn Trade and on the Corn Laws, to which is added a Postscript on the Present Commercial Stagnation*, (second letter to Lord Grenville); (1838), *A History of Prices and of the State of the Circulation from 1793 to 1837* (Volumes I and II).

[11] Thus, Skaggs summarizes Tooke's early views and their relations to Ricardo: "one can hardly disagree with Arnon's (1989, 1991) conclusion that the two [the early Tooke and Ricardo] were allied only policy, not on theory." Skaggs (2003, p. 183). See also Tooke's critique of Ricardo in 1826.

[12] See Skaggs (2003, pp. 188–190).

does not share Ricardo's view of the length of time that would pass until exports and imports are affected, arguing that it would take longer than people imagine:

So that taking the time occupied in the shipment, the transmission, the interval between arrival and sale, and again between the sale and the expiration of the credit, a period of a year-and-a-half, or two years, may elapse before the funds arising from such shipments can be made applicable to foreign payments. (1826, p. 103)

Once Tooke had demonstrated the error in Ricardo's assumption of instantaneous equilibrium in the value of gold and had argued for the existence of a substantial time lag, it was clear that the entire Ricardian theory of the working of the international mechanism, which was shared by the Currency School, was open to question. In Tooke's view, the main drawback to Ricardo's proposal is that it is not clear what mechanism will work when gold has to move out of the country. Ricardo and McCulloch, "those distinguished writers," support paper circulation on the basis of its being cheap, and argue for a small reserve of gold. "I am aware," argues Tooke, "that it is commonly argued by the advocates for an exclusive paper currency, that foreign payments to any amount may be provided, by such a contraction of the paper, as will raise the value of the currency and depress the prices of commodities, thus causing an additional exportation, which will make the payments to the extent required" (1826, p. 101).

In an additional critique, Tooke argues that exports will not grow rapidly; expectations of falling prices and reduced ability to give credit to customers would stunt growth. Moreover, whereas in metallic circulation, that part that is reduced would immediately become part of the export because gold is a commodity, in paper circulation, this would not happen. The export of gold would result in price rises in foreign countries and would accelerate the equilibration process. The answer to this problem lies in the Bank having sufficient reserves to meet the new demand for gold. Tooke's argument here is in favor of the preservation of convertibility, and he held this view also as a Banking School supporter. He considered the damage from raising prices and of overpricing imported goods to be enormous. This damage would be increased by fluctuations in the demand for labor, fluctuations in the demand for foreign loans, the existence of unprofitable export programs, and the fact that certain commodities were not produced. Such extensive damage was not worth the savings provided by a paper circulation (1826, pp. 116–117).

In contrast with these reservations about Ricardo's assumption of equilibrium under convertible regimes, Tooke expresses agreement with Ricardo's later position that convertibility in itself may not suffice to regulate bank-ing. Interestingly enough, as we have seen, Ricardo seems to have arrived at such a position in his last, posthumously published 1824 paper, *A Plan for a National Bank*. In this paper, Ricardo argues for the monopolization of note-issuing by a national bank. In the 1826 pamphlet, possibly under Ricardo's influence, Tooke suggests that maybe the Bank ought "to be entirely re-modelled." Furthermore, Tooke argues that until such a remod-eling occurs, the Bank's power should be limited. The persons who have "the privilege of issuing paper money" and have the power to change the pros-perity of every individual should be under the control of public opinion. The first step would be to abolish the secrecy behind which the Bank hides and to publish reports every six months. In other words, society's interests do not always correspond to those of the Bank, even under convertibility:

> Next to the administration of the state, there is no administration of any office so immediately and extensively affecting the interests of the community, as that which is intrusted to the persons who are invested with the privilege of issuing paper-money...No man, nor a set of men, ought, in my opinion, to be intrusted with that privilege: but being so intrusted, their exercise of it ought to be subjected to the constant control and correction of the public. Such publicity would enforce a steady and consistent adherence to some settled rule, the uniform operation of which the mercantile world might understand and be prepared for. There is no reason what-ever why the accounts of the Bank of England should not be published with as much fulness of detail as is exhibited in the accounts published half yearly by the Bank of France. (1826, pp. 124–125)

The views that Ricardo developed in his 1824 pamphlet were to become the basis for the Currency School's positions. However, when Tooke changed his views on Free Trade on issuing notes and thus finally parted ways with the Currency School, he rejected this proposal as well.

In 1844, Tooke published *An inquiry into the currency principle*,[13] a pam-phlet in which he expresses monetary views entirely different from those of his first period, both in his mind and in the view of his contemporaries. These new positions constituted a theoretical declaration of the principles of the famous Banking School. In brief, Tooke now argued that there was no theoretical or empirical basis for the Currency School's distinction between bank notes and other means of payment, such as checks on deposits and bills of exchange. Tooke argued further that the Quantity Theory, which stated that prices are determined by the quantity of the medium in circulation,

---

[13] The full title of this pamphlet, which was reissued in 1959, is *An Inquiry into the Currency Principle: the Connection of the Currency with Prices and the Expediency of a Separation of Issue from Banking*.

was wrong. Tooke and the Banking School thought that in fact the quantity of the medium in circulation was determined by prices. Prices, he now argued, are determined ultimately by the incomes of the consumers.

The change in Tooke's theory was gradual, and in order to understand it fully one has to analyze the complicated issue of the application of free-trade principles to banking. Beyond his detailed study of prices and his skepticism concerning the Quantity Theory, to which we will return, it was this fundamental issue more than any other that divorced Tooke from the Currency School and conventional theory. Tooke's mature position changed from his early writings, in which he opposed the application of free-trade principles to issuing notes, as did Ricardo in 1824 and the Currency School later. In his later years, Tooke became an advocate of competition in the supply of notes outside of London and its vicinity while supporting continued monopoly in the metropolis. Thus, he supported the status quo, pre–1844 Bank Act arrangements. The Currency School wanted monopolization of note-issuing; Tooke wanted note-issuing outside London to remain entirely in the hands of the many country banks and note-issuing in London in the hands of the Bank of England. Thus, his position seemed more favorable to the application of free-trade principles to note-issuing than that of the Currency School, though both schools supported the monopoly status of the Bank of England in London. Thus, Tooke was not a supporter of free banking.[14]

At the same time, during his transition to the new, innovative Banking School theory, Tooke was convinced of the utmost importance of other financial mediums in the economy. Although he had originally ignored the role played by banks in determining the quantity of credit instruments, also leaving this function to the competing banks, in his mature years he struggled continuously with this difficult issue. Thus, though his position on money did not lead him in 1844 to propose discretionary monetary policy, this view gradually changed between 1844 and 1858. In these years, Tooke published the fourth volume of *A History of Prices* in 1848; the pamphlet *On the Bank Charter Act of 1844* in 1856; and then, in collaboration with Newmarch, the last two volumes of his monumental work in 1857.[15] In the sections written by Tooke, as well as in his last committee appearance in 1848, he devoted much effort to clarifying his position on the limits, if any, to free trade in banking. However, his analysis in those years, although incomplete because

---

[14] We will elaborate on the Free Banking School of the 1830s and 1840s in Chapter 13.

[15] Tooke (1848), *A History of Prices and of the State of the Circulation from 1839 to 1847* (Vol. IV); Tooke (1856); *On the Bank Charter Act of 1844, its Principles and Operation;* Tooke and Newmarch (1857); *A History of Prices and of the State of the Circulation from 1848–1856* (Vols. V, VI).

he did not develop a comprehensive theory of monetary policy, showed the first signs of understanding that the Bank should manage its reserves. Thus, Tooke does not deserve some of the criticisms that Schumpeter and others direct at him for being a-theoretical, in particular in this context of a lack of a theory of monetary policy. As we shall see, Tooke's thinking about policy in those later years was closer to what Bagehot advocated in the 1870s than the secondary literature commonly realizes.

The 1844 Text: A Banking School Manifesto

Tooke's mature Banking School conceptualization appears in its most fully elaborated form in the famous 1844 pamphlet, *An Inquiry into the Currency Principle*. This pamphlet was received with great interest by Tooke's contemporaries, who saw it as the definitive criticism of the Currency School. J.S. Mill, who became sympathetic to the Banking School, recognized that Tooke's new views were "irreconcilably at variance" with the accepted doctrine and called on his contemporaries to award Tooke's innovative statement "a respectful hearing."[16] Torrens, one of the three leading figures of the Currency School, who in 1840 had already identified and addressed the change in Tooke's thought in his *A Letter to Tooke*, continued to debate him in 1844 in his own *Inquiry*.[17] Whether his "hearing" was indeed respectful is less than clear. Tooke had been an early advocate of convertibility and the Bullion Committee principles and thus, up until the 1840s, had advocated theoretical principles similar to those of the Currency School. Torrens seemed to be worried that Tooke might use his past "deserved reputation" to influence the public against those same principles.

Tooke's main innovation and the cornerstone for what was to become the Banking School approach lay in the view that the quantity of money needed for circulation is an endogenous, not an exogenous, variable. Moreover, Tooke now argued against the Quantity Theory, which states that prices are determined by the quantity of the medium in circulation. Tooke and the other Banking School members thought that, in fact, the quantity of the medium in circulation was determined by prices. Prices, he now argued, are ultimately determined by the incomes of the consumers. Tooke now questioned the theoretical as well as empirical basis for the Currency School's distinction between bank notes, which were considered by its adherents

[16] See J.S. Mill's review of Tooke's book in Mill (1844). See also the appendix to the chapter with a note on Mill.
[17] Torrens (1840).

to be "money," and other means of payment such as checks and bills of exchange, which were not. Thus, the new theory rested on a reappraisal of prevailing views on banking and particularly on a reexamination of the concept of money. Contrary to the Currency School, Tooke stated clearly that the quantity of the aggregate they called "money" (bank notes and coins), was determined by the demand. Thus, Tooke rejected one of the fundamental classical positions: that the level of prices is determined by the relation of the quantity of money in circulation relative to the volume of transactions. This left his theory without the classical mechanism that determined the price level.

Tooke's 1844 pamphlet was published after his views had crystallized during the great debate of 1837–1844 over banking policy. In the background were the crises of 1836 and 1839, for which the financial system was at least partially blamed. The pamphlet was prepared quickly on the basis of notes made by the author between 1841 and 1844, so that it would be ready by the May 1844 debate in Parliament on the proposed reform in the banking system. In this pamphlet, Tooke presented his arguments against the Currency School principles that formed the theoretical basis for the 1844 Act.

The Act, which passed after the debate, aimed at shaping a banking system that would guarantee the right amount of currency in circulation, with currency defined as that which the Currency School theorists understood by the term, that is, notes and coins. The result, in terms of the twentieth-century terminology of "rules" versus "discretion," fell clearly on the rules side. Moreover, the Act attempted to create a mechanism that would work automatically so that no decisions would be taken by the authority. Using Simon's (1936) language of "rules" versus "authorities," the authority had no power and no role. It had to function like a modern money changer: The public offers gold and receives notes, or offers notes and receives gold. Hence, "automatism" was a common description of the reform.

Two main reforms were introduced to further this aim. First, the Bank was divided into two departments, the Issue Department and the Banking Department; second, legal steps were taken to concentrate note-issuing in the hands of the Bank of England, prohibiting other institutions from issuing their own convertible notes. The Act stated that the two departments should be managed separately, according to simple principles. The Issue Department should issue Bank notes to the amount of L- 14m (against fixed amount of securities) plus the amount of precious metals it held. The latter amount would be calculated according to the fixed rate of exchange for those metals: Gold ounce would exchange for 3l.17s.10.5d. The Banking Department should deal freely in deposits and loans just as any regular bank did. From now on, argued the supporters of the new legislation, every change in the quantity of Bank of England notes would equal the change in the amount of precious metals in the reserve of the Issue Department. Thus, such changes would not depend on the banking system's discretionary behavior but on the public will, thus reflecting "natural" economic forces. More specifically, the quantity of money would be determined through the working of the Price-Specie-Flow mechanism and would always be the right amount.

The Currency School Trio of Lord Overstone (Samuel Loyd), Norman, and Torrens believed that their doctrine was a straightforward continuation of Ricardo's monetary theory. They based this conclusion on Ricardo's adherence to the Price-Specie-Flow mechanism as well as on his famous analysis of the two functions fulfilled by any bank of issue, found in his last text on this topic, *A Plan for A National Bank* (1824). However, they seemed to overlook Ricardo's change of mind and his growing mistrust of those "natural" forces in this last pamphlet, which led him to recommend a discretionary policy.[18] Hayek (1929b) argues that in the 1824 text, the Currency School found "one of the basic ideas that gained prominence ... [that] had already been expressed by Ricardo ... and constituted a sort of legacy on his part" (p. 219); this was the "separation" of departments concept.[19]

In the introduction to the 1844 pamphlet, Tooke explains that his main aim is to clarify the theoretical background of the Bank Act, especially by providing rigorous definitions of the concepts hitherto used so loosely – particularly regarding the distinction between money and currency. Tooke saw himself, not the Currency School, as continuing the tradition of the authorities on this topic, those whose views had remained unchallenged until the emergence of the controversy around the reform of the Bank of England in the late 1830s. He characterizes supporters of the Currency School as believing that "good management" and the convertibility of bank notes are not sufficient guidelines for banking policy. However, the meaning of "good management" was a major focus of debate. Tooke, argues Fetter (1965), "came to the very brink of the proposition that the only limitation needed on the monetary supply was that banks lend only on real bills" (p. 193). This view of Tooke, which is shared in varying degrees by others, implies that he

---

[18] For a detailed account of Ricardo's position, see Chapter 8 and Arnon (1987).

[19] Hayek adds that Joplin was the first one who advocated "the fundamental idea of the Currency School that note issue should be proportional to the inflow or out flow of gold from the bank..." (ibid., pp. 219–220). More on this issue in Chapter 13.

thought that the Real Bills Doctrine provided a sufficient guideline for issuing notes as well as advancing other instruments: A bank should accept as a security any "good bill." We will argue that Tooke's acceptance of the Real Bills Doctrine was in fact explicitly limited only to the business of issuing notes and, like Fullarton's, was in line with what became known as the Law of Reflux.

The Currency School wanted to avoid discretion and "good management" altogether through a rule that would ensure an automatic correspondence between the quantity of "money" and the quantity of gold that would have circulated had there been no notes at all. Its adherents rejected the idea that the banks' self-interest, including that of the Bank of England, provided sufficient guidelines for controlling the quantity of the medium in circulation. Tooke's rejection of the 1844 Act was twofold: He argued that the recommendations of the Act would not work in practice as its advocates predicted, and he rejected its underlying principles on theoretical grounds.

How Would a "Separated" Bank Work?

On the practical level, Tooke's pamphlet addresses Torrens's views on the working of the "separated" Bank. These views had been expressed in an example that appeared in the *Letter* written to Tooke in 1840, which provides the best summary of their disagreements. In this *Letter*, Torrens claims that the separation of the Bank of England into two departments would achieve control of both the issue of the notes and the amount of deposits. Torrens explains his position using the following example[20]: Let us assume an issuing bank which owns 18 million pounds securities and 9 million pounds bullion against 18 million pounds outstanding notes and 9 million pounds deposits. Now, let us further assume that as a result of an "adverse exchange" (imports surplus), depositors withdrew 3 million pounds of their deposits in bullion to send them abroad. Under the banking system as it existed prior to the 1844 Bank Act, no effect whatsoever was to be felt in the "amount of the circulation," a clear sign for the Currency School, that the system was malfunctioning. However, under a reformed system, such an occurrence would have different results.

According to Torrens's example, the Issue Department would have started with 9 million pounds bullion and 9 million pounds securities (the latter quantity – the Dead Weight – was not to be changed) against which 18 million pounds of outstanding notes were issued. The Banking Department

---

[20] See Torrens (1840), *A Letter to Thomas Tooke*, pp. 11–17; See also my Chapter 11.

would have had 9 million pounds deposits against 6 million pounds of securities and 3 million pounds notes. Now, the same initial withdrawal of 3 million pounds from deposits would have produced first a decline of the quantity of notes held by the Banking Department, and then a decline in bullion held by the Issue Department. Thus, the desirable correspondence between gold flows and the circulation would have been maintained. However, Torrens went on to state that the Banking Department would have changed the amount of its "reserve" and securities so as to return to the initial proportions. The final amount of reserves in the form of notes would have been 2 million pounds and the securities would have been cut to 4 million pounds. Thus, the Deposit Department would have given 3 million notes to its depositors and sold 2 million pounds worth of securities in order to return to the initial reserve ratio (L 6m deposits against L 2m bank notes). In other words, Torrens was satisfied that the circulation would contract and that there was a "limitation to the power to over-trade in discount and loans."

The following schematic balance sheet summarizes the changes from the initial to the final situation:

Deposit Dept. (Banking Dept.)	First Period	Second Period	Issue Dept. (Circulating Dept.)	First Period	Second Period
Deposits	9	→ 6	Circulation	18	→ 15
Securities	6	→ 4	Securities	9	→ 9
Reserve in Bank notes (in millions of pounds)	3	→ 2	Bullion	9	→ 6

In his 1844 text, Tooke declares that he is "willing to admit this statement [Torrens's] as exhibiting in substance the difference between us." Tooke argues that the described contraction of circulation would have a major influence on trade, a point about which Torrens "has no adequate idea." Tooke maintains that before the 3 million notes would have left circulation, the banks would have experienced a great pressure to limit discounts and loans. Thus, the new system would result in a contraction in credit and trade and in a crisis arising from such a contraction, even though "enough" bullion is still at the disposal of the Issue Department.

Thus, paradoxically, the Currency School would have reached the control it desired, but along with it emerged the possibility that the Banking

Department would have to stop payments, even though 6 million pounds bullion was still in the Issue Department. What would occur then?

[The] deposit department would have no alternative but to stop payment. A most absurd, however disastrous a state of things. But it would be too disastrous, and too absurd to be allowed to take its course. If such a crisis were to happen, as most probably it would at the time when the dividends on the public funds became due, the Government would be imperatively called upon to interfere and prevent so ridiculous, however lamentable, a catastrophe. *And the only interference that could meet the emergency would be to authorise a temporary transfer of coin from the issuing to the banking department.* (Tooke 1844, p. 109; my emphasis)

Of course, such interference would run counter to the basic idea behind the 1844 Act, which was to shape a system where the two departments always obey the "rules." The two crises of 1847 and 1857–1858, after the Bank reform was enacted, provide illuminating empirical proof of Tooke's prediction, even though the direct cause for those crises was different from that assumed by Tooke in this quotation. It was not the payments of the dividends on the public debt, but rather the movements of gold that triggered the need to consider temporary departures from the Bank Act in 1847 and 1857. However, these movements came as no surprise to Tooke because this was exactly the major cause for instability, the main shock, which he had already analyzed in this exchange with Torrens.

Assume, again, that a demand for gold to be sent abroad arose, albeit "under a system of unity of issuing and banking," that is, under the pre-1844 conditions. Then, if the Bank had held a proper reserve, the demand for gold would have been answered "with no inconvenience whatever." However, under the separated system, such pressure would have led to "violent effort of the Bank on its securities … with inconvenience to the public. And all this inconvenience may have been purely gratuitous, as a sacrifice to the currency principle" (ibid., p. 110). Such sudden demands for gold were not rare, and each time they occurred they would have endangered the banking system, risking a financial crisis as well as a real one. In many instances, gold movements reflected short-run phenomena caused by ever-changing economic conditions. The answer, in Tooke's opinion, was to hold a significant reserve of bullion, big enough to answer these transitory demands.

The problematic issue was determining whether a gold reflux was transitory or not. Tooke, aware of this problem, had a simple – one may even say simplistic – answer. The quantity of the drain would serve as the criterion. This is a relatively easy criterion to follow. If gold movements exceeded a certain amount, it would be time for a policy change. The policy target was the amount of securities held by the Bank. The policy tools recommended by Tooke were the rate of discount and open-market operations. Before the bullion reserves shrank enough to cause the public to worry, the Bank had to stop the bullion drain either by increasing its discount rate, and thus reducing the amount of its securities, or simply by selling its public securities.

To avoid such painful shocks to the money market and to the economy in general as a result of sudden changes in the Bank's policy, Tooke recommended having a big reserve of bullion. This would answer most cases of sudden demand and would prevent most discretionary interferences. The number Tooke most often used was 10 million pounds "on the average," meaning that as long as the quantity of gold in the Bank's coffers was between 5 and 15 million pounds, the Bank was to remain passive. Thus, in terms of the desired reform in the banking system, Tooke was a supporter of the status quo. The only reform that he thought desirable was that relating to the quantity of the Bank of England's reserves. Other than this important issue, he preferred the unreformed system to any of the proposed reformed ones.

Rejection of the Currency School Theories
Let us turn now to the second level, that of the theoretical disagreements between the two schools that lay behind their policy differences. We can see that the arguments really revolved around the complicated relations between the three basic elements of the famous Price-Specie-Flow mechanism: prices, international gold movements, and the internal circulation. Concern with this threefold relationship is common not only to both the Currency and Banking Schools, but to contemporary economists as well.

The Currency School's basic assumption in their formulation of these relations was that of the perfect circulation. They argued that the perfect currency, the "natural" one as Loyd put it, is that in which gold alone circulates. If the circulation includes bank notes or paper money because these are cheaper and more convenient, they should function as if they were gold. This was the Currency Principle. "Good management" on the part of banks is that which retains all the properties of gold for the circulation, and in particular, ensures that the circulation will expand and contract together with bullion movements, influxes, and refluxes. The Currency School, explained Tooke in 1844, attempted to achieve an imitation of the pure circulation: "By an unnatural state of the circulation, and the want of due regulation, must be understood, in the sense in which Mr. Loyd uses the term, a non-conformity of the amount of banknotes to the amount of bullion" (p. 6).

Tooke questioned the Currency School theory: Why should only bank notes correspond to gold? What is the difference between notes and deposits? Are not bills of exchange used (at least in part) as means of payment? Tooke claimed that the Currency School had not made a valid case for any clear-cut distinction between bank notes and other forms of paper-credit. Because they based their whole case on this assumption, their proposals were limited to controlling the amount of bank notes alone. If one desired to control the circulation, one would have to control *all* forms of paper-credit – checks on banks, bills of exchange, and bank notes – because all function as money (1844, pp. 21–22, 32). In other words, Tooke argued that even if one were to accept the idea of a perfect circulation and tried to shape a system where the amount of coins and notes would imitate that of gold alone, the Act's recommendations would not be effective in controlling the money supply, as money *should* be defined.

Tooke's thorough critique of the Currency School's theoretical principles concentrated on three subjects in particular. First, he reevaluated the "perfect circulation." Second, as mentioned earlier, he questioned the Currency School's tendency to treat all means of payment except gold and bank notes as nonmoney. Third, he criticized the Currency School's unquestioning acceptance of the Quantity Theory. Rejection of these accepted conventions led Tooke to question the Currency School's Theory of Prices and to develop one of his own.

The Perfect Circulation

Tooke's first main theoretical argument with the Currency School concerned the concept of a perfect circulation. The Currency School members assumed that the perfect, or "pure," circulation always reacted to changes in international exchanges. In other words, they maintained that the flow of gold to and from the country must be reflected in the amount of a circulation that is perfect. Thus, their theory was based on a necessary link between international trade and the amount of gold functioning as currency. Furthermore, they assumed that the amount of gold functioning as currency was either the exclusive "money" (as in a metallic circulation) or that it determined the quantity of money in a mixed circulation. Tooke questioned the existence of such a link, which should have been in effect under a metallic circulation, as well as the additional assumption that a mixed circulation would function like a metallic one.

Tooke argued that international gold movements have no direct influence on the amount of gold functioning as currency, but rather influence the amount of bullion outside circulation (bank reserves, plates, jewelry, and so forth). Thus, even the ideal metallic circulation would not function like the Currency School supposed. Tooke thought that one had to distinguish "... for the purpose whether of theory or practice, between gold considered as merchandise, i.e. as capital, and gold considered as currency circulating in the shape of coins among the public" (1844, p. 10). Tooke's discussion of this point, as well as of the operation of a metallic circulation in general, was far from complete. However, he made valuable distinctions between the different and confusing functions of gold, and he criticized the Currency School for ignoring those well-known distinctions. The transfer of gold in international trade does not always correspond to changes in the amount of money in circulation; it does not have the character of currency transfers.

If one accepts this criticism, the perfection of the metallic circulation is no longer beyond question, as the Currency School assumed it to be. However, Tooke's questioning of the second relation – that between the quantity of gold and the amount of the money in a mixed circulation – is of even greater significance. The Currency School maintained that the banks interfered with the working of the desired correspondence between gold movements and what they defined as money. They argued that the existence of convertible notes in the pre-reformed banking system was an obstacle to the equilibrating movements of gold, because the interest of the issuing bankers was opposed to the public interest. The banks, which were supposed to contract the circulation when there was a reflux of gold (when gold reserves diminished), were in fact trying to add notes to the circulation because, in general, prices rose in such a period, bringing prosperity and enabling the banks to issue more notes. Similarly, when there was an influx of gold (when gold reserves rose), banks did not add notes to circulation, because prices usually fell and the economy was in depression.

This point in the controversy was relevant to the economic reality of England in the first half of the nineteenth century. Gold movements occurred frequently, fluctuations in the exchanges were expected, and the policy question of what should be done when the exchanges were favorable or unfavorable was a worrying one. The Currency School had its conventional answer, based on the well-known Price-Specie-Flow mechanism associated with Hume and accepted by Ricardo and almost all of the classicals. In 1844, Tooke no longer accepted this mechanism.[21]

---

[21] This line of criticism had already been adopted by Tooke, although in a weaker form, in his 1826 pamphlet. See Arnon (1991, pp. 87–89) and in the section on the rate of interest later.

Tooke's strongest argument against the notion of a perfect mixed circulation was his argument that the banking system cannot influence the quantity of notes. Notes were considered by the Currency School to be the only medium besides coins in need of regulation, because notes function as "base money." The logic behind this conclusion was twofold. It had its roots in Tooke's analysis of the behavior of the banks as well as in his treatment of the characteristics of the different mediums of payment. The bankers, argued Tooke, are not directly influenced by the exchanges or other general considerations, but in fact react only to the public will. If the exchanges influence the public's behavior, then the banks will react. In short, the banks are passive, only reacting to the exchanges, to price changes, or to other changing economic conditions through their relationship with the public. In particular, as we have seen, an influx of gold will cause a reduction in the quantity of notes because the lower prices will typically result in a lower demand for notes. Thus, prices affect the banks and not vice versa. Furthermore, the banks as a whole are unable to react otherwise. Tooke cited the testimonies given by many bankers before parliamentary committees to prove his point. These bankers argued that they were not influenced by the state of the exchanges and maintained that it was impossible to control the quantity in circulation.

The same conclusion holds for the Bank of England. Even this powerful institution is unable to determine or directly control the quantity of its own notes in circulation: "... in no case could the Bank, by its own volition, add one hundred thousand pounds, perhaps not one hundred pounds to the amount already in circulation among the public"(Tooke 1844, p. 60). Tooke qualifies this unconventional position to leave the Bank some power over its notes for short periods. But even then, the Bank's power is limited to changes in the quantities of notes that are *not* part of what is known as circulating money. Thus, Tooke maintains his fundamental rejection of the view that banks can, at their discretion, change the quantities of their circulating convertible notes. If the banks are incapable of influencing, much less controlling, the quantity of their notes in circulation, why should anyone attempt to regulate the banks?

The controversy over the question of the banks of issue versus those not issuing notes was crucial in this context. The Currency School argued that banks of issue increase circulation in cases where the circulation ought to shrink. According to Tooke, it was not in their power to increase the circulation. If they were to try to add more notes than the public wanted, the notes would simply return to the banks. This is the Banking School's famous "theory of reflux," which claims that there is a mechanism that maintains the amount of convertible bank notes in circulation at a certain volume, *dependent only on the public will*.[22] Therefore, Tooke argues, the present freedom of the banks is advantageous for society and cannot cause any harm. The banks supply the desired amount of currency in an efficient and safe way. This argument was presented clearly by Fullarton.

Fullarton and the Law of Reflux

John Fullarton (1780–1849) was a wealthy banker and surgeon who traveled extensively in India, China, Egypt, and other parts of the empire. His contributions to the debate can be found in his 1844 book, *On the Regulation of Currencies*.[23] Those who study Fullarton agree that he was an original and independent contributor to the debate. He himself modestly underplayed his role. In the introduction to his book, he writes critically of Tooke's slow change of mind: "he adhered to these [prevailing Currency School] doctrines even after he had refuted them by his discoveries"; according to Fullarton, Tooke should have changed his views much earlier (p. 18). Fullarton states that his own efforts are made "chiefly in the hope of contributing something, however imperfect" toward the "completeness and consistence of [Tooke's] theory." Skaggs and Cassidy make a convincing argument for the independent simultaneous discovery of Banking School principles by Tooke and Fullarton. Whether Fullarton was influenced by Tooke or discovered his theory independently, as both Skaggs and Cassidy argue, is beyond the scope of the present study. What is clear is that Fullarton's major contribution and novel addition to the debate was the Law of Reflux, for which he is best known.

Under the title "The impossibility of Over-Issue" (his fifth chapter), Fullarton explains how convertible notes will return to the issuer if he were to try to issue too many of them. The public would return those excessive notes:

It may be stated, therefore, as a stated principle, that the efforts of the banks of issue to extend their circulation know no remission; that the whole system, in fact, is continually on stretch; and that, *but for the antagonist force* which is always in

---

[22] On the Theory of Reflux and Fullarton and on the Real Bills Doctrine and the Law of Reflux and the development of these concepts in classical monetary theory, see Glasner (1992) and Skaggs (1991). The latter discusses the role of Fullarton's contributions in detail.

[23] The full title is *On the Regulation of Currencies; Being An Examination of the Principles on which it is proposed to restrict the Future Issues on Credit of the Bank of England*, second edition, 1845. For an elaborated account of Fullarton, see two comprehensive and sympathetic articles by Skaggs (1991) and Cassidy (1998).

action to correct and repress it, the overflow of notes will be irresistible... (p. 84; my emphasis)
It may rest with the banker to issue, but it is the public which circulates; and without the concurrent action of the public, neither the power nor the will to issue can be of any avail. (p. 87)

Thus, bank notes are similar to other "forms of credit" (bills of exchange, Exchequer bills) where "no question of over issue can possibly ever arise" (p. 85). All those instruments are controlled by market forces; the demand of the public determines the quantities. If there are too many notes in circulation, the banks know with "certainty of having their notes immediately returned to them," as they know with "almost equal certainty of vacancy being filled up from some other sources" (p. 86). Thus, the quantity of convertible notes in an economy with competing banks will be demand-determined and will be the right quantity. Skaggs specifically applies the modern competitive banking model to Fullarton.

The Law of Reflux, which is the name by which this mechanism is known, reminds some of the Real Bills Doctrine. But as Skaggs is careful to explain, the two concepts are different. The Law of Reflux relates to the quantity of bank notes and advances and is an argument about their quantity when competition rules; people will not hold an asset (or liability) that they can exchange. The Real Bills Doctrine relates to the loan policy of the competing banks. It is true that Smith and other supporters of the Real Bills Doctrine thought that it guaranteed that the banks would not only advance the right amount of loans, but that the quantity in circulation would also be the right one. However, loans can take different forms and notes can penetrate the circulation through channels other than loans. Hence, the Law of Reflux is in some way both weaker and stronger: It is weaker because it relates only to one specific medium (bank notes), but it is stronger because for that specific medium it predicts persistent optimal quantity. Skaggs argues that the Law of Reflux is "part of a theory of portfolio choice" that relates to a particular credit instrument but says nothing about the total quantity of credit (Skaggs 1991, p. 470). Tooke advocated a similar Law of Reflux and specified three channels through which it works: Notes could be deposited; notes could be used to pay maturing bills; and/or notes could be exchanged for coins. Skaggs argues (p. 471) that because Fullarton emphasized the second channel, Laidler (1972) and Fetter (1965) wrongly accuse him of accepting the Real Bills fallacy. Skaggs does not agree and finds convincing passages that prove his case concerning the many competing banks; but they do not make his case for the Bank of England.

The role of the Bank of England is thus different and receives separate treatment from Fullarton. Skaggs argues that this is where Fullarton develops his second major contribution: a theory of central banking (1991, pp. 472–476; see also Cassidy, pp. 520–522). This theory hinges on two examples: one where an inflow of gold occurs (Fullarton 1845, pp. 78–81), and one concerning the Bank's purchase of long-term securities – not Real Bills, which are short term (pp. 95–97). In the first example, the Bank maintains a constant Bank rate in the face of gold inflow and hence maintains the reflux; the market rate remains temporarily under the Bank rate; and if the gold inflow is not temporary, the Bank is forced to change its Bank rate, causing prices to rise. In the second example, the Bank again maintains its Bank rate but deals on longer term securities, thus enabling the reflux through them. In short, the Bank has to maintain a Bank rate at an "appropriate" level. However, according to Skaggs, Fullarton did not argue for discretionary monetary policy: "Constraining discretion with firm principles can prevent major errors in credit policy. Seen in this light, Fullarton's attitude toward central bank policy is strikingly similar to that of the currency school" (p. 478).

Fullarton, in his *On the Regulation of Currencies* (1844), relates to Tooke as a source of inspiration, describing himself as following in Tooke's footsteps; although it is clear that on the Law of Reflux, it is Fullarton rather than Tooke who was the innovator. In the fourth volume of *A History of Prices* (1848), the law is defined by Tooke as follows:

This Law operates in bringing back to the issuing banks the amount of their notes, whatever it may be, that is not wanted for the purposes which they are required to serve. The reflux takes place chiefly in two ways: by payment of the redundant amount to a banker in a deposit account, or by the return of notes in discharge of securities on which advances have been made.

A third way is that of a return of the notes to the issuing bank by a demand for coin. The last seems, in the view of the currency theory, to be "the only way by which a redundancy, arising from the unlimited power of issue, which they assume to exist, admits of being corrected in a convertible state of the paper. It is certainly the one least in use" (Tooke 1848, Vol. IV, p. 185). Skaggs (1991) makes a distinction between Fullarton and Tooke on the Law of Reflux: Whereas Tooke "extended the argument without reservation to include notes of the Bank of England, Fullarton made the reflux of Bank notes conditional on the pursuit of proper Bank policy" (p. 462). Let us return to Tooke and his analysis of the various means of payments. His analysis can shed some light on the ideas of these two major Banking School thinkers on central banking.

Tooke on Other Mediums of Payment

In addition to the above analysis of the banks and their relationship with the public concerning bank notes, Tooke carefully examines the various mediums that function in exchange. He opens this important part of his argument with a description of the different functions fulfilled by bank notes. His main point is that when notes are withdrawn from circulation, their place is not always taken by coins, as the Currency School believed. Tooke distinguishes between low-denomination notes, about which the Currency School might have been right, and high-denomination notes, about which they were certainly wrong. Tooke defines low-denomination notes as the one-pound notes that still circulated in Ireland and Scotland, five-pound notes, and a small proportion of the ten-pound notes in the United Kingdom. "All the larger amounts might be, and most probably would be, supplied [if such notes were withdrawn] by cheques and bills of exchange..." (ibid., p. 21).

To convince the reader that this was really the case, Tooke listed seven "purposes" for which higher-denomination notes were used. He then explained how these notes' place would be taken by mediums other than coins if they were withdrawn from circulation.

The inclusion of deposits as an integral part of "money," so natural to the modern reader, was much less so in 1844. Even Tooke felt that "[it] sounds oddly, to say the least of it, to speak of deposits or lodgements of money as being active." Because money has to be active, deposits could not be counted as constituting part of it. However, because active payment was done through checks, these did deserve to be included in what is considered as money. Thus, Tooke concludes:

> It is not the deposits, but the transfer of them; or, in other words, the cheques, that constitute the actual instruments of interchange, and effect payments concurrently with bank notes. *They perform the functions of money not only as perfectly as bank notes, but in the description of transactions to which they are applicable, they are more convenient than bank notes.* (ibid., p. 23; my emphasis)

The only necessary condition for checks to function as money is for the deposits on which the checks are drawn to be "strictly payable on demand." The implications were, of course, far reaching: "[Whatever] influence may be ascribed to bank notes, whether on prices, or on the rate of interest, or on the state of trade, cannot be denied to cheques or their substratum, deposits payable on demand." It might seem to the modern reader that Tooke must stop extending the definition of money at this point, but he did not. Bills of exchange also function like money, he argues, laying his case this time with Thornton and Horner. Bills of exchange perform all the functions performed by notes, including payments for goods or cancellation of debts. They circulate "in consequence chiefly of the confidence placed by each receiver of it in the last endorser." In this they hardly differ from bank notes, which are also circulating debts. The need to endorse the bills does not change this fact. The counter-argument, "the last resort in the argument" as Tooke described it, was that the bills "require the intervention of bank notes for the ultimate payment." But this is "a mere fiction"; bank notes and bills of exchange can and do substitute for one other. What determines their relative popularity is the cost associated with each medium relative to its convenience in performing the functions of money.

Supplying the various mediums that are used to execute payments is a very complicated process. However, complex as it may be, the banks would remain passive throughout this process. If depositors withdrew their deposits, the bank would have to pay them in bank notes, coins, or Bank of England notes. The bankers could not affect the amounts deposited with them. If the banks tried to limit advances, they would succeed only if other mediums of payment – for example, bills of exchange – circulated instead. Tooke's main argument denies the power of either the government or the banks to determine, or even to merely influence, the amount in circulation.

On a more abstract level, it is important to note that Tooke does not argue that distinctions between the various mediums are not important or useful in general. However, he thinks that the distinctions made by the Currency School are the wrong ones and are completely different from the correct categorizations and the useful distinctions (see 1844, p. 33). The alternative analysis that Tooke provides is based on a distinction that the Currency School ignored. We will describe this alternative in the next section.

An Income Theory of Prices

Although Tooke devotes much attention to his critique of the idea of a "perfect circulation" and to an analysis of the similarities and differences between various means of payment, he is even more concerned with the question of what determines prices. As the previous section shows, Tooke and the Banking School in general had an original view of the interrelations between the various means of payment. They also had a novel idea about the relationship between the quantity of money, whatever it may be, and prices. It is important to elaborate on this last point as it appears in the 1844 pamphlet, because it contains the most complete exposition of Tooke's alternative theory, known as an Income Theory of Prices.

Tooke follows Smith in dividing transactions into those "between dealer and dealer" and those between "dealers and consumers." This categorization seems critical to Tooke because it corresponds to the distinction between currency and capital. Moreover, generally speaking, different mediums were used in executing the different types of transactions. "Dr. Adam Smith has noticed the distinction, and has accordingly, in his views of the operation of paper money, steered clear of the confusion between currency and capital which pervades and disfigures nearly all modern reasoning on the subject" (1844, p. 33).

Transactions between dealers are characterized by reliance on bills of exchange and a minimal use of bank notes, that is, by a higher proportion of what is usually described as credit and not included in money. This was clearly manifested in regular dealings, with some exceptions, in markets such as the provision and livestock markets, where the proportion between credit and money tended more to the latter. In any case, in most transactions between dealers where credit is given, there is "little or no intervention of bank notes in purchases or sales." Thus, the argument, which Tooke thought to be an original one, depends on the distinctions between currency and capital and between the two types of transactions. The additional fact that capital transfers, which characterize transactions between dealers, are carried out with the help of credit rather than money closes the argument. A similar distinction characterizes the trade between dealers and consumers. There, currency circulates and only coins and bank notes are used.

Tooke adds a further important consideration to his observation of the correspondence between the type of transactions (only between dealers or also involving consumers), the nature of the transfer that takes place (capital versus currency), and the medium used. He states that "the total amount of the transactions between dealers and dealers must, in the last resort, be determined and limited by the amount of those between dealers and consumers" (1844, pp. 35–36). The reason is that "whatever is bought by the dealers... [is] ultimately destined to be sold to the consumers." Thus, the incomes of the final consumers are the ultimate regulators of prices. In other words, in the final analysis, prices are determined by consumption. This holds true both for the final commodities consumed and for intermediate commodities. The sole source of consumption, the level of the demand for commodities, is determined almost entirely by the income of the consumers, that is, by wages (see 1844, pp. 71–72).

Thus, what Tooke calls "general prices" are determined not by the quantity of money, however money is defined, but by that sum of money that constitutes the income of consumers; hence, the theory is described as an

Income Theory of Prices. Tooke's famous seventeen conclusions that summarize the first edition of the *Inquiry* contain a clear formulation of his rejection of the Quantity Theory (see conclusions 12 and 13). One should note that Tooke rejects the Quantity Theory only for convertible situations. He clearly distinguishes between two types of paper money: government compulsory paper and convertible bank notes. He rejects the Quantity Theory only for the latter and not for compulsory paper, which is inconvertible. His argument is consistent with the Income Theory of Prices. Paper money issued by a government, which consists of inconvertible notes, was used as payment for "Public Works," "Building," "Salaries," "Maintenance of Military and Naval Establishment," and "Expenditure of the governing power." This paper money "will constitute a fresh source of demand, and must be forced into and permeate all the channels of circulation" (1844, p. 69). Under such conditions, "every fresh issue" will be followed by the "rise of commodities and wages and a fall of the exchanges," because *income has changed.*

On the other hand, convertible bank notes are issued to those "entitled to demand gold" but who for some reason prefer notes. In this case,

[the] quantity, therefore, is an effect, and not a cause of demand … In a convertible state of the currency, given the actual and contingent supply of commodities, the greater or less demand will depend, not upon the total quantity of money in circulation, but upon the quantity of money constituting the revenues, valued in gold, of the different orders of the state under the head of rents, profits, salaries, and wages, destined for current expenditure. (1844, p. 71)

According to the Currency School, a shortage of money will cut prices and an excess will push them up whether this occurs under convertibility or inconvertibility. Tooke's disagreement was the result of his complete rejection of the mere possibility that a shortage or an excess of notes or coins could occur under convertibility. The demand for means of payments would be answered, under the conditions then prevailing, by the creation or destruction of the various mediums. Thus, if there were a shortage of notes, bills of exchange in the right amount would be created and would function instead. The Currency School's reaction to this oft-quoted example, wherein a sale is made against a bill of exchange, is enlightening. Let us suppose, they argue, that after three months, there is no money to pay the bill. The result would then be a decrease in prices. Tooke's answer is that the right interpretation is that the consumer simply did not want to buy the commodity, thus the reason for the decrease in price was reduced demand.

Banking, Monetary Policy, and the Economy:
An Incomplete Analysis

Tooke rejected the proposals to regulate money. He believed that the best way to deal with the supply of money was to leave it to market forces as they operated in the preformed system. However, he also recognized the major role played by credit in the growing economy. Could the creation of credit instruments be left to market forces as well? Tooke's answers to this important question were far from complete and satisfactory.

The role of credit and the financial system more generally in the economy was particularly important with regard to their apparent link to prices and their place in Tooke's "waves" or "cycles" theory.[24] Tooke's forceful argument that money, whatever its exact definition, plays no role in determining prices and thus should not be regulated, raises an immediate question: What is the status of credit? Should other mediums used in payments be regulated? Are their quantities a determinant of prices or of some other economic variable?

Tooke's 1844 pamphlet explicitly recognizes the importance of credit. Price levels and other economic aggregates depend on credit to a much greater extent than most people think. For example, when discussing major factors that determine the price level, Tooke shifts his emphasis from the "Seasons" to "Credit." This change probably reflects not only the changing focus of his inquiries, but also the rise in the importance of credit from the 1820s to the 1840s (see ibid., pp. 86–87).

Tooke's analysis of the three different functions fulfilled by banks is of great interest in this regard. The first function, which is carried out only by the issuing banks, is to issue "promissory notes on demand." The second function is to "receive deposits of the incomes of their customers, and to pay out the amount, as it is wanted for expenditure." The third function "is to collect capital from those who have not immediate employment for it, and to distribute or transfer it to those who have" (ibid., p. 36). The second function, carried out "over the counter," is responsible for the circulation of currency, whereas the third one, carried out "behind the counter," is relevant to the circulation of capital and reflects the role of banks in what is known as "intermediation." This distinction is identical, Tooke claims, to the distinction between the two types of transactions previously discussed, those between dealers and those between dealers and consumers. Thus,

---

[24] See Arnon (1991) for a detailed account of Tooke's theory of "waves" as well as Skaggs (2003). On the role of the business cycle in the debate, see O'Brien (1995, 1997, 2007) and Chapter 13.

banks deal with two different subjects beyond issuing: One is the collection of capital from those who have no use for it and its transfer to those who do have use for it; the other is the acceptance of deposits and, through transfers of those deposits, management of payments.

Tooke recognizes that banks do have a limited influence on advances and thus on the creation of credit instruments. Through the use of their own capital, though not through their notes, they could make advances in the hope of getting a bigger share of the market. Those advances were not always made against good securities and were considered dangerous to the smooth functioning of the banking system. Taken together with Tooke's assumption that credit influences other variables in the economy, the natural consequence of this observation is either to explain how market forces will determine the right quantity of credit or to suggest some control of credit. Tooke, however, does neither. His silence on the determination of the quantity of credit remains the weakest point in his analysis. The determination of the rate of interest, whether in the banks' second role, giving credit, or in its third role, intermediation, receives proper and outstanding treatment by Tooke.

Tooke's Theory of Interest: Consistency in 1826 and 1844

During the pre–Banking School period, Tooke produced one publication that deserves more attention: the 1826 pamphlet, *Considerations on the State of the Currency*. This pamphlet was prepared by Tooke under the shadow of the 1825 crisis. Although much of the pamphlet is devoted to a presentation of his early 1823–1824 views on prices and how best to remedy their fluctuations, one new factor is Tooke's treatment of interest. In fact, the major novelty to be found in Tooke's 1838 analysis of price changes compared with that of 1823 lies in this new argument about the rate of interest.

Tooke rejected the "commonly-received opinion" held by political economists, like McCulloch, among others, that the rate of interest "is governed" by the rate of profit in the sense that a high (low) rate of interest reflects a high (low) rate of profit. Tooke ridicules this claim through the example of war and peace: Experience shows and common sense dictates that in times of war, profit rates are low and interest rates are high, whereas the opposite is the case in times of peace. Tooke starts his critique by trying to clarify whether the rate of interest reflects past, present, or future rates of profit. He concludes that the rate of interest cannot reflect past or present rates because "*present* profits, as contra-distinguished from past or future, cannot be said to exist. When they have been realized, they are past; as long as they depend on a contingency, they are future or *expected* profits." Thus, the rate of interest only "indicates the degree of expectation of profit"; this is an "average" or a "long run" concept and "may be supposed to bear some proportion to the rate of profit" (1826, p. 7). However, even this weak link is rejected by Tooke on the grounds that, whereas the rate of interest is measured in money terms, the rate of profit is measured in kind. McCulloch, argues Tooke, has first to show that the two rates change together:

> ... to point out the invariable connection between the return to national capital, estimated in kind, and the returns to individual capitals, estimated in money; and in the next place, the invariable equality of the proportion of the whole national capital, compared with its productiveness, and of the supply of monied capital seeking secure investment, compared with the demand for the use of such capital, by persons having good security to offer, this latter being the condition by which the rate of interest is determined. (1826, p. 10)

Thus, the accepted doctrine has to establish a link between the real profit rate, determined in production, and the money interest rate, determined in the supply and demand for loans – what Tooke calls the "money market," and what we will describe as intermediation. Tooke claims that money is not only demanded for "reproduction, or in other words, for profitable employment"; a situation could arise in which "money capital may increase in greater ratio than the means of employing them." In that case, interest "may fall, as the returns to mercantile, or other professional skills rise." After criticizing McCulloch's views, Tooke proposes his own definition:

> I should define the rate of interest to be that proportional sum which the lender is content to receive, and the borrower to pay, annually, or for any longer or shorter period, for the use of a certain amount of *monied capital*,* without any consideration for trouble in the collection of the income, or for risk as to the punctual repayment of the interest or principal at the stipulated periods. (Tooke 1826, pp. 11–12).

The attached note that appeared in the original expands the distinctions and is at the core of the debates that we will follow:

> * To distinguish with perfect accuracy between *monied capital* and *currency* is a matter of some difficulty ... In general terms ... *monied capital* ... is lent on the security of bills, that is, on discount, on mortgage, or on any kind of security; – while *currency* is that *medium*, whether consisting of gold, notes, bills, or credit by which the purchase of commodities is effected (ibid., note).

In everyday language ("ordinary discourse"), both monied capital and currency are called money, but the former functions in production and the

latter in exchange. In making this distinction, Tooke declares that he is following Say:

In this view, the *rate of interest is the measure of the net profit on capital.* All returns
beyond this, on the employment of capital, are resolvable into compensations under
distinct heads, for risk, trouble, or skill, or for advantages of situation or connexion.
When the owner of a capital employs it actively in reproduction, he does not come
under the head of these capitalists, the proportion of whom, to the number of borrowers, determines the rate of interest. It is only that class of capitals, the owners
of which are unwilling or unable to employ their money actively themselves, which
has any immediate influence on the rate of interest. (1826, p. 12)

These "disposable monied capitals" come from three sources: (a) those who
do not want to take any risks or trouble when they "conduct their business according to correct banking principles"; (b) those who are willing to
take some trouble and maybe small risks (on mortgages and "good securities"); and (c) those who are willing to take higher risks. More monied
capital in the hands of the first two groups will tend to increase the share of
the "profits industries" as distinguished from "profits de capitaux," in Say's
terms (1826, pp. 15–16). All three groups are lenders of monied capital,
representing the supply side.

The demand for monied capital comes from: (a) those who can employ
more capital than they hold (and pay interest above their revenue); (b)
those who need this capital to complete a project (paying the interest from
their revenue); and (c) those "who have occasion to borrow, in order to supply the means of unproductive expenditure beyond their income" (p. 19).
Among the last group, Tooke includes what we call today foreign investment against "foreign governments' securities."

Tooke suggests that a method of investigating the rate of interest and
the rate of profit is to examine each of these factors "separately, the others
remaining the same, and then to trace the influence of any variation in each
class on all the others" (p. 20). This process is too lengthy, so Tooke explains
only the relation between the currency and the rate of interest. Suppose
the equilibrium – the "ordinary state" – is disturbed by "a sudden increase
in the issue of paper, by banks of circulation," while other circumstances
remain the same (p. 21). This could substantially reduce the rate of interest because the important factor is not the proportion of this addition to
the total "national capital," but its proportion to "the capital seeking investment, at any given time," which is much smaller. This drives lenders to risky
projects, to "hazardous investments"; for example, lenders will move from
investment (demand) of type (a) to type (c). If there are expectations for

price rises, then borrowers who can employ monied capital with profit (the first type) will demand more monied capital.

Tooke suggests measuring the rate of interest simply by the price of consols; when he tries to do so, he claims that the last period before the crisis of 1825 was marked both by rising demand from those who could employ more capital (type [a]) and by rising supply due to note-issuing and credit expansion by the banks. This is why the rate of interest did not fall, in spite of the fact that monied capital was augmented (in the demand for monied capital, he includes the demand by joint-stock banks, a point to which we shall return later). The increase in the currency in the form of gold, paper, or credit must reduce the rate of interest, "increase the number of lenders, or diminish the number of borrowers" and "raise the price of commodities and labor. But as almost every increase of paper, excepting what is paid by the bank for bullion, is issued in the way of loan, either to government, or to individuals, it is likely to affect the rate of interest in the first instance, before it comes in contact with commodities" (pp. 23–24, note).

This is a fairly sophisticated theory of the rate of interest, and one is tempted to suggest that Tooke places himself outside the mainstream of classical thought by suggesting that monetary phenomena have an effect on the "real" side of the economy. Usually this is understood to mean a causal relationship between money and "real" factors such as employment, accumulation, or distribution. The classicists considered the rate of profit to be one of the "real" phenomena; because for most of them, including Ricardo, the rate of interest reflected the rate of profit, this was also part of the real side of the economy. Positing that the rate of interest could be influenced by monetary phenomena could undermine their basic belief that monetary phenomena, though important for the new society, do not change real economic phenomena, which continue to act as they do in a barter economy.

At this stage in the development of his theory, Tooke does not question this proposition. First, his rate of profit is a monetary phenomenon and does not reflect the real rate of profit. Second, like Ricardo, he claims that the influence of monetary factors on the rate of interest is transitory:

When the amount of the currency has become settled, for any length of time, at a particular level, it is immaterial, as relates to the rate of interest, whether the level of the currency be at one half or at double of its former value: the rate of interest will then be governed entirely by the supply of, and demand for, capital ... every alteration in the amount of currency produced a temporary effect upon the rate of interest. (p. 24n)

It is interesting to note that the theory of interest was one of the few aspects of Tooke's theory to remain unchanged through the major revisions of later years.

In his 1826 text, Tooke uses his wave theory in conjunction with this newly developed analysis of the rate of interest to explain the 1825 crisis. After 1822, prices, especially in agriculture, rose as a result of less-than-average harvests on the one hand and increasing population on the other. This caused an increase in circulation that lowered the rate of interest: "The fall in the rate of interest, which was to a certain extent, the effect of the increased issue of paper, became, in its turn, a cause of speculation, and thence of a further increase of the circulation, by the facilities which it afforded for the use and abuse of credit" (1826, p. 42). This chain reaction, moving from commodities whose prices had risen to those whose prices had yet to rise, encouraged "speculators" and brokers "to look minutely through the General Price Currents, with a view to discovering any article which had not advanced, in order to make it the subject of anticipated demand" (1826, p. 48). Many people were involved in these speculations which, Tooke estimates, expanded the circulating medium, including credit, by 50 percent; he bases this estimate on the fact that without any scarcity in terms of quantity, prices went up by about this percentage (1826, pp. 52–53).

As was clear to "any person not possessed by the mania," there was "no solid foundation for the general rise of prices." The mechanism that reduces prices works through gold movements: High prices cause reflux of gold, which reduces prices. The events "proved" this reasoning. Seventy banks failed in December 1825; people refused to use bank notes and used gold, which was in great shortage, together with Bank of England notes. The Bank of England was very close to a new suspension, and only a new issue of one-pound notes and the influx of gold after the reduction in prices saved the country.

As noted, Tooke's analysis of the rate of interest remains consistent before and after the development of his new Banking School views. The development of the banking system and the rise of credit, together with the successive crises (1836–1837, 1839), attracted attention to the relation between prices and the rate of interest. Tooke argued in 1844 that confusion on this subject is even greater than on others. The term "money" is used both in the Stock Exchange and in the Money Market synonymously with capital, but it is not the same (see chapter 13 in the 1844 text).

Tooke rejects the Currency School argument that when money is "abundant" or "cheap," it is followed by a low rate of interest. In his view, the value of money refers both to the "value of exchange of commodities" and to the "value in use of capital" or, in other words, to purchasing power and the rate of interest respectively. Tooke quotes Gilbart (*Westminster Review*, January 1841) to illustrate the prevailing confusion:

... suppose the circulation is at its proper amount and the Bank should purchase a million of exchequer bills, the notes *thus put in circulation* not finding immediate employment might be returned to the Bank, and be lodged on deposit. *Here there would be no increase in the circulation, but an increase of a million in the deposits. A power of purchase to the extent of a million sterling* ... would have the effect of advancing the prices of commodities... (Tooke 1844, p. 78)

Tooke does not accept Gilbart's argument:

A power of purchase might thus doubtless be created; but why should it be directed to the purchase of commodities if there was nothing in the state of supply, relatively to the rate of consumption, to afford the prospect of gain on the necessary eventual resale? ... The error is in supposing the *disposition* or *will* to be co-extensive with the power. The limit to the motive for the exercise of the power is in the prospect of resale with a profit. (ibid., p. 79)

Tooke argues that though it is customary to connect a low rate of interest with high prices on the grounds that low interest encourages advances that create deposits and thus "power of purchase," this is not in fact the case. A low rate of interest increases advances against securities and therefore does not raise prices. On the contrary, a low rate of interest reduces costs, and the result is a fall in prices.[25] "A general reduction in the rate of interest is equivalent to or rather constitutes a diminution of the cost of production" (p. 81). The situation with shares is different: "A low rate of interest is almost synonymous with high price of securities (including shares)" (p. 86). Thus, Tooke's approach to the determination of the rate of interest as well as its relationship with prices did not change from his early formulations. We will return to Tooke's analysis of the rate of interest and its impact on prices when we address the writings of Wicksell, a person who studied Tooke's approach to the rate of interest and prices thoroughly.

Monetary Policy and the Bank after 1844[26]

Tooke's and the Banking School's defeat in the 1844 debate left them wondering about the future success of the Act. The two crises that followed in 1847

---

[25] See my Chapter 18 on Wicksell as well as Wicksell (1935, pp. 131–187); also see Laidler (1972).
[26] This section draws on Arnon (1991, chapter 9).

and 1857 convinced them that although they had lost the debate, they were not on the wrong side. They did not believe, either before the passing of the Act or later, that the Currency Principle and the strict rule of conduct for the Issue Department of the Bank of England that followed from it would make good monetary policy. But what is a good policy? The answer to this crucial question, which requires a theory of monetary policy, was not clear. Tooke struggled with an answer in the years after 1844 until his death in 1858.

As we have seen, the role played by the different forms of assets and liabilities and whether they should be treated differently was at the forefront of the disagreements between the Currency and Banking Schools. In Tooke's view, the Currency School had overlooked two points in the relationship between convertible bank notes and inconvertible paper money: the mode of issue and what Fullarton had called the Principle of Reflux, which Tooke adopted after 1844. Convertible bank notes were issued through the mechanism of discounts and loans, but in no way was the amount of bank notes in circulation equal to the amount of loans and discounts. The reason for this was that the sum given by the Bank of England could be in the form of book credit, gold, or notes; the actual form depended upon the needs of the person receiving the loan. This was the reason why the Bank of England could not regulate the amount of notes in circulation through the mechanism of discounts and loans. The country banks were in the same position. Their advances could be taken either in their own notes, in Bank of England notes, or in a bill on London or some place else. Even if more notes, either Bank of England notes or country notes, "could be forced into the hands of the public, there is an operation constantly going on which would almost instantaneously reduce the amount" (Tooke 1848, p. 185). This operation was the outcome of the Law of Reflux discussed first by Fullarton.

The crisis of 1847 had many features similar to that of 1825, and in Tooke's view, it furnished further proof for the correctness of his position in his argument with the Currency School. "The charge against the act is not that it was the originating cause, but that it greatly aggravated the operation for all the other existing causes of commercial failures and distress" (IV, p. 328). This, claimed Tooke, was what he had expected on a theoretical basis in 1844 (1844, p. 124). In the fourth volume of *The History of Prices*, published in 1848 as well as before the Commons' Committee of the same year, Tooke explained how the 1847 crisis was aggravated by the 1844 Act.

Will you explain to the Committee your view of the manner in which the Act of 1844 operated in 1847, so as to render the crisis more severe? – It operated by diminishing the power of the Bank to grant accommodation in consequence of the narrow limit of its banking reserve, instead of allowing the Bank, as it would have had the power of doing but for that Act, to grant extended accommodation at a moderately increased rate of interest. (Parliamentary Papers, 1848, Q.5310, p. 411)

Thus, Tooke's criticism mainly focused on the inability of the banking system to react properly to the unfolding events. The fact that the 1844 Bank Act was effectively canceled, relaxing those clauses that restricted the issue of Bank notes, caused Tooke to comment, somewhat triumphantly:

> Were the occasion less grave, it would be calculated to excite a smile to observe the great anxiety of ministers to justify their sanction of a contingent infringement of the law, when the real, and as I conceive, the unanswerable charge against them, was that of having withheld it too long. (Tooke 1848, p. 320)

The "infringement of the law" in 1847 was in the form of a letter to the governor and deputy governor of the Bank, "recommending to the directors to enlarge the amount of their discounts and advances upon approved security, but suggesting that the rate of interest should not be less than 8 per cent" (Tooke 1848, p. 319). Thus, the 1847 crisis brought back to the forefront the question of the right policy of the Bank's directors. However, this time it was much clearer to the participants that they were in fact debating the desired level of discretion, if any, that should be allowed the Bank's directors, as well as the best tools to be used by them.

Instead of the strict rules of the 1844 Bank Act, Tooke continued to support a more flexible banking system stabilized by and based on a big reserve of bullion. This would leave the Bank's directors much broader margins in the face of (transitory) gold drains. In case the drain should continue beyond what was considered "transitory," the directors would react by increasing the rate of interest, which was their first policy tool. If this discretionary action should prove insufficient and the drain continued, the Bank's directors would have complete discretion to take whatever "corrective measure" they deemed necessary. They would evaluate the economic conditions and enjoy absolute power as to how and when to react, if at all. Any guidelines, such as the exact amounts of reserves that justify a change of course regarding the rate of interest or, later, the implementation of the unspecified "corrective measures," were explicitly rejected by Tooke.

> Q. And you would begin to take corrective measures as soon as you pass 6,000,000l.? – Yes, and the extent of those measures, and the degree of restriction of accommodation must be left to the judgment of the directors, it being quite impossible to point out beforehand any limit, and to say it shall not go below a certain amount under any circumstances. (Parliamentary Papers 1848a, pp. 419–420)

When asked whether predetermining an amount as the "upper" limit, below which changes in the rate of interest should be considered, would not lead to an "alarm" in case the reserves should actually fall below this amount, Tooke replied: "I would not say that that should be a regulation; I am quite sure that you must leave it to the discretion of some man or some body of men; no doubt they are fallible in their judgment, and the Bank directors have sometimes signally failed in their judgment" (ibid., p. 420).

Tooke's conclusion, that since 1844 the Bank's directors had complete discretion regarding their liabilities other than notes, as well as in their other powers such as determining the rate of interest, led him to suggest "improvements of the Governing Body of the Bank." Whereas in 1848 Tooke trusted the directors of the Bank and favored "discretion of the existing body," eight years later he expressed his disappointment. He thought that they were not ready for their important tasks, mainly because he had a "very unfavorable opinion of their judgment." Improving the governing body of the Bank was also Tooke's major answer to some of his critics, who wanted him to propose a "Scheme or Plan" of his own in case the 1844 Act was repealed.

The natural next step was to suggest some form of credit policy. This was done, implicitly and indirectly, through leaving total discretion to the Bank's directors regarding all their liabilities. One should understand Tooke's efforts to improve the management of the Bank in this light. In a way, Tooke inverted the assumptions contained in the famous Palmer rule and supported complete discretion on the Bank's credit, instead of the rule on all the various liabilities. This was a major change, because he himself thought in 1844 that "no one would be mad enough to attempt to interfere ... with the management of establishments for borrowing and lending money." Thus, in later years, Tooke came very close to accepting this "mad" idea. However, as close as he was to formulating central banking policy on credit, a full discussion of such a policy is missing. In his view, the Bank's directors should be directed by the prevailing economic conditions in formulating their policies. No specific model on targets and tools was provided. It was left entirely to the intuition of the directors, in the best tradition of complete discretion, to shape their different reactions under various circumstances

Before the Lords' Committee of 1848, which inquired into the causes of the distress, Tooke pointed out his rivals' inconsistency with regard to legislation of credit:

Would not your Evidence rather go to show that a Restriction should be imposed upon the Bank of England in respect to the Management of its Banking as well as its Issue Department? To be consistent it would. The only Mode in which any Restriction could be imposed upon the Banking Department would be to say that for their liabilities they should hold a certain Amount of Bullion; not that I conceive that it would be practicable, but that would be the consistent Course; it would however be perfectly impracticable. I only point out the Inconsistency. I never could understand, from the Moment it was proposed, why there should be a different Guarantee to the Public for the Notes of the Bank as compared with its other Obligations. (Q.3136, p. 352)

Tooke raises this point again that same year in Volume IV of the *History of Prices*. In a discussion of Peel's speech of 1844, Tooke quotes Peel as saying: "We think that the privilege of issue is one which may fairly and justly be controlled by the state, and that *the banking business*, as distinguished from issue, *is a matter in respect of which there cannot be too unlimited and unrestricted a competition.*" Tooke comments:

[This is] *exactly the reverse* of the conclusion which can alone be legitimately derived from a correct view of the nature of the separate functions of, and of the distinction between, currency and capital. To the extent to which regulation is desirable or admissible, it is, fact, much more required to avert the dangers of excessive competition of banking than of issue. (Tooke 1848, pp. 250–251; Tooke's italics)

However, Tooke did not go all the way with this conclusion and recommend, as he probably should have, the desirability of controlling credit. On the contrary, he recommended giving complete discretion to the competitive bankers, leaving no one responsible for the outcome of the various decisions. This left his position open to the many attacks that followed.

In 1856, Tooke published a pamphlet *On the Bank Charter Act of 1844*, a retrospective on the previous twelve years of the Bank's policy.[27] Since the passing of the 1844 Bank Act, the directors of the Bank of England had assumed that they were free in their "Banking Business" like any other joint-stock bank. This mistake, argued Tooke, was even greater than the one concerning the erroneous rule that they imposed on issuing notes. The main reason for this mistaken assumption was that they had overlooked the central role of the Bank in the payments system and the Bank's influence on the exchanges, the state of credit, and, most of all, the convertibility of notes. Paradoxically, the Bank directors were restricted after 1844 in their

---

[27] Many of the arguments were repeated in 1857 when the last two volumes of *History of Prices* appeared. These volumes were written in collaboration with William Newmarch. In the introduction, Tooke explains that they wrote different parts, with Tooke writing the first part on the prices of corn and the seasons in the years 1842–1856 and the fifth part "On the Management and Policy of the Bank of England during the period 1844–1856." This last section was mainly a repetition of his 1856 pamphlet.

actions in that department over which they had no power whatsoever, while at the same time, they had complete freedom in the department where their discretionary actions were most important:

> As a general proposition, it may be laid down, and has been shown, that the Issue Department is (as it was before 1844) *acted upon by* the Public; – while the Banking Department continues (as it did before 1844) to *act upon the Public*. – Thus producing a result *the very reverse* of that contemplated by the propounders of the scheme of separation. If, then, the due regulation of the currency, in any intelligible sense of the expression, depends, as it undoubtedly does, upon the Banking Department and not upon the Issue Department, it is the height of inconsistency to restrict the latter, and to leave the former wholly at the discretion of the Directors. (Tooke and Newmarch 1857, Vol. V, pp. 546–547)

The 1856 pamphlet and the final volumes of the *History of Prices* contain even clearer thoughts about the Bank's responsibilities and the need to defend the monetary system. We will return to these early manifestations of defensive monetary policy in Chapter 18.

Wilson, the *Economist*, and the Public Debate

James Wilson (1805–1860) was an important contributor to the debate on the side of the Banking School, especially after 1844 and mainly through the public debate. He came from a Quaker family, the fourth of fifteen children of a family involved in the wool industry. He and his brother set up a hat manufacturing firm in London in 1824. He soon became involved in the Anti–Corn Laws movement; he published a pamphlet in favor of Laissez Faire in 1839 entitled *Influences of the Corn Laws* and published another in 1840 entitled *Fluctuations of Currency, Commerce and Manufacturers*. The two publications established him a "chief theoretician of the Anti-Corn Law League" (Boot 1983, p. 567). In 1843, he created the famous *Economist* newspaper to advance free trade on the basis of "pure principles" and open debate. His many contributions appeared often in the newspaper's editorials, and a collection of them was published in the 1847 volume, *Capital, Currency and Banking*. From the time of its creation until the present day, the *Economist* has had a very significant influence on the public debate. The family was heavily involved in the paper; Wilson's daughter Eliza married Walter Bagehot, who edited the *Economist* after Wilson's early death in India, and to whom we will return in Chapter 14.

Wilson was well connected and appreciated in the free-trade movement. He was a Liberal MP from 1847, first for Westbury and later for Devonport, and he held many important positions in Parliament and government.

He was a member of the Commons select committee on commercial distress in 1847–1848; a secretary at the India Board of Control, where he helped the development of the Indian railway system; and was financial secretary to the treasury. He was close to Lord Palmerston, who in 1856 offered him the governorship of the Australian colony of Victoria, an offer that was retracted in the face of the queen's objections. In 1859, he was asked to become the de facto Chancellor of the Exchequer in India. He had worked there for less than a year on a set of reforms on taxation, paper currency, and the financial system when he died from a sudden illness in July 1860 in Calcutta.

Wilson did not receive much attention for his role in promoting the free-trade movement, his activities and ideas concerning the Anti–Corn League, his interest in the miserable Irish economic condition, or his contributions to the debate on money and banking around the Bank Act. However, as Norman – the third persona in the Currency School Trio – was in many ways that school's important link to the real world through his position as a governor at the Bank, so Wilson was in many ways an essential link to the real world of public life for the Banking School.

Conclusion

Rereading and reinterpreting the monetary debate of the 1840s has produced quite different evaluations over the years. As Laidler commented in his account of Tooke (1972), one can find in the secondary literature those who are more sympathetic to the Currency School, like Gregory, and those who seem to be more sympathetic to the Banking School, like Fetter. In the same paper, Laidler mentions that it would be "a fascinating study in itself to trace the evolution of opinion about nineteenth century monetary controversy" from the various later interpretations (p. 168 n 2). He did not take up this task, but Skaggs accepted the challenge and in 1999 published a typology of twentieth-century views of the debate. It is of course, by definition, an unfinished business.

The issues with which Tooke struggled are of utmost importance in any monetary economy and are still debated today. Thus, it is not surprising that his views influenced many later economists of various traditions. Both Marx and Wicksell, for example, read Tooke carefully and were influenced by his writings. His later Banking School positions, wherein Tooke defended the endogeneity of money, the "inverse" causality between money and prices (from P to M and not, as traditional theory assumes, from M to P), and the immense importance of credit, have resurfaced frequently during the one hundred fifty years since Tooke first stated them. Echoes of similar views can be found today in the writings of the new classical economics, the new monetary economics, and the post-Keynesian tradition. The same is true concerning Tooke's more general position on free trade in banking. Rules versus discretion, or no intervention at all, are still open questions in monetary theory. Modern "Quantity Theorists" like Friedman accepted the need to control the quantity of the medium in circulation, and preferred rules over discretionary policies on the part of the central bank. However, with the transformation in his thought and increasingly toward the end of his life, Tooke, somewhat like Hayek, was drawn to the possibility of applying free-trade principles to banking, at least to the note-issuing business, if not to credit in general. These changing positions and views are relevant for the present-day's evolving financial system, where deregulation and financial innovation are reshaping the meaning of money and credit.

Appendix: A Note on J. S. Mill's Monetary Thinking

J. S. Mill (1806–1873) was probably the best-known and most influential political economist during the third quarter of the nineteenth century. His influence has been described as coming from his canonization of classical economics through novel interpretations of others' works, efforts to synthesize the classicals, and some of his own original achievements.[28] Mill's status was partly due to the central place his *Principles of Political Economy* came to occupy after its publication in 1848. As the son of a political economist whose strict education became legendary, Mill started reading and writing early on in life. In the field of money and banking, he was considered to be one who tended toward the Banking School point of view without being associated with that school's more controversial and opinionated positions. He had a personal relationship with Thomas Tooke through Tooke's son Eyton, who was the same age as Mill and was one of his closest friends until Eyton's suicide in 1830.

Mill's monetary writings appeared in early reviews of monetary tracts, among them Tooke's first book, *Thoughts*, in 1823, the review of which Mill wrote when he was only seventeen, as well as Tooke's and Torrens' *Inquiry* in 1844; in an 1826 paper, "Paper Currency and Commercial Distress," written after the 1825 crisis and influenced by Tooke's 1826 pamphlet; in two famous papers, "On the Influence of Consumption Upon Production" and "Of Profits, and Interest," written in 1829 but published only in 1844 in

---

[28] See Hollander (1985) and Skaggs (1994).

Essays on Some Unsettled Question of Political Economy; in several papers
on the Bank Act; and, of course, in monetary sections in the *Principles*.[29]

As Skaggs observes, Mill aligns himself with the Banking School during
the 1844 debate but in later writings he moves to a more centrist position
between the two schools, so much so that by the 1870s, he is considered a
key founder of the British monetary orthodoxy – an orthodoxy that is not
that of the Banking School – on certain important issues.[30] Skaggs (1994)
makes an interesting, though controversial, case for reading Mill's 1826 text
as an early Banking School position, making Mill the historical father of the
school. It is clear that neither Mill nor his contemporaries read this paper as
such a radical analysis, and other students of Mill, like Hollander (1985), do
not share this view. As Fetter (1965, pp. 225–227) and Laidler (1991, chapter 2) observe, in the 1860s and 1870s, Mill's views represent the orthodoxy
that accepted neither the Currency School nor the Banking School views.
Certainly on some key issues, like the attitude to the Quantity Theory, Mill
was not aligned with the Banking School. As important a figure as he was, it
is beyond the scope of this book to fully cover Mill's monetary writings. We
will return to Mill and the British monetary orthodoxy briefly in Chapter
14 on Bagehot.

---

[29] On J. S. Mill's monetary thinking, see Hollander (1985, chapter 8); Skaggs (1994); and
      Laidler (1991).
[30] See Hollander (1985), Laidler (1991), Skaggs (1994) and my discussion in Chapter 15.

THIRTEEN

Neither Currency Nor Banking School:

Joplin and the "Free Banking" Parnell

Introduction

The debate around the 1844 Bank Act, with its strong camp of victorious supporters and its very visible opposition, hides the fact that there were scholars who were not associated with either the Currency School or the Banking School. In fact, a perusal of the literature of the 1830s and 1840s reveals that there were probably more people who did not identify themselves with one of the two quarreling positions than who did. However, as is the case with such formative and public debates, the pressure to take sides was high; because the debate continued in some form into the 1850s and even 1860s, those who rejected both positions faced difficult times and were in many cases neglected. Two currents of thought outside of both the Banking School and the Currency School deserve our attention. The first is represented by Thomas Joplin and the second by a group that received the label "Free Banking School." I will address the latter mainly through Henry Parnell.

Thomas Joplin (1790–1847)

Joplin's importance in the history of monetary theory has been enhanced in recent years by the scholarly efforts of Denis P. O'Brien, who in 1993 published an important monograph entitled *Thomas Joplin and Classical Macroeconomics*. O'Brien has since continued to promote Joplin as a more significant scholar than those of the two Trios, and argues that Joplin deserves more credit than he received from his contemporaries or has received in the secondary literature. In this survey of Joplin, we will follow both Joplin's unique views and the changes in the thinking of his major interpreter, O'Brien.

After almost three decades of scholarly research into classical economics, starting in the mid-1960s, O'Brien filled a gap in the history of monetary thought with a fascinating book on Joplin. When O'Brien published his monograph, Joplin was a relatively neglected economist. This is no longer the case. O'Brien has not only brought Joplin to the attention of historians of economic thought, but has tried valiantly, and in my view quite success-fully, to establish him as one of the most original thinkers among the classi-cals. O'Brien admits that he himself was taken by surprise by what he found when he read Joplin carefully – so much so that he declares the outcome of his research to be "a highly subversive document for it suggests that previ-ous work on classical monetary economics, including my own (for Joplin has changed my mind), has adopted a faulty perspective" (1993, p. 1).

The "faulty perspective" was clearly outlined by O'Brien himself in his textbook *The Classical Economists* (1975), in a chapter entitled "Classical Monetary Theory."[1] According to accepted wisdom at the time, including O'Brien's, two major schools of thought struggled to shape British mon-etary institutions in the second quarter of the nineteenth century: the Currency School and the Banking School.[2] Joplin, O'Brien argues later, was not an advocate of either the Currency School or the Banking School, but rather constituted his own one-man camp and had a better understanding of money and banking than both schools.[3] Joplin's personal story partially explains his lack of influence over his contemporaries, who did not register him as an important theoretician. He was personally lonely and isolated and had little influence on policy makers throughout his life; O'Brien goes so far as to describe him as socially miserable. He also had serious finan-cial difficulties. However, according to O'Brien's work in 1993 and since, Joplin managed not only to change the course of British banking institu-tions through his contribution to the creation of joint-stock banking, but formulated a very modern and sophisticated macroeconomic model and

---

[1] Chapter 6, pp. 140–169; a second, somewhat revised, edition appeared in 2004.
[2] In recent years, some of the modern advocates of free banking argued that during those years there existed a third Free Banking School. I will return to this claim later.
[3] In the 2004 second edition of *The Classical Economists*, O'Brien basically repeats his 1975 arguments, including this claim: "no doubt that the Currency School had the better of the argument with the Banking School on a theoretical plane." He added, "Nevertheless the Banking School were correct to stress the difficulties of contraction, and the vulnerability of the Banking Department, as well as the importance of deposits and (after a while) the last-resort role of the Bank" (2004, pp. 189–190). But because of his research he adds a new section on Joplin that begins: "One dissenter from both the Currency School and the Banking School deserves special mention, however. Thomas Joplin, the abrasive pioneer of joint stock banking, was convinced by the analysis of neither side, though his model was much closer to that of the Currency than that of the Banking School" (see pp. 190–191).

discovered some of the most important concepts in monetary theory – all without being given due credit.

The "faulty perspective" that in O'Brien's new view needs to be changed concerns the determinants of the price level and the latter's role in the economy. The conventional perspective, certainly that of the Currency School, attributed the central role in determining the price level to the amount of Bank of England notes in circulation. Joplin emphasized the role of country banks' notes, which were neither regulated nor controlled by the Bank. Thus, Joplin maintained that the country banks played a crucial role both in determining the price level and in influencing real activity and the balance of payments. This original perspective was contrary to that of the Currency School but did not match that of the Banking School either, because Joplin accepted the Quantity Theory. Paradoxically, Joplin objected to the 1844 Bank Act, although already in 1823 he had argued for the concept of "metallic fluctuations," which – according to O'Brien – others including Loyd and even Ricardo, shamelessly borrowed from him while denying him due credit (O'Brien 1993, pp. 70–72). In a later paper (2003), O'Brien added that at almost the same time, in 1825, Joplin discovered and advocated the principles of central banking, making him a kind of intellectual bridge between Thornton and Bagehot. Furthermore, Joplin developed a comprehensive macromodel that O'Brien describes as neo-Keynesian in nature.[4] Let us elaborate on these topics.

The Newly Discovered Joplin

In *Thomas Joplin and Classical Macroeconomics*, O'Brien claims that Joplin's writings represent, in fact, a sophisticated model that can be described as neo-Keynesian. It is not clear whether the implication is that a modern, "neo-Keynesian" position existed among the classicals or that Joplin presents a theory different from that of the other classicals. The macroeconomic model presented by O'Brien using the modern tradition of equations and identities that deal with income, expenditure, and aggregate demand, does not seem to us to be classical (see chapter 5, O'Brien, 1993).

For the purposes of our discussions of monetary theory and control, part III of O'Brien's book, "The Banking System," has the greatest significance. It starts with chapter 8 on "The Principle of Metallic Fluctuation," which maintains that the quantity of money should behave as if it is made up of only gold coins; money is defined to include coins and bank notes – those of the Bank of England and the country banks as well – but not other mediums of payment. Thus, Joplin's Metallic Fluctuations Concept is similar to the Currency

---

4   O'Brien (1997) also tested statistically the claims made by Joplin.

Principle discussed in our Chapter 11, which states that actual money (in the Currency School view of money as bank notes and coins) should imitate that which would have circulated were no other means of payments used. The Currency School also believed that the country banks distorted the workings of the principle and hence should be excluded from issuing notes. According to Joplin, and O'Brien strongly concurs, the Metallic Fluctuations Principle was first formalized by Joplin himself in 1823 as a criticism of the Bullionists and their adherence to convertibility. The Bullionists, as noted in my Chapter 6 and Chapter 8, considered convertibility to be a sufficient safeguard or guideline for the proper behavior of the money supply. In the 1820s and 1830s, many political economists rejected the idea that convertibility alone could provide a sound enough mechanism for regulating the quantity of money. These critics wanted money to behave as a metallic circulation would have; hence the importance of the Metallic Fluctuations Principle. Since the principle played such an important role in the debate on monetary reform that eventually led to the 1844 Bank Act, it is worth elaborating further on its history.

Did Joplin Discover "Metallic Fluctuations"?

My view is that the Metallic Fluctuations Principle, or Currency Principle, had in fact been the implicit and sometimes explicit basis for the monetary theories of economists such as Hume and maybe even Adam Smith. Hume's famous Price-Specie-Flow mechanism links gold flows and the price level via money supply. The adherence of Hume and the Bullionists, including Ricardo, to convertibility was intended to leave the determination of the quantity of money to the "natural" forces at work in Hume's mechanism. They assumed that these natural forces would guarantee the metallic fluctuations that they desired. Furthermore, the opponents of inconvertibility maintained that Hume's mechanism failed to work during the Restriction because of the separation of the internal from the international means of payments. Thus, the Metallic Fluctuations Concept was present in discussions well before the 1820s.

O'Brien tells us that Joplin restated the "charge of plagiarizing" against Ricardo no less than eight times over the period from 1824 to 1846. The charges, although softened somewhat over the years, still left "a number of puzzles about the whole episode," writes O'Brien; "[It] seems unlikely that [Ricardo] would consciously have engaged in intellectual theft" (1993, p. 72). O'Brien goes on to remind us that, as later scholars pointed out, the *High Price of Bullion* was also not an original contribution. However, the real puzzle, argues O'Brien, is that modern scholars did not investigate the origins of metallic fluctuations.

Joplin's case had been made by Joplin himself and not by others. His contemporaries did not give him credit, and the secondary literature also did not recognize his priority.[5] A partial explanation for the puzzle, provided by Joplin himself (1832, pp. 178–189), brings in the notorious tradition of withholding credit. The fact that Ricardo himself had not received due credit for the Bullion Report, argued Joplin, may have caused him to infer that he could behave similarly:

> But the concealing of his [Ricardo] name, when it was well known, gave a greater sanction to such frauds, than if it had not been known: for it showed that the concealment was dictated by no wish to rob him, but was right in itself. That, in short, it would be neither proper nor dignified in a Committee to make such acknowledgments; and it was beneath the dignity of a Parliamentary Committee to acknowledge any obligation to an individual, though that individual might be Mr. Ricardo, by an easy transition it was beneath the dignity of Mr. Ricardo, a member of parliament, and a distinguished author, to acknowledge an obligation to an obscure person like myself. (Joplin 1832, p. 184, quoted in O'Brien, p. 71)

Thus, there are proper and improper credits, and to acknowledge Joplin would have been incorrect. One tends to cite those persons whose reputations will lend weight to an argument.

We would like to propose a different, somewhat less accusatory explanation for this enigma. As mentioned earlier, the idea of metallic fluctuations had been discussed in many circles during the Restriction Period and, subsequently, after the transition from inconvertibility to convertibility. The issue is still under debate; some scholars believe that the notion of metallic fluctuations can be found in Ricardo's writings before 1823.[6] The ideas concerning the "right" amount of paper money under conditions of convertibility seem to be present in Ricardo's 1816 text:

> The amount of notes in circulation depends in no degree on the amount of capital possessed by the issuers of notes, but on the amount required for the circulation of the country; which is regulated, as I have before attempted to shew, by the value

---

[5] Robbins noted the accusation, "but dismissed it without argument" writes O'Brien). See O'Brien (1993, p. 72) Robbins (1958, p. 101n). Viner is quoted favorably by O'Brien as the "only commentator to give Joplin any credit for this important intellectual development." But many others did not: Neither Horsefield nor Sraffa, who edited Ricardo's collected works, nor any other modern scholar, looked into Joplin's accusations.

[6] O'Brien does not agree: "[It] is quite clear that his [Joplin's] development of the principle of 'metallic fluctuations' did not derive from Ricardo, not least because, despite the efforts of later commentators to find the principle in Ricardo's works it is not in fact there" (O'Brien 1993, p. 70). A note attached to this paragraph refers to Horsefield (1944) who cites Ricardo, 1816, section IV, which we cite next.

of the standard, the amount of payments, and the economy practised in effecting them. (Ricardo 1816, IV, p. 109)

Thus, convertibility is perceived as the mechanism that will assure that the amount in circulation is "right." Moreover, a year later, in the chapter on "Currency and Banking" of the *Principles*, in a section that Sraffa claimed contains an early formulation of the 1824 ideas (see Ricardo IV, p. 272), one can read: "A currency is in its most perfect state when it consists wholly of paper money, but of paper money of an equal value with the gold which it professed to represent." The claim that what Ricardo had in mind was probably the substitution of a *quantity* of gold coins by paper notes is supported by the following argument from the *Principles of Political Economy*:

Suppose that a million of money should be required to fit an expedition. If the State issued a million of paper, and displaced a million of coin, the expedition would be fitted out without any charge to the people; but if a Bank issued a million of paper, and lent it to Government at 7 per cent ... the society would in either case be as wealthy. (Ricardo 1817, I, pp. 361–363)

The advantage is in the "improvement of our system, by rendering capital of the value of a million productive." This is a well-known Smithian position. Shortly after, in the evidence presented before the 1819 committees that inquired into the Resumption of cash payments, Ricardo stated:

I always call paper depreciated when the market price exceeds the mint price of gold, because I conceive that there is then a greater quantity of circulating media than what there would have been if we were obliged to make our paper currency conform to the value of coin, and which we are obliged to do, whenever the bank pay in specie. (PP 1819, p. 140)

Thus, convertibility is the mechanism that imposes the working of metallic fluctuations. The link to international transactions is clearly manifested in this evidence. The major difference between inconvertible and convertible notes is that the former are not used in international transactions: "a bank note not payable in specie is confined to our circulation, and cannot make a foreign payment ..." The crucial point is the equilibrating mechanism which functions only under convertibility. This brings in the balance of payments:

You must be convinced, that between two trading countries, there must be a balance one way or the other?
- Those purchases and sales appear to me to be guided a great deal by the relative value of the currencies of the two countries; that any cause which shall operate to encrease the value of one, would have an effect upon its commercial transactions

with the other, and consequently the exchange would be affected by an increase or diminution in the value of the currency of either. (ibid., p. 141)

Thus, the Price-Specie-Flow mechanism is the mechanism which will create the natural distribution of gold and restore equilibrium.

Interestingly, a further confirmation of the claim that the Currency Principle or the metallic fluctuations were present in discussions of monetary issues before 1823 can be found in Joplin himself. In his *An Analysis and History of the Currency Question* (1832), he quotes Adam Smith favorably on the proper amount of paper money in circulation. Assuming convertibility, that amount "'... never can exceed the value of the gold and silver of which it supplies the place, or which (the commerce being supposed the same) would circulate there, if there was no paper money.' (Smith Book II chapter 2) This, of course, as he [Smith] elsewhere lays down, is the proper amount of paper required," argues Joplin (1832, p. 20). In the same text, summarizing Smith's views, Joplin writes: "3. That the amount of Notes which the country required was an amount equal to the sum of metallic money which would circulate if there were no paper" (ibid., p. 27). Thus, even according to Joplin's own reading of the history of monetary thought, the concept of metallic fluctuations had been present in discussions for quite some time.

As we argued earlier, Ricardo's thinking before 1824 was based on the Price-Specie-Flow mechanism. The mechanism was perceived as providing an automatic procedure that would be effective in determining the right amount of money under the conditions of a mixed circulation, as long as notes were strictly convertible. Ricardo's change of mind in 1824 was provoked by his doubts about whether convertibility had provided sufficient conditions for the mechanism to work. His answer turned out to be negative, a change of mind that could have been influenced by Joplin. In one of his later accounts of the encounter between Ricardo and himself, Joplin wrote:

I also communicated with the late Mr. Ricardo on the subject, and found him favorable to the proposition, though he denied its necessity; for he had written a pamphlet to prove, that the agricultural distress had not been produced by any contraction of the currency, but by over-production.

I requested him to take the matter up, which he engaged to do, and after his death in the following year, it appeared he had prepared a pamphlet on the subject, which was published, and which contains the principles of my plan, with alterations of his own as to the manner of carrying it out. (Joplin 1840, pp. 14–15).

The discussions between Ricardo and Joplin might have contributed to Ricardo's last efforts, efforts that culminated in writing his new monetary theory. The implications of the new theory were not fully understood by many contemporaries or by many later observers (see Arnon 1987 and Chapter 8). Joplin, in contrast, recognized the importance of the new 1824 thinking. Our claim, however, is that there is no proof, beyond Joplin's own statements, that Ricardo plagiarized Joplin.

In all events, Joplin's plan and Ricardo's proposals were quite similar. Joplin's metallic plan included his famous proposal for the creation of joint-stock banks as well as detailed recommendations for how the money-supply process should be controlled. The basic plan was based on the idea of Bullion Commissioners who would supervise and control the issue of bank notes. First, the quantity of notes in equilibrium would be estimated and distributed between the joint-stock banks, which would pay seigniorage (3 percent) to the government in exchange for the right to issue notes. The Bullion Commissioners would be the only ones who dealt in gold; they would issue receipts against the purchase of bullion. Presentation of these receipts to a joint-stock bank would enable that bank to issue notes; the receipt would be deposited with the Bullion Commissioners, and the bank would credit the sum. The banks could write checks on the Bullion Commissioners in exchange for their notes, and the checks could then be used either to claim bullion from the Bullion Commissioners for exporting purposes, or could be deposited in another bank. In such an event, the latter (receiving) bank's credit with the Bullion Commissioners would increase and more of its notes would enter circulation, while the notes of the former (paying) bank would decrease. The basic idea is that note circulation would behave like an ideal pure circulation ruled by the metallic principle.

In Joplin's view, the major obstacle to the appropriate functioning of the system was the missing link between bullion flows and the money supply. That missing link had been caused by the fact that gold flows influenced the "money market" and not the money supply. The "money market" was located in London, where the banks and other financial institutions functioned. When bullion flowed in, the impact was felt in the center, increasing the supply of funds and pushing interest rates down, while the "national supply of money" remained, in many cases, disconnected. His plan, argued Joplin, corrected this unfortunate state of affairs and offered the country a way to have a supply of money controlled by metallic fluctuations. The basic plan did not change over the years, although some flexibility was introduced, partly to accommodate the Bank of England and the private banks in London (see O'Brien 1993, pp. 148–158).

The proposals put forward by Ricardo in his 1824 posthumously published paper were very similar, and were also designed to create conditions under which the money supply would be influenced by bullion movements. There were several differences between the two plans, though. First, Ricardo recommended the abolition of the country banks' notes. Second, he proposed that the department responsible for issuing notes do so only against bullion; thus, notes would be monopolized. However, the notes issued by the Bank of England had a very similar function in the system to the receipts of the Bullion Commissioners. They provided the "monetary base" on which the money supply was built.

The disagreements between the plans concerned the degree to which Bank of England notes were actually functioning as money in the counties. Joplin thought that the Bank of England's notes were not a significant part of the reserves of the country banks and that the Bank's actions were therefore irrelevant to those institutions. Furthermore, Joplin thought that the country banks were of utmost importance to the supply of money. Accordingly, he proposed joint-stock banks, which would be much stronger than the then-current partnerships in banking; he also proposed the development of branch banking.

In 1840, after the introduction of joint-stock banks that issued notes, Joplin concluded that the circulation would "regulate itself upon the principles of metallic circulation" (1840, p. 5). Thus, he was close to the position of the Currency School in adopting a "rule" rather than "discretion." However, Joplin sided with the Banking School on one crucial point of disagreement between the Currency School and the Banking School in the 1840s: Deposits, he wrote in 1845, were similar to notes and were thus part of the money supply. This, as he explicitly stated, was in contradiction to the views of the Currency School and their leader, Loyd (see Joplin 1844, p. 35)

In another paper, O'Brien (1997) extends the argument that both he and Joplin have with the Currency and Banking Schools about the supposed working of the monetary system before and after the 1844 Bank Act. O'Brien provides empirical tests based on price data and monetary aggregates from which two conclusions can be drawn. One conclusion concerns the period before the 1844 Act: "...neither the currency school nor the banking school can take much from this study of the data for the years leading up to the 1844 Bank Charter Act. The only person who could, if he were alive, take comfort from this is Joplin ..." (p. 613). The tests for the years after 1844 suggest that the Act did not succeed in creating a more stable system, as the Currency School had promised it would. Neither could the Banking School find comfort in the extensive statistical tests, argues O'Brien, because the tests for the post-1844 period seem to contradict their assumptions as well. Again, the only theoretician who came out relatively "clean" from the statistical tests was Joplin.

O'Brien's interpretation is open to question on two levels. First, the analytical foundations of both schools can be persuasively defended when compared with Joplin's theoretical structure. Second, one can question the degree to which we should accept the value of these particular statistical tests in this context. Our main argument is that though the confrontation between the Currency School and Joplin does favor the latter, the results of a contest between Joplin and the Banking School are less convincingly on Joplin's side. The theoretical disagreements between Joplin and the Currency School were less significant than O'Brien seems to argue, and the practical reforms Joplin offered had weaknesses and gaps similar to those that remained even after the reforms enacted in the 1844 Bank Act. Moreover, both Joplin and O'Brien seem to play down some of the major issues debated between the Banking and Currency Schools. Whereas the Banking School tried, unsuccessfully in many respects, to understand the financial innovations of the period and especially the role and increasing use of deposits, both Joplin and the Currency School left deposits out of their proposed reforms. It is not therefore surprising that in all the statistical tests carried out by O'Brien, deposits are not in the picture. Lack of data is the usual explanation, raised also by O'Brien, but if deposits are money, how can one derive any conclusions from the tested economic relations unless one believes that they are *not* really money?

As interpreted by O'Brien, Joplin is positioned as neither a Currency School nor a Banking School advocate; he is, in the language of the twentieth-century debates and in particular the famous 1959 Radcliffe Report, an "active money" rather than a "passive money" person. O'Brien's Joplin is closer to the Currency School than the Banking School, a supporter of the Quantity Theory and, later, some form of monetarism, as is O'Brien himself.[7] But Joplin does not make the mistake of focusing on one aggregate – Bank of England notes – and ignoring all other notes, deposits, and other instruments, as did the Currency School. He also opens the door to discretionary monetary policy in ways that make him more appealing to moderns than Loyd or, more generally, the Currency

---

[7]   O'Brien in his 2007 introduction to the collection of his papers writes: "in chapter 5 ... a discussion of the mid-19th century debate between the Currency School, which favoured a counter-cyclical control of the money supply, and the Banking School which ... had more than a little in common with the passive money supply view which underlay the thinking of the authors of the Radcliffe Report. It is argued that, subject to an important qualification concerning the efficacy of monetary base control, the purely theoretical position of the Currency School was much the stronger" (2007, p. 3). In chapter five's conclusions, which are also O'Brien (1995), he writes: "There seems to be a willingness on the part of some Banking School writers – John Stuart Mill is the leading example – to broaden the concept of means of payments to the point where it stretches to an almost Radcliffean vagueness" (2007, p. 104). Clearly, O'Brien objects to the Radcliffe Report's anti–Quantity Theory, anti–Currency School view.

School. I shall address O'Brien's further claims regarding Joplin's contributions to the development of central banking theory in Chapter 18. Meanwhile, let us move to another line of thought that was neither Currency School nor Banking School, that known as the Free Banking School.

Parnell and the Free Banking School[8]

Several modern advocates of "free banking" have argued in recent years that their call for unregulated competitive banking has forerunners in classical monetary literature. Some further maintain that the free-banking approach was abandoned in the mid-nineteenth century not because of theoretical inadequacies, but because of the concerted opposition of "interventionists" helped by the rise of the activist state.

The laissez-faire view of money and banking has been advanced in recent years both at the theoretical level, with several researchers attempting to prove the feasibility and efficiency of a competitive banking regime,[9] and at an historical level, where researchers have sought and analyzed precedents for such a regime.[10] In Lawrence White's influential book, *Free Banking in Britain: Theory, Experience and Debates, 1800–1845* (1984), he emphasizes the Scottish experience and argues that not only was there a (successful) free-banking regime functioning in Scotland before 1845, but that an important group of political economists active during the 1820s and 1830s, the Free Banking School, approved of it. As did Vera Smith before him, White singles out Parnell as a leading member of this school. White writes: "Parnell's [*Observations on Paper Money, Banking and Overtrading* (1827)] should indeed be considered the first major work of advocacy by the Free Banking School" (1984, p. 62). Vera Smith describes Parnell as "the chief adherent" of extending free trade to banking.[11]

Several modern commentators have reexamined the historical case of Scottish banking and have cast doubt on whether it really proves the case

---

[8] This section draws on Arnon (1999).
[9] See Black (1970), Klein (1974), Hayek (1976), Fama (1980); for a review of the literature, see Selgin and White (1994).
[10] See Sechrest (1991), White's response (1991b), White (1991a), Munn (1991), Dow and Smithin (1992) where references to other relevant papers can be found.
[11] The subject was discussed several times in the Political Economy Club. "This club had been founded by Tooke to support the principles of Free Trade, and it was not unnatural that reference should be made to the possibilities of extending Free Trade to banking. The chief adherent of such an extension was Sir Henry Parnell, who moved a discussion on whether 'a proper currency (might not) be secured by leaving the business of banking wholly free from all legislative interference'" (Vera Smith 1936, p. 62).

for the existence of free banking (Dow and Smithin 1992; Sechrest 1991). However, White's claim that free banking has significant ancestors in classical political economy during the 1820s and 1830s has remained virtually unchallenged, as has his explanation for the disappearance of this tendency from mainstream thinking.

"Why did the Free Banking School lapse into near silence in 1844?" asks White. His answer: "One of the school's leading pamphleteers and spokesmen, Parnell, had died in 1842. It is likely that most of the others were, to put it baldly, co-opted by the way in which Peel's acts offered to cartelize the bank note-issuing industry" (White 1984, p. 78). Thus, according to White, the Free Banking School lost the battle in the 1840s and lapsed into such a long silence due to coincidence and capitulation.

In what follows, we provide a critical reexamination of this view, surveying some aspects of the history of classical free banking and, in particular, of its decline. First, we shall ask whether we can identify classical forerunners to modern free banking. Here we will reexamine the views of Parnell, who was accorded such significance by both White and V. Smith, and discuss to what extent he really was a pioneer of free banking. In addition, we shall argue that there was an earlier free-banking position represented by Adam Smith and Ricardo before the latter's *Plan for a National Bank* (1824), and shall ask why White chose to focus mainly on Parnell. Third, we shall reexamine the fall of the Free Banking School in order to develop the argument that its decline was due not only to the causes noted by White, but also to recognition of certain theoretical weaknesses. We do not discuss all the figures White cites as members of the Free Banking School; however, our analysis can be seen as a step toward a critique of the view that a separate Free Banking School existed in the mid-nineteenth century, a possibility that Schwartz (1987) also raises.

We will first briefly examine free banking as it is treated by Vera Smith and White. In spite of important differences between them, they agree that Parnell should be considered a classical forerunner to free banking. We will then follow Parnell's views as they evolve in his major texts and in his debate with McCulloch. Lastly, we will examine the relationships between the figures White describes as "free bankers" and the better-known theorists associated with the Currency and Banking schools.

Vera Smith and White

As noted, the modern Free Banking School has many supporters who differ among themselves in their theoretical and methodological foci. The departure point for the present discussion is the analysis offered by White

(1984) in his important work on free banking. Not only is White one of the leading modern advocates of free banking, but he is also unusual in his historical perspective. White defines free banking as a "system under which there are no political restrictions on the business of issuing paper currency convertible into full bodied coin" (1984, p. 1). Thus, according to White, laissez-faire in banking is equivalent to lack of intervention in the business of issuing convertible notes. Moreover, White interprets the history of economic thought on money and banking as basically a reflection of different positions on note-issuing. This leads him to the novel argument that in addition to the familiar Currency and Banking Schools, one can identify among the classical political economists a separate Free Banking School whose members advocated reforms in banking that would enable competition in note-issuing.[12] In this interpretation of the debates on money and banking since Adam Smith, White is, in fact, departing from a thesis developed by Vera Smith in her pioneering work entitled *The Rationale of Central Banking* (1936). Although these two scholars share the same basic sympathy for free banking and criticism of central banking, Vera Smith did not interpret the monetary debates of the nineteenth century in such a one-dimensional manner. Reading her book carefully, one does not reach the conclusion that note-issuing was the main subject dividing theorists and that there was a separate Free Banking School. Rather, Vera Smith finds supporters for free banking among both the Banking School and the Currency School (see her table, p.127). However, despite this difference (to which we shall return later) one should clarify that on the major issue that concerned them both, that of free versus central banking, V. Smith and White are very similar in both their definition and their advocacy of free banking.

Both Vera Smith and White identify the best mechanism for issuing notes as one where competition prevails; that is, one in which many issuers of convertible notes are free to act according to their discretion. From both analyses, it is clear that their support for such a regime is based on several arguments:

A. The quantity of money, which in their view includes coins and convertible notes, in such a system will be the "right" one. Such optimality is generated through an automatic mechanism where no authority interferes: If too many notes are issued, the holders of those notes will return them to the issuer, either directly or indirectly, through a

---

[12] For a concise and clear summary of White's interpretation see his scheme on p. 135 (1984) in a table which is reproduced at the end of this chapter.

clearing system. To prevent the threat to their solvency and in particular to their gold reserves, the banks will not issue too many notes. Thus, it is the threat of gold outflows that regulates the system as a whole. In this sense, their argument is based on a mechanism similar to the famous Price-Specie-Flow mechanism, which is also automatic.

B. Other forms of bank liabilities, such as deposit accounts, and bank assets, such as loans, should not be a target for those concerned with the smooth functioning of the economy. In other words, it is sufficient to determine the conditions under which money is created. The competing banks will then provide not only the right amount of money but also the right amounts of other liabilities and assets.

Taken together, this kind of reasoning put Vera Smith and White, their differences aside, in a unique position concerning the famous debates of the Classical School, debates to which we will return shortly.

The mechanism at work under a regime where competitive banks issue convertible notes is described by Vera Smith through the exchange between Parnell (1827,1832), the chief advocate of free banking in her view, and McCulloch (1831), representing the interventionists. White also views Parnell as the pioneer of free banking. At this point, one should note that other modern advocates of free banking (for example, Glasner, 1985, 1992) trace their ancestry to Adam Smith. The lack of any reference to Adam Smith by Vera Smith, and the limited importance that White ascribes to him in the rise of the free-banking tradition, is intriguing and will be discussed later. This discussion will also help account for the importance ascribed to Parnell by both V. Smith and White.

Henry Parnell

Henry B. Parnell (1776–1842), from 1812 Baron Congleton, an Irish landowner, was active in British political economy as both a politician and a theoretician. He entered Parliament in 1802, was a member of the Bullion Committee, and was involved in various other committees. He served for a short time as secretary of war and for several years as treasurer of the navy and paymaster general. He was mainly interested in financial reform and wrote his most influential book on this topic.[13] From1822 until his death in 1842, he was a member of the famous Political Economy Club.

To examine the issues raised in the debates around free banking, we will turn to the two pamphlets which associate Parnell with laissez-faire

---

[13] *On Financial Reform* (1830).

in banking. The first is his *Observations on Paper Money, Banking, and Overtrading* (1827), which according to White "should be considered the first major work of advocacy by the Free Banking School" (1984, p. 62). The second is his *A Plain Statement of the Power of the Bank of England* (1832). Parnell approved of Adam Smith's approach to banking and complained that his principles had never been fully applied. "Notwithstanding the length of time that has elapsed since the publication of the Wealth of Nations, there is not perhaps any work in which all the leading principles, which relate to paper money and banking, are more fully and clearly stated than in the chapter of Adam Smith's work" (1827, pp. 2–3). The important missing reform was that which would end the Bank monopoly in London. Since 1819, Parnell tells us, he demanded that in addition to convertibility, of which he of course approved, an end to monopoly was necessary. The responsibility for the 1825 crises lay, according to Parnell, with the Bank of England. On this he quotes Tooke, who suggested that "at the expiration of the present charter of the Bank of England, the whole system, as connected with the circulation of promissory notes, should be entirely remodelled" (Tooke 1826, p. 123; quoted in Parnell 1827, p. 16). One should note that this position reflects Tooke's pre–Banking School views. Parnell suggests that in order to prevent

the recurrence of similar distress [to that of 1825] ... it is necessary – That the banking system should be wholly changed; first, by diminishing the capital of the Bank of England, so as to admit of new banks entering into competition with it; secondly, by allowing joint-stock companies to be established in London, with the power of opening branch banks in the country, so that the capital of the metropolis may be brought into operation in supporting the country circulation; and thirdly, by requiring that every bank should give security. (ibid., p. 21)

Thus, the most important reform in banking was to change the law that prevented more than six partners from joining in an issuing company. The existing law "has taken away, as to the Bank of England, the great check over abuses in issuing paper money, namely, the competition of rival banks" and "led to the establishing of weak banks in the country" (p. 35).

A perfect system of banking must be a secure system, Parnell tells us. However, security cannot be guaranteed, and there is always a certain danger in the banking system. Why? Because "[the] chief part of the difficulty of establishing a safe system of banking, arises from the trade being profitable according to the proportion in which the amount of notes, that is kept in circulation by a bank, exceeds the amount of capital which is kept in reserve for the payment of them" (p. 84). This might cause banks to over-issue because this unique state of affairs in banking is a "powerful stimulus in tempting bankers to issue more notes than in prudence they ought to do." Even if they resist this temptation, bankers are "exposed to great difficulties by sudden and unforeseen demands." Parnell then explains why and how, in spite of this temptation, free banking would be safe. He argues that in a system of banking where several banks exist, each one with sufficient capital, the mechanism of clearing notes between the banks will provide the safeguard against improper functioning. This point is of major importance to today's Free Banking School. In Parnell's words,

> each bank will daily have paid into it the notes of some of the other banks; but no bank will reissue these notes, because it would be throwing away, by doing so, the opportunity of making profit by issuing its own notes; The banks will therefore be driven to exchange the notes so paid in with each other; and every bank, that has a balance against it, will be under the necessity of paying the amount of that balance in gold. ... In this way an efficient check is established against over issues. (p. 87)

Such a system, argues Parnell, would protect the economy from fluctuations as well as from panics. The rival banks would correct each other; even if they all acted as a cartel and "were to combine to increase the quantity of paper beyond what the circulation required," the system as a whole would remain secure. Although this cartel action might increase the note circulation beyond the "right" amount for a short time, Parnell argues that the mechanism that corrects this collusion would soon apply, and such disturbances would be short-lived. The mechanism which would discipline the colluding banks is the exchange of gold against the banks' excess notes. Moreover, the resulting correction would cause the banks to "suffer more in the end from their combination than they could gain by it" (p. 89); thus, rational bankers would not start such a process.

Parnell, an experienced politician and well-informed economist, knew that this competitive system was not perfect. He was aware of the danger of over-issue, because the working of the system depended on human beings who have the tendency to miscalculate, among them respected bankers. They were sometimes taken by a spirit of unfounded optimism that was felt through the whole economy.

> But although a system of banking might be established, by leaving free the operation of the influence of the principles of convertibility, of profit, and of private interest, which would admit of paper money being extensively used, with perfect security from bank failures, the banks would still be able to make those large issues of paper when prices are high, and a spirit of speculation existed, which would encourage overtrading. But this is no reason against employing bank notes, because, under

such circumstances, if the currency were wholly metallic, over-trading would go on, as it has always gone on, in Lancashire, with the help of bills of exchange, and the system of indorsing them from one party to another. (p. 90)

Thus, the free-banking system was not perfect, but neither was the pure metallic system. The reason for the additional danger caused by issuing banks is clearly explained by Parnell: "The improvident conduct of banks, in issuing paper too freely when prices are high, arises from the same cause as the miscalculations of merchants upon the future state of prices, namely, negligence in inquiring into the causes of their being high, and too much confidence in their permanency."

At this point Parnell seems confident that the system would work. However, it is important to note that he does not suggest here a theoretical mechanism by which the problem of over-issue, caused by the previously mentioned imperfect bankers, would be overcome. Rather, he expresses his hope that the bankers will eventually learn from their mistakes: "But as the late distress has taught the banks their past errors, it may be expected that they will adopt a different line of conduct when prices again become very high ..." Thus, it is the belief that private individuals will soon learn how not to err in their future actions which justifies free banking.

It is not surprising that White saw in Parnell and in this paper a fore-runner of modern free banking. Parnell expresses here unequivocal support for the principle of free banking in note-issuing. Moreover, one must remember that Parnell was writing at a time when the Bank of England had a monopoly on note-issuing in London, so, unlike Smith, Parnell's position also incorporated policy recommendations to change the banking system (as do those of modern free bankers). However, under the influence of political economists such as McCulloch, Parnell developed a somewhat different analysis which also led him, in our view, to modify his position on free banking and propose some limitations on competition in banking.

Parnell's Argument with McCulloch

McCulloch (1831) provided, according to Vera Smith, the "first important theoretical argument for the case against free banking." McCulloch questioned whether belief in the tendency of private bankers to learn to avoid over-issue could alone provide a sufficiently solid base for leaving the business of money and banking in the hands of private interests. Does this belief constitute a convincing argument for applying the invisible hand to the business of banking while withholding any policy tools from the Bank of England's directors?

McCulloch agreed that convertibility would provide a mechanism of control over the supply of notes by the Bank of England, as well as over any other individual bank. In Vera Smith's words:

An over-issue can admittedly depress the value of the whole circulation, gold as well as paper, in the country concerned, but immediately this over-issue takes place, gold starts going abroad, notes are presented to the issuer for payment, and they, in order to prevent the exhaustion of their reserves and to maintain their ability to redeem their obligations, are obliged to contract their issues, raise the value of money and stop the gold efflux. There is, therefore, in his [McCulloch's] opinion always a check on over-issues by way of the public's bringing notes to the banks for redemption. (Vera Smith 1936, pp. 63–64)

However, McCulloch argued that this mechanism would not suffice in the case of numerous competing banks. Rather, McCulloch thought, as many theorists have since, that there are forces in a competitive banking system that will cause the system as a whole to over-issue. Competing banks will often be forced to decrease the discount rate and expand their note-issuing in reaction to one of their competitors who was doing the same. The banks will be forced to "follow the leader" on this dangerous route for fear of losing market share. The result would be over-issue. Moreover, it is doubtful whether over-issuing bankers would learn to mend their ways. The initiator would not be punished because customers would convert notes of all banks, and not just those of the troublemaker. This analysis led McCulloch to endorse the continuation of the Bank of England's monopoly over note-issuing.

In contrast, in his 1832 pamphlet, Parnell seeks to combine his rejection of such a monopoly with his recognition of at least some of McCulloch's warnings about the over-issue inherent in unrestricted competition. The monopoly power of the Bank "gives it an unbounded influence: – first over the Currency; secondly, over Commercial Credit; thirdly, over the prices of the Funds; and, fourthly, over the Government" (p. 4). The first was the focus of this pamphlet; Parnell gathered historical data to prove that the "real source of the misconduct of the Bank was the motive of realizing the largest possible profit on the Bank capital" (p. 49). This pattern, in Parnell's view, was the cause of the changes in the quantity of money that were behind many of the financial and economic crises in England.

Parnell was also influenced by McCulloch's argument that convertibility was insufficient to prevent over-issue in the event of free competition. On the one hand, Parnell argues that a clearing mechanism like that at work between the banks in Scotland provides some restriction on over-issue. However, he also agrees that as long as public redemption of bank notes remains the primary force on which the control of banks depends, there is always the possibility of imperfections. Either the public will not be informed at all or it will not be informed in due time. One should note that Parnell is not concerned here with financial crises, but rather with the potential for over-issue during times of normal business.

Parnell's solution is to let joint-stock issuing banks operate in London. These banks will bring discipline to the issuing business through a mechanism described by Parnell as "federative capacity":

> Each of them knows perfectly well to what injuries he is exposed, and what ought to be done to avoid them; but instead of each Banker depending upon his own independent power to protect himself, they all combine together, and employ their united powers, to stop, at once, the loss which they would all sustain, immediately, or remotely, by the failure of a single Bank of mere speculation, and unprovided with a proper amount of capital. (pp. 72–73)

This is basically an argument against both numerous small banks and one large one, and in favor of a system where a few big banks act in a coordinated, "federative" manner. Thus, the "banking trade" should be "managed" by a few banks who will consider the state of the exchanges as well as other factors. Such a market structure, whereby a few banks combine activities on a regular basis, and not just in times of financial crisis, characterizes what modern terminology refers to as a cartel.[14] Such a cartel would, in Parnell's view, prevent risky banks from entering the trade and would prevent over-issue by strong banks. Moreover, the coordinated decisions of a few strong banks would provide the country with the right amount of money, whatever that amount might be. Thus, a few private banks would assume the role and function of a public central bank:

> As these Banks would all be injured by one or more of them issuing paper in excess, they would, as in Scotland, act in a *federative capacity*, in checking every deviation from true Banking principles; and they would certainly have the means of keeping the currency at all times at a proper amount; for with all this paper, issued to accommodate trade, a moderate limiting of it, in a way to make it operate generally

---

[14] At this stage, Parnell argued that the Scottish system was managed by few strong banks; see in particular Parnell 1832, pp. 66–76. Parnell did not like small banks: "What has been the cause of the failure of Country Banks in England? The facility with which every cobbler and cheesemonger has been able to open a Bank, in consequence of the limitation of the number of partners having forbidden the existence of numerous opulent Banks. What has been the cause of so few failures in Scotland? The freedom of the Banking Trade, and the establishment of opulent Banks" (p. 73). However, the main issue remained the control and determination of the money supply and not this hint at minimum capital requirements.

and equally, would admit of a contraction being quietly and easily made, when the price of bullion, or the state of the exchanges, indicated that the circulation had become redundant. (p. 76; emphasis added)

This is an argument in favor of discretionary control of money, and not for automatic rule or free banking, albeit with a unique twist concerning the allocation of power between the public and private sectors. It is not clear how these banks would reach and apply their decisions.

The interpretation that Parnell is arguing in favor of a discretionary monetary policy here is supported by his appeal to Ricardo's 1824 paper. Parnell approvingly quotes Ricardo, "whose practical authority on a matter of this kind cannot be disputed." Parnell argues that in his 1824 text on a national bank, Ricardo "made his whole case depend upon what he conceived to be the facility of dealing with the currency with reference to the foreign exchanges. The way by which he proposed to give steadiness of value to his circulation, to consist wholly of paper, was, by contracting, or increasing the amount, according to the fall or rise in the foreign exchanges, and in the price of bullion" (ibid., pp. 65–66). While raising this argument, Parnell also defends the Scottish system, wherein several banks, not only one as in London, assume the "management" task:

Now, in order to understand how far this system is fit for London, let us suppose that the twenty millions of paper which are now issued by the Bank of England, were issued by five opulent London Banks, that they acted entirely on the Scotch system, as to deposits, cash credits, exchanges of notes, and settling of balances. 1. These Banks would have full power to prevent any Bank, without capital, from establishing itself. (ibid., p76)

Parnell is clearly opposed to free entry to banking; however, he is also opposed to leaving decisions entirely to competitive forces even in the case of adequately capitalized banks. "Federative capacity" is necessary to "control … against over-issues of paper." For Parnell, the true banking principles were those advocated by Ricardo in his 1824 paper, which, as I argued earlier, do not represent a free banking position. Moreover, Parnell's enthusiastic support for a system which he understands to represent managed rather than free banking supports the interpretation that by this stage Parnell was no longer an unequivocal "free banker."

He also was not, of course, a convert to monopoly note-issue. The last section of Parnell's 1832 pamphlet is devoted to a reply to McCulloch, and his message is clear. A banking system where several strong banks with adequate capital compete with each other cannot deviate from the public's interests. None of those banks would be able to expand when the economic conditions are not suitable; neither would they contract when not expected to. Parnell clearly explains why a particular bank might over-issue, arguing that the others will correct this greedy bank:

> But this effect of an over-issue will be a direct injury to the other Banks; the means by which the over-issue has been brought about will be considered by them as unfair and hostile to their interests, and as a breach of an implied compact [contract]. When, therefore, the Banks discover, by the exchanges, that the over-issuing Bank has violated the rules of fair dealing, they will seek to obtain redress, and to protect their own interests, by taking those means which they possess to force the transgressing Bank to retrace its steps. (pp. 87–88)

This line of reasoning assumes that there is a natural allocation of production in a cartel as well as a clear agreement as to the amount of total production.

It is interesting that Parnell insists that he is following in the footsteps of both Adam Smith and Ricardo (prior to the latter's 1824 text) on the issue of laissez-faire in banking, although at this point he favors restricted competition and advocates discretion. However, one must remember that he still rejects the Bank of England's monopoly over convertible note-issuing in London. He seems to be relying on Adam Smith and Ricardo to convince his readers that the founding fathers were closer to him than they were to McCulloch, who rejects the application of laissez-faire to banking altogether and defends the monopoly power of the Bank over note-issuing in London.

To conclude, we suggest that in this last important paper, Parnell appears as neither a "free banking" nor a "one bank" advocate. In this case, one can question White's identification of Parnell as an unequivocal classical forerunner of modern free-banking positions. Moreover, it seems that Parnell himself modified his position not as a result of coincidence or capitulation, but because he was influenced by certain theoretical weaknesses in his original position. In this context, we suggest that Parnell's support of the Scottish system be understood not as evidence for his advocacy of unrestricted competition, but rather as evidence for his acceptance of some discretion. Thus, the foregoing discussion also raises questions about White's use of the Scottish example as evidence that a free-banking system has worked in the past. A careful reading of Parnell seems to support modern writers such as Sechrest (1991) and Munn (1991) who question White's interpretation on the grounds that the Scottish experience was not an example of pure free banking (see also Checkland 1975; Cowen and Kroszner 1989; Munn 1981).

We are now in a position to ask whether theoretical problems such as those that seemed to have troubled Parnell featured in the debates around the 1844 Bank Act, and what role, if any, they played in the eventual abandonment of competitive note-issuing.

The Banking and Currency Schools on Laissez-Faire in Banking

The return to convertibility in 1821 did not bring with it the desired stability in the monetary system. Crises in the economy continued to trouble both theoreticians and practical persons active in "real" economic life. The crisis in 1825 triggered the debate between Parnell and McCulloch and also led to a reform in banking legislation in 1826 (see Fetter 1965). The various reforms did not stop the cycles in the economy and "bad" years returned in 1836/7, 1839, 1847/8, 1857/8, and 1866. The belief that the monetary system was at least partly responsible for this dismal performance was widespread and led to heated debates about a new and better reform. These debates culminated in the 1844 Bank Act.

As we have seen, the Bank Act marked the victory of the Currency School over the rival Banking School. The Currency School rejected the application of laissez-faire to banking and in particular to note-issuing. The Currency School's strong distrust of bankers led its advocates to reject competition in note-issuing and to agree with Thornton that the monetary system should be managed and not left to the invisible hand. However, they did not follow him in endorsing some form of discretion. but rather sought an alternative method for determining the quantity of convertible notes in circulation. They adopted the principles of Ricardo's *Plan*, but endorsed a strict rule with no discretion. Their position is most clearly expressed in the 1844 Bank Act, according to which every change in the quantity of Bank of England notes would equal the change in the amount of precious metals in the reserves of the Issue Department. Thus, changes in the quantity of notes would *not* depend on the banking system's discretionary actions, but rather on the public's will. The Act freed the bankers from all responsibility other than obeying the "rule." The Act thus provided an *automatic mechanism* for controlling the money supply, with money understood as coins plus convertible bank notes.

Thus, the Currency School held a strange position. Although the rejection of competition for money should have led its advocates to reject free banking and accept some form of visible-hand policy and central banking, they clung to the alternative solution of "rules" even in the years following the Bank Act, when a succession of crises (1848, 1857, 1866) necessitated discretion. Moreover, they did not think it important to control aggregates other than notes. Thus, although they rejected competition for notes, and their proposals for reform paved the way for central banking, they paradoxically accepted laissez-faire in banking for other liabilities such as deposits. As we saw earlier, Parnell also focused mainly on note-issuing but did not, of course, endorse a rule. In this, his position was close to that of the rival Banking School. However, in contrast with both Parnell and the Currency School, the Banking School was concerned with more than just note-issuing. The Banking School's strong commitment to free trade and its advocates' acceptance of a competitive mechanism for money (notes), at least outside London, brought them close to a free-banking position for note-issuing. However, though this aspect of their thought has led to a common perception that they were close to Smith's laissez-faire views, their consideration of other assets and liabilities complicates the picture. In 1844, Tooke, the leading Banking School theorist, rejected both the Real Bills Doctrine and competition as mechanisms for regulating other liabilities and assets of the banking system, a position that should have led to some form of visible-hand policy. However, although Tooke continued to refine this distinction between money and credit, he did not translate his implied endorsement for competition in note-issuing (but not in credit) into clear policy recommendations.[15] Although he was concerned about preventing what he considered to be over-legislation and unnecessary interference in the banking system, he did not recommend complete free banking, nor did he specify how to control deposits or other assets and liabilities.

Parnell, who wrote on similar issues before the heyday of the famous Currency versus Banking School debate, focused mainly on the appropriate issuing policy in London. Like Adam Smith, Ricardo (before his 1824 text), and the Currency School, Parnell accepted free banking for assets and liabilities of the banking system other than convertible notes. However, although he endorsed less competition in note-issuing than did Adam Smith, he clearly endorsed more competition than did the Currency School, and so, had he not died in 1842, he probably would have joined the Banking School in opposing the 1844 Bank Act. However, whereas the Banking School did not propose a significant reform concerning the Bank of England, Parnell preferred a reform: a nonmonopoly regime.

---

[15] Tooke developed a unique attitude among the classicals towards the relation between credit and cycles in the economy. According to Tooke, there exists no automatic mechanism by which the banks can control and "fine tune" the cycles in the economy. However, led by the Bank of England, they can, and should, act as stabilizers in the economy after their managers have determined the direction of the cycles.

Summary

We can now return to our opening questions: Were there forerunners to the new free-banking view, and, if so, why were they neglected for so long? The natural candidate as a forerunner is Adam Smith. He recommended the application of laissez-faire to banking in both the creation of notes and other liabilities and assets. The fact that Vera Smith did not consider him a forerunner and the limited importance which White ascribed to him are puzzling. A possible explanation for the puzzle can be found in the weak theoretical structure that Adam Smith provided. The Real Bills Doctrine was harshly criticized by nineteenth-century political economists and could not serve as a respected cornerstone on which the old – or new – Free Banking School could build their arguments. In other words, the Real Bills Doctrine is not defensible, and hence Smith is problematic as a founding father of the new view.[16]

On the other hand, a competitive mechanism for issuing notes, whereby the determination of the quantity was left to market forces and particularly where a clearing system was in effect, provided a defensible argument for free banking. White and Vera Smith ascribed the introduction of this mechanism to political economy to Parnell; hence, their claim that he was the founding father of free banking. However, did Parnell really ascribe to free banking? Did he recommend free entry and no regulation of note-issuing? My reading of Parnell does not provide a clear answer of yes. Parnell struggled with the arguments of the interventionists and eventually recommended a privately owned cartel that would direct the issuing business. Not only was entry limited, but, as we have seen, Parnell expected the cartel to take responsibility for and to correct the errors of individual banks; moreover, he did not reject the idea that the cartel would regulate the banking system in line with macroeconomic conditions, as Ricardo proposed in 1824. In addition, Parnell did not believe in the Currency Principle, that is, in the need to create a system where correspondence between gold and notes would always be maintained. Thus, it is not surprising that Vera Smith (1936) regarded Parnell as a Banking School member, albeit one who tended more to free banking than to central banking (see a summary table on p. 127; the table is reproduced in the appendix) and White classified him as a free banker.

---

[16] I am indebted to D. O'Brien for drawing my attention to another possible explanation, which emphasizes Hayek's indirect influence on Vera Smith. Hayek did not seriously discuss Adam Smith writings on money, and Vera Smith, who was his student, followed him. Still this remains an interesting puzzle.

It is beyond the scope of this paper to elaborate on all the other candidates for the Free Banking School. However, two other leading figures, Bailey and Gilbart,[17] do not seem to have been pure free bankers either. Bailey, in his 1840 text, can be read as a Banking School supporter; although he raised the issue of competition within the London area, he concluded his penetrating analysis with this lukewarm recommendation:

With regard to any change at the expiration of the present charter in the power of issuing notes within the circle now exclusively supplied by the Bank of England, it scarcely comes within the object of these pages to discuss it. ...
Whether the times are ripe for adopting the salutary principles of free trade ... in this important department of economical policy, is a question which requires for its decision a more familiar acquaintance with the commercial spirit of the metropolis than the author of these pages can boast. (Bailey 1840, pp. 99–100)

Gilbart's support for free banking was initially clearer, but he modified his position later on, after the Bank Act was passed. We do not deny the claim that one can find supporters of competition in note-issuing; there were some, but they were marginal to the main debate.

To summarize, Parnell's position was not a pure free-banking position. It was an anti–Bank of England position, and on several major issues he was close to the Banking School. Although it is true that Parnell expressed sentiments in favor of competitive note-issuing, he was often criticized by his contemporaries, took their criticisms into account, and as a result supported a privately regulated mechanism for the supply of notes. Thus, the decline of the Free Banking School can be explained as the result of theoretical weaknesses, and not as the consequence of coincidence and capitulation.

The modern Free Banking School might expect to find a new hero in Joplin, but he was too smart for this. O'Brien explains Joplin's nondogmatic position on laissez-faire in banking in "Competition and Regulation," chapter 10 of his book. Joplin rejected competition in note-issuing, but at the same time, he fought the monopoly status of the Bank of England. Joplin was the person who discovered that the Bank's monopoy vis-à-vis other joint-stock banks in London was limited to note-issuing and did not include other banking operations. He wanted to increase competition between the banks but thought note-issuing to be a matter for regulation and discretion. His position is, again, a very modern one.

If, as it seems, Joplin indeed formulated such a modern analysis of a monetary economy, the answer to a question posed by O'Brien in the

[17] See White (1984).

conclusion needs to be addressed thoroughly: "Why, despite these achievements, did Joplin fail, and remain and indeed die an outsider?" His personality certainly played a role but, if we may speculate, more can be learned from a detailed examination of his relationships with fellow political economists. O'Brien looks at some of these relationships, but in our view, has left much to future scholars, especially concerning Joplin's encounters with the members of the Banking School. They did not share the "metropolitan perspective" adopted by many of the Currency School supporters, which emphasized the role of London and the Bank of England in determining monetary developments. Thus, in principle, they should have been more receptive than they were to his arguments. Whether they ignored him altogether or they explicitly rejected his point of view, the interesting question to be answered is why. O'Brien hints on several occasions that views that are at odds with the interests of the "economic establishment" are doomed to be neglected. If true, this speculation sheds further light on the complicated relationship between science, interests, and influence. These factors will play a major role in the story of the two scholars who contributed more than any one else to the rise of a theory of monetary policy: Walter Bagehot and Knut Wicksell.

PART FOUR

THE ROAD TO DEFENSIVE CENTRAL BANKING

FOURTEEN

Bagehot and a New Conventional Wisdom

Introduction

The passing of the Bank Act in 1844 did not stabilize the financial system as the framers of the Act had expected; but in spite of this disappointing outcome – one that should have opened a new round of discussions – the next quarter century saw much less interest in monetary debates than had the 1840s. Two financial crises, one in 1847–1848 and the second ten years later in 1857–1858, resulted in two committees of inquiry that invited many witnesses to comment on the events of the crises; they in many ways merely repeated the formative debate held before the 1844 Act; their contribution was in adding new data sets collected especially for them. The two post-1844 crises forced those in control in the government and at the Bank to depart from the Act's clear prescription to always follow a simple rule. In the first crisis, the announcement that the Bank's Issue Department would issue more notes than the bullion it received – contrary to the Bank Act's strict rule – was enough to calm the markets; the promised action didn't have to be taken. In the second crisis, a similar announcement was not enough to return stability and had to be followed by action: The Issue Department actually injected notes into the circulation beyond the bullion reserve it had. This time the announcement was not enough, but the action that followed, apparently, calmed the markets. Thus, it was obvious to all observers that the Bank would not always follow the Bank Act, especially when it mattered most – in a crisis. The Banking School and others saw the two events and the new understanding about the Bank's willingness to break the strict rule as confirmation of their views. As expected, some of the Banking School advocates went one step further and provided a fuller, new analysis concerning the proper policy for the Issue Department and the Deposit (Banking) Department; some new ideas started to surface, as

277

we saw in Chapter 12 in the section on monetary policy after 1844, but no comprehensive analysis was generally accepted before the 1870s. The person who filled this lacuna was Walter Bagehot.

Bagehot (1826–1877) was born to a wealthy and well-connected family in Somerset. He was educated in Bristol and University College, London, where he studied the classics as well as political economy; he was involved all his life in the political questions of the day. He started a career in banking after avoiding a career in law – he found both dull – and was really attracted to writing. He wrote on politics and economics as well as literary criticism. His meeting with the *Economist* editor James Wilson (see Chapter 11) changed his life: He married Wilson's daughter and soon became a writer for and then an editor of this famous and influential newspaper. In 1867, he published *The English Constitution*, his most famous noneconomic book, which still has a standing with political scientists. He was well-connected and influential in the political elite, a discreet consultant to many, and always close to power, hence the catchy phrase describing him as the "spare chancellor," which was also the title of one of his biographies (Buchan 1959).[1]

Since its publication in 1873, Walter Bagehot's *Lombard Street* has been perceived as presenting the position of the British monetary orthodoxy (to use Fetter's famous title) on banking and monetary policy. The full title of Bagehot's influential text – *Lombard Street: A Description of the Money Market* – suggests that it was not planned as a theoretical treatise providing an analytical perspective, but rather was written from a practical, policy-oriented perspective. Bagehot's emphasis on the practical should not lead us to underestimate the depth and clarity of his ideas; neither should the fact that the book's influence had much to do with the author's unique role in British public life. Bagehot's choice of a descriptive, historical methodology in *Lombard Street* and in his many economic articles can be partially explained by his personal intellectual journey. He grew up during the years when the debate around the 1844 Bank Act was always in the background, and it clearly shaped his monetary views. In fact, one of his first pieces, written when he was only twenty-two, was a review of that debate.[2] The

---

[1] The economic works of Bagehot are published in three volumes entitled *The Economic Essays* within *The Collected Works of Walter Bagehot* (volumes 9–11 in the fifteen-volume set), N. St John-Stevas (ed.). On Bagehot the economist, see Sayers' (1978) introductory article to vol. 9, pp. 27–43 and also the editor's preface, vol. 9, pp. 19–26.

[2] Bagehot's article reviewing Wilson, Tooke, and Torrens, "The Currency Monopoly" was first published in the *Prospective Review* (1848, vol. IV, pp. 197–337); see vol. 9 in the *Collected Works*, pp. 235–271. For the economic secondary literature on Bagehot, see Hirsch (1977), Rockoff (1986), O'Brien (2001), Laidler (2004), and references therein. On the history of the concept of the Lender of Last Resort, see our Chapter 18.

unfruitfulness of many of the "theoretical" debates – both those during the 1830s and 1840s around issues relating to the 1844 Bank Act and certainly those since – led Bagehot in a different direction from the theoreticians. He believed that even those who thought the debates in 1844 were productive – and in retrospect Bagehot did not – should have understood by the 1870s that the changes in the financial system since 1844 made these old debates outdated, irrelevant, and even misleading. Thus, in 1873 Bagehot promised to deal as little as possible with the old issues, and even then, only when they help to explain how we arrived at the 1870s financial system.[3]

The resulting historical approach, very similar in both method and style of writing to that of Adam Smith, is an attempt to understand the English money market with all its peculiarities. The description of past and present money markets helps the reader appreciate what, to Bagehot's mind, is the single most important fact, one that is emphasized throughout the book: the centralization of the market so that it has a pivot around which the activities are executed. Specifically, the various institutions dealing with other people's money – those institutions that take in deposits on the one hand and advance funds on the other – rely on the center in London. They had become accustomed to keeping their reserves there for the times when an outstanding demand would arise; it is to London that they could apply for relief. It was a unique structure, not designed with any theory in mind and, in Bagehot's view, did not exist in any other country.

Bagehot carefully describes the circumstances out of which the English financial system grew. In London, the City came to function as the center; within it, the Bank of England was the center's center of gravity: The reserves of the financial system, unlike any other institution in the world and without precedent in England as well, were now concentrated in the Deposit Department of that old and respected institution. This unprecedented power was dangerously concentrated in the hands of an institution that had never been intended to hold it and whose governance denied it even had such power; hence, the Bank never really accepted or even understood its unique role. Based on this foundation, *Lombard Street* and Bagehot's formulation of central-banking policy, known as the Bagehot Principle or Rule, gave the final shape to what has since been described as

---

[3] "Half, and more than half, of the supposed 'difficulty' of the Money Market has arisen out of the controversies as to 'Peel's Act,' and the abstract discussions on the theory on which that act is based, or supposed to be based. But in the ensuing pages I mean to speak as little as I can of the Act of 1844; and when I do speak of it, I shall deal nearly exclusively with its experienced effects, and scarcely at all, if at all, with its refined basis" (p. 2). References are to the 1896 edition of *Lombard Street*.

the British monetary orthodoxy. As we shall see later, the Bagehot Principle was the most advanced concept concerning central banking and monetary policy of its time, certainly since Thornton, and was closely associated with the Bank's role as a Lender of Last Resort. Strangely enough, especially for a person so well acquainted with the history of monetary theory, one can find almost no reference in *Lombard Street* to the history of the concept; neither Thornton nor any other political economist who wrote about discretionary policy is credited with discussing it.[4] However, contrary to some later interpretations, Bagehot's Principle was not intended as an active, full-fledged monetary policy; it had a very restricted aim. It was intended to prevent a possible dangerous collapse of the financial system. We will return to the narrow policy target, relative to what we usually ascribe to monetary policy, in this chapter and in our summary discussion in Chapter 18.

The British Monetary Orthodoxy

Fetter's seminal study, the *Development of British Monetary Orthodoxy 1797–1875* (1965), written more than fifty years ago, defines the orthodoxy and associates its rise in the 1870s with J. S. Mill, who took a position that was neither pure Banking School nor Currency School (pp. 225–226). Mill supported convertibility, as did the two big rival schools and also Bagehot, and advocated a monetary policy that reacts to disturbances in the balance of payments. His (mature) position defines the orthodoxy's view. Fetter quotes a passage from Mill's *Principles of Political Economy* that has since been "read by tens of thousands of students":[5]

And if the balance due is of small amount, and is the consequence of some merely causal disturbance in the ordinary course of trade, it is soon liquidated in commodities, and the account adjusted by means of bills, without the transmission of any bullion. Not so, however, when the excess of imports above exports, which has made the exchanges unfavourable, arises from permanent cause. In that case, what disturbed the equilibrium must have been the state of prices, and it can only be restored by acting on prices. It is impossible that prices should be such as to invite to an excess of imports, and yet that the exports should be kept permanently up to the imports by the extra profit on exportation derived from the premium on bills; for if the exports were kept up to the imports, bills would not be at a premium, and

---

[4] Thornton is not mentioned at all by Bagehot, which is another indication of Thornton's disappearance from the literature by the 1870s. Joplin is not mentioned either (see O'Brien (2003). We will return to this point later.

[5] The quote is from the seventh edition, the last issued in Mill's lifetime; the relevant chapters on money were modified in 1865. Unfortunately, we are not sure there are tens of thousands of students who continue to read this quote.

the extra profit would not exist. It is through the prices of commodities that the correction must be administered.

Disturbances, therefore, of the equilibrium of imports and exports, and consequent disturbances of the exchange, may be considered as of two classes; the one casual or accidental, which, if not on too large a scale, correct themselves through the premium on bills, without any transmission of the precious metals; the other arising from the general state of prices, which cannot be corrected without the subtraction of actual money from the circulation of one of the countries, or an annihilation of credit equivalent to it; since the mere transmission of bullion (as distinguished from money), not having any effect on prices, is of no avail to abate the cause from which the disturbance proceeded. (From Fetter 1965, pp. 226–227, quoting Mill 1848/1871, Book III, chapter 20, sec. 3)

Fetter writes that the defenders of the Bank Act, the Currency School and also Mill – "the leading economist of the age, though a critic of the act" – advocated a credit policy that was supposed to regulate the exchanges by "altering commodity prices." Hence, "it is little wonder" that twentieth-century economists perceived the British classical orthodoxy as supporting a "specie-flow price-adjustment mechanism"[6] (p. 227). The truth, argues Fetter, is that most spokespersons, whether from the Currency School or the Banking School, assumed that mechanisms other than price changes – mainly capital flows and interest rates changes – would restore equilibrium to the balance of payments. The various discussions in both schools of the adjustment mechanism assumed a gold standard; however, neither school explained why a gold standard is superior to a managed currency, leaving the argument to Thornton, that innovative (though long-dead and unfortunately unknown) theoretician.[7] The mainstream theoreticians did not waste their energy on arguing with a position that only "lunatics and enemies of society" held, as Fetter, quoting Robbins' (1958) famous study of Torrens, tells us.

Since the passage of the Bank Act in 1844, the only significant theoretical development to become part of the 1870s orthodoxy related to the behavior of the Bank of England and its relations with the government. Fetter believes that the growth of "a philosophy of central banking" belongs to the years after 1844. Any trace of such a policy before "1840 is hardly more than a footnote" (p. 257). After 1844, the major new theoretical issues related to the Bank's relationship with the other banks, especially its role as a Lender

---

[6] On Taussig's role in promoting this idea see Fetter (1965, p. 228).

[7] See Fetter, pp. 223–224: "The closest English approach in the first three quarters of the nineteenth century to what the economist of today would consider a theory of an inconvertible currency came not from those who favored an inconvertible currency, but from a supporter of the gold standard, Henry Thornton." On the interpretation of the later position, see Chapter 7.

of Last Resort and its position vis-à-vis the government. The person who presented the emerging new theory was Bagehot. Thus, according to Fetter, it was to Mill and Bagehot that we owe the British orthodoxy of the 1870s.

Laidler's important study, *The Golden Age of the Quantity Theory* (1991), covers developments in monetary orthodoxy from the 1870s on, beginning where Fetter's study ends. The opening chapter of Laidler's evaluation, entitled "The orthodoxy of the 1870s,"[8] lays the groundwork for his larger discussion that takes the reader to the first quarter of the twentieth century; naturally, Laidler discusses Fetter's seminal work there. For Laidler, the major tenets of monetary orthodoxy are the outcome of an analysis of the exchange process, where the major function of money is that of a means of payment rather than a store of value; that is, the emphasis in the orthodoxy's approach to money is different from that of modern post-orthodoxy economists. Laidler's book is in fact a study of the rise of the modern approaches. In Laidler's view, the authorities who contributed to shaping and defining the orthodoxy of the 1870s are, again, Mill, Bagehot, and also Jevons.

The question of the price level was the "central scientific problem of classical monetary theory" (p. 9), writes Laidler. By the 1870s, theoreticians understood the interplay between long run and short run. Long-run price level was determined by cost in the production of gold; the short-run explanations, which had been heavily debated up to the 1870s, were now broadly agreed upon. In Laidler's opinion, Mill's formulations provide the definite mainstream view on both the long run and the short run. That view was a sophisticated quantity theory of money; in Mill's words: "the amount of goods and the transactions being the same, the value of money is inversely as its quantity multiplied by what is called the rapidity of circulation" (Laidler, pp. 14–15 from Mill, pp. 513–514). This sophisticated version took into account mediums other than notes and coins, unlike the Currency School. It also took into account changing and not just uniform velocities, the impact of credit mediums on prices, and so on. The orthodoxy also agreed on the way that changes in the price level were caused by changes in monetary aggregates; this is the so-called transmission mechanism. Mill summarized the classical theory of cycles as well, the tenet that was so central to Loyd and the Currency School (p. 23). The links between money and the balance of payments and bimetallism were two additional tenets of the orthodoxy; the theory of monetary policy was the last, though not least in importance, to be added. This last element had been added by Bagehot, who "completed the edifice of classical monetary economics with a theory of central banking" (Laidler 1991, p. 36).

---

[8]   See also Laidler's earlier version of 1988.

In the concluding chapter of Fetter's seminal study, entitled "The Victory of the Bagehot Principle," he presents a summary of the development of the orthodoxy on monetary policy in the years after the Bank Act, from 1845 to 1875. In his view, this new element shaped and consolidated the new orthodoxy:

The theoretical controversies of the period had little positive influence. The really significant development of those years, in which *monetary and banking orthodoxy was consolidated*, was the acceptance of a set of traditions governing the behavior of the Bank of England and its relations with the Government. (Fetter 1965, p. 257; my emphasis)

Fetter acknowledges that there were some early scholars who recognized "some principle of central banking," but he is quick to state that what happened before 1844 on this key issue – and here he specifically mentions Baring, Thornton, the Bullion Committee, and Attwood – "was hardly more than a footnote." In Fetter's view, the "emergence of the philosophy of central banking ... did not have a continuous growth, but was for all practical purposes born anew out of the controversies that followed Peel's legislation" (pp. 257–258).

Denis O'Brien (2003) advocates a different perspective on the rise of central banking; he sees continuity and a steady growth of the concept of central banking, starting with Thornton (1802) and then, in 1825, after the crisis of that year, advocated by Joplin. Moreover, O'Brien strongly suggests that Bagehot may have been influenced by Joplin's views, probably indirectly through Stuckey.[9] Thus, the concept owes more to predecessors than Fetter grants, and Joplin deserves more credit than he had received so far. The credit this time is not for Joplin's discovery of the Metallic Fluctuations Principle (see Chapter 13) before Ricardo and the Currency School, but for the discovery and promotion of the concept of Lender of Last Resort.

The influence of and similarity between Bagehot's and Thornton's discussions of monetary policy have been discussed by Fetter (1965), Humphrey (1989), Laidler (1991, 2002), Skaggs (1995), and O'Brien (2003), as well as by many others. Skaggs (2003) suggests that Thornton's influence can be traced through Tooke. O'Brien (2001) argues that in *Lombard Street*, Bagehot devised a counter-cyclical monetary policy: "Bagehot argued that use of Bank

---

[9] "It seems reasonable to infer from all this that Stuckey's intervention owed not little to Joplin's article; that Joplin article produced the dramatic intervention by the Bank; and that thus Bagehot's classic statement of the role of the lender of last resort stems from the intervention of the outsider Thomas Joplin" (O'Brien 2003, p. 7). I think this inference to be highly speculative, as I will argue below.

Rate as an active tool to protect the reserve in the Banking Department of the Bank would stabilize the economy" (p. 426). The aim was to avoid the damaging results of a panic caused by an exogenous, real agricultural cycle. We will argue that Bagehot did not construct an anticyclical policy in the sense of modern monetary policy, where instruments are used to reach some targets, but rather a defensive monetary policy whose sole objective was to avoid dwindling reserves and evaporating trust. We will term this innovative idea "passive monetary policy" or "defensive central banking," which was to substitute the inaction of the Bank embedded in the Bank Act. Thus Bagehot, who tried to run away from that old debate, in fact complemented its shortcomings. However, his analysis goes far beyond the simplistic approach of the Bank Act and the Currency School, with their focus on money and exchange. We will show that Bagehot's concept of Lender of Last Resort is different from a full-fledged theory of central banking, or what moderns usually describe as monetary policy. Bagehot developed his concept to enhance the stability of the financial system and to defend against its sudden collapse, not to fine tune the economy. Neither was his concept primarily an instrument to fight the real cycles in the economy, as O'Brien claims.

Laidler (2004) sees Bagehot as "an exponent of the hard-money Banking School ideas," whereas Thornton, "on the other hand, in many respects looked further forward than that, to the quantity theory based approach to stabilization policy developed by Hawtrey (1919) and Keynes (1923)" (p. 52). Moreover, Thornton's approach to central banking, developed many years before in "a remarkable intuitive insight," reflects a more general theory of central banking than does Bagehot's (p. 46). Laidler highlights the different focuses of the two analyses, with Bagehot emphasizing the bank assets and Thornton emphasizing the bank liabilities. What is even more important than the difference in focus is that Bagehot's analysis rehabilitates the importance of finance in any monetary economy, and does so without focusing the analysis on the exchange process as the Currency School did. Bagehot emphasizes intermediation and shows a deep understanding of the crucial place of credit and trust in the process of wealth creation in the real economy. While reading these innovative discussions in *Lombard Street*, one cannot but remember those parts of Thornton's *Paper Credit* that relate to the many mediums used in a monetary economy and the utmost importance of trust and credit. This makes the surprising fact that Thornton is missing from *Lombard Street* an even deeper puzzle that calls for an explanation.

We will speculate that Bagehot owes more to the Banking School critique of the Bank Act than he is ready to admit. We will see that from being an early supporter of the Bank Act and the Currency School, even after the

1847 crisis that raised disturbing questions, he later came to appreciate the Banking School's policy proposals. In particular, the ideas raised by Tooke after 1844, discussed in Chapter 12, were known to Bagehot and apparently shaped his more pro-interventionist stance of the 1860s and 1873. We will return to these issues later in the section entitled "Lombard Street: Defensive Monetary Policy" and in the final chapter.

Lombard Street: Addressing Intermediation

The full title of *Lombard Street*, "a description of the money market," should not mislead us. Bagehot discusses monetary policy based on an analysis of the market for loans; in other words, his fundamental layer is the "credit market" and not, as expected, the traditional analysis of the mediums used in exchange – coins and convertible (or inconvertible) notes. These latter mediums and the exchange process, or what the classicals sometimes described as "circulation," were treated by him as of a clearly secondary importance. He simply assumes that money exists, and thus departs in a very important way from the long-established traditions of analysis, certainly since the Banking and Currency schools took center stage. Bagehot clearly understood and provided many fascinating examples for the fact that a well-functioning modern economy depends on the smooth working of the complicated financial structure. That structure was at the core of intermediation, the transfer of funds from units with surplus resources to those that face shortages. Intermediation explained the growth and vitality of the English economy, which through the utilization of its developed financial system could compete as no other country could, and which could use the energies of entrepreneurial people who lack capital:

Thus English capital runs as surely and instantly where it is most wanted, and where there is most to be made of it, as water runs to find its level.
    This efficient and instantly ready organisation gives us an enormous advantage in competition with less advanced countries – less advanced, that is, in this particular respect of credit. In a new trade English capital is instantly at the disposal of persons capable of understanding the new opportunities and of making good use of them. (pp. 13–14)

Elaborating on the advantages that England possesses due to its unique intermediation system – an important advantage in what Bagehot saw as the globalizing, competitive world economy – Bagehot comments:

There are many other points which might be insisted on, but it would be tedious and useless to elaborate the picture. The main conclusion is very plain – that English trade is become essentially a trade on borrowed capital, and that it is only by this refinement of our banking system that we are able to do the sort of trade we do, or to get through the quantity of it.

But in exact proportion to the power of this system is its delicacy – I should hardly say too much if I said its danger. (pp. 16–17)

Thus, credit and intermediation are the driving forces behind English economic power. However, one has to understand that alongside these enormous benefits, there is a huge danger that is the result of the risks facing the intermediation structure. The English "one reserve" system contributed to an increase in risks, because the whole system became dependent on one, sometimes too-small reserve. When this reserve failed to answer the various demands, which occurred from time to time, it caused widespread and significant damage. Thus, how to safeguard the centralized credit system became the crucial question facing the English financial system. What Bagehot describes is not an activist monetary policy intended to influence the economy via monetary instruments, but rather a passive, defensive policy intended to maintain the system's stability. Those who put their trust in the existing practices did not understand that, in fact, there were no good practices, no rules or set of directions that the Bank could rely upon; there was not even a clear agreement and understanding of the problem. The official rules of conduct were still those of 1844, but the financial system had changed so rapidly since then that

We cannot appeal, therefore, to experience to prove the safety of our system as it now is, for the present magnitude of that system is entirely new. Obviously a system may be fit to regulate a few millions, and yet quite inadequate when it is set to cope with many millions. And thus it *may* be with "Lombard Street," so rapid has been its growth, and so unprecedented is its nature.

I am by no means an alarmist. I believe that our system, though curious and peculiar, may be worked safely; but if we wish so to work it, we must study it. We must not think we have an easy task when we have a difficult task, or that we are living in a natural state when we are really living in an artificial one. Money *will not manage itself*, and Lombard Street has a great deal of money to manage. (p. 20; my emphasis)

That path to safety, or at least to a safer system, necessitated a new "study" with a starting point and focus that were unique and very different from the problem that the Bank Act supposedly solved. The focus of the new study was credit, not in its usages in exchange covering the gap between sales and payments, but in intermediation. Thus, Bagehot managed to break away from the established, dominant tradition that analyzed banking through the problems of exchange in the economy. He understood the fragility of the banking sector as it related to an entirely different source: intermediation based on the credit system. Thus an initial question that Bagehot asked was, "What is the credit system?" His answer: "a set of promises to pay" based on trust (p. 22). Trust was a basic concept in credit:

The main point on which one system of credit differs from another is "soundness." Credit means that a certain confidence is given, and a certain trust reposed. Is that trust justified? and is that confidence wise? These are the cardinal questions. To put it more simply – credit is a set of promises to pay; will those promises be kept? Especially in banking, where the "liabilities," or promises to pay, are so large, and the time at which to pay them, if exacted, is so short, an instant capacity to meet engagements is the cardinal excellence.

All that a banker wants to pay his creditors is a sufficient supply of the *legal tender* of the country, no matter what that legal tender may be. Different countries differ in their laws of legal tender, but for the primary purposes of banking these systems are not material. A good system of currency will benefit the country, and a bad system will hurt it. Indirectly, bankers will be benefited or injured with the country in which they live; but practically, and for the purposes of their daily life, they have no need to think, and never do think, on theories of currency. (p. 22)

Thus, neither the bankers nor Bagehot had to worry too much, as the English traditionally did, about the status of currency. They should invest more energy in understanding that mysterious and fragile system of trust that lies behind banking. Its essence is the promise to pay back liabilities with the legal tender whenever called upon to do so, whereas the institution owing the debt has no means to issue the legal tender. In normal business processes, the bankers know how much they are expected to pay and they arrange a way to cover those obligations. But "normal" times, when regular transactions are performed, do not test trust and the strength of the credit system. It is when conditions are abnormal, when crises are present, that trust is built or, unfortunately, destroyed. When such challenging times arrive, and history tells us they tend to repeat their appearances, merchants and institutions cannot rely on their own resources and reserves but must rely on those of the Deposit Department of the Bank of England. Paradoxically, the Bank's Deposit Department did not consider itself to be fulfilling this crucial role. Its directors thought of themselves as managers of a regular bank, aiming for its own profits and safety and not responsible in any meaningful way for those either of other banking institutions or of merchants, and certainly not responsible for the well-being of the country.

Lombard Street: One Reserve System

The banking system and credit arrangements evolved so that every one of the participants linked in the huge interdependent chain was relying on reserves held at the Bank's Deposit Department. The descriptions of the institutions – their functions, growth, and interdependencies – are the focus of Bagehot's study, and they are described in a brilliant and clear manner. This description and Bagehot's analysis led to his major conclusion: The strength of the center is well documented, but so is its fragility. The main goal of *Lombard Street* is an attempt to find answers to the problems posed by the financial system's fragility.

One obvious approach may have been to propose a total change to the system: to create a multicentered reserve system with competition between many institutions, each keeping its own separate reserve, instead of the de facto single-centered reserve system. Although Bagehot expressed reserved sympathy for this free-banking approach, he considered it impractical, contrary to the historical development of the English system, and a waste of its hard-earned achievements.[10] One should not underestimate the significance of the fact that historically, the English system came to rely on one reserve whose importance could not be exaggerated: "In consequence all our credit system depends on the Bank of England for its security. On the wisdom of the directors of that one Joint Stock Company, it depends whether *England shall be solvent or insolvent*" (p. 36). The Bank directors are the "trustees for the public" and should recognize their role. However, not only do they not perform this trustee role, some of them deny its existence. This particular critique is directed at Thomson Hankey, a director of the Bank with whom Bagehot had a continuing debate; Hankey, in his own book, claims that the Banking Department is just like any other bank. In reality and contrary to Hankey's claims, others in the Bank had changed the practice of managing its business since 1844; it was the theory, the understanding of this change in practice, which had not yet changed in the Bank:

The practice of the Bank has, as we all know, been much and greatly improved. They do not now manage like the other Banks in Lombard Street. They keep an altogether different kind and quantity of reserve; but *though the practice is mended the theory is not.* There has never been a distinct resolution passed by the Directors of the Bank of England, and communicated by them to the public, stating even in the most general manner, how much reserve they mean to keep or how much they do not mean, or by what principle in this important matter they will be guided. (p. 38; my emphasis).

Fetter (1965) describes the evolution of this new practical, though not theoretical, understanding both inside and outside of the Bank after 1844.[11]

---

[10] See more on Bagehot and free banking later.
[11] See Chapter 9, pp. 259–283 on the 1847, 1857, and 1866 crises and the views in the Bank and outside it.

It was a long process, accelerating after the 1857 crisis and even more so after that of 1866. Bagehot discusses the Bank's responsibility in the *Economist* within the context of a debate over free banking versus a state bank. Fetter argues that after the banking crisis of 1866, Bagehot thought it "wise," though not necessarily natural, to accept that England has one reserve. In *Lombard Street*, it was the cornerstone of his theory:

The result is that we have placed the exclusive custody of our entire banking reserve in the hands of a single board of directors not particularly trained for the duty, - who might be called "amateurs," - who have no particular interest above other people in keeping it undiminished - who acknowledge no obligation to keep it undiminished - who have never been told by any great statesman or public authority that they are so to keep it or that they have anything to do with it - who are named by and are agents for a proprietary which would have a greater income if it was diminished, - who do not fear, and who need not fear, ruin, even if it were all gone and wasted. (p. 44)

Bagehot focuses on the reserves held by the Bank, defined as whatever the "legal tender" may be. In his mind, legal tender includes coins and convertible notes, and he is quick to avoid the traditional issues which were so typical to the 1840s debate and Peel's Act (pp. 46–47). Instead, he concentrates on which tool can bring in enough reserves:

What I have to deal with is, for the present, ample enough. The Bank of England must keep a reserve of "egal tender" to be used for foreign payments if itself fit, and to be used in obtaining bullion if itself unfit. And foreign payments are sometimes very large, and often very sudden. ... A bad harvest must take millions in a single year. In order to find such great sums, the Bank of England requires the steady use of an effectual instrument.

That instrument is the elevation of the rate of interest. If the interest of money be raised, it is proved by experience that money does come to Lombard Street, and theory shows that it ought to come. (p. 47).

The increased rate of interest attracts "loanable capital," and does it quickly and forcefully. It also has an impact on other important economic dimensions: "there is also a slower mercantile operation. The rise in the rate of discount acts immediately on the trade of this country. Prices fall here; in consequence imports are diminished, exports are increased, and, therefore, there is more likelihood of a balance in bullion coming to this country after the rise in the rate than there was before" (p. 48). The Bank discovered this instrument only in 1857: "The panic of that year for the first time taught the Bank directors wisdom, and converted them to sound principles." The discovery, however, did not suffice for sound policy; it remained "defective" for lack of full understanding.

Lombard Street: Defensive Monetary Policy

The acknowledgment that England is a "monarchy" in its money market, relying on a one reserve system, paved the way for management of the financial system. However, Bagehot formulated the problem in terms different from those of the Currency School, with which he was of course very familiar. According to Bagehot, one has to create the conditions that will prevent a financial breakdown when a panic presents itself, and the monetary policy that Bagehot formulated was intended to do just that.[12] The Currency School, the promoters of the Bank Act, and Joplin all had external drain in mind when they constructed their respective answers. Internal drain, where the pressure does not come from demand to send money abroad, complicated the scene.

The reasons for internal drain can vary. Sometimes the external pressure brings about internal pressure; at other times the cause is different. The important point, not sufficiently understood at the time, was that the dynamics of the drain depend to some extent on opinion, on what people think about the position of their creditors: Even a slight sense that their reserves were at risk or remote rumors that they might face difficulties were enough to put the credit system in trouble. The first instinct of banks, the Bank of England included, was to hold on to the reserves and to contract lending. However, this natural reaction was the exact wrong one. The banks had to lend in order to create the impression that everything was right and safe. In order to implement such a strategy, the system had to prepare itself ahead of time by creating the funds, the reserves on which one could rely when the test comes. Thus, argues Bagehot, "A panic, in a word, is a species of neuralgia, and according to the rules of science you must not starve it" (p. 53).

When reduced to abstract principle, the subject comes to this. An "alarm" is an opinion that the money of certain persons will not pay their creditors when those creditors want to be paid. If possible, that alarm is best met by enabling those persons to pay their creditors to the very moment. For this purpose only a little money is wanted. If that alarm is not so met, it aggravates into a panic, which is an opinion that most people, or very many people, will not pay their creditors; and this too can

---

[12] Rockoff (1986) sees some inconsistencies and problems in Bagehot that are linked to the problem that "There are two Bagehots, ... one who tells us to 'lend freely at high rates' in a panic, but there is also the Bagehot who tells us to 'protect the reserve' when the market is merely apprehensive" (pp. 160–161). As I will argue, Bagehot is well aware of the gap between these two conflicting requirements and addresses them. There are theoretical weaknesses in *Lombard Street* to be sure, but they do not hang on any confusion between two states of the economy. What Rockoff describes is, in fact, the difficulties that any discretionary policy, in any field, will always face.

only be met by enabling all those persons to pay what they owe, which takes a great deal of money. No one has enough money, or anything like enough, but the holders of the bank reserve. (p. 55)

The fundamental issue of course is that banks cannot, by the nature of their business, be prepared for all occasions because this would mean 100 percent reserves in money (legal tender) at their disposal, always. Thus, Ricardo, whom Bagehot quotes throughout the discussion, was naturally right when he wrote that "against a [general] panic ... banks have no security *on any system*" (p. 57; quoting Ricardo 1816, *Economical and Secure Currency* [*Collected Works*, IV, p. 68]). However, that risk can be reduced and satisfactorily addressed with proper policy. The first element of proper policy was a large reserve built ahead of the difficult times. Clearly such a policy sacrifices short-term profits for securing the long-term solidity of the credit system. The advantages, social and general in nature, are worth the price. Bagehot is fully aware of the gap between private interests and costs and public ones. This was not so clear, certainly not on the theoretical level, to the Bank and its governing bodies.

Bagehot's recommendation, his well-known "rule," is simple: The Bank should extend loans at the start of a crisis, but at escalating interest rates. The exact quantity of the prepared reserve and the schedule of such interest-rate increases should be the prerogative of the Bank directors. The directors were not yet fully ready to fulfill this responsibility, though, because they did not recognize that they had a responsibility. Thus, although the Bank actually made substantial advances[13] and behaved properly during the panic years of 1847, and even more so in 1857 and 1866, it did not yet acknowledge the principle for doing so. Hence, wrote Bagehot, one should be very worried about the Bank despite its reasonable behavior:

But, on the other hand, as we have seen, though the Bank, more or less, does its duty, it does not distinctly acknowledge that it is its duty. We are apt to be solemnly told that the Banking Department of the Bank of England is only a bank like other banks – that it has no peculiar duty in times of panic – that it then is to look to itself alone, as other banks look. And there is this excuse for the Bank. Hitherto questions of banking have been so little discussed in comparison with questions of currency, that the duty of the Bank in time of panic has been put on a wrong ground. (p. 64)

The proof for the shaky foundations of the Bank directors' policy lies in all the earlier instances. For example, at a certain point the Bank gave the impression that it was not going to advance on Consols. That impression alone countered all other efforts, because it contributed to a decline in confidence and the

---

[13] See *Lombard Street* table on p. 64.

spread of discredit and panic. If the system had been well understood by the directors, their efforts would have been aimed in the opposite direction: "What is wanted and what is necessary to stop a panic is to diffuse the impression, that though money may be dear, still money is to be had" (p. 66).

Bagehot's conclusions are clear. First, the Bank should be aware of its position in the system and its responsibilities. The directors and the governor, a job kept in rotation among the directors, should work according to the Bagehot Rule, on which more will be said later. They should become "real trustees" for the nation, not "semi-trustees" as they were then (p. 75). The second conclusion relates to the professionalism of the directors; they were unacceptably "amateur." The third conclusion aims at reducing the dependency of the various banks on the Bank of England's reserve (pp. 75–76).

The most advanced and innovative sections in Bagehot's analysis are those in which he takes a totally different path than that taken by the Currency School and by many in the secondary literature. Reading these sections, one looks for a reference to Thornton – but in what is really a puzzle, Thornton appears to have disappeared from the canon and seems unknown to Bagehot. This well-known disappearance of Thornton from the literature is surprising. Like Thornton, Bagehot emphasizes the importance of financial institutions to the functioning of a market economy. The fundamental asset of such institutions is trust, and the danger they face is their inbuilt fragility. The process that historically created the trust is described in terms that make it seem close to a miracle, and the necessary maintenance of trust is at the core of Bagehot's study. Trust facilitates effective intermediation throughout the financial system, and this is what Bagehot considers to be the crucial advantage of the English economy over its rivals. Thus, Bagehot's focus of analysis is not the exchange process or even price stability, as was the case with Hume, the Bullionists, and the Currency School. Bagehot shifts the emphasis clearly to intermediation. If there was an influence on him, it is Thornton, but Bagehot apparently never knew of him. That Thornton's influence may have traveled to him indirectly through the Banking School, as Skaggs (2003) has persuasively argued, is possible. However, in my view, it is far less likely that Bagehot was influenced by Joplin, as O'Brien (2003) argues.

The historical rise of the English banking system is explained by Bagehot through the role of deposits. The rise of deposits in its turn is the outcome of money and the exchange process. Smith is the authority on whom Bagehot relies here.[14] According to this interpretation, banks first stepped in to deal

---

[14] "Adam Smith describes it so admirably that it would be stupid not to quote his words" (p. 81).

in currencies and to bridge the gaps between standard and degraded coins. They then accepted coins of various values and issued their credit, called bank money, to the depositors (Bagehot, pp. 81–84, from Smith Book IV, chapter iii, "Digression concerning Banks of Deposit"). According to Bagehot, the banks' function of "remitting money" is still fulfilled by them but is now "subsidiary to their main use." The most important function is not payments and the exchange process any longer, but what Bagehot terms "deposit banking":

> Again, a most important function of early banks is one which the present banks retain, though it is subsidiary to their main use; viz. the function of remitting money. A man brings money to the bank to meet a payment which he desires to make at a great distance, and the bank, having a connection with other banks, sends it where it is wanted. … [The] instant and regular remittance of money is an early necessity of growing trade; and that remittance it was a first object of early banks to accomplish.
>
> These are all uses other than those of deposit banking which banks supplied that afterwards became in our English sense deposit banks. By supplying these uses, they gained the credit that afterwards enabled them to gain a living as deposit banks. *Being trusted for one purpose, they came to be trusted for a purpose quite different, ultimately far more important, though at first less keenly pressing.* But these wants only affect a few persons, and therefore bring the bank under the notice of a few only. The real introductory function which deposit banks at first perform is much more popular, and it is only when they can perform this more popular kind of business that deposit banking ever spreads quickly and extensively. This function is the supply of the paper circulation to the country, and it will be observed that I am not about to overstep my limits and discuss this as a question of currency. In what form the best paper currency can be supplied to a country is a question of economical theory with which I do not meddle here. I am only narrating unquestionable history, not dealing with an argument where every step is disputed. (pp. 84–86)

The last remark hints at the old 1840s debates. The structural changes since then have been overlooked by too many people for far too long, including, unfortunately, the directors of the Bank. The irony of history turns these payments services into something totally new, with far-reaching consequences; for quite some time, argues Bagehot, banks had been performing more services that are not related at all to payments, yet most people did not understand this.[15] Notes and coins attracted the attention in

---

15 "But probably up to 1830 in England, or thereabouts, the main profit of banks was derived from the circulation, and for many years after that the deposits were treated as very minor matters, and the whole of so-called banking discussion turned on questions of circulation. We are still living in the *débris* of that controversy, for, as I have so often said, people can hardly think of the structure of Lombard Street, except with reference to the paper currency and to the Act of 1844, which regulates it now" (p. 87).

much of the relevant literature, maybe because they were the two original payment mediums; the rise of deposits that dramatically changed banking and the financial system received almost no attention.[16] That notes and coins appear first is also no accident:

> A system of note issues is therefore the best introduction to a large system of deposit banking. As yet, historically, it is the only introduction: no nation as yet has arrived at a great system of deposit banking without going first through the preliminary stage of note issue, and of such note issues the quickest and most efficient in this way is one made by individuals resident in the district, and conversant with it. And this explains why deposit banking is so rare. Such a note issue as has been described is possible only in a country exempt from invasion, and free from revolution. (pp. 91–92)

The reasons for the rise of the English system are explained by its specific history, in particular the nation's relative stability and security. That led to the widespread note-issuing institutions and to their direct contact with a strong and reliable center; hence, "the monarchical form of Lombard Street" (p. 94). The business of note-issuing developed in such a way that it was monopolized in London and its vicinity. The reasons that Bagehot gives for this development are the "exclusive possession of the Government balances"; that the Bank had a long-time "monopoly of limited liability in England"; and that the Bank "had the privilege of being the sole *joint stock company* permitted to issue bank notes in England" (pp. 97–99). Bagehot draws a clear distinction between what was considered banking in the mid-eighteenth century and what is considered banking in the 1870s. In the earlier period, "exclusive banking," a term from the 1742 law, referred only to note-issuing; now the term refers to "the present system of deposit banking … [that] was not then known on a great scale, and was not called banking" (p. 100). The old system

---

[16] "The reason why the use of bank paper commonly precedes the habit of making deposits in banks is very plain. It is a far easier habit to establish. In the issue of notes the banker, the person to be most benefited, can do something. He can pay away his own 'promises' in loans, in wages, or in payment of debts. But in the getting of deposits he is passive. His issues depend on himself; his deposits on the favour of others. And to the public the change is far easier too. To collect a great mass of deposits with the same banker, a great number of persons must agree to do something. But to establish a note circulation, a large number of persons need only *do nothing*. They receive the banker's notes in the common course of their business, and they have only not to take those notes to the banker for payment. If the public refrain from taking trouble, a paper circulation is immediately in existence. A paper circulation is begun by the banker, and requires no effort on the part of the public; on the contrary, it needs an effort of the public to be rid of notes once issued; but deposit banking cannot be begun by the banker, and requires a spontaneous and consistent effort in the community. And therefore paper issue is the natural prelude to deposit banking" (pp. 88–89).

paved the way for the new one and created the note-issuing monopoly in the metropolis. The old system was also responsible for the "practical monopoly of the circulation," although as people discovered in the 1830s, not the legal one. Until that discovery was made, the Bank already accumulated power in both issuing and deposits.

With so many advantages over all competitors, it is quite natural that the Bank of England should have far outstripped them all. Inevitably it became *the* bank in London; all the other bankers grouped themselves round it, and lodged their reserve with it. Thus our *one*-reserve system of banking was not deliberately founded upon definite reasons; it was the gradual consequence of many singular events, and of an accumulation of legal privileges on a single bank which has now been altered, and which no one would now defend. (pp. 101–102)

The Government and the Bank

The role of the government in the English banking system was a critical one. Bagehot writes that "in theory," banking is a trade and "nothing can be more surely established by a larger experience than that a Government which interferes with any trade injures that trade. The best thing undeniably that a Government can do with the Money Market is to let it take care of itself" (p. 103). However, he immediately adds a reservation that in fact makes a case against free banking. Much had been written on this first priority, describing what he calls a "natural system of banking," where many banks have each their own reserve and manage themselves:

Under a good system of banking, a great collapse, except from rebellion or invasion, would probably not happen. A large number of banks, each feeling that their credit was at stake in keeping a good reserve, probably would keep one; if any one did not, it would be criticised constantly, and would soon lose its standing, and in the end disappear. And such banks would meet an incipient panic freely, and generously; they would advance out of their reserve boldly and largely, for each individual bank would fear suspicion, and know that at such periods it must "show strength," if at such times it wishes to be thought to have strength. Such a system reduces to a minimum the risk that is caused by the deposit. If the national money can safely be deposited in banks in any way, this is the way to make it safe.
But this system is nearly the opposite to that which the law and circumstances have created for us in England. (p. 109)

The role of government was and is crucial; no one with real influence would propose "to 'wind up' the Bank of England. A theorist might put such a suggestion on paper, but no responsible government would think of it" (p. 110).

The rejection of free banking, an issue to which Bagehot returns repeatedly in his writings, is the result of what he sees as the functions of modern government. As long as the money market is not "entirely to be relied on," the government cannot depend on privately owned banks for its transactions; "it must keep its own money." The importance and size of the government forces it not to rely on one bank: "If a Finance Minister, having entrusted his money to a bank, begins to act strictly, and say he will in all cases let the Money Market take care of itself, the reply is that in *one* case the Money Market will take care of *him* too, and he will be insolvent" (pp. 104–105).

The relationship between the government and the banks, argues Bagehot, is a complex topic, but as a result of the historical occurrences in England, no one can propose to "wind up" the Bank of England, and the government "cannot let the Money Market take care of itself because it has deposited much money in that market, and it cannot pay its way if it loses that money" (p. 110). Theorists can discuss this option, but responsible government cannot. Hence, the system faces "evils": It requires "State help" more than does a natural system; it relies on a small reserve due to the monopoly conditions, making the system "more delicate"; the one reserve is managed by only one board with less wisdom than that of many competitors; and that one board is "pressed on by its shareholders to make high dividend, and therefore to keep a small reserve, whereas the public interest imperatively requires that they shall keep a large one" (p. 111). To these four "evils" Bagehot adds another one, created by an error on the part of the government, which in 1797 introduced the Restriction. That decision was crucial because it changed the Bank's behavior and made it behave as if "it *could* not be in any danger. And naturally the public mind was demoralised also" (p. 113). Since 1797, the "public have always expected the government to help the Bank if necessary." The crises in 1847, 1857, and 1866 made "people think that the government will always help the Bank if the Bank is in extremity. And this is the sort of anticipation which tends to justify itself, and to cause what it expects" (p. 113). Hence, the Chancellor of the Exchequer cannot "banish [the Money Market] from his thoughts ... He must aid the Bank of England in the discharge of its duties." In order to do this, he has to understand Lombard Street.

The first theoretical issue that Bagehot explains is that of the value of money. Money is a commodity, and like all commodities, its value is determined by supply and demand. However, because most money is concentrated in the hands of one big holder, this holder would ask for a minimum price and the other smaller banks would follow. The Bank was an important seller, but since 1844, it did not have full control over issuing its notes, and it had virtually no control over the rate of interest; it could affect the rate momentarily but not for a long time.[17] Additional lending by the Bank would cause temporary decline in the value of money, but their "counter-action" would push the rate of interest back to its "average rate." Lower interest rates would work through three channels: First, he argues that people would want to borrow more because money is less efficient; second, more loans would be made on stocks that would now be worth more; and third, assuming convertibility, the temporary lower value of money would generate their "own counteraction" that would work even more quickly through the balance of payments. More imports and fewer exports due to price changes would lead to outflow of bullion. As a result, banks "keeping the reserve" would suffer a decline in reserves and would increase the rate of interest (p. 119). Thus, money behaves like any commodity: Its value obeys the demand and supply conditions, but in this case in a monopoly situation and with more volatile changes in its value. The rate of interest – the price of money – would deviate momentarily from the average rate. Banks cannot determine their average rate of interest, but they can "completely control its momentary value" (p. 123).

The reliance of the credit structure in England on a relatively small reserve of cash explains the delicacy of the financial system. Even "accidental events" can "easily break up and shutter" the system. The various causes for the particular events are less important than many people think. What is more significant is that the answer to all such events is clear: "We must be prepared for all of them, and we must prepare for all of them in the same way by keeping a large cash reserve" (p. 125). The reason for the reality that "good times" and "bad times" come and go (for the recurring crises), is more fundamental than most people understand: It is the advanced division of labor that makes us wealthier but at the same time causes every producer to depend on the smooth, uninterrupted sale of his products:

[As] every producer is mainly occupied in producing what others want, and not what he wants himself, it is desirable that he should always be able to find, without effort, without delay, and without uncertainty, others who want what he can produce. ... Taken together, they make the whole difference between times of brisk trade and great prosperity, and times of stagnant trade and great adversity, so far as that prosperity and that adversity are real and not illusory. (pp. 127–128)

---

[17] Bagehot adds that also before 1844, the Bank could not determine the long term "average rate of interest," contrary to what many observers erroneously argued; they confused the Bank's power over issuing notes before 1844 with what they thought was his power to determine the average interest rate.

Bagehot's description and analysis of a typical cycle (pp. 124–131) combines the real and what can be considered nonreal dimensions. In the real dimension, a crisis can occur in a barter economy as well as in a monetary economy. But in modern societies where a monetary economy functions, credit can be the cause of a cycle independent of and on top of real causes. Bagehot asks if "credit" is capital; does it have "productive power"? It is clear that he thinks the state of the economy is sensitive to the state of credit in the economy. The state of credit and the rate of interest are closely linked. Bagehot explains the supply of and demand for credit as derived from the savings and investments in society: The savers postpone the use of their funds to the future, trying to increase their funds by lending them. The investors use the funds to make profits, out of which they pay the interest. The dynamics of the rate of interest explains the behavior of the savers and investors, as well as the peculiar and violent changes in crisis years (1825, 1866). The description is familiar to anyone who has read about speculative cycles: More savings leads to more lending and to price rises (pp. 133–140). Thus, when the interest rate is low, prices tend to rise; when interest rates are high, prices tend to fall.[18]

This is the meaning of the saying "John Bull can stand many things, but he cannot stand two per cent": it means that the greatest effect of the three great causes is nearly peculiar to England; here, and here almost alone, the excess of savings over investments is deposited in banks; here, and here only, is it made use of so as to affect trade at large; here, and here only, are prices gravely affected. In these circumstances, a low rate of interest, long protracted, is equivalent to a total depreciation of the precious metals. In his book on the effect of the great gold discoveries, Professor Jevons showed, and so far as I know, was the first to show, the necessity of eliminating these temporary changes of value in gold before you could judge properly of the permanent depreciation. He proved, that in the years preceding both 1847 and 1857 there was a general rise of prices; and in the years succeeding these years, a great fall. The same might be shown of the years before and after 1866, *mutatis mutandis.* (p. 141)

The Bank's Structure and Policy

Lombard Street then turns to an explanation of the ups and downs in the economy, which is the focus of Bagehot's attention in chapter 7: "Why

---

[18] Sayers (1978, p. 29) follows the history of this idea in Bagehot's writings, originating in Fullarton's (1844) chapter 8.

Lombard Street Is Often Very Dull, and Sometimes Extremely Excited." The recurring real changes in the economy should be perceived as the normal course of life and "we should cease to be surprised at its seeming cycles … [and] sudden panics" (p. 160). The effects of such real changes on trust and credit are crucial: Credit can affect trust and make the real changes even stronger; to answer that negative feedback, the banking system needs a large reserve. The most important role in maintaining the right reserve belongs to the Bank of England. However:

If we ask how the Bank of England has discharged this great responsibility, we shall be struck by three things: *first*, as has been said before, the Bank has never by any corporate act or authorised utterance acknowledged the duty, and some of its directors deny it; *second* (what is even more remarkable), no resolution of Parliament, no report of any Committee of Parliament (as far as I know), no remembered speech of a responsible statesman, has assigned or enforced that duty on the Bank; *third* (what is more remarkable still), the distinct teaching of our highest authorities has often been that no public duty of any kind is imposed on the Banking Department of the Bank; that, for banking purposes, it is only a joint stock bank like any other bank; that its managers should look only to the interest of the proprietors and their dividend; that they are to manage as the London and Westminster Bank or the Union Bank manages. (p. 162)

The reason for this abrogation of responsibility goes back to past formulations that remind one of the Real Bills Doctrine. The Bank in previous times

believed that so long as they issued "notes" only at 5 per cent, and only on the discount of good bills, those notes could not be depreciated. … Unluckily … the directors of the Bank of England were neither acquainted with right principles, nor were they protected by a judicious routine. They could not be expected themselves to discover such principles. The abstract thinking of the world is never to be expected from persons in high places. (p. 179)

However, not through abstract thinking, but through practical experience, the Bank learned how to use the instrument of interest rates to build the reserves. They did not know how to do this in 1857, but by 1864 they had learned how to stop the panic (pp. 183–185).

Bagehot's well-known policy rule appears in this context: In a panic, the Bank has to lend while raising the price of its advances (interest rates). However, there are no rules or prespecified plans for executing such actions. The reserve should be built up in good times, and a clever policy should be implemented in bad times. It all depends on the Bank management, and this management suffered from "grave defects in its form of government"

(p. 187). The rapid rotations at the governor post make the decisions made in the early period of each governor's "reign" particularly open to errors:

The usual defect then is, that the Bank of England does not raise the rate of interest sufficiently quickly. ... A cautious man, in a new office, does not like strong measures. Bank Governors are generally cautious men; they are taken from a most cautious class; in consequence they are very apt to temporise and delay. But almost always the delay in creating a stringency only makes a greater stringency inevitable. The effect of a timid policy has been to let the gold out of the Bank, and that gold must be recovered. It would really have been far easier to have maintained the reserve by timely measures than to have replenished it by delayed measures; but new Governors rarely see this. (pp. 187–188)

The role of the Bank is to prevent panics, and the reserves are the instrument to be used. Having appropriate reserves is not enough; one has to know how to use them. The Bank has to decide when to step in and extend loans and when to refrain; in a panic the decision is crucial. The complex interdependencies of the financial institutions and the nonbanking customers make the financial system more fragile than people usually understand. The pressure is on the Banking Department; the demand in crises is for Bank notes which are "*legal tender*." The reserve of those notes would soon disappear:

Nothing, therefore, can be more certain than that the Bank of England has in this respect no peculiar privilege; that it is simply in the position of a Bank keeping the banking reserve of the country; that it must in time of panic do what all other similar banks must do; that in time of panic it must advance freely and vigorously to the public out of the reserve.

And with the Bank of England, as with other Banks in the same case, these advances, if they are to be made at all, should be made so as, if possible, to obtain the object for which they are made. The end is to stay the panic; and the advances should, if possible, stay the panic. And for this purpose there are two rules:

First. That these loans should only be made at a very high rate of interest. This will operate as a heavy fine on unreasonable timidity, and will prevent the greatest number of applications by persons who do not require it. The rate should be raised early in the panic, so that the fine may be paid early; that no one may borrow out of idle precaution without paying well for it; that the Banking reserve may be protected as far as possible.

Secondly. That at this rate these advances should be made on all good banking securities, and as largely as the public ask for them. The reason is plain. The object is to stay alarm, and nothing therefore should be done to cause alarm. (pp. 198–199)

The Bank should not refuse "good securities" because then "the alarm will not abate, the other loans made will fail in obtaining their end, and the panic will become worse and worse. ... The only safe plan for the Bank is the brave plan, to lend in a panic on every kind of current security, or every sort on which money is ordinarily and usually lent. This policy may not save the Bank; but if it do not, nothing will save it" (p. 201). In a historical discussion of crises since 1825, Bagehot attempts to prove this limit on the Bank's prowess.

Bagehot's analysis of the body that manages the money market is full of modern insights concerning ownership and management.[19] "In theory, nothing can be worse than this government for a bank – a shifting executive; a board of directors chosen too young for it to be known whether they are able; a committee of management, in which seniority is the necessary qualification, and old age the common result; and no trained bankers anywhere" (p. 219). The reform in management that Bagehot proposes is aimed at professionalizing the Bank. He suggests adding a "permanent Deputy-Governor," representing the best traditions of a civil servant within the government structure, to the decision-making process.

The problem of managing banking activities was also a major worry with the joint-stock banks. Bagehot, in contrast to Loyd but like Joplin, supported those institutions; however, their speedy growth had been accompanied by disproportional reliance on the Bank of England's reserves. Like many other issues, this fact remained hidden in the shadows of the overemphasized currency and Bank Act discussions. Thus, the rise of joint-stock banking contributed significantly to the concentration of the reserves, the major change in the English money market. Although Bagehot supported these institutions, he noticed a weakness in their management (pp. 257–268).

The issue of proper management was also the focus of his treatment of two additional institutions: private banking and the bill brokers. The crucial management role of the Banking Department of the Bank of England concerned the Bank's reserves. The traditional approach was to have a rule-of-third reserves against liabilities – the famous Palmer Rule. According to Bagehot, however, a more serious analysis should take into account the various liabilities and distinguish between those that can be presented without giving advance notice and those that require some time interval before withdrawal; it should assess their impact on others in the market. Thus, the Bank's liabilities to the government were sensitive because they could change dramatically, but "Bankers' deposits" were very sensitive as well, contrary to what many people thought, and were especially so during panics:

A deposit which is not likely to vary in ordinary times, and which is likely to augment in times of danger, seems, in some sort, the model of a deposit. It might seem not only that a large proportion of it might be lent, but that the whole of it might be so. But a further analysis will, as I believe, show that this conclusion is entirely

---

[19]   See in particular chapter VIII, "The Government of the Bank."

false; that the bankers' deposits are a singularly treacherous form of liability; that the utmost caution ought to be used in dealing with them; that, as a rule, a less proportion of them ought to be lent than of ordinary deposits. (p. 310)

The conclusion then was clear:

The result comes round to the simple point, on which this book is a commentary: the Bank of England, by the effect of a long history, holds the ultimate cash reserve of the country; whatever cash the country has to pay comes out of that reserve, and therefore the Bank of England has to pay it. And it is as the Bankers' Bank that the Bank of England has to pay it, for it is by being so that it becomes the keeper of the final cash reserve. (pp. 316–317)

As for the correct policy, Bagehot denies any possible simple rule or blueprint on either the risk facing the Bank, which was impossible to calculate, or the right amount of reserves. The reaction of the Bank in times of crisis had again to follow a very general path and make advances at higher interest rates; but Bagehot refrains from any clear specifications as to the exact schedules. It is up to the discretion of the management of the Bank to determine the policy.

What is almost a revolution in the policy of the Bank of England necessarily follows: no certain or fixed proportion of its liabilities can in the present times be laid down as that which the Bank ought to keep in reserve. The old notion that one-third, or any other such fraction, is in all cases enough, must be abandoned. The probable demands upon the Bank are so various in amount, and so little disclosed by the figures of the account, that no simple and easy calculation is a sufficient guide. A definite proportion of the liabilities might often be too small for the reserve, and sometimes too great. The forces of the enemy being variable, those of the defence cannot always be the same.

I admit that this conclusion is very inconvenient. In past times it has been a great aid to the Bank and to the public to be able to decide on the proper policy of the Bank from a mere inspection of its account. In that way the Bank knew easily what to do and the public knew easily what to foresee. But, unhappily, the rule which is most simple is not always the rule which is most to be relied upon. The practical difficulties of life often cannot be met by very simple rules; those dangers being complex and many, the rules for encountering them cannot well be single or simple. A uniform remedy for many diseases often ends by killing the patient. (pp. 320–321)

Along with the well-known rule to keep reserves as a "third of liabilities" was the common rule about interest rates: Look to the market rate of interest for guidance and make the Bank rate equal to it. Bagehot argues that this rule was "always erroneous" and had recently become even more so:

The first duty of the Bank of England was to protect the ultimate cash of the country, and to raise the rate of interest so as to protect it. But this rule was never so erroneous as now, because the number of sudden demands upon that reserve was never formerly so great. The market rate of Lombard Street is not influenced by those demands. That rate is determined by the amount of deposits in the hands of bill-brokers and bankers, and the amount of good bills and acceptable securities offered at the moment. (pp. 321–322)

The rate is the equilibrium of the market for loans, reflecting intermediation, and was not related to defending convertibility. Thus, discretion must replace the search for a clear directive capable of answering many contingencies:

There is no "royal road" to the amount of the "apprehension minimum": no abstract argument, and no mathematical computation will teach it to us. And we cannot expect that they should. Credit is an opinion generated by circumstances and varying with those circumstances. The state of credit at any particular time is a matter of fact only to be ascertained like other matters of fact; it can only be known by trial and inquiry. And in the same way, nothing but experience can tell us what amount of "reserve" will create a diffused confidence; on such a subject there is no way of arriving at a just conclusion except by incessantly watching the public mind, and seeing at each juncture how it is affected. (pp. 324–325).

The Bank's considerations should always aim at maintaining the "apprehension minimum" while remembering that this might change from time to time; that the damages for keeping too-small a reserve are much higher than keeping too much; and that expectations play an important role in the complicated game between the public and the Bank.[20] After several hesitant attempts, Bagehot proposes a figure for the reserves, an "estimate" which is "arbitrary" – "conjectures" to be presented to "the judgment of others" who will be capable of assessing and deciding. The others should be the governing body of the Banking Department of the Bank of England:

I shall perhaps be told also that a body like the Court of the Directors of the Bank of England cannot act on estimates like these: that such a body must have a plain rule and keep to it. I say in reply, that if the correct framing of such estimates is necessary for the good guidance of the Bank, we must make a governing body which can correctly frame such estimates. We must not suffer from a dangerous policy because we have inherited an imperfect form of administration. I have before explained in what

---

[20] "… the 'apprehension minimum' is not always the same. On the contrary, in times when the public has recently seen the Bank of England exposed to remarkable demands, it is likely to expect that such demands may come again. Conspicuous and recent events educate it, so to speak; it expects that much will be demanded when much has of late often been demanded, and that little will be so, when in general but little has been so. A bank like the Bank of England must always, therefore, be on the watch for a rise, if I may so express it, in the apprehension minimum; it must provide an adequate fund not only to allay the misgivings of to-day, but also to allay what may be the still greater misgivings of to-morrow. And the only practical mode of obtaining this object is to keep the actual reserve always in advance of the minimum 'apprehension' reserve" (pp. 325–326).

manner the government of the Bank of England should, I consider, be strengthened, and that government so strengthened would, I believe, be altogether competent to a wise policy. (p. 329)

Furthermore, argues Bagehot, in order to never go below that mark of 10
million pounds, at least 11 to 11.5 million should be kept in reserve, because
"experience shows that a million, or a million and half, may be taken from us
at any time." In order not to go below 11.5 million, the Bank should "take pre-
cautions when the reserve is between 14,000,000l. and 15,000,000l." Thus, the
reserves should be in fact between 14 and 15 million pounds, because it was
known that a sudden move could push the amount toward a dangerous level.
"[When] it begins to be diminished by foreign demand, the Bank of England
should, I think, begin to act, and raise the rate of interest" (p. 330). Bagehot
stops the chain of estimates here, but he could have of course continued.

Thus, Bagehot concludes the book and his description of the money market with the following lesson:

We must therefore, I think, have recourse to feeble and humble palliatives such as I
have suggested. With good sense, good judgment, and good care, I have no doubt
that they may be enough. But I have written in vain if I require to say now that the
problem is delicate, that the solution is varying and difficult, and that the result is
inestimable to us all. (p. 336)

Who Influenced Bagehot?

O'Brien (2003) sees the missing link in the history of the concept of the
Lender of Last Resort (LLR) between Thornton and Bagehot in Thomas
Joplin, who indirectly may have had an influence on Bagehot via Vincent
Stuckey. According to this interpretation, Joplin's discovery of the LLR
concept occurred at the height of the 1825 crisis, in a short article Joplin
published in the *Courier* of December13, 1825. The Bank was reluctant
to "support financial institutions" and Joplin urged the Bank "to alter its
course dramatically" (O'Brien 2003, p. 6). As Joplin argued repeatedly in
later years, and O'Brien concurs, this article and a series of others that followed changed both public opinion and the Bank's course of action. The
crisis is due to "want of confidence," he writes; the public demands Bank
notes and the Bank's directors should supply them. The newly issued notes
would not enter the circulation but would be kept outside of it by the public, and would not have any impact on either prices or the exchanges:

In the state of the money market, the Directors have a very easy test by which to
regulate their issues. So long as the pressure is unnatural (of which they will be able

to form a tolerable judgment) the demand must be unnatural, and may be supplied without any increase to the quantity of money, which would otherwise have been in actual circulation. On the other hand, when confidence is restored, the Directors will perceive, by the depreciated value of money in the market, the period when the money hoarded and supplied to the Country Bankers is beginning to find its way back into the circulation of London, and this, of course, will be the proper time for withdrawing their surplus issues. ... The Bank, indeed, is, in a great measure, bound to administer the relief necessary upon such occasions. (Joplin 1832, pp. 222–223)

The issue of additional notes would not affect the exchanges. The one authority that Joplin cites is Smith, who explained that more circulation would overflow and not have any impact on the exchanges. Joplin clearly talks about a short-term policy with a "temporary purpose," not lasting for "many months." It is interesting to note that in 1832, Joplin refers to Thornton's work on public credit, which he cites as supporting the idea that "in a period of panic, the Bank ought rather to lean to the side of enlarging, than contracting its issues." However, Joplin complains that Thornton did not fully understand his own argument and "the advice is given with caution" (Joplin 1832, p. 235). But the advice was "more strongly and concisely" adopted by the Bullion Report.

O'Brien dramatizes the effect of Joplin's *Courier* article and speculates that it indirectly influenced the Bank's change of mind. O'Brien also argues, however, that the change was probably achieved through a different means of intervention, that of a banker who was less of "an outsider" than Joplin, Vincent Stuckey, who wrote a letter to the Bank on December 14 on the need for a policy reversal. Despite this recognition and Stuckey's own claim to fame in the 1832 Committee and other places, O'Brien insists that it was Joplin who "produced the dramatic intervention of the Bank" (O'Brien, p. 7). Moreover, O'Brien argues that an "incidental fact" suggests that there might have been an indirect intellectual link between Joplin and Bagehot, because Stuckey was Bagehot's maternal uncle, and Bagehot worked at Stuckey's bank.

O'Brien argues that the Banking School did not develop "the case for a lender of last resort" (p. 7 n) and "did not develop the insights bequeathed by Thornton"; in making this case he relies on Tooke's evidence from 1832, when the latter was not yet a Banking School member. In the years after 1844, as we have seen in Chapter 12, the Banking School, and Tooke in particular, proposed a concept of defensive monetary policy similar to that of Bagehot's in 1873. Thus, in 1848 as before, Tooke advocated a more flexible banking system, stabilized by and based on a big reserve of bullion. This would leave the Bank's directors, as we have seen, much broader margins in the face of (transitory) gold drains. In case the drain should continue beyond what was considered "transitory," the directors should react by increasing the rate of interest, argues Tooke, which was their first policy tool. If this dis-cretionary action should prove insufficient and the drain should continue, a "corrective measure" should be taken that is completely in the discretion of the Bank's directors.[21] Like Bagehot in 1873, Tooke in 1848 placed growing emphasis on the quality of the Bank's management. In fact, this aspect of Bagehot's thought was most likely influenced by Tooke. In *Lombard Street*, Bagehot quotes Tooke once, and the context is the Bank's structure:

> It has been said, with exaggeration, but not without a basis of truth, that if the Bank directors were to sit for four hours, there would be "a panic solely from that." "The court," says Mr. Tooke, "meets at half-past eleven or twelve; and, if the sit-ting be prolonged beyond half-past one, the Stock Exchange and the money market become excited, under the idea that a change of importance is under discussion; and persons congregate about the doors of the Bank parlour to obtain the earliest intimation of the decision." (Bagehot 1873, p. 243)

Bagehot does not tell us, but the quote comes from one of the last texts written by Tooke in 1856, *On the Bank Charter Act of 1844, its Principles and Operation, with suggestions for an improved administration of the Bank of England*. In this text, Tooke elaborates on the role of the Bank and expands his ideas for monetary policy, probably developed after the 1844 Bank Act's failure in the crisis of 1847. We will return to these mature monetary ideas in Chapter 18 while discussing the slow rise of a concept of active monetary policy.

Lombard Street on Free Banking

Bagehot tries to rationalize the existing banking system, which is a monop-oly; he prefers, in principle, competition in banking.

> But it will be said – What would be better? What other system could there be? We are so accustomed to a system of banking, dependent for its cardinal function on a single bank, that we can hardly conceive of any other. But the natural system – that which would have sprung up if Government had let banking alone – is that of many banks of equal or not altogether unequal size. In all other trades competition brings the traders to a rough approximate equality. In cotton spinning, no single firm far and permanently outstrips the others. There is no tendency to a monarchy in the cotton world; nor, where banking has been left free, is there any tendency to a monarchy in banking either. In Manchester, in Liverpool, and all through England, we have a great number of banks, each with a business more or less good, but we have no single bank with any sort of predominance; nor is there any such bank in

---

[21] See Chapter 12 for an elaborate discussion. The claims were made for example in the Parliamentary Committee (1848, pp. 419–420). We will elaborate in Chapter 18.

Scotland. In the new world of Joint Stock Banks outside the Bank of England, we see much the same phenomenon. One or more get for a time a better business than the others, but no single bank permanently obtains an unquestioned predominance. None of them gets so much before the others that the others voluntarily place their reserves in its keeping. A republic with many competitors of a size or sizes suitable to the business, is the constitution of every trade if left to itself, and of banking as much as any other. A monarchy in any trade is a sign of some anomalous advantage, and of some intervention from without. (pp. 69–70)

Bagehot's well-known position in favor of competition was an abstract argument. It was not an argument for a radical reform in the system but rather, we would say, a clever scoring point with no practical and very limited theoretical weight. He recommends acceptance of the system as it in fact historically grew, appreciating the advantages it had:

I shall be at once asked – Do you propose a revolution? Do you propose to abandon the one-reserve system, and create anew a many-reserve system? My plain answer is that I do not propose it. I know it would be childish. Credit in business is like loyalty in Government. You must take what you can find of it, and work with it if possible. A theorist may easily map out a scheme of Government in which Queen Victoria could be dispensed with. He may make a theory that, since we admit and we know that the House of Commons is the real sovereign, any other sovereign is superfluous; but for practical purposes, it is not even worth while to examine these arguments. Queen Victoria is loyally obeyed – without doubt, and without reasoning – by millions of human beings. If those millions began to argue, it would not be easy to persuade them to obey Queen Victoria, or anything else. Effectual arguments to convince the people who need convincing are wanting. Just so, an immense system of credit, founded on the Bank of England as its pivot and its basis, now exists. The English people, and foreigners too, trust it implicitly. Every banker knows that if he has to prove that he is worthy of credit, however good may be his arguments, in fact his credit is gone: but what we have requires no proof. The whole rests on an instinctive confidence generated by use and years. Nothing would persuade the English people to abolish the Bank of England; and if some calamity swept it away, generations must elapse before at all the same trust would be placed in any other equivalent. A many-reserve system, if some miracle should put it down in Lombard Street, would seem monstrous there. Nobody would understand it, or confide in it. Credit is a power which may grow, but cannot be constructed. Those who live under a great and firm system of credit must consider that if they break up that one they will never see another, for it will take years upon years to make a successor to it. (pp. 69–71)

Summary

Bagehot's policy rule articulates what the Bank's directors should have known and should have done had they not blinded themselves to what they perceived as their legal role in the banking system, and were they more accepting of their actual position. In some cases, rarely, they behaved in fact as if they managed the banking system, particularly in 1866, but they did not have a theory to justify their actions. Bagehot, a careful observer for many years of the Bank's actions, and well informed about the directors' unsatisfactory theory, explained to the Bank and the public why Bank interventions were justified. The British banking system, centralized as it was around the Bank, was prone to crises, and the central body needed to understand its role and step in. The causes for the recurring crises were the result of inherent instabilities rooted in the actual complexity of the money market. When many different institutions are involved in accepting funds and extending them (intermediation), the resulting fragility is unavoidable. The instability arises in the sphere of intermediation but also threatens the exchange process. The problems that call for interventions in banking are caused to a large degree by intermediation, but threaten exchange. Like his predecessors Hume, Smith, and Ricardo, Bagehot understood the advantages of a monetary economy over barter; however, he concluded that the modern, complex money market cannot rely on decentralized, uncoordinated mechanisms. The threats are too great.

The policy rule discussed in *Lombard Street* is not monetary policy in the modern sense; it does not aim to improve macroeconomic performance, but rather aims to defend the system. The weakest part of the money market, the one that caused the most trouble over the one hundred years before Bagehot published *Lombard Street*, was the reserves backing the system. Runs on the banking system always led to pressure on the centralized reserves of cash, whether gold or silver or other "hard money" mediums; Bagehot answers by strengthening the ability of the Bank to answer those demands. Hence, it is a defensive policy that Bagehot proposes, not the more active policy that Thornton and to some degree Ricardo (1824) offered. Wicksell is the one who returns to active monetary policy, but before exploring his monetary thought in Chapter 17, let us discuss Marx and Marshall, two men who studied classical monetary theory very carefully.

FIFTEEN

Does Karl Marx Fit In?

Introduction

Many volumes have been written on Marx's life, on his intellectual development, and on different aspects of his political and economic writings. In this chapter, we limit the discussion only to those aspects that will facilitate understanding of a relatively neglected topic: Marx's monetary theory and how it relates to classical monetary theory.[1] In 1846–1847, Marx wrote his critique of Proudhon, in which he accepted both Ricardo's labor theory of value[2] and his monetary theory (Rosdolsky 1977, p. 2). Although Marx's first work on political economy did not appear until 1859, he had felt his studies to be drawing to a close as early as 1851;[3] by this time, Marx had already developed a critique of Ricardo's money theory.[4] The first known important work to include a comprehensive analysis of money – the *Grundrisse* – was written between August 1857 and March 1858 but was only published in German in 1953.

The first chapter of *Grundrisse*, entitled "On money," and the chapter entitled "On money as capital" formed the core of the book published in 1859, *A Contribution to the Critique of Political Economy*. After this, the *Contribution*, in its turn, formed the core of the chapters on money in *Capital* I, which was published in 1867. Thus, we can see three milestones in the development of Marx's monetary theory during his lifetime: the *Grundrisse*, the *Contribution*, and *Capital* I. After Marx's death in 1883, *Capital* volumes II

[1] The chapter draws on Arnon 1984. (See Brunhoff 1976; Foley 1983, 2003; Rosdolsky 1977, part II.)
[2] See Marx 1963, pp. 87–88, 154 ff. For a detailed account of Marx's development regarding the labor theory of value, see Mandel (1971, pp. 40–51) and Rubin (1972).
[3] Marx to Engels, April 2, 1851, *Marx-Engels Werke (M.E.W.)*, 27:218.
[4] See *M.E.W.*, 27: pp. 173–177, 200–201; Rosdolsky 1977, p. 5.

(1885) and III (1894) were published by his friend Frederick Engels. These volumes were primarily written before the publication of volume I in 1867, and were just edited posthumously by Engels.

Much of the somewhat limited discussion of Marx's monetary theory has concentrated on the *Contribution* and *Capital* I (Brunhoff 1973; Foley 1983, 2003). This chapter will focus instead on the development of his monetary theory from the preliminary, rough presentation of 1857 in the *Grundrisse* to the fairly complete presentation of 1859 in the *Contribution*, and to the mature formulations as they appear in 1894 in *Capital* III. Analysis of Marx's development will clarify his attitude toward the Classical School and reveal the extent of his debt to the Banking School and to Thomas Tooke.

Marx's Thoughts on Money – 1857

Marx's theories cannot be treated separately from his methodology. Marx thought that correct method could in itself determine the difference between true and false theories. While writing the *Grundrisse*, he set down his views on methodology as the correct way to arrive at an understanding of a complex reality (Marx 1857, pp. 100–108). While we will not deal directly with Marx's methodology, it is important to note that the methodological conclusions that he drew in 1857 determined his point of departure in analyzing capitalism: the commodity. This in turn determined his discussion of money and led to what is known as his *general* theory of money. As de Brunhoff (1976, pp. 19–25) explains, Marx's analysis of money opens with a discussion on money that could fit every economy in which commodities – products for exchange – exist and in which the exchange is not barter. For Marx, money is the general equivalent, a commodity standing against all others. Thus, money must necessarily be a commodity like all others, but at the same time, set apart from them. These two aspects are essential and complementary.

The general theory of money, which in Marx's view is a precondition for understanding money in capitalism, was at least partially formulated in 1857. As in many other instances, the general theory developed from a critique, in this case of the theory of labor-money popular at the time. The chapter "On money" in the *Grundrisse*, which was written by Marx in October and November 1857 (notebook I and the first pages of II), opens with a discussion on the proposal to create money that would represent labor time. The source for this idea, as well as its popularity, derived of course from the notion of labor as the sole creator of value and determinant of prices. According to its supporters, such money – labor-money – would remove the defects from the existing monetary system and with them the basic distortions of capitalist society. This suggestion was based on the view that money has to have the same status as commodities, that is, money should not have any privileges. This solution was popular among the Proudhonists, who argued that the economic crisis in France was caused by pressure in the money market arising from a shortage of gold. The solution to this shortage was, in their view, to supply free credit. The Proudhonists thought that a supply of credit representing labor time would remove both the causes of crisis in the economy and the basis for inequality in society. This of course fit their value theory and their more general view of the ideal society, a society in which communities of independent laborers who own their means of production would live in harmony. Marx's criticism of their support for labor-money was based on two points: (a) Because no form of money can change the basic relation between production and circulation, it is impossible to get rid of crises by creating a new form of money[5]; (b) the suggestion that paper money represents labor time rather than gold does not resolve the problem of rises and falls in prices, as the originators of this proposal claimed it did. The assumption made by the supporters of labor-money, that "time-chits" would equalize values and prices, was false. This equality of price and value, a distinction that played such an important role in the arguments around the famous "transformation problem," holds only as an average; value is the determining factor behind prices and is the direct cause of specific price, but value is not identical with price. Thus, the creation of "paper chits" representing labor time will not solve any of the problems that emerge during the process of circulation:

The first basic illusion of the time-chitters consists in this, that by annulling the nominal difference between real value and market value, between exchange value and price – that is, by expressing value in units of labour time itself instead of in a given objectification of labour time, say gold and silver – that in so doing they also remove the real difference and contradiction between price and value. Given this illusory assumption it is self-evident that the mere introduction of the time-chit does away with all crises, all faults of bourgeois production (Marx 1857, p. 138).

The comparison between commodities is made by means of a third commodity, first in the mind and then through actual exchange. "Time-chits"

---

5. "Various forms of money may correspond better to social production in various stages: one form may remedy evils against which another is powerless; but none of the, as long as they remain forms of money, and as long as money remains an essential relation of production, is capable of overcoming the contradictions inherent in the money relation, and can instead only hope to reproduce these contradictions in one or another form" (Marx, 1857, p. 123).

would not be able to perform this function because they are "not a third commodity but ... rather their own measure of value, labour time itself" (see ibid., pp. 139, 140–142).

As mentioned earlier, the Proudhonists saw the main defect in the monetary system as lying in the outstanding privileged status of gold. The strict connection between means of circulation and gold prevented any elasticity in the Bank's policy and created a situation in which society at large could not control its circulation because it was prevented from fixing the amount of means in circulation. On the other hand, the Proudhonists objected to the unlimited printing of paper money. They thought that as prices, in the final analysis, represent the labor time invested in the product, so money, including paper money, should represent labor time. Successful creation of such money was the key to a new society. One of the direct conclusions of this view was the suggestion that all commodities should have the same status vis-à-vis gold, in the sense that all commodities should have the same privileges in operating as the medium of exchange. "Let the pope remain, but make everybody pope," Marx remarked on this view.

From the standpoint of what was to become the general theory of money, Marx "negates the question" raised: Gold, as specific money, could not be a commodity like all other commodities. The "bourgeois system" needs an instrument of exchange and this instrument needs to be in the form of an exclusive commodity. If one suggests that no commodity should be exclusive, then one is in fact suggesting: "Abolish money and don't abolish money! Abolish the exclusive privilege possessed by gold and silver in virtue of their exclusive monetary role, but turn all commodities to money, i.e. give them all together equally a quality which no longer exists once its exclusiveness is gone" (ibid., p. 127).

This position clearly sums up Marx's general theory of money: Money is both a commodity like all others and a unique commodity. Money as the general equivalent, as a particular commodity and a general exchange value, emerges out of this view. Rosdolsky (1977) argues that in the *Grundrisse*, which he prefers to call the Rough Draft, Marx sees money "as the embodiment of value in the sense of 'the Ideal, the Universal, the One' in contrast with commodities, which in Hegelian terms represent 'the Real, Particularity, the Many.'" This view reflects Hegel's influence and it led Marx, incorrectly, "to regard money as a mere sign of value" (Rosdolsky 1977, p. 113). In Rosdolsky's view, the error lies in "equating the concepts 'representing' and 'symbolising.'" He also claims that from the *Contribution* (1859) onwards, there is "no trace of this 'symbol theory' in Marx's works." We would argue that the symbol theory of money is not false and Marx himself in his various drafts on credit did not abandon it. It did not appear in *Capital* I because Marx was explicitly treating a system without credit.[6]

Money functions in the process of production and exchange in several different ways. The first function of money, which arises directly from Marx's analysis of money as the universal equivalent (from money as the form in which exchange value is materialized against commodity as use value), is to measure value. The value of every commodity, the social abstract labor time embodied in it, is equated to the value of the money commodity (gold). This appears in the *Grundrisse* in the section devoted mainly to criticism of labor-money. When money functions as a measure of value, the possibility of its functioning as a medium of exchange already exists. Marx discusses the relationship between these two functions and raises the possibility of a contradiction between them.[7] In its function as a measure of value, money has to have value in itself, and this, of course, can only be variable value. Money as a measure of value provides the common denominator for commodities, which are qualitatively different because of the different concrete labors embodied in them (Marx 1857, p. 189). The concept of abstract labor is not yet mentioned here by name, but the idea of abstract labor as the basis of a value theory, against Ricardo's concept of general labor, does exist.[8] Whereas in its function as a measure of value the actual quantity of money is not significant, and what is important is *the value of the money commodity*, as a medium of exchange, *the quantity of money in circulation* is important, whereas its value is insignificant.

The core question is how the actual quantity of the medium of exchange in circulation influences the determination of prices (absolute prices). Ricardo

[6] As long as the system is such that gold and convertible paper circulate side by side, a clear principle of limitation on the credit system is in operation. In their management of credit, banks must be guided by their need to maintain convertibility. In this situation, paper money does represent a commodity (gold); via this association, it is equated with other commodities both in the mind – as a unit of account, a measure of value – and in reality, as a means of exchange. It is not difficult to see that in an inconvertible situation, paper money does not represent gold, but in fact symbolizes commodities. In other words, its value is determined in circulation "as a mere sign of value." The importance of the subjective moment becomes clear when we examine intermediate situations that are really inconvertible, but in which there are continuous expectations of a return to gold. In such situations, inconvertible paper money still represents gold; only when there is no such expectation of a return to gold does it act as a symbol. Rosdolsky's view that paper money never acts as a symbol leads him to conclude that money is always based on gold.

[7] "In its quality of being a measure, money is indifferent to its quantity, or, the existing quantity of money makes no difference. Its quantity is measured in its quality as medium of exchange, as instrument of circulation. Whether these two qualities of money can enter into contradiction with one another – to be looked at later" (Marx 1857, p. 196).

[8] The concept of abstract labor appeared in 1859.

and Hume supported the position that the quantity in circulation determines prices. Marx opposes this position, because he thinks that, in general, abstracting from the oscillation of prices of commodities around their values, (production) prices are determined before the process of exchange. Marx uses the terms "real money" and "accounting money" to explain the process by which prices are determined. The key point is that "real money" is not needed in this process: "Money is needed here only as a category, as mental relation."[9]

For readers not familiar with Marxian terminology, Marx had his own method for describing the flow of commodities and money. In exchange, people sell a commodity for money (C-M) and use the money to buy another commodity (M-C); in short, C-M-C. In production, people use money to buy commodities, in this case, means of production and labor (M-C). The commodities they produce are then sold for money (C-M); in short, M-C-C-M. The circulation of money is, in Marx's view, determined by the circulation of commodities. Although this did not mean that the former is unable to affect the latter,[10] Marx's conclusion is that "This much is clear, that prices are not high or low because much or little money circulates but that much or little money circulates because prices are high or low" (Marx 1973, p. 195). Shades of the Banking School and in particular of Tooke's formulation are apparent in this important anti–Quantity Theory principle, which will be developed further later.

The main difficulty that Marx is dealing with in this context is the possibility of crisis. The existence of money brings with it the possibility of a discrepancy between production and the realization of this production through a gap between sale and purchase (Marx 1857, 148, pp. 199–200). The third function of money appears as a solution to the discrepancy between the quantity of money needed for circulation and the quantity that actually exists, subject to the condition that the value of money itself, as a commodity, is determined in production, that is, "before" circulation. This contradiction rises from the circuit M-C-C-M, and Marx derives the third function of money from this circuit: buying commodities in order to sell them. This kind of interpretation of the third function of money, money

---

[9] "Money only circulates commodities which have already been *ideally* transformed into money, not only in the head of the individual but in the conception held by society (directly, the conception held by the participants in the process of buying and selling). This ideal transformation into money is by no means determined by the same laws as the real transformation." (Marx 1857, p. 187)

[10] "The circulation of commodities is the original precondition of the circulation of money. To what extent the latter then reacts back on the circulation of commodities remains to be seen." (Marx 1857, p. 187)

that escapes circulation, appears only in the *Grundrisse,* and not in the *Contribution,* as Rosdolsky points out (1977, p. 150):

[It] already implies that money functions neither only as measure, nor only as medium of exchange, nor only as both; but has yet a third quality. It appears here *firstly* as an end in itself, whose sole realization is served by commodity trade and exchange. *Secondly,* since the cycle concludes with it at that point, it steps *outside* it, just as the commodity, having been exchanged for its equivalent through money, is thrown out of circulation. (Marx 1857, pp. 202–203)

Marx argues that when there is a surplus in the amount of the medium in circulation, this surplus is "accumulated." Marx uses the term "piling up" (*Anhaufen*) for that money (gold) which is extracted from circulation and represents general wealth (Marx 1857, pp. 229–233). This "piled-up" money is not capital, argues Marx. In order to be capital, it has to be a moment in the accumulation of capital when returning to circulation. This is not yet money as a hoard, as it was developed in 1859, either in its content or even in its name. When Marx in 1857 analyzes the "original form" of circulation, C-M-M-C, the third function of money still does not exist (see ibid., p. 212). The term "hoarding" was introduced in the *Grundrisse* around the middle of 1858. The term was borrowed from Thornton and referred to *a moment in the process of circulation,* as the following passage shows clearly:

"Guineas are *hoarded* in time of distrust" (Thornton, p. 48). The *hoarding principle,* in which money functions as independent value, is, apart from the striking forms in which it appears, necessary as *one moment* of exchange resting on money circulation; since everyone, as A. Smith says, needs, beside his own commodity, the medial quantity, a certain proportion of the "general commodity." (ibid., p. 816)

Thus, Marx in the *Grundrisse* still argues that the third function of money, in which money appears not just as a *medium* or *measure,* but as an end in itself, and hence stops outside circulation just like a particular commodity that ceases to circulate, "is developed from the circuit M-C-C-M" (ibid., p. 215). In the next section, we shall see that the 1859 text explains hoarding quite differently. The new explanation serves to complete Marx's theory of money as it appears in *Capital* I. In addition, the change is of importance because it was significantly influenced by the mature Banking School views of Thomas Tooke.

Marx's Mature Formulation – 1859

Less than two years elapsed between the Rough Draft and *A contribution to the critique of political economy,* where Marx first used the concept of "abstract labor" to complete his original version of the labor theory of value. It is clear that the introduction of "abstract labor" marked a departure from Ricardo's version of value rather than just a modification or revision of it. As is clear from Marx's Historical Notes (Marx 1859, pp. 52–63), he considered the concept of "abstract labor" to be necessary for a correct conception of money. "Abstract labor" is the theoretical solution to the real contradiction between value in use, which is created by concrete labor, and value in exchange, which is the result of unquantifiable abstract labor. Marx thought that money, as the crystallization of exchange value, could not be understood without this distinction.

A second significant change to appear in 1858, on which we will concentrate here, concerned Marx's conception of the third function of money. In this section, we shall present Marx's mature formulation of 1859 and compare it with the earlier 1857 draft. This comparison will also form the basis for evaluating the extent of Tooke's influence during Marx's transition between these two formulations. A third, less important point of difference concerns the critical treatment in the *Grundrisse* of the theory of labor-money. The critique of this theory provided the impetus for the development of Marx's own theory, but was hardly mentioned in later formulations after it had outlived its purpose.[11]

The point of departure for both the *Contribution* and for *Capital* I was the analysis of a commodity. Money emerges with the emergence of "social labor as universal labor," meaning that when, with the growing division of labor, the role of exchange value rather than use value becomes dominant (Marx 1859, p. 52). In order to understand "the inherent laws of monetary circulation," one has to study money in its complete form. Thus, it is not enough to study only paper money or other forms of "tokens of value," such as coins (Marx 1859, pp. 121–122). It is necessary to begin with the basic form of money, commodity-money. The laws governing paper money can only be understood within the framework of a correct theory of what Marx sometimes called "real money," that is, commodity-money. For Marx, commodity-money is almost synonymous with gold; when gold is a measure of value to which all commodities are compared, it becomes money. Gold is the "embodiment of universal labor-time" from which the function of unit of account directly emerges. Thus gold functions both as a measure of value and as a standard of price:

Gold as materialized labour-time is a measure of value, as a piece of metal of definite weight it is the standard of price. ... Gold is the measure of value because its

---

[11] In fact, Marx devoted only a few paragraphs to this topic in 1859, and in 1867, it was relegated to a footnote. See also Rosdolsky (1977, p. 99).

value is variable; it is the standard of price because it has been established as an invariable unit of weight. (Marx 1859, p. 71)

The determination of the quantity of gold in circulation occurs in two stages. The sum of prices of commodities is determined by the production and the circulation of commodities, whereas the velocity of money is determined by the circulation of money itself. These two processes determine the quantity of gold in circulation:

Prices are thus high or low not because more or less money is in circulation, but there is more or less money in circulation because prices are high or low. This is one of the principal economic laws, and the detailed substantiation of it based on the history of prices *is perhaps the only achievement of the post-Ricardo English economics*. ... Since the quantity of gold in circulation depends upon two variable factors, the total amount of commodity-prices and the velocity of circulation it follows that it must be possible to reduce and expand the quantity of metallic currency. (ibid., pp. 106–107; my emphasis).

The rejection of the Quantity Theory was not a new idea. Marx is hinting at the criticisms of the Quantity Theory so typical of the Banking School, and in particular, of Tooke. The mechanism for changes in the quantity of gold so that it would adapt to commodity circulation provided by Marx in 1859 is that of hoarding and dishoarding. In the development of this concept between 1857 and 1859, Marx was considerably influenced by the mature writings of Tooke.

The third function of money is discussed by Marx in both 1857 and 1859 under the odd heading "Money as money." The term money as money really means that in its first two functions, money is not yet money; that is, when it functions as a medium in circulation, it has the form of a coin, of a symbol. Money as money, that is, gold as money, arises with the independent existence of money:

... a commodity in which the functions of standard of value and medium of circulation are united, accordingly becomes money, or the unity of standard of value and medium of circulation is money. But as such a unity, gold in its turn possesses an independent existence which is distinct from those two functions. As the standard of value gold is merely nominal money and nominal gold, purely as a medium of circulation it is symbolic money and symbolic gold, but in its simple metallic corporeality gold is money or money is real gold. (ibid., p. 124)

Turning to money as money in 1859, Marx seeks to derive it from the circuit C-M-C rather than from M-C-C-M. In the circuit C-M-C, one should look for the only possible source of the nonequivalence of M at the beginning of the circuit M-C-C-M and at its end: "money as distinct from the medium of circulation must be derived from C-M-C, the immediate form of commodity circulation," Marx writes in the *Contribution* (p. 123). Here, we have a new approach to the third function of money.

In April 1858 this point of departure for analyzing the third function of money had not yet appeared. In a letter to Engels[12] under the title "Money," Marx distinguishes between "(a) 'money as measure' and (b) 'money as a means of exchange, or simple circulation.'" In this letter to Engels, the third function, money as money, is derived from the circuit M-C-C-M, meaning *money as money arises from the monetary circuit*. However, in the last part of this letter, Marx already hints at the missing argument: Money during this process changes its quantity – it expands. The only source for this should be sought in the higher circuit, that of C-M-C.

In 1859, Marx discusses the third function of money under three subheadings: Hoarding, Means of Payment, and World Money. Hoarding, both historically and logically the first form of money as money, is based on the separation of purchase and sale. Hoarding is "the first form in which exchange value assumes an independent existence as money." In this sense, "hoard" is used in quite a different sense in 1859 than in 1857. In 1857, a hoard was the "piling up" of money outside circulation; now, a hoard is the creation of more use values than are consumed. "The fact that gold as money assumes an independent existence is thus above all a tangible morphosis of commodities into two discrete and separate transactions which exist side by side" (Marx 1859, p. 125). This is identical to the meaning Tooke gives to the term "hoarding." However, argues Marx, hoarding should not be confused with the reserves of coin needed to maintain the ability to buy at any time (liquidity), which are not yet money. This "first transformation of the medium of circulation into money constitutes therefore merely a technical aspect of the circulation of money" (ibid., p. 126).[13]

Money as money appears with the production of use values which are not consumed at once, that is, with the creation of a surplus exceeding immediate necessities. This surplus use value is represented by money: "Every use-value fulfills its function while it is being consumed, that is destroyed,

---

[12] See a letter to Engels on April 2nd, 1858, in Marx and Engels (1934, pp. 105–109).

[13] See also Marx (1859, p. 137): "Hoards must not be confused with reserve funds of coin, which form a constituent element of the total amount of money always in circulation, whereas the active relation of hoard and medium of circulation presupposes that the total amount of money decreases of increases."

but the use-value of gold as money is to represent exchange-value, to be the embodiment of universal labour-time as an amorphous raw material" (ibid., p. 127; my emphasis). Commodities in circulation are to be transformed into gold in order to remain wealth, to be "ossified" into gold, whereas gold becomes money only by not functioning as means in circulation.

One of the important features of gold as money is the impossibility of returning it to circulation, in contrast to coin. Gold in the form of hoard is "prevented from functioning as means of circulation and thus from becoming a merely transient monetary aspect of commodities" (ibid., p. 129). Or course, the hoard is "constantly in tension with circulation," otherwise it would have become a "heap of useless metal." Hoards provide the mechanism through which the amount of coins, the means of circulation, adapts to the needs of circulation, which in its turn "is merely a manifestation of the metamorphosis of commodities" (p. 136): "If prices fall or the velocity of circulation increases, then the money ejected from the sphere of circulation is absorbed by the reservoirs of hoarders; if prices rise or velocity of circulation decreases, then these hoards open and a part of them stream back into circulation" (Marx 1859, p. 136). On this proposition, Marx completely agreed with Tooke's mature stand that prices are the cause and not the result of changes in the circulation. Marx thought that banks in "advanced bourgeois countries" concentrated the hoards in their "reservoirs," thus functioning as the regulator of the quantity of the medium in circulation.

With the development of the capitalist mode of production, "New relations of intercourse arise in the process of circulation." These relations manifest themselves in the emergence of creditors and debtors, those persons who sell a commodity against future money and those who pay money against a past commodity. These transactions are carried out by money, which functions as *means of payment* (not to be confused with money which functions as means of exchange). This new function of money is in addition to the functions we have already met and complicates the analysis of money, because it appears to many writers as if this function is not only the "basic" function of money, but its definition.

Marx emphasizes the distinction between money functioning as means in circulation (sometimes called means of purchase) and the forms of money functioning as means of payment. "The difference between means of purchase and means of payment becomes very conspicuous, and unpleasantly so, at times of commercial crises" (ibid., p. 141), that is, when the apparent means of payment are exposed as only *representing* money, rather than as money itself.

Whereas in its function as a hoard-money, it is external to circulation in its function as means of payment, money remains in circulation. Here, it fulfills two necessary and contradictory roles. If all payments cancel each other out, it functions as a mere measure of value; if payments do not cancel each other out, it functions as means of circulation – not as a "transient" one (like coins), but as an "absolute commodity" (see Marx 1859, p. 146).

Up to this point, we have seen how the same material, gold, functions in three different ways and takes on three different forms. First, it takes the form of coin functioning as means of exchange (means of circulation). Second, it is "suspended coin" in the form of "coin reserves" ready for future transactions caused by the diachronic quantities of sales and purchases. In this form, gold is still in circulation. Third, we have gold in its pure material aspect, functioning as a hoard outside circulation. One has to analyze the function each form of gold performs in order to be able to determine its role in the process of circulation and outside the sphere of circulation. No technical measurement of the quantity of gold can help us to determine that quantity of gold that plays so significant a role in circulation.[14]

The fourth function of gold is discussed by Marx under the title "World Money." Thus, when gold is "breaking the barriers of domestic circulation," it functions as the "universal equivalent in the world of commodities." Weight is the important attribute in this function, as it is in the emergence of gold as a measure of value. In the fourth function, gold is used as means of purchase only when purchase and sale are separated; otherwise, the transaction is of the kind that belongs to barter – commodities against commodities.

Thus, we can see that the main difference between the 1857 and 1859 theories of money lies in Marx's changed view of the third function of money. Whereas in 1857 he thought that money as money derives from the monetary circuit, in 1859, he came to the conclusion that it derives from commodity circulation. This new approach ensured that *the commodity aspect of money* would henceforth be retained over all its functions, including even the third function. This formulation is equivalent to that of the General Theory of Money developed at its fullest by Marx in *Capital* I.

Mandel states that "Marx's completion of the theory of money was simply a logical application of the labour theory of value to money" (1971, p. 89), an application that took place, according to Mandel, between autumn

---

[14] Like Tooke, Marx thought that different forms of money were used in different types of transactions; "coin is almost entirely confined to the sphere of retail trade and to petty transactions between producers and consumers, whereas money as means of payment predominates in the sphere of large commercial transactions" (Marx 1859, p. 143).

1857 and the beginning of 1859. The implicit assumption held by Mandel is that what was missing in Marx's 1857 text was a criticism of the Quantity Theory. The application of the labor theory of value to commodity-money, argues Mandel, contradicts the relationship between prices and the amount of currency in circulation assumed by Montesquieu, Hume, and Ricardo. Because precious metals are commodities, they have exchange value or "intrinsic value," and they "cannot modify *by their own movements* the fluctuations in the prices of other commodities." Mandel supports this conclusion with a quotation from Marx's 1859 text: "Hence, prices are not high or low because there is more or less money in circulation, but on the contrary, there is more or less money in circulation because prices are high or low" (Mandel 1971, p. 89 from Marx 1859, p. 136). However, as we have seen, the rejection of the Quantity Theory was stated clearly in 1857 in an almost identical form.

Mandel is right in stating that "it was above all [Marx's] study of Thomas Tooke's great work on the history of prices that provided Marx with his material for the critique of Ricardo's theory of money" (1971, p. 90), but this occurred before 1857. The "completion" of Marx's monetary theory was not the rejection of the Quantity Theory, but rather the new analysis of the third function of money as arising from the circuit C-M-C and the *new* concept of hoard associated with it.

Traces of Tooke in Marx's Developing Theory of Money

After completing the Rough Draft of 1857, Marx was still dissatisfied with his own understanding of the role of gold in internal and international circulation. As a result, he returned to the libraries and to a study of economic history, even returning to texts through which he had previously only glanced. In particular, his search for the origin of money led Marx to earlier economists who had dealt with this question, and in particular, to those writers who had criticized the Quantity Theory and who, like Marx, treated the monetary circuit as secondary.

Marx had first come across Tooke's name some years earlier, when he had been studying political economy in the Manchester Library in 1845. During this period he read Petty, Cooper, Thompson, Cobbett, and also Tooke (Marx 1934, p. 96). In March 1851, Marx studied Ricardo's *High Price of Bullion* (1810) and Tooke's *Inquiry* (1844) (ibid., p. 103). Although there was much in these writings of Tooke that was relevant to Marx's developing ideas, at this point, Marx paid attention only to Tooke's views of the commodity aspect of money, with which he completely agreed.

While reading Tooke, Marx arrived at one of the main bones of conten-
tion between the Currency School and the Banking School: the relationship between metallic circulation and the international mechanism. Marx
accepted without reservation the position of Tooke and the Banking School,
as is shown in the following comment in a letter to Engels in February
1851:

> What I am trying to explain here returns to the basics. I argue that even if there is
> metallic currency, the quantity, extension and contraction of the currency, are in
> no way linked to the export and import of metals or to a positive or negative bal-
> ance of payments or to positive or negative exchanges, except in exceptional cases
> which never occur in reality but which can be determined theoretically. *Tooke says
> the same*; I found no proof in the History of Prices (1843–47). You see the matter is
> important. This negates the very base of the whole theory of circulation. (*M.E.W.*
> 27: pp. 173–77; my emphasis)

It is odd that Marx claims not to have found a proof, because this volume of *the History of Prices*, published in 1848, already includes a proof
of Tooke's thesis. Thus, Marx agreed with Tooke without at this point fully
understanding him. This suggests that Marx had not yet read Tooke's works
in full and in depth, but was only using what he had grasped of Tooke's
writings to add weight to his own claims that gold as money is primarily
a commodity. Moreover, it seems that Marx completed notebooks I and
II of the *Grundrisse*, in which the subject of money is treated, before he
had fully understood Tooke's theories. In April 1857, before completing the
notebooks, Marx wrote to Engels that he would eventually have to investigate the relation between the exchanges and bullion and the role of money
in determining the rate of interest, and that Tooke's works would be of value
in understanding these matters:

> An experienced broker in the London Stock Exchange told me that the form of the
> present chronic crisis has not been known for 40 years. I haven't reached it, but I
> will eventually have to investigate the relation between the exchanges and bullion.
> The role of money as it is regarding interest and the money market is striking and
> quite antagonistic to all laws of political economy. The volumes of Tooke which
> are now appearing of the *History of Prices* are important. It's a pity that the old fel-
> low gives all his researches a one-sided interpretation aimed against the Currency
> School.[15]

We know that during this same period in 1857, Marx read and summarized these two volumes of Tooke, and at this time Tooke's theories made

---

[15] *M.E.W.* 29: pp. 129–131, Marx to Engels, April 23, 1857.

a profound impression on him. Tooke had been living in the same city as Marx; when Tooke died, Marx was moved to mention it to Engels, in a rare positive evaluation of someone else's work. "Friend Thomas Tooke, the last English economist of any value, has died."[16] The same admiration is reflected in other references to Tooke in later years. Of course, the main indication of Marx's appreciation of Tooke lies not in such passing references, but in the impact Tooke had on Marx's own theories, especially in the ways they changed between the *Grundrisse* and the *Contribution*, and the important place assigned to Tooke by Marx when discussing the history of economic thought.

By 1859, Marx had finally understood Tooke's position on the international mechanism and was convinced by his arguments as to the role of gold. Marx realized that an adequate explanation of gold movements could be achieved only after drawing a clear distinction between the different functions of gold. Even though Tooke was less explicit than Marx was to be, it is clear that Tooke's main argument against the "perfect circulation" and the international mechanism was his treatment of gold as having different functions. On this point, as on many others, Marx sided with Tooke against Ricardo and the Currency School. Different forms of gold play different roles in exchange, and their respective quantities are determined by the needs of the different types of exchange that they help to carry out.[17]

After completing his formulation in 1859, Marx turned his attention to discussing the views of previous writers on the subject of money. It is at this point in the history of monetary theory that Marx used his own detailed distinction between the different functions and forms of money to shed light on some well-known views of money. He began with Steuart, whom he treated with much sympathy. Steuart explained the demand for money as caused by the need for liquidity, which he called "ready money demands." However, this demand has no influence on prices. The surplus or shortage of gold in circulation will be balanced by "hoards" or "luxury articles":

[Steuart] is indeed the first to ask whether the amount of money in circulation is determined by the prices of commodities, or the prices of commodities determined by the amount of money in circulation ... he discovers the essential aspects

[16] *M.E.W.* 29: p. 198, Marx to Engels, March 5, 1858.
[17] In 1859, Marx also distinguished between different forms of money for different kinds of transactions. More specifically, he gave the example of England, where "coin is almost entirely confined to the sphere of retail trade and to petty transactions between producers and consumers, whereas money as means of payment predominates in the sphere of large commercial transactions" (Marx 1859, p. 143). This approach was originally developed by Tooke to prove his own theory of prices.

of money, because he does not mechanically place commodities on one side and money on the other, but really deduces its various functions from different moments in commodity exchange. (Marx 1859, p. 165)

Marx then turned to the Quantity Theory and explained its origin as lying in the extreme position taken by the critics of the monetary system, who related to the second function of money while neglecting its third function. It is true, argued Marx, that the supporters of the monetary system gave a one-sided account of the functions of money, in that they regarded it only as money (the third function). However, this is by no means a sufficient reason for reaching another one-sided conclusion that money functions only as means of circulation. The conclusion reached by the critics of "the Monetary and Mercantile systems," that is, by the new political economists, including Ricardo, was therefore a false one.

The examples given by Marx when criticizing Ricardo's theory will help us to see the similarities between Tooke and Marx. In his Banking School period, Tooke rejected the Quantity Theory and developed a distinction between the different functions that gold fulfills in internal and inter-national monetary systems. This led him to reject Hume's mechanism and to oppose the 1844 Bank Act that was based on it. Marx first mentions the Bank Acts of 1844–1845, which were based on Ricardo's "discovery" that "gold and notes taken together" will determine the value of the currency (Marx 1859, pp. 184–185). He then returned to the famous example of crop failure. When crops fail, the subsequent import of corn and export of gold is, according to Ricardo, the result of the cheapness of gold caused by its abundance relative to the amount of commodities produced:

As opposed to this paradoxical explanation, statistics shown that in the case of crop failures in England from 1793 up to the present, the existing amount of means of circulation was not excessive but on the contrary it was insufficient, and therefore more money than previously circulated and was bound to circulate. (Marx 1859, 177–178)

The footnote to this remark is "Cf. Thomas Tooke, *History of Prices* and James Wilson[18] Capital, Currency and Banking." This is no coincidence; in criticizing Ricardo's theory, Marx followed Tooke on many points. In an attack directed at the Currency School and especially at Lord Overstone, Colonel Torrens, and Norman, Marx again agreed with Tooke. Discussing

[18] James Wilson, founder of *The Economist*, was the third main leader of the Banking School, together with Tooke and Fullarton; see Chapter 12.

the relationship between internal and external circulation on the basis of metallic currency, Marx claimed that Ricardo's theory of money was a tautology and not an explanation. The rise in prices is explained by the change of the value of money, whereas the change of the value of money is attributed to changes in prices. "The theoretical assumption which actually serves the school of economic weather experts as their point of departure is the dogma that Ricardo had discovered the laws governing purely metallic currency" (Marx 1859, p. 182). These experts tried to explain crises "within the sphere of currency, the most superficial and abstract sphere." They tried, simply, to include credit money under the same laws.

The reason for Ricardo's failure to analyze money correctly is that he missed the distinction between the various functions and forms of money. Ricardo treated money as "currency – the fluid form of money," whereas Tooke is described by Marx as the inheritor of Steuart's view: "After Hume's theory, or the abstract opposition to the Monetary System, had been developed to its extreme conclusion [by Ricardo], Steuart's concrete interpretation of money was finally restored to its legitimate position by *Thomas Tooke*" (Marx 1859, p. 185). Marx described Tooke in 1823 as one who is "still completely engrossed in the Ricardian theory and vainly tries to reconcile the facts with this theory." Tooke, who did not begin from a theory, but from the facts – prices from 1793–1856 – was "compelled" by the facts "to recognize" that the "direct correlation between prices and the quantity of currency … is purely imaginary … that altogether the circulation of money is merely a secondary movement and that, in addition to serving as medium of circulation, money performs various other functions in the real process of production" (Marx 1859, p. 186).

Marx does not try here to analyze Tooke's thought in detail, because he was not dealing with credit. However, his view of the Banking School in general and of Tooke in particular is illuminating. First, Marx argues that the Banking School supporters did not take a "one-sided view of money but dealt with its various aspects, though only from a mechanical angle without paying any attention to the organic relation of these aspects either with one another or with the system of economic categories as a whole." The main confusion in their system is the relationship between currency, money, and capital. The export of gold, which is money and not just currency, is viewed by them as the export of capital, whereas the most important thing about the export of gold is that it is money and not just commodity.

The same is true in internal circulation, where gold or bank notes "act as means of payment" and are at the same time capital. "But it would be impossible to use capital in the shape of commodities instead, as crises very strikingly demonstrate." Marx's criticism is summed up as follows:

> It is again the difference between commodities and gold used as money and not its function as capital which turns gold into a means of payment. ... Generally speaking these writers do not first of all examine money in its abstract form in which it develops within the framework of simple commodity circulation and grows out of the relation of commodities in circulation. As a consequence they continually vacillated between the abstract forms which money assumes, as opposed to commodities, and those forms of money which conceal concrete factors, such as capital, revenues, and so forth. (Marx 1859, p. 187)

This concluding remark is not very clear, and in a footnote, Marx promises to elaborate on it in a future chapter to be devoted to the "conversion of money into capital." Although he did write such chapters (cf. *Capital* I, chapters 4 and 5), they do not in fact include an elaboration of these remarks. However, a further clarification can be found in his chapters in part V of *Capital* III, which were in fact written before *Capital* I. This promised elaboration on the distinction between capital and currency and the various types of money associated with them appears under the title, "The medium of circulation (currency) and capital. Tooke's and Fullarton's conception" (*Capital* III, chapter 28). Here, one finds another example of the use Marx made of his theory of money.

What was "wholly overlooked by Tooke," argues Marx, was that the same form of money is used sometimes as revenue and sometimes as capital. There is no one-to-one relation between the form taken by money, the function it fulfills, and the distinction between revenue and capital. Thus, it is not true that coins (means of purchase) are used only as currency, whereas bank notes (means of payment) are employed in the transfer of capital (see *Capital* III, pp. 523–524). Marx thought that in the "case of Tooke," the reason for this confusion was that Tooke "simply places himself in the position of a banker issuing his own bank-notes" (ibid., p. 526). Marx understood Tooke as saying that, for the bankers, a coin or Bank of England note was currency, incapable of expanding by itself, whereas the banks' notes were a source of income. For the bankers, bank notes function as capital, meaning bank notes were able to expand. Marx thought that this distinction was a false one. Although it is true that a general correspondence does exist between money (coin) as a means of circulation that functions mainly in transferring revenues, and money (notes) as a means of payment that functions mainly in transferring capital within the business world, Tooke's distinction between coin and notes is not equivalent to the distinction between money and capital.

Marx bases his criticism of Tooke on a quotation from Tooke's 1844 pamphlet:

The business of bankers, setting aside the issue of promissory notes payable on demand, may be divided into two branches, corresponding with the distinction pointed out by Dr. [Adam] Smith of the transactions between dealers and dealers, and between dealers and consumers. One branch of the bankers' business is to collect *capital* from those who have no immediate employment for it, and to distribute or transfer it to those who have. The other branch is to receive deposits of the *incomes* of their customers, and to pay out the amount, as it is wanted for expenditure by the latter in the objects of their consumption ... the former being a circulation of capital, the latter of currency. *(Capital* III, p. 523; note from Tooke 1844, p. 36).

This passage shows that Tooke located the distinction between capital and revenue (income) in the identity of the different people involved in transactions. Transactions between dealers are transfers of capital, whereas transactions between dealers and consumers are transfers of revenue. The false link is, in Marx's view, the association of notes as *the* medium by which the former are carried out, whereas only coin is used in the latter. Thus, Tooke can distinguish between capital and currency, whereas Marx distinguishes between capital and revenue on the one hand, and between notes and coins on the other, without assuming any relationship between them.

Marx argues that in times of prosperity, more money is needed for transactions between dealers and consumers (type I) and less for those between dealers and dealers (type II). In times of crisis, transactions of type I need less money, while those of type II need more money, because credit usually collapses in times of crisis. The increase in type II money is described by Marx as the "demand for pecuniary accommodation," a concept very close to the modern concept of liquidity. This demand can be answered, even in times of crisis, by the same amount of currency, a fact from which Tooke, Fullarton, and others concluded that "the circulation of money (of bank notes) in its function as a means of payment is not increase and extended." Marx argues that they arrived at this erroneous conclusion because they saw "pecuniary accommodation" as "identical with taking up capital on loan as additional capital" *(Capital* III, p. 542). The opposite is true, because the demand for money as means of payment in fact rises in periods of crisis. However, what is really necessary in such periods is more money to meet "the growing demand for pecuniary accommodation," and not more capital.

The situation becomes more complicated because, in Marx's view, "one sole reserve fund," or hoard, has four different functions:

(i)   A reserve fund for payments of due bills in the interior business;
(ii)   A reserve fund of currency;
(iii)   A reserve fund of world money;
(iv)   A guarantee of the convertibility of bank notes in countries in which the credit system and credit money are developed. (*Capital* III, pp. 536–567).

As a result, in order to draw a valid picture of a monetary process, one has to reach beyond the changes in the reserve itself to inquire into the changes in each of its different functions. This, argues Marx, has nothing to do with the distinction between notes and coins.

Despite the developments in his monetary theory, Marx remained faithful throughout his life to his original points of departure: a general theory of money, and commodity-money as the basic form of money. The foregoing discussion locates the most significant change in Marx's thought in the refinement of his concept of the functions of money, and in particular, in the development of the third function of money as arising from commodity circulation. Marx was influenced by Tooke both in his own early formulations, which were based on rejection of the Quantity Theory, and in his final statement of the functions of money.

Summary

Many modern economists doubt Marx's relevance and feel that his economics is not only outdated, but has also been proven wrong over the years. A serious reevaluation of Marx's analysis of the "unreal" side of the economy locates his thinking in the context of classical monetary theory and shows how close he was to the classicals' problems and thinking. Marx's starting point is very clear: Money has to be understood as it evolved from the exchange of commodities. The basic form of money, both analytically and historically, is commodity-money. This conceptualization, typical of Marx, is not a natural starting point for analyzing modern forms of money and finance, which seem to be divorced from the exchange of commodities. But many of the classicals started from the same point and took the same path. Some would argue that a more promising starting point would be money as a symbol, hence the attraction to "credit theories of money" in place of the more common "monetary theories of credit," a distinction emphasized, as we have seen, by Schumpeter (1954). Whether Marx himself moved from one conceptualization to the other will remain a point of disagreement and heated debates. Nelson (1999), for example, argues for a consistent Marx, one who remained loyal to money's commodity properties. This was also the common approach among the British orthodoxy – but it was not a unanimous approach among the classicals. Henry Thornton and, as we shall see in Chapter 17, Knut Wicksell both offered an alternative that Marx did not seriously consider.

SIXTEEN

Marshall's (Oral) Monetary Tradition and Bimetallism

Introduction

Alfred Marshall (1842–1924) contributed to the rise and canonical status of the new, marginalist tradition in economics after the 1870s; more than any other individual, he helped in many ways to create modern, professional economics in Cambridge, England, in the last quarter of the nineteenth century. His major book, *The Principles of Economics* (1890) – not primarily devoted to monetary issues – soon inherited the canonical status of J. S. Mill's classic treatise and remained the major text of marginalism for many years. Marshall's contributions to the fields of monetary theory and policy were also exceptional. This, in spite of the well-publicized and curious fact that Marshall's monetary thinking was mainly passed down in the form of an oral tradition; his first published book on monetary issues did not appear until 1923, when he was over eighty years old. In the meantime, the Cambridge oral tradition that he shaped had been written down and published by others. Marshall became interested in monetary subjects early in his career; long before his book on money finally appeared, he had expounded original and well-advocated ideas; lectured often on monetary subjects; gave evidence before official committees of inquiry; and established the Cambridge oral tradition on money.[1]

---

[1] Keynes wrote in Marshall's obituary: "We must regret still more Marshall's postponement of the publication of his *Theory of Money* until extreme old age, when time had deprived his ideas of freshness and his exposition of sting and strength. There is no part of Economics where Marshall's originality and priority of thought are more marked than here, or where his superiority of insight and knowledge over his contemporaries was greater. There is hardly any leading feature in modern Theory of Money which was not known to Marshall forty years ago" (Keynes 1925, p. 27). The first written versions of the Cambridge oral tradition were written by Fisher (1911), Pigou (1917), and Keynes (1923); see Patinkin (1965) and Laidler (1990). Keynes also commented in his famous obituary that Marshall's (1923) text was written when Marshall was already past his intellectual best.

Historians of economic thought have studied Marshall's early monetary thinking mainly through two early texts that were published only in 1975.[2] These texts prove that the oral tradition was not only influential, but well thought out and even formulated in written, though not published, form early on. These early texts can help confirm what the oral tradition was in the early years, at the time when the British monetary orthodoxy of the 1870s took shape (see our Chapter 14). Our focus, however, is on the influence of Marshall's oral tradition on later thinkers; therefore, this chapter will emphasize those of Marshall's monetary views that were accessible to interested scholars in the 1880s, such as Wicksell. We will focus on Marshall's views as they were presented in the few texts that were available to those who were not personally exposed to the oral tradition in Cambridge but were able to access the few written documents – especially one paper and some published evidence given to committees – in which his views were presented. For a full study of Marshall's monetary thinking, an elaboration on its early phase, its relation to the classicals, and its influence on later thought, the reader is referred to Laidler (1990).

The Oral Tradition

Marshall's early texts, unpublished at the time but now available, include a short "mathematical" presentation entitled "Money" from 1867 and an "Essay on Money," apparently from 1871.[3] Bridel (1987) and Laidler (1991, chapter 3), two scholars who studied Cambridge (and Marshall's) monetary thought, observe that the major tenets of his analysis were stated in this mathematical note and in the short essay. The economy Marshall assumed was a corn-producing one that used "shells of a certain extinct fish" as money. First, the total available quantity of the shells is given, and Marshall assumes that an individual has the desire to hold a certain proportion of his income (flow) as money (stock). Thus, the value of each shell will be determined by the now famous Cambridge equation: $1/P=kY/M$ where $1/P$ is the value of a shell, k is the desired proportion to Y, the (flow) income, and M, the stock of money (shells). Marshall explicitly describes the relation as that of rectangular hyperbola, which captures the demand for money and a (fixed) supply. In the "Essay on Money," Marshall combines this description from his "mathematical notebook" with short-term and long-term

---

[2] See Whitaker (1975).

[3] On Marshall's monetary thought, see Bridel (1987), *Cambridge Monetary Thought*, chapter 3 and Laidler (1991), *The Golden Age of the Quantity Theory*, chapter 3, and references therein.

dynamics in gold production, and addresses the well-known classical tension between the Quantity Theory and the Cost of Production approaches to the determination of the value of money. As Keynes noted, the influence of this early, unpublished formulation was unmistakable (See Laidler 1991, pp. 54–56).

The only possible access to Marshall's monetary thinking in the last quarter of the nineteenth century besides exposure to the oral tradition was via some sections in the *Economics of Industry* (1879); one monetary paper published by Marshall in 1887; and the published evidence he gave before a few committees of inquiry. The paper, which Keynes describes as "perhaps, the most important of A. M.'s occasional writings,"[4] clearly relates to the debate in the 1880s about bimetallism. Britain experienced deflation beginning in the 1870s, and the argument in favor of a reform in the monetary system – a suggestion to add silver to gold to create a supposedly better standard – was at its height. The title of the paper, "Remedies for Fluctuations of General Prices," hints at the issue. However, the importance of the paper goes well beyond that specific policy problem, to which we will return. It opens with a section on "The Evils of a Fluctuating Standard of Value," wherein Marshall describes two functions of money, as a medium of exchange and as a standard of value. Marshall discusses the links between nominal and real rates of interest and price changes; trade fluctuations are linked to monetary changes and are sometimes magnified by them. Having a "proper standard of purchasing power" could help the economy avoid some of the worst damages caused in a monetary economy:

The fluctuations in the value of what we use as our standard are ever either flurrying up business activity into unwholesome fever, or else closing factories and workshops by the thousand in businesses that have nothing radically wrong with them, but in which whoever buys raw materials and hires labour is likely to sell when general prices have further fallen. (1887a, p. 192)

In the second section of the paper, Marshall rejects the precious metals as "A Good Standard of Value" for the short term. In the long term, the changes in value are

chiefly caused by changes in the amounts of the precious metals relatively to the business which has to be transacted by them, allowance being of course made for changes in the extent to which the precious metals are able at any time to delegate their functions to bank-notes, cheques, bills of exchange, and other substitutes. And

---

[4] See the "Bibliographical List of the Writings of Alfred Marshall" published by Keynes in the *Memorials* volume, edited by Pigou in 1925, a year after Marshall died.

they would certainly be much mitigated if each decade's supply of the metallic basis of our currency could be made uniform – i.e. to grow proportionately to our commercial wants. Bimetallism would tend somewhat in this direction, but it would not go very far; for at best it would substitute the mean between two fluctuating supplies in place of one fluctuating supply. (ibid., pp. 192–193)

Any possible remedy for the long term will not solve the short-term problems that arise from causes other than changes in the supply of gold. The supply of gold does not change much, and the relation between its quantity and prices is not the significant relation. The changes in the value of money are caused "by wars and rumors of wars, by good and bad harvests, and alternate opening out of promising new enterprises, and the collapse of many of the hopes founded on them" (ibid., p. 194). Marshall produces a diagram containing the basic facts to support this claim; it presents average prices of commodities once in gold and then measured in a composite of gold and silver (bimetallic standard) over one hundred years. The discrepancy between these two indexes when gold and silver values were stable (relative to each other) after 1873 are greater than before 1873, when the values of gold and silver changed (again, relative to each other).

I maintain, then, that there is no reason to believe that a bimetallic standard would give us in the long run much more stable prices than we have now. No doubt it would do some good, and, if no other course were open to us, it would be worth while to go through a great deal in order to gain even the small additional steadiness that would result from a stable bimetallism. But I contend that, before taking so great a step as entering into treaties with other nations for the establishment of a new currency, we ought to inquire whether our standard of value ought not to be altogether independent of our currency. (Marshall 1887a, p. 196).

Marshall's innovative proposal is to establish a standard based not on gold and silver but on an artificial unit calculated to preserve the purchasing power of money, called by him simply "The Unit." The calculations concerning the unit should be done by an official and reliable government statistical agency and published so that all the economic agents would be able to take this true measure into account. "Ere long the currency would, I believe, be restricted to the functions for which it is well fitted, of measuring and settling transactions that are completed shortly after they are begun" (ibid., p. 199).

In a detailed proposal entitled "Stable Bimetallism," Marshall begins by turning to Ricardo's Ingot Plan. Marshall's "currency scheme" differs fundamentally from that of Ricardo's because the basis of Marshall's is bimetallic and Ricardo's is monometallic. In Marshall's scheme, the Issue Department would issue notes convertible to bars of gold and silver; Marshall mentions (about) £28-£30 for 100gr gold and 2kg silver. He recommends that the currency "would not be allowed to exceed, say, three times the bullion reserve in the Issue Department." However, in a note, Marshall hints at the problematic discretionary debate: He explains that "in times of emergency, when the minimum rate of discount was, say, 10 percent ... then the rule might be broken, either, as now, by the authority of the Government, or, which I think would be better, by a self-acting rule" (p. 205). Marshall modifies this scheme but maintains its basic structure in his evidence to the Gold and Silver Committee, as we shall see.

The scheme, argues Marshall, would create "secured" paper that is backed by "hard metal" and not "soft Money," as was the case in Ricardo's time of the Restriction. Many people would find the scheme strange and would not consider it, but in Marshall's view, it has many advantages, which he lists as follows:

(1) It would be economical and secure; (2) Though economical, the largeness of its reserve would obviate the sharp twinges that now frequently occur in the money market; (3) It would vary in value with the mean of the value of gold and silver; (4) As it would in no way attempt to control the relative values of gold and silver, and would not be affected even if an ounce of gold became worth fifty ounces of silver, it could begun at once and without risk to any one nation; (5) If adopted by several nations it would constitute at once a perfect international basis of currency and prices; (6) Lastly, ... it is a movement in the direction in which we want to go of a tabular standard for deferred payments" (ibid., pp. 205–206).

Marshall presented the essence of this argument to the Royal Commissions in 1886 and 1887–1888. In the former, in the "Answers to Questions on the Subject of Currency and Prices Circulated by the Royal Commission on the Depression of Trade and Industry" (1886), Marshall relied heavily on Tooke's data on prices. In the second, "Memoranda and Evidence before the Gold and Silver Commission" (1887), he presented to the committee a written Preliminary Memorandum (see Marshall 1887b, pp. 19–31) in which, as Marshall states, he repeats many of the arguments made in the 1887 article. Marshall's thinking is further revealed in his evidence to the *Royal Commission on the Values of Gold and Silver (1887, 1888)* that Wicksell, as we shall see, refers to.

The determination of the rate of interest is a complex process that brings into play short-term and long-term forces as well as supply and demand for both capital and loans. The real rate of interest is determined by the supply and demand for "free" capital. The discount rate (or sometimes known as the loan rate) is determined by the supply and demand for loans. The complicated dynamics are determined by the interplay between these two rates and the different time frameworks. Whereas the real rate is covered fully by Marshall in the *Principles*, the loan rate gets some treatment in the evidence. Four main factors determine the discount rate: the real rate; changes in metallic money; changes in loanable funds in the banking system; and the stock market mood:

> Equilibrium is found at that rate of interest for long loans (and the corresponding rate of discount for short loans) which equates supply and demand. But next, this equilibrium being established, we set ourselves to inquire what will be the result of a new disturbance, viz. the influx of a good deal of bullion into the City. This does not increase the amount of capital, in the strict sense of the word; it does not increase the amount of building, materials, machinery, etc., but it does increase the amount of command over capital which is in the hands of those whose business it is to lend to speculative enterprise. Having this extra supply, lenders lower still more the rate which they charge for loans, and they keep on lowering it till the point is reached at which the demand will carry off the larger supply. When this has been done there is more capital in the hands of speculative investors, who come on the markets for goods as buyers, and so raise prices. (1887b, pp. 51–52)

The expectation that further price rises will increase demand for loans will continue the process. A "cumulative process" will develop, argues Bridel (p. 41), that supports his argument that Marshall had a "primitive version of the 'cumulative process'" that we now usually associate with Wicksell. The support for this claim is found in the following quotation: "[the] cycle ... seems to be this. The new currency, or the increase of currency, goes ... to the banking centres; and, therefore, it increase the willingness of lenders to lend in *the first instance*, and lower discounts; but it *afterwards* raises prices, and therefore, tends to increase discount. This latter movement is *cumulative*" (1887b, 274). Based to some degree on the last word in the quotation, Bridel argues that one can find support in Marshall's evidence for the claim that he had a primitive version of the famous cumulative process associated with Wicksell that we will discuss in Chapter 17. It is important to emphasize that the italics in the above quotation are not in the original; it is equally important to note that the quotation is from later evidence, that of 1899, not 1877–1888 – that is, a year after the publication of Wicksell's seminal book. Furthermore, the process is very different from that of Wicksell's cumulative process.

Marshall's monetary thinking clearly belongs to the classical tradition; it deals with the value of money, the choice of a standard, the link between the balance of payments and money, and policy issues. It is clearly influenced by Ricardo, and even more by J. S. Mill; and, like the classical doctrine, Marshall's monetary thinking accepts the famous classical dichotomy, or, the claim that money is neutral in the long run.[5] He also expresses classical positions on the rate of interest: "the supply of gold excercises no permanent influence on the rate of discount. The average rate of discount is determined permanently by the profitableness of business. All that the influx of gold does is to make a sort of ripple on the surface of the water" (1887b, p. 41). The impact of an influx of gold is to raise prices, as we have seen.[6] The Humean mechanism is explained and defended in two memorandums submitted to the Gold and Silver Commission[7]; the imbalance in international trade is linked to the money supply, and through changes in the exchanges the equilibrium is restored. As Laidler concludes,

> ... the Humean analysis of the international distribution of the precious metals, not to mention its extension to the determination of exchange rates between inconvertible currencies and currencies convertible into different metals, are doctrines utterly central to the Classical tradition. Marshall upheld them, and in so doing demonstrated how deeply the roots of his monetary theory were embedded in that tradition. (1990, p. 52)

The modification that Marshall introduced to the classical doctrine concerns the value of money. He did not hold to the idea that in the last analysis, it is the cost of production of gold (or the average of gold and silver) that determines the price level. As Marshall writes in his 1887 paper:

> ... gold and silver have no natural value. They are so durable that the year's supply is never more than a small part of the total stock, and therefore their values do not conform closely to their cost of production. And, insofar as their values are regulated by the relations between the demands for them and the existing stocks of them, their value is artificial, because the demand for them as currency is itself artificial. (1887a, pp. 200–201)

In his memorandums and evidence, Marshall uses the unpublished apparatus, a demand function for a stock of money put against a supply that is fixed in the short term. In the "Preliminary Memorandum" to the 1887 commission, he is posed a question about "the extent ... and way ... prices are

[5] In the Gold and Silver Commission, Marshall answers a question about the "older economists, who say that all trade tends to be conducted as a system of barter, and that money is only a mechanism by which that gigantic system of barter is carried out," with "So far as permanent effects go I accept that doctrine without any qualification" (1887b, p. 115).
[6] For the influence of Cairnes and Mill and that of Hume on Marshall, see Laidler (1990, pp. 48–52).
[7] "Memorandum as to the Effects which Differences between the currencies of different Nations have on International Trade" (1887b, pp. 170–190) and "Memorandum on the Relation between a Fall of the Exchange and Trade with Countries which have not a Gold Currency" (1887b, pp. 191–195).

affected by the quantity of the metal or metals used as standard of value."
He writes in response that "[while] accepting the doctrine that, '*other things
being equal* prices rise or fall proportionately to every increase or diminution
in the metal or metals which are used as the standard of value,' I consider
that the conditioning clause, 'other things being equal,' is of overwhelming
importance and requires careful attention" (1887b, p. 21). Among the other
factors, one can find many of the most important issues debated for more
than a century among supporters of the old doctrine: the various means of
exchange, credit instruments, confidence, the business cycle, and so forth.

Monetary Policy

Marshall was clearly drawing on the classical tradition for his views on
monetary policy as well; like the classical monetary theorists, he wanted
to achieve price stability. This common aim of monetary policy is stated
repeatedly in his 1887 paper and throughout the evidence he gave that same
year. As we have seen, Marshall recommends "stable bimetallism" as the
best method to reach this goal. His policy proposals relate to the debate
around the 1844 Bank Act. Marshall would like to have a stable system via
a sufficiently large reserve: "The new law will be different in form from the
old. What I want is that there should be about 20,000,000 l. of bullion and
coins in the banking reserve above what is wanted for current business in
ordinary times; in order to prevent a small exportation of bullion from
causing a stringency in the discount market" (1887b, p. 110). In answer to
a question, Marshall does not exclude silver from the reserve and makes it
clear that he does not support additional private banks. As to who would
manage the reserve, he mentions two possibilities: "persons who were ultimately responsible for the management of the basis of notes ... as at present,
the Bank of England, or a committee of Lombard Street" (p. 111). Marshall
states that he relies on "the arguments at the end of Bagehot's *Lombard
Street*, and pushing them rather further than it does." Elaborating on this
point in response to repeated questions, Marshall recommends now having
50 percent reserves against notes of all denominations on top of the additional 20,000,000 l.; he also advocates allowing the directors to "neglect that
restriction in times of great pressure: they might, for instance, be empow-
ered to issue notes in excess of twice the value of their metallic stores when
the minimum rate of discount has risen to 10 per cent"[8] (pp. 111–112).

[8] Reading the evidence, it is clear that these figures are just examples and that Marshall
leaves the exact calculations to others (see for example p. 164).

In his evidence, Marshall elaborates on the use of discretionary policy. First, he mentions the possibility of raising the discount rate in the face of a gold outflow before expanding the note issue. But there are no simple rules in policy matters; they are left to the managers of issuing and the reserve: "I have in my mind not so much an obligation defined in set legal phrase, as a moral obligation, in which much would be left to their discretion, they acting on their knowledge of the special circumstances of each case" (p. 112).

This thinking represents a decisive break with the Currency School and the 1816 Ricardo, whom Marshall quotes repeatedly. The discussion is a clear expression of central banking as an art, not a rule or predesigned set of instructions that can be summarized in a blue book. It is central banking as a discretionary decision taken by human beings based on actual circumstances. Asked if that means that the Bank's two departments "would be fused together and would be reconstituted one," Marshall answers plainly, "yes" (p. 112).

A week after this evidence, on January 23, 1888, the committee returned to the issue. A series of questions raised by Sir Lubbock sought to elaborate on the rationale behind the 1844 Bank Act and the consequent Bank actions in the crisis years of 1847, 1857, and 1866. Marshall tries to shy away from the historical argument; the consistent goal was to stabilize the system, but the solutions should be thought through anew each time. Asked if "[y]ou are aware that one reason against that [reuniting the departments] was ... [its] effect in times of stringency," he answered:

Well, I know that was held, but it seems to me that the whole business of banking is one which each generation has solved for itself. I have myself very little interest in the past controversies on the Bank Act, because almost all the arguments that were brought forward on either side seem to me to be based on conditions that do not exist now, or at all events not exactly in the form in which they existed then. Of course it is true that in case we ever should be invaded there might be an almost unlimited demand for bullion, but unless we should meet with some disaster which was next door to the destruction of the nation, I cannot myself think that with our present application of the telegraph any such run would be probable. (pp. 162–163)

The belief that technology would prevent the next crisis remained. The essence of Marshall's answer is to seek "the right constitution of the banking reserve" under ever- changing conditions; in fact, that was the same question that had bothered the classicals in their policy debates since Smith. Like Bagehot, Marshall claims to have little interest in the Bank Act controversies, and like him, he would prefer to focuses his interest first and foremost on preventing a collapse of the monetary system. In 1899, in front of the Indian Currency Committee, Marshall refers to Bagehot:

There are a vast number of able minds at work on her financial problems. Mr. Bagehot, than whom there is no higher authority on such a matter, says that there never was, since the world began, so high and massive a brain-power applied to any one question as is applied to these question in England... (1887b, p. 282)

As Laidler concludes, although Wicksell's *Interest and Prices* is not an essay "in Marshallian economics," Wicksell had read Marshall and "a case may be made for a Marshallian influence on the details" of Wicksell's analysis; this will occupy us in our next chapter.

In the famous bibliography to the *Memorials of Alfred Marshall* (1925), Keynes writes that Marshall's 1887 article was one of his most important. He summarizes its contributions as follows:

It includes his proposals (1) for a Tabular Standard of Value, independent of gold and silver, called 'The Unit,' to be established officially for optional use in contracts; (2) for a "Symmetallic" system of currency, the unit being made of twenty parts silver and one part gold; (3) for the "chain" method in the compilation of Index Numbers of Purchasing Power. He points out (a) that the evils of a fluctuating standard for deferred payments are chiefly of modern origin, but that now they are of overwhelming importance; and (b) that bi-metallism, even if successful, aims only at curing long-period fluctuations in the value of money, whereas the harm was done by the short-period fluctuations, corresponding to the Trade Cycle, which no metallic system could cure. (Keynes 1925, p. 502)

The evidence of the 1880s, as we have argued, makes those lessons clear to the decision makers, and had a lasting influence not only on the audience but also indirectly on Wicksell's monetary thinking.

PART FIVE

A NEW BEGINNING: TOWARDS ACTIVE CENTRAL BANKING

SEVENTEEN

Wicksell's Innovative Monetary Theory and Policy

Introduction

The Swedish economist Knut Wicksell (1851–1926) wrote in German and Swedish and is, at least in this regard, an exception to our mainly British story. His career was not what one would expect from someone who is perceived today as an outstanding and influential academic. Throughout his life, he was somewhat of an outsider in his contemporary academic world. He did not get a chair in economics until late in life, in Lund when he was fifty. Indeed, his name was first known in Sweden not as an economist, but as a radical pamphleteer. Wicksell's serious interest in economics began in the mid-1880s when he was over thirty years old; he taught himself economics first in Sweden and then during visits to London and Europe, where he focused on reading both classical and modern, post-1870s economics. He started publishing in economics relatively late, in the 1890s, and his celebrated *Interest and Prices* appeared when he was forty-seven years old.[1] As we shall see, Wicksell's analysis should be read and understood against the background of the British debates, the British institutions, and the British monetary orthodoxy. Hence, Wicksell fits well into the history of monetary thought from Hume and Smith through Ricardo, Tooke, Loyd, and J. S. Mill to Bagehot and Marshall. In some important dimensions, as we shall see, he completes our journey on the ascent of the British monetary orthodoxy, especially in formulating central banking theory (to which we will return in Chapter 18).

---

[1] Gardlund (1958) and Uhr (1960) are the two authoritative biographers of Wicksell; the first is a translation of the original 1956 Swedish biography. See also the introduction to the translation of *Interest and Prices* by Ohlin (1936), and the introduction by Lindahl to Wicksell (1958). It is interesting to note that Wicksell studied mathematics for many years before moving to economics.

Wicksell's most famous monetary writings appeared in English only many years after they had been published in German. Early on, before he studied economics, he was interested primarily in population issues, on which he wrote some pamphlets and often lectured, and in Malthusian thinking on "general gluts." His attention turned to monetary questions in the 1890s. *Geldzins und Guterpreise*, his treatise on monetary theory published in 1898, was written when he was supported by a private foundation, not a university; it was translated into English as *Interest and Prices* only in 1936. *Lectures on Political Economy* was his next major work on monetary theory and was written with an eye on the history of monetary thinking; it was produced in Lund, where he lectured from 1901 until his retirement.[2] *Money*, the second volume of *Lectures*, is more relevant to our subject than the first volume. It was published in 1906; a revised 1915 edition was translated into English in 1935. One short paper, "The Influence of the Rate of Interest on Prices," originally appeared in English in 1907 in the *Economic Journal* after it was presented before the Economic Section of the British Association in 1906. As we shall see, the historical background and the analytical content of Wicksell's monetary thought draws on classical monetary theory and should be read as a critique and development of the British orthodoxy.[3]

The 1898 *Geldzins und Guterpreise*

Interest and Prices: A Study of the Causes Regulating the Value of Money originally aimed, as Wicksell states in the preface, at an "examination of the case for and against the Quantity Theory." Many secondary commentaries

---

[2]   Wicksell's approval process in joining Lund became a public issue between liberals and conservatives in Sweden. Typically for a principled persona, Wicksell almost lost the appointment for refusing to sign his final application with the traditional "your humble servant," choosing instead "respectfully." See Gardlund (1958, pp. 20–24).

[3]   More of Wicksell's papers on monetary issues in English were published in 1958 by Erik Lindhal, who edited *Knut Wicksell: Selected Papers on Economic Theory* and in 1999 by Bo Sandelin, who edited *Knut Wicksell: Selected Essays in Economics* (volume ii). On the monetary aspects of Wicksell's thought, see Patinkin (1952, 1965), Leijonhufvud (1981), Laidler (1991, chapter 5), Chiodi (1991, chapter 2–4), Boianovsky and Trautwein (2001), and references therein. Boianovsky and Trautwein's paper is an introductory essay to "An Early Manuscript" they found in the Lund University Library (Wicksell 1889/2001) that was never before published. In their paper, they compare that MS to an article published in 1897 (in Swedish) and to *Interest and Prices*. The dating of the MS is based on a note prepared in the 1970s by the librarian in Lund, and their reading of the MS that confirmed the date. If that date is confirmed, it will make Wicksell's basic line of monetary analysis appear immediately after he studied the British texts in London in the 1880s, earlier than scholars thought before. The MS however, is relatively short and seems more of an outline of Wicksell's major monetary ideas at the stage it was written or a research plan. See more later.

emphasize this issue, although Wicksell's "reflections" caused him "to give up this simple plan":

I already had my suspicions – which were strengthened by a more thorough study, particularly of the writings of Tooke and his followers – that, as an alternative to the Quantity Theory, there is no complete and coherent theory of money. If the Quantity Theory is false – or to the extent that it is false – there is so far available only one false theory of money, and no true theory. (p. xxiii)

The criticism of the Quantity Theory by Tooke and his followers did not result in a theory, a "connected whole" as Wicksell describes it, but remained at the level of negative "aphorisms." Ricardo, on the other hand, who presented the Quantity Theory in its classical form, left it "open to too many objections." Thus, it is the debate between Ricardo and the closely associated Currency School on the one hand, and Tooke and the Banking School on the other that attracted Wicksell's attention and led, in due course, to his innovative analysis. That analysis, as we shall see, represents a coherent connected whole, a theory, which provides an alternative to the Quantity Theory that is, at least under certain circumstances, more than just a negative aphorism.

At the center of the shortcomings of the two approaches represented by Ricardo and Tooke lies the theory of interest and its relation to the theory of the price level. Summarizing the core message of his study in the preface to *Interest and Prices*, Wicksell writes: "The Quantity Theory is correct in so far as it is true that an increase or relative diminution in the stock of money must always *tend* to raise or lower prices – by its opposite effect in the first place on rates of interest" (p. xxviii). In Wicksell's view, the focus of the inquiry should change; though the analysis traditionally addressed the relationship between the quantity of money and prices, he thought that the analysis should move to explain the link between interest and prices. Wicksell begins with an elaborated distinction, now familiar, between relative prices and monetary prices; the latter define the purchasing power of money, or, the value of money. Whereas the analysis of relative prices had been promoted by "modern investigations," these have "done nothing to promote directly the theory of money – [i.e.] of the value of money and money prices" (p. 18). Jevons, Walras, and Menger are the moderns that Wicksell had in mind; their new marginalist theories changed the way we understand exchange values or relative prices.[4]

---

[4] Wicksell's first book, published in 1893, dealt with these topics; it was translated into English in 1954 as *Value, Capital and Rent*.

In the exchange of commodities, where relative prices are determined, money plays a "*double* role": One is its role as a *medium of exchange*, which prevents the inefficiencies in barter where the need for "double coincident of wants" increases transaction costs (see our Chapters 1 and 3). The second role, or function, that of a "store of value," is explained by the fact that the exchange of commodities in a monetary economy (not in barter) is not instantaneous, and in reality, the purchase of a commodity may take some time after the sale has been completed. The use of money introduces the split between buying and selling, with possible divergences in their overall sum and discrepancies that do not show up in barter (pp. 20–23). Wicksell analyzes several mechanisms for the exchange process: from less sophisticated, where only cash is used, to more developed and sophisticated processes, where credit exists. In the discussion of the former, Wicksell assumes, "for the sake of simplicity," that money serves only as a "medium of exchange"; later, money is analyzed as serving also as a store of value, but the development of credit facilities makes this function of money less important. Wicksell discusses the case where credit is used, in the context of a fully developed credit system. It is important to emphasize that at this stage, Wicksell analyzes the exchange of commodities that have been already produced; he does not discuss production and relative prices, nor does he discuss the process of intermediation whereby economic units – savers and investors – trade purchasing power.[5] The first issue, that concerning relative prices, is only briefly discussed in *Interest and Prices*; the latter issue, that concerning intermediation, is addressed later in Wicksell's book and later in this chapter.

Wicksell argues that for his subject of investigation, the price level, "[the] exchange of commodities in itself, and the conditions of production and consumption on which it depends, affect only exchange values or *relative prices*: they can exert *no direct influence whatever on the absolute level of money prices*" (p. 23). Changes in the level of prices originate "*outside* the commodity market proper" (p. 24). One should either look into the specific market of the commodity that serves as money, for example gold, or take into consideration conditions that, at this stage, Wicksell assumes do not

---

[5] There may be some confusion reading the following: "So the function of money is here purely that of an intermediary; it comes to an *end* as soon as the exchange has been effected" (p. 23). The confusion is due to the meaning attached to "intermediary" in this sentence; here, it is money as an instrument that prevents the need for a direct exchange of two commodities, using the well-known coincident of wants, and instead exploiting money as a bridge between the seller and the buyer; hence, intermediary. Later, we will refer to intermediation as does Wicksell: as the process that bridges between savers and investors.

exist – specifically, that money does serve as a store of value. In two separate chapters, chapter 4 and chapter 5, he addresses two, not mutually exclusive alternatives, "one of which is connected to the so-called Cost of Production Theory of Money and the other with the so-called Quantity Theory" (p. 24). We will address them next.

The first theoretical explanation for possible changes in the value of money, that is, in the price level or purchasing power of money, emphasizes the commodity aspects of money. Where money is money, "i.e. it fulfils the functions of money, [and] is of significance in the economic world only as an intermediary," its purchasing power is not determined by the other commodities (p. 29). However, where money is not money, but is itself a commodity intended for use, its value relative to other commodities may change. The causes can differ, but a "cheapening … of the precious metal in terms of commodities will at least set up a tendency for its production to decrease and for its consumption to increase" (p. 31). The purchasing power of money will change as well. Wicksell quotes Senior's *Three Lectures on the Value of Money* as playing "a preeminent part in developing the theory that the exchange value of gold must be determined by its cost of production." Roscher tries to uphold the theory and rejects the alternative Quantity Theory, as does Marx.[6]

In the case of Marx, the rejection is, of course, associated with his value theory and the fact that "Marx refuses to admit that the quantity of money may possibly exert an influence on prices" (p. 35). Money is for Marx first and foremost, a commodity like all commodities. It has value (relative price), which will not change in the exchange process. We have seen in Chapter 15 that Marx was attracted to the criticisms of the Quantity Theory put forward by Tooke and the Banking School. Wicksell was familiar with Marxian thought; he does not dismiss Marx but criticizes his monetary thinking as well as his value approach. Wicksell believes in the superiority of the marginal analysis of exchange value, that is, relative prices, and also rejects Marx's monetary theory. Theoretically, it is possible to argue that the "exchange value of gold" will be temporarily constant; "But in the actual locality where gold is produced … increased output will result at first in a certain lowering of the value of money" (p. 36). The proof that this is actually the case, not just locally, but globally, and not for a short time, but for long intervals, has been shown by the discoveries of gold in California and Australia in 1848–1849 and the resulting changes in prices.

---

6   Wicksell writes: "Among the attempts that have been made to attribute to the cost of production of money the dominating influence on its value in exchange, that of Karl Marx deserves special notice" (p. 35). See a discussion of Marx's monetary thought in Chapter 15.

Wicksell's position on the Quantity Theory attracted many commentators who present him alternately as either for or against that theory.[7] His position was more complex. The opening statement of his famous chapter 5, "The Quantity Theory and its opponents," should be read carefully:

It is clear that the higher is the price of a commodity the greater the amount of money required for the purpose of its sale and purchase. But the whole function of the available supply of money – so long at any rate as it retains the form of money – is to be exchanged, sooner or later, for commodities. It is now but a small step to recognizing that the total volume of money instruments in existence in an economic system, or rather their volume taken in relation to the quantity of commodities exchanged, is the regulator of commodity prices. (p. 38)

This doctrine is ascribed to Hume but originated earlier, Wicksell tells us. It grew against the Mercantilist concept wherein money had an invariable, intrinsic value. But although "*under given conditions* the Quantity Theory is capable of being correct" it must not "be imagined" to determine the level of prices (pp. 38–39). Such a conclusion is valid only under the assumption that money does not create a gap between sales and purchases. Wicksell now complicates the analysis by emphasizing the possibility of a time gap between a sale and a purchase. If there is no time gap, and the transactions are executed simultaneously, the stability of the value of money, its purchasing power, is insignificant. However, because in reality simultaneity does not always occur, the value of money does affect the exchange process and the prices of commodities. An oft-quoted paragraph states Wicksell's position under these circumstances:

Now let us suppose that for some reason or other commodity prices rise while the stock of money remains unchanged, or that the stock of money is diminished while prices remain temporarily unchanged. The cash balances will gradually appear to be *too small in relation to the new level of prices* ... I therefore seek to enlarge my balance. This can only be done – neglecting for the present the possibility of borrowing, etc. – through a *reduction* in my *demand* for goods and services, or through an *increase* in the *supply* of my own commodity ... or through both together. The same is true of all other owners and consumers of commodities. But in fact nobody will succeed in realising the object at which each is aiming – to increase his cash balance; for the sum of individual cash balances is limited by the amount of the available stock of money, or rather is identical with it. On the other hand, the universal reduction in demand and increase in supply of commodities will necessarily bring about a continuous fall in all prices. This can only cease when prices have fallen to the level at which the cash balances are regarded as *adequate*. (p. 40)

---

[7]   See Patinkin (1952), Leijonhufvud (1981), Laidler (1991), and a review of the positions in Humphrey (2003); see also later and note 15.

This famous discussion has since been labeled the "cash-balance" or "real-balance" approach, and presents the "strength and weakness" (p. 41) of the Quantity Theory.[8] Wicksell argues that the Quantity Theory is logical in theory, but he lodges several objections. The first is that the Quantity Theory is based on an assumption that has "little relation" to practice: that cash balances are held individually, as in a system that we have described as "a pure gold circulation." In reality, however, more and more transactions are done through deposits; in those cases, the story, as we shall see, is different. Wicksell's second objection is that the Quantity Theory makes the unrealistic assumption that velocity is constant. A third objection is that it assumes a constant ratio of the use of money "in the sense of coins or notes" in transactions when in reality, "true instruments of credit (ordinary book credit, bills, cheques, etc.)" sometimes substitute for the use of money in exchange, in particular in periods of crisis. A fourth objection is the assumption that one can distinguish between the use of money as money and its usages outside the monetary function, as commodity or in hoards.

To sum up: The Quantity Theory is *theoretically* valid so long as the assumption of *ceteris paribus* is firmly adhered to. But among the "things" that have to be supposed to remain "equal" are some of the flimsiest and most intangible factors in the whole of economics – in particular the velocity of circulation of money, to which in fact all the other can be more or less directly referred back. It is consequently impossible to decide *a priori* whether the Quantity Theory is *in actual fact* true – in other words, whether prices and the quantity of money move together in practice. (p. 42)

The supporters of the theory are blamed for being too soft on its difficulties; they sound sometimes as if the quantity of money has a "*direct* and *proximate* price-determining force." Others, like J. S. Mill, are guilty of at least confusion on this point, arguing both sides of the Quantity Theory; Marx accused Mill of arguing both sides, and Wicksell seems to concur. But it is "far easier to criticize the Quantity Theory than to replace it by a better and more correct one," argues Wicksell. That is both his critique of Tooke and the difficult task that he attempts himself.

The cost-of-production approach, argues Wicksell, is now (1898) dead except for in the "orthodox Marxist circles." The alternative "*Credit Theory of Money*, which is supposed to originate from Thomas Tooke and provide a scientific antithesis," does not convince Wicksell (p. 43). He cannot find a "positive theory of money" in Tooke's writings. The only statement that attempts to provide an answer, the thirteenth conclusion in Tooke's 1844 *Enquiry*, is "obscure." It explains prices by incomes (see our Chapter 12 for

[8]   See Patinkin (1952) and Laidler (1991).

The Income Theory of Prices) but, in an unconvincing circular argument, also leaves incomes to be determined by prices (pp. 44–45). Wicksell adopts the first half of the circular argument, that incomes affect prices, but rejects the second half. Tooke refers often in his writings to price changes, and he links the explanations almost exclusively to changes in the conditions of production; this is an "unscientific and illogical" approach (p. 45), argues Wicksell, because it is neither a cost-of-production nor a Quantity Theory explanation of absolute prices.[9] Tooke's explanation is based on a disturbing confusion between relative and absolute prices, which Wicksell would try to correct throughout his life.

Different Payment Arrangements and Intermediation

Wicksell turns his attention to velocity, which appears in the literature as the equilibrating variable that makes the exchange with the existing supply of money possible. He specifically directs his criticism at J.S. Mill's idea that velocity depends on prices; clearly, at this stage, Wicksell is still analyzing the exchange of commodities and not intermediation: "So our definition of velocity of circulation is simply this: the average number of times the available pieces of money change hands during a unit of time, say a year, in connection with buying and selling (*excluding lending*)" (p. 52; my emphasis). The crux of the matter is whether the velocity is determined by "*independent factors*" or is a "*resultant*, given the quantity of goods exchanged and the available money, [and] of the particular level of commodity prices, themselves determined by *quite different* causes" (p. 54). Wicksell chooses to address this question separately under three payments systems: (a) Pure Cash Economy; (b) Simple Credit; and (c) An Organized Credit Economy.

Under the all-cash-economy system, the velocity clearly depends on the factors discussed in the previous paragraph; however, velocity changes are restricted by the "physical conditions under which money can be paid and transported" (p. 54). The discussion of money holdings under a system like (a) is straightforward: It depends on the exchange technology for the planned transactions, the holdings for unforeseen transactions, and some hoardings that leave the circulation of money (pp. 56–59).

The second case, that of "simple credit," is less hypothetical in Wicksell's mind because "at no stage of economic progress can the phenomena of

---

[9] Wicksell quotes Marshall's and Jevons' criticisms of Tooke; he also criticizes the German Tookeans – the early Wagner and Nasse – who did not manage to bridge the gaps in his argumentation. It seems that from Wagner he got the idea of a pure credit system, a "giro" system. See Wicksell 1898, p. 46 and other places.

credit have been entirely absent" (p. 59). This case raises the possibility that the Quantity Theory will be refuted, although a careful evaluation will show that it is not. The discussion continues to revolve around the exchange process excluding intermediation, while allowing credit to affect the velocity of money in the exchange of commodities. In fact, Wicksell argues that the impact of credit can be unlimited, so that a very small amount of money can suffice; the reason for this is that "merchandise credit" and "loans"[10] will enable the traders to save on holding money. In theory, this process has no restrictions but for the fact that at some point money has to be physically transferred; hence, the physical restriction is associated with the "speed of transport" of money. The simple credit system can make this transport fast, but not as fast as the organized, banking credit system. The velocity of money in the simple credit system is elastic and flexible but does not change fully with changes in the money supply so that "the conclusions of the Quantity Theory ... retain the appearance of substantial validity" (p. 62). That validity is not maintained in the third case Wicksell analyzes.

The "organized credit system" makes the impact of credit on money infinite; the two restrictions mentioned before, the access to credit by individuals and the need to hold some cash, disappear.[11] The mechanisms that enable this disappearance are "the *transfer of claims* (the use of bills of exchange) and the *centralisation of lending* in monetary institutions"; the modern system of finance combines the two methods and together banks, the bourses, and so forth progress toward an organized credit economy. Debts that function as mediums of payments, that is, as money, and money that is not held by individuals but returned to the banks, change the way we do exchange. "There is no real need for any money at all if a payment between two customers can be accomplished by simply transferring the appropriate sum of money *in the books of the bank*" (p. 68). The consequences for the Quantity Theory are dire.[12]

It is important to emphasize that up to this point the discussion has focused solely on exchange; from now on, beginning with the section dedicated to the

---

[10] We will return to the distinction between "merchandise credit" that belongs to the exchange process and "loans" that are part of intermediation.

[11] "In a developed credit economy both these obstacles are removed, and either actually or *virtually* a higher velocity of circulation is provided – or, more correctly, the velocity of circulation is *capable* of being increased more or less at will" (p. 62).

[12] That the abstract organized system has implications for the real systems analyzed in the 1840s by the Currency School seems clear to Wicksell. When he refers to a bank-note system he concludes: "Notes provide in themselves the basis for a more or less elastic system of credit, and they circulate with a velocity which is more or less variable. It is for this reason that it was never possible for even the older supporters of the Quantity School to provide a satisfactory demonstration of the exact relationship which they held to exist between the price level and the quantity of notes (and coin)" (pp. 69–70).

organized credit economy, Wicksell analyzes intermediation as well.[13] After a discussion of the various interest rates in an organized credit economy, he returns to his major question: What determines prices? Now the link of the general price level to interest rates takes center stage. Wicksell asks: Can the rate of interest regulated by the banks influence "the exchange value of money and commodity prices?" (p. 75). The context of Wicksell's discussion is obviously the British monetary debates. On the one hand is Ricardo and what Wicksell calls the "Classical Theory," and on the other, the "school of Tooke." According to Wicksell, Ricardo's *Reply to Bosanquet* gives a positive answer to his question; Tooke and Fullarton deny such a possibility; and Mill takes a disappointing, weak middle position. But all of them miss the main point which is at the center of Wicksell's 1898 theory (pp. 81–87).

The Price Level, Interest Rates, and the Cumulative Phenomena

Wicksell's analysis provides an innovative link between the rate of interest and prices, and associates the market for loans and credit with the determination of absolute prices. Wicksell assumes in this famous theory that "all payments are made by means of cheques," as is done in the organized credit economy. When conditions change in the loans market, for example when credit is extended, the market rate of interest will decrease. However, the effect of the market rate of interest on prices depends on another rate, which Wicksell denotes the "natural rate of interest." That natural rate is determined outside the financial sphere, by conditions in the production sphere. Wicksell thinks of this rate as determined by the marginal product of capital, or as the real profit rate in production. If in the original situation, before any changes in the loans market, the economy faced a market rate of interest that was equal to the natural rate, and now, due to credit expansion, the market rate has gone down and is below the natural rate, a process of rising prices will begin. Prices will continue to rise as long as the market rate stays below the natural one. Hence, the economy will experience continuous price changes, a process that Wicksell terms "the cumulative process." The cumulative process will only come to an end when the market rate increases, the natural rate decreases, or both rates change so that they are once again uniform.

---

[13]   Its first appearance: "We have so far dealt with the interval of time, dependent on nature and technique, which separates purchase from the corresponding sale. But actual long-term credit itself has a part to play. Many people require in their business, either regularly or at certain periods, more capital than they themselves possess, while others possess more capital than they are able or willing to find use for. The resultant lending and borrowing can be supposed to be effected through the intervention of our Bank" (p. 73).

Wicksell's innovative cumulative process must be understood in the context of the British monetary debate of the first half of the nineteenth century. When explaining the theory, Wicksell refers repeatedly to Ricardo, Tooke, and J. S. Mill. It is not, as Tooke and Mill argue, the rate of interest itself, low or high, that impacts prices; it is its relation to the natural rate that helps to explain price changes.[14] The theory aims at explaining money prices and not relative prices, thus arguments about relative costs and relative values, which Tooke raises, miss the major point that Wicksell makes. Two oft-quoted metaphors elegantly describe the differences between the equilibrium of relative prices and that of money prices:

[T]he movement and equilibrium of actual money prices represent a fundamentally different phenomenon, above all in a fully developed credit system, from those of *relative* prices. The latter might perhaps be compared with a mechanical system which satisfies the conditions of *stable* equilibrium, for instance a pendulum. Every movement away from the position of equilibrium sets forces into operation – on a scale that increases with the extent of the movement – which tend to restore the system to its original position, and actually succeed in doing so, though some oscillations may intervene.

The analogous picture for *money* prices should rather be some easily movable object, such as a cylinder, which rests on a horizontal plane in so-called *neutral* equilibrium. The plane is somewhat rough and a certain force is required to set the price-cylinder in motion and to keep it in motion. But so long as this force – the raising or lowering of the rate of interest – remains in operation, the cylinder continues to move in the same direction. Indeed it will, after a time, start "rolling": the motion is an accelerated one up to a certain point, and it continues for a time even when the force has ceased to operate. Once the cylinder has come to rest, there is no tendency for it to be restored to its original position. It simply remains where it is so long as no opposite forces come into operation to push it back. (pp. 100–101)

The mechanism that brings the economy to equilibrium is that of the many competing capitalists and entrepreneurs who function within a developed banking system. Changes in the loan (market) rate of interest, making it different from the natural rate, will push the economy into disequilibrium, increase profits for the entrepreneurs, and put in motion rises in prices. This is true, of course, as long as we are assuming that the natural

---

[14] "We have seen that a casual and temporary change in the discount rate would not in itself exert any marked influence on prices. To this extent it can be granted that Tooke was quite right in maintaining, in contradiction to Ricardo, that the banks' discount policy is in itself of direct significance in respect only to such matters as international or interregional movements of capital and the postponement of payment of fluctuating liabilities, but that it is of smaller importance in respect to the structure of prices" (p. 92). Wicksell refers to Tooke's arguments repeatedly in the book; he is often critical of Tooke's positions but sometimes approving of them.

rate has not changed. Thus, what is pushing the economy into disequilibrium is the "relative rate," or the gap between the two rates; the analytical difficulty is to establish the conditions in which the relative rate will be zero. The natural rate, as explained before, is determined in the real, productive economy, independent of the market rate, and functions like an anchor. Thus, if there is equilibrium in the economy, the market rate should gravitate to the natural rate. The force that is at work is that of changing money prices: "When the money rate of interest is relatively too low all prices rise. The demand for money loans is consequently increased, and as a result of a greater need for cash holdings, the supply [of loans] is diminished. The consequence is that the rate of interest is soon restored to its normal level, so that it again coincides with the natural rate" (pp. 109–110).

The equilibrating mechanism thus depends on a mechanism that can work only under traditional money markets, where the supply and the demand are independent of each other and together determine the price level. Wicksell is of course aware that under the conditions of the assumed modern "giro" system ("pure credit"), where the supply of money is accommodating demand (also called an "elastic monetary system"), this equilibrating mechanism will not work. Thus: "It follows that if the rest of our theory is correct the banks can raise the general level of prices to any desired height" (p. 111). The opposite scenario, in which banks keep the rate of interest above the natural one and prices fall, is also possible. The rise and fall of prices in these respective cases are restricted by the freedom of the banks to determine their interest rates. In Wicksell's view, international competition and the actual existence of cash reserves are the factors that restrict the banks in determining whether the money rate is below or above the natural rate. In other words, actual conditions are different from those of a pure credit system; under these circumstances the money rate will tend "to coincide with an ever-changing natural rate" (p. 117).

In a chapter entitled "Systematic Exposition of the Theory" (chapter 9), which Wicksell describes as based on "methods of abstraction," and which some readers will find "no love for" and may omit, he elaborates on the causes that determine the two rates and their relation to price changes:

The two rates of interest still reach *ultimate* equality, but only after, and as a result of, a previous movement of prices. Prices constitute, so to speak, a spiral spring which serves to transmit the natural and the money rates of interest; but the spring must first be sufficiently stretched or compressed. In a pure cash economy, the spring is short and rigid; it becomes longer and more elastic in accordance with the stage of development of the system of credit and banking. (pp. 135–136)

The abstraction brings the capitalists, who own capital; the entrepreneurs, who work with borrowed money from the banks; and the laborers and property owners, who receive wages and rent, into the production process. At the beginning of the year, the entrepreneurs borrow "sum of money K," which is the amount of available "real capital"; the sum is paid to workers and land owners and to the entrepreneurs themselves. The consumers buy and the sum K returns to the bank as deposits. In this simplification of one year's transactions, the entrepreneurs receive a one-year loan, which they will pay back to the banks after the production has been completed. The bank has assets, in the form of loans to entrepreneurs, and deposits to the same amount. Further, Wicksell assumes the same interest rate on the loans and on the deposits, which equals i.

In an "undisturbed and stationary state," assuming the entrepreneurs receive normal profits and make i percent, price level of the product will be $K(1+i/100)$. The various transactions are done through the banks, and the system is ready to repeat itself the next year. What if the rate of profit rises by 1% to $(i+1)$ while the bank rate remains i? The first beneficiaries of this change are the entrepreneurs; their nominal product is worth more than they owe the banks. The consequences discussed by Wicksell, in great detail and based on many assumptions, are a rise in demand for loans, which the banks supply at the "old" interest rate (i) and at rising prices, although with only minimal "real" changes in the economy. The case of a higher bank rate than the natural rate will cause prices to fall, again, until the two rates will converge (pp. 142–150).

The cumulative process under a pure credit economy, the core of Wicksell's theoretical approach, attracted many scholars in the twentieth century. Humphrey (2003) observes that these scholars can generally be divided between those who see Wicksell as having an "active money view" and those who describe him as advocating a "passive money view"; thus, roughly, as a Quantity Theorist or an anti–Quantity Theorist.[15] Humphrey concludes that Wicksell "wrote passages that support both interpretations" (p. 217).[16] In 1993, in a conference in honor of Don Patinkin, Laidler

---

[15] In the Active Money group Humphrey includes Marget (1938), Myhrman (1991), Patinkin (1965), Trautwein (1996); in the Passive Money group are Haavelmo (1978), Niehans (1990), and Leijonhufvud (1981). The distinction reflects, of course, in many respects that between the the Bullionist and anti-Bullionist and that between the Currency and Banking Schools.

[16] In a relatively short section, Humphrey (2003) describes "Wicksell's Own View" (pp. 207–210); only two quotations from Wicksell in support of the Quantity Theory are mentioned, both in the case of a pure credit economy. One quotation is from the Swedish 1898 article "Influence of the Rate of Interest on Commodity Prices," (see Wicksell 1958) where Wicksell writes that prices adapt "themselves to the increase in the amount of money"

presented a paper entitled "Was Wicksell a Quantity Theorist?"[17] He seems to me to be right in answering the question in the title: "Only sometimes, and not when he was writing the contributions that, as it was to turn out, were to matter" (1993, p. 172). "Sometimes" probably refers to those cases where some cash circulated. Thus, we would argue as we did in discussing Laidler's paper, that when Patinkin answered this question with "yes," he had the pure cash economy in mind; Laidler, perhaps after encountering both theoretical developments (Gurley and Shaw and maybe Hicks) and the changes in the financial system, considered the credit economy to be "the" system Wicksell analyzed, and said, "probably not."[18]

Wicksell on Monetary Policy

Under the title "Practical Proposals for the Stabilisation of the Value of Money" in chapter 12 of *Interest and Prices*, one will find a discussion that comes closest to policy. The motivation for the discussion seems to be the policy conclusions of bimetallism. The bimetallists proposals to bring "order and security" to the international monetary system failed, as did other proposals for "composite standard" by Marshall, Edgeworth, and others (pp. 178–183). Wicksell's own proposals are derived directly from the theoretical discussion in chapter 9 of *Interest and Prices*: What can be done to stabilize the price level and to provide order and security is to "exert an indirect influence on the *money rate of interest* and bring it into line with the natural rate, or below it, more rapidly than would otherwise be the case" (p. 188). Stable prices, the objective of such policy, could be reached "more cheaply, and far more securely through the monetary institutions of the various countries" (p. 189).

Wicksell does not recommend free banking, which was by then even less appealing than before; he calls for a rival strategy: international coordination between central banks of their rates of interest, which is the only

(p. 208, from Wicksell [1958] p. 80). The other is from *Lectures* volume II, p. 164; Humphrey writes, "he [Wicksell] implies money-to-price causality when he writes 'of the influence of credit [demand deposits] on prices.'" But in the next section of the *Lectures*, "The Influence of Credit on Commodity Prices: The Dispute between the Currency School and the Banking School," Wicksell does not argue for the Quantity Theory. Humphrey argues, based on reading Cassel's paper of 1928, that Wicksell was in fact arguing for the Quantity Theory even in the pure credit case, where money does not exist; but the "proof" is by implication, and Wicksell himself did not say so. We believe that more will be said on this issue in the future.

[17] This is a slightly different version of chapter 5 from his 1991 book.
[18] See my discussion of Laidler's paper (Arnon 1993).

effective method that will "bring the average money rate into coincidence with the natural rate" worldwide. One does not have to know the natural rate, which is certainly hard to calculate on a worldwide scale, in order to achieve such an objective. It would suffice to look at world prices and determine whether they are rising or falling:

> The procedure should rather be simply as follows: *So long as prices remain unaltered the banks' rate of interest is to remain unaltered. If prices rise, the rate of interest is to be raised; and if prices fall, the rate of interest is to be lowered; and the rate of interest is henceforth to be maintained at a new level until further movement of prices calls for a further change in one direction or the other.* (p. 189; emphasis in the original)

This policy rule, which we may call "Wicksell's Rule," is aimed, like some of the old monetary policy rules that we have encountered, at the general public good; its implementation may contradict the private interests of the banks. The banks may lose profits if, as recommended, they decrease the interest rate while prices are falling; in the opposite case, they may lose customers. "I should like then in all humility," writes Wicksell, "to call attention to the fact that the banks' prime duty is not to earn a great deal of money but to provide the public with a medium of exchange – and to provide this medium in *adequate measure*, to aim at stability of prices. In any case, their obligations to society are enormously more important than their private obligations" (p. 190). Sarcastically, or as a matter of his social philosophy, Wicksell adds that if the banks could not fulfill their obligations to society as private institutions, the task would be "a worthy activity for the State."

Such a policy proposal calls for cooperation between the banks of the world, or at least between those of the gold-standard countries. Wicksell asks whether such cooperation is realistic. A central bank in one specific country fixes its interest rate according to the balance of trade and the exchanges and would not agree to others fixing its rate, because the country would face "efflux of precious metal." The central bank must "retain a free hand to be used *in the last resort*, if not earlier, over bank-rate policy" (p. 191). Wicksell's proposed solution to this dilemma comes in the form of another "mechanical metaphor," this time one that he describes as "two degrees of freedom":

> There is first of all the individual regulation of *relative* rates of interest, which aims at maintaining the rates of exchange, the balance of payments, and the *relative* level of prices, and which, by the nature of the case, must proceed in *opposite* directions in different countries or groups of countries. At the same time, and more important, there can, and should, on occasion come into being a co-operative regulation of the rate of interest, proceeding everywhere *in the same direction* with the object of maintaining the *average* level of prices at a constant height. (p. 192)

Such a bold proposal for international cooperation, based on a theory that systematically links intermediation and exchange, the rate of interest, and the level of prices, was rare. Up to this point, Wicksell had maintained the gold standard, although in the pure credit economy, clearly, the role of gold was less and less important.[19] However, while assessing the role of gold flows in his discussion of international cooperation on policy, Wicksell suddenly introduces an intriguing reservation that should send us back to the Restriction Period. What if, he asks, gold production increases to the extent that pressure on the banks forces them to reduce the rate of interest, causing prices to rise? "For my part," writes Wicksell, "I regard such an eventuality as no less undesirable than a further fall in prices. ... [It] would be possible to avoid such a rise of prices only by the *suspension of the free coinage of gold*. This would mark the first step towards the introduction of an ideal standard of value" (p. 193). Such an "international paper standard," he claims, is welcome and is certainly not a cause for "consternation." The current gold standard system is suddenly ridiculed by Wicksell, who describes it as a "fairy tale, with its rather senseless and purposeless sending hither and thither of crates of gold, with its digging up of stores of treasure and burying them again in the recesses of the earth" (p. 193). A paper system of the type he proposes can function if the credit institutions obey the Wicksell Rule and adopt an interest-rate policy that will guarantee both equilibrium in the balance of payments and stable world prices.

These objectives are very similar to those Hume tried to achieve one hundred and fifty years earlier in a convertible system with no policy at all. Ricardo, Wicksell argues, gave up on price stability, but this objective is theoretically feasible and practical. The realization of such a "monetary reform on rational lines definitely remains among the most important of economic problems," writes Wicksell. It can be achieved, however, only via international cooperation.

History of Monetary Policy in the *Lectures*

Wicksell published an English-language paper on his monetary theory in the *Economic Journal* in 1907, where a short review of *Interest and Prices* had

---

[19] An interesting discussion of the relationship between Wicksell's and Woodford's (2003) *Interest and Prices* can be found in the *Journal of the History of Economic Thought*, 2006 (special issue). In his contribution, Laidler (2006) argues that the Wicksell's pure credit approach was not intended as a substitute to the traditional demand and supply for money as Woodford assumes. Thus, it was an "analytic fiction" (p. 158) to be used carefully, only when the environment was stable; in particular, "it is not a sufficient foundation for a theory of monetary policy" (p. 159). It is beyond the scope of the present book to enter this important discussion.

appeared a few years earlier.[20] But neither of the two pieces attracted much attention in the English-speaking world, and Wicksell remained relatively anonymous outside Sweden for many years. In the 1907 piece, Wicksell outlined what he thought were the major analytical novelties of his approach and why they had practical consequences for policy. Possibly the most difficult and important analytical point relates to the distinction between the rates of interest and profit when banks ("modern forms of credit") exist. Because banks can create as many loans as they wish and are not restricted by their own resources like in a private loan-transactions system, the "connecting link between interest and profit" poses an analytical difficulty. "In my opinion there is no such link, except precisely the effect on prices," writes Wicksell. He argues that an equilibrating process will be at work: If the bank-loan rate of interest is lower than the profit rate, prices will rise, the bank reserves will fall and the banks will be forced to raise their loan rate.

After a brief discussion of actual history, Wicksell concludes with his radical, internationally coordinated policy proposal, but admits that this will work only when and if the gold standard stops functioning. In the one note to the article, one can locate the point that continued to bother Wicksell in later years; new gold enters the banks in two forms: as additional "lending capital" that can be loaned and as payments for goods by the gold-producing countries. The latter mode may cause higher prices and in some circumstances a rise of interest on loans; the former mode will bring a decline in interest rates. Hence, in his view, data indicating that an increase in gold reserves could be accompanied by either lower or higher interest rates did not refute his theory.

Wicksell's second major work on monetary theory, which he wrote a few years after 1898, while already in academic life in Lund, and which he revised several times, can shed more light on the historical context of his ideas. There are some differences between *Interest and Prices* and the *Lectures on Political Economy* (*Lectures*) (1906, two volumes; the second, entitled *Money*, is the relevant text for this discussion), although most scholars agree that the basic theoretical message remains the same.[21] The

---

[20] A short review of *Interest and Prices* was published in the *Economic Journal* in 1900; it was "a warmly appreciative review," writes Garlund (1958, p. 279). The 1907 paper was read in 1906 before The Economic Section of the British Association.

[21] The English translation is of the revised 1915 edition and appeared only in 1936, a year after *Interest and Prices* was translated. Ohlin wrote the introduction to the *Lectures'* translation. He explains that the "chief reason why Wicksell changed his views so little was undoubtedly that the criticisms which his theory met did not go down to fundamentals" (p. xii). Ohlin mentions three major changes in the 1906 edition compared to *Interest and Prices*, quoting Wicksell who was aware of them; they relate to: (a) the role that saving and investment play in determining the natural and normal rates; (b) the strengthened

latter work, however, expands on Wicksell's readings of past theories and outlines his innovative theory in the context of a survey of monetary economics.[22] In chapter III of the *Lectures*, "The Velocity of Circulation of Money, Banking and Credit," Wicksell expands on the actual rise of modern banking and the use of credit in exchange and in intermediation (pp. 79–87). He explains clearly how the "Law of Large Numbers" makes the reserves the banks need smaller and smaller; in addition, the interactions between the customers of the banks tend to stabilize the system, even when they have small reserves. These forces tend to create the "Ideal Bank," though there are certain obstacles to its creation that Wicksell analyzes.

In chapter IV, "The Exchange Value of Money," Wicksell explains both the motivation and background for his study and the essential theoretical ingredients. These are, on the one hand, Ricardo's *High Price of Bullion* and the *Reply to Bosanquet*, Senior's writings, and Peel's 1844 Bank Act; and on the other, the ideas of Tooke and Fullarton. Wicksell argues that stability of the value of money, whether as manifested in its exchange value or the level of prices, is desired in any monetary reform. The Quantity Theory is probably the only theory with a claim to "scientific importance" (p. 141), but there are defects in that theory. The price of any commodity is the result of its supply and demand; where money is concerned, unfortunately, the tendency even among scholars is to expand the same argument:

A general rise in prices is therefore only conceivable on the supposition that the general demand has for some reason become, or is expected to become, greater than the supply. This may sound paradoxical, because we have accustomed ourselves, with J. B. Say, to regard goods themselves as reciprocally constituting and limiting the demand for each other. And indeed *ultimately* they do so; here, however, we are concerned with precisely what occurs, *in the first place*, with the middle link in the final exchange of one good against another, which is formed by the demand of money for goods and the supply of goods against money. Any theory of money worthy of the name must be able to show how and why the monetary or pecuniary demand for goods exceeds or falls short of the supply of goods in given conditions. (pp. 160–161)

Advocates of the Quantity Theory did not understand this point, but opponents of the Quantity Theory never came up with a positive theory. In the

emphasis on "bridging the gap between price theory and monetary theory"; and (c) the actual impact of additional gold production on prices. One important change in the 1915 edition in Ohlin's mind, but not in Wicksell's, concerns the *mutual* effect the two interest rates have on each other (pp. xiii-xvii). An additional change concerns the definition of capital.

[22] See Laidler (1991, pp. 119–120); for another view, see Uhr (1960, chapter 10).

Lectures, Wicksell expands his criticisms of those who represented the two opposing views in the British debates, Ricardo and Tooke. His detailed critique of their respective errors is a prelude to his critique of the current divergent views, because the "divergence of opinion persists even to-day, despite discussion which has lasted for almost a century" (p. 175).

Ricardo, whom Wicksell ranks highly as a political economist, was right on the relation between notes and gold during the Restriction, a point which Tooke also accepted, but wrong on the relation between notes (and coins, or money) and commodity prices[23]:

> Ricardo's proof on this point is all too slender, and even superficial. He wishes to show that an excessive issue of notes and a real excess of gold have the same effect on commodity prices, and for this purpose he has recourse to the picture of an imaginary goldfield discovered in the vaults of the Bank of England (in the "Reply to Mr. Bosanquet").... To the objection of his opponents that there must be an essential difference between notes – and, they might have added, the gold coinage originating from the Bank's imaginary goldmine – which were only loaned and must be repaid, and the actually freshly produced gold which belongs *ab initio* to the holders and is mainly used for the purchase of goods, Ricardo answers that there is no difference, since it is the function of even the freshly produced gold to loaned out. (p. 177)

For Wicksell, the error concerns this last point. Gold that has been produced does not arrive as "capital to be loaned"; it arrives as payment for goods. Hence, its ability to cause higher prices is like that of additional notes or even checks; however, additional loans made by the banks play a very different role. That distinction seems to escape Ricardo. Moreover, Wicksell complains that "[it] is remarkable that Ricardo never examined in detail by what means the banks could succeed in putting a larger amount of their stocks of money or notes into circulation and especially what effects the lowering of the loan rate would have on the demand for credit instruments and on the level of prices" (p. 178).[24]

---

[23] "Too liberal credit on the part of the banks by means of lower discount rate may cause a flight of domestic capital and consequently, as we may well assume, an outflow of gold, even if, meanwhile, the domestic price level does not simultaneously undergo any fluctuations." See section 8, "A criticism of the Theories of Ricardo and Tooke," pp. 175–190.

[24] Wicksell tells us that in one passage Ricardo argues that if a link between excess money and a lower rate of interest exists, the price rises that will follow will cancel the excess ("the surfeit of money") via price rises. "As soon as this occurs there no longer exists any surfeit of money, relatively to the requirements of turnover, and consequently there is no reason to keep interest rates below normal level, which, he [Ricardo] remarks, is regulated by the supply of and demand for real capital" (p. 179). One would think that in this passage Wicksell is looking for a respected forerunner for his theory.

A change in the loan rate may have some influence on relative prices, but the issue is its influence on absolute prices, or the "general price-level." Wicksell describes a case that Ricardo analyzes, that of a goldmine in the Bank: If there is more money in circulation, it means that the Bank lowered its loan rate; if prices fall, there will be less "need for credit instruments," and the Bank will not be able to extend the circulation. Hence, prices will rise. "But Ricardo's argument by no means explains why, how, and to what extent a lower rate of interest has this effect, which is the essence of the whole problem. In his zeal to provide a striking proof of a fundamentally self-evident thesis Ricardo advanced a vague and partially erroneous argument, which could not fail to exercise an unfavourable influence on the subsequent discussion of the subject" (pp. 181–182).

Tooke had shown statistically that high prices were not the result of increases in the quantity of money, but rather preceded them. However, Tooke denied that low interest rates contributed to price rises. In fact, in many instances, he makes the erroneous argument, in Wicksell's view, that the rate of interest affects prices through cost; that is, a lower interest rate will tend to decrease prices.[25] "A fall in loan rates caused by increased supplies of real capital (increased savings)," concludes Wicksell, "should thus in itself cause neither a rise nor a fall in the average prices level" (p. 183). However, in the case just discussed, there is no increase of "real capital," but rather of "artificial capital created by bank credit," which will cause a general rise in prices.

Tooke's analysis addressed real incidents where speculation was brought in as a form of explanation. Wicksell's treatment of expectations in this context is outstanding. For our purposes, this does not change his view that Tooke was wrong and Ricardo right on the inverse link between the rate of interest and the "abundance of money" (p. 186). The consequences of "unstable equilibrium," where lower interest rates lead to less demand for loans and further declines in rates "to nil," whereas higher interest rates lead to more demand for loans and "ever higher" interest rates (because prices induce the respective changes in loans demands), were never addressed by Tooke's disciples (p. 187).

---

[25] "In general, however, Tooke's thesis is certainly wrong; it is of exactly the same kind as the view put forward by Ricardo, which we have just criticized, with the difference, however, that whereas in Ricardo it appears as a hasty interpolation and has no connection with his general point of view, in Tooke it is the foundation and forefront of his theory. The argument is based on the inadmissible, not to say impossible, assumption that wages and rent would at the same time remain constant, whereas in reality a lowering of the rate of interest is equivalent to a raising of the shares of the other factors of production in the product" (p. 183).

Wicksell now proposes a "Positive Solution" that both Ricardo and Tooke failed to provide, and while he discusses the same basic ideas of 1898, he goes deeper into both the fundamentals and monetary policy. He makes a distinction between "interest on capital" and "interest on money"; the former – the "real rate" – is determined in the production sphere, whereas the latter – the "loan rate" – is the outcome of the loan market. The real and loan rates "more or less coincide," although there is no "complete correspondence" between them (p. 191). The loan rate in the credit market, which represents (on average) the real one, is the normal rate; it "is a direct expression of the real rate" (p. 192). The real rate that Wicksell now has in mind is that raised by "real capital" that is "mobile capital in its free and uninvested form." This is not tangible capital as we usually think about it, but a stock of commodities that can be used "either for consumption or for further processes of production," or investment[26] (p. 192). The real rate is determined by savers and investors in the process of intermediation, whereas the real rate on the free, notional capital functions like an anchor:

> The accumulation of capital consists in the resolve of those who save to abstain from the consumption of a part of their income in the immediate future. Owing to their diminished demand, or cessation of demand, for consumption goods, the labor and land which would otherwise have been required in their production is set free for the creation of fixed capital for future production and consumption and is employed by entrepreneurs for that purpose with the help of the money placed at their disposal by savings. ... The rate of interest at which *the demand for loan capital and the supply of savings* exactly agree, and which more or less corresponds to the expected yield on the newly created capital, will then be the normal or natural real rate. (pp. 192–193)

The market rate of interest will settle sooner or later at this real rate, but the process is not simple. Wicksell starts with a simple credit market in which individuals make loans to each other, and then moves to "organized credit" including, especially, banks. Then the "connection between loan interest and interest on capital will become much less simple." The reason for the complexity is due to the fact that, unlike individuals who can loan only their available free funds, banks "possess a fund for loans which is always elastic and, on certain assumptions, inexhaustible" (p. 194). As a result, the relationship between the natural rate (on capital) and market-loan rate will be established "by virtue of the connecting link of price movements" (p. 194):

> If the banks lend their money at materially lower rates than the normal rate as above defined, then in the first place saving will be discouraged and for that reason

---

[26] "Under such circumstances free capital will not really have any material form at all – quite naturally, as it only exists for a moment" (p. 192).

there will be an increased demand for goods and services for present consumption. In the second place, the profit opportunities of entrepreneurs will thus be increased. ...

Equilibrium in the market for goods and services will therefore be disturbed. As against an increased demand in two directions there will be an unchanged or even diminished supply, which must result in an increase in wages (rent) and, directly or indirectly, in prices. (pp. 194–195)

This is the essence of the two-rates approach; if and when the loan rate departs from the real, normal rate on capital, prices will move. Wicksell is careful to address the different processes initiated by such conditions when the economy is in full employment or not; his "first approximation" is full employment and hence results in price movements alone and no income changes. The level of general prices could reach any height, as explained by the cylinder equilibrium already mentioned (p. 197).

Following this discussion in the *Lectures*, Wicksell addresses monetary policy assuming inconvertibility; this may become the only answer to a dwindling gold supply.[27] The countries that decide to take this path will be able to create internally stable system by managing their currency along the lines discussed earlier. The problems discussed are those of the international payments system. The central banks will have to make changes in their interest rates so as to "counteract movements either occasional or more persistent, in the balance of payments" (p. 223). This necessity to react, says Wicksell, will linger even if there will be an "intimate monetary union ... and even if the proposal for a common world paper currency, issued by one central bank, were adopted." The right policy refers to the "*two degrees of freedom*" mechanical metaphor discussed earlier. It makes cooperation between the central banks of the world responsible both for balancing their credits and debits and for fixing world prices, the last target that would be achieved via the coordinated efforts to make the international loan rate equal to the international real rate. Clearly, Wicksell is not satisfied with the role of gold in the system. Like Smith more than one hundred years earlier, he complains about the "pure waste" of using gold. But that is not the main point; "As an independent measure of value, independent of material substance, whether gold or silver, and kept stable in value both in space and time in the manner described above, the banknote, or in more general terms bank money, is undoubtedly the ideal which currency systems should endeavor to approach" (p. 224). That calls for an ambitious reform in

---

[27]   See "Conclusions. The Practical Organization of Currency," pp. 215–225.

international monetary arrangements, assuming certain conditions, mainly in the gold market, will make it impossible to reject such an endeavor. Wicksell, writing at the turn of the century, was not discouraged.

Ohlin (1936) argues that in Wicksell's last paper, "The Monetary Problem of the Scandinavian Countries" (1925), he alters his original position on the stability of the price level in those cases where the two interest rates are equal. The essence of Wicksell's new argument is that what determines price changes are total income and total supply of commodities, and that these can change while the rates do not change. The context for this revision is the developments in prices during World War I.[28] Be that as it may, Wicksell's theory as the profession remembers it is the one he advocated before that last paper.

A Note on Wicksell's Independent Discovery

Wicksell's seminal 1898 book draws heavily on the British debates and should be read in that context. As is the case with most British writers after J. S. Mill, Thornton is not mentioned; but what is more surprising is that Bagehot seems to have disappeared from the discussion as well; also, the impact of Marshall on Wicksell, if at all, is not well recorded.

The relationship between Wicksell's and Thornton's views, which are both neither Currency nor strictly Banking School, though, as we will argue in the final chapter, closer to the latter, has intrigued economists since the rediscovery of *Paper Credit*.[29] Wicksell himself does not mention Thornton in his writings; to the best of our knowledge, he only learned of Thornton after 1916, when his colleague Davidson wrote a piece on Thornton.[30] This is not surprising because Thornton was already by then a neglected economist, to be rediscovered only in the 1920s and 1930s. What is more puzzling, in our view, is that Bagehot's name does not appear in 1898's *Interest*

---

[28] Ohlin is impressed with Wicksell's "truly scientific and humble attitude toward monetary problems," as revealed by Wicksell's comment in this last paper on his dissatisfaction with his own explanations of the "irrational and often puzzling price fluctuations, I am loth [sic] to confess that I would far sooner listen to somebody who could express an authoritative opinion of these matters than essay an explanation myself" (Ohlin, p. xxi, in Wicksell 1925, p. 210).

[29] See Humphrey (1989, 2003) and Laidler (1991, 2002, 2004, 2006).

[30] Gardlund (1958), after studying "Wicksell's notebooks and letters and the footnotes to *Interest and* Prices," concludes that it is unlikely that Wicksell was acquainted with Thornton (p. 275). Uhr (1960) writes that "On reading this [Davidson paper], Wicksell said he was agreeably surprised at finding that ideas similar to his own were of such comparatively ancient origin as to antedate Ricardo." There is no further source about to whom or where Wicksell expressed his surprise. See (Uhr 1960, pp. 200–201).

and Prices, and he merely earns a mention in 1915, without any discussion of his analysis of the money market or especially his monetary policy views. He is mentioned in passing in the *Lectures*, in the bibliography that opens chapter III on "The Velocity of Circulation of Money, Banking and Credit." This neglect is all the more puzzling because, as we have seen in Chapter 14, Bagehot's treatment of the interest rate was both well known and closely linked to Wicksell's thinking.

According to Gardlund (1958), Wicksell had read *Lombard Street* in 1886 in his first London study tour (p. 106). Though, Gardlund's conclusion is clear: "Wicksell's monetary theory was essentially an original achievement, despite the fact that once he had begun to work on it, he found some germs of it in earlier economic literature" (p. 277). Gardlund observes that Wicksell did not read much on monetary issues before 1897, and that it seems that *Interest and Prices* was "constructed as though it were an extended examination of a basic idea conceived before the author sat down to write" (p. 278). The rediscovery of the 1889 draft by Boianovsky and Trautwein confirms that speculation. The draft reads like a research "idea"; probably what motivated the idea was the interest in the Ricardo–Currency School versus Banking School debate.

Uhr (1962) writes that "it seems rather unlikely that Marshall's early monetary writings 'influenced' Wicksell" (p. 206). Clearly, Wicksell was familiar with the evidence given by Marshall in 1886 and 1887 (see Chapter 16), but he "was probably not acquainted with Marshall's remarkable article 'Remedies for Fluctuations of General Prices [1887].'" Thus, there is no clear evidence that beyond a very general familiarity with Marshall, there was an intellectual debt to be recorded. The conclusions of Gradlund and Uhr, as well as others who studied Thornton, Bagehot, and Marshall, (Laidler, Humphrey), tend to affirm the statement that Wicksell discovered his path-breaking theory independently. In fact, without knowing that, he reintroduced Thornton's forgotten innovative ideas back into the economics discourse.

The Classical Dichotomy and Wicksell's Unorthodox Trichotomy

Wicksell's monetary theory was the basis for much of the twentieth century's repeated questioning of the famous classical dichotomy. The classical dichotomy supposedly claimed that relative prices and absolute prices are determined independently from each other, by quite different mechanisms and in different spheres of the economy; or, as it is sometimes phrased, the classical dichotomy held that value and monetary theories are separate.

Hence, many of the monetary theories of the twentieth century were motivated by Wicksell's insights when they attempted to better explain the functioning of modern economies through the integration of value and monetary theories. A survey of these efforts is beyond the scope of the present book, as is the proof that they were motivated or linked to Wicksell's theory, but one should remember Wicksell's important place in these modern efforts. We have in mind the Swedish monetary theories, Austrian innovations, Patinkin's pioneering work after the Second World War, and Woodford's (second) *Interest and Prices*.

The classical dichotomy hangs on the idea that relative prices, in their language referred to often as "exchange values," do not depend on the monetary sphere; they will not change whether the economy is a barter economy or a monetary one, and they are determined in the sphere of production. More specifically, relative prices do not depend on the state of the monetary arrangements, that is, whether the economy uses pure commodity circulation, mixed circulation, or, in Wicksell's case, pure credit. On the other hand, absolute prices (average prices or the price level or the purchasing power of money) are determined, according to the classical dichotomy, in the exchange sphere, which includes the payment arrangements in society, the medium of exchange, and monetary institutions. Thus, the dichotomy reflects two separate processes in the economy: production and exchange.

Wicksell's model of the economy addresses not two, but three distinct processes: that of the production of goods and services, that of the exchange of commodities, and that of intermediation. The monetary theory deals mainly with the last two, abstracting in most of the analysis from production. Whereas in the exchange analysis, he assumes first a cash economy and then a credit economy, he never analyzes intermediation in a cash economy, as if he considers it as an empty possibility. His most creative achievement is to analyze the three processes in the imaginary pure credit setup. Under these conditions, the different roles and functions played by the monetary system make it clear that absolute prices have not been determined at a specific level, leaving them hanging in the air or, more properly, subject to a "cylinder" type of equilibrium. That kind of equilibrium means that the economic conditions could set the level of absolute prices anywhere.

Thus, the simplified classical dichotomy was in fact rejected by Wicksell and turned into a "trichotomy" between: (a) production, where relative prices and the natural profit rate are formed; (b) exchange, where absolute prices are formed; and (c) intermediation, where the loan-market rate is determined. In production and intermediation, two different rates are determined in the case of an economy with a pure credit system; the two are not necessarily always equal. The two rates could continue to be in disequilibrium, thus sending the price level up or down continually. Intermediation, the process of bringing the savers and investors together through loans supplied and demanded in the banking sector, was not fully analyzed by either the classicals or by Bagehot. Marshall did introduce it into his analysis, but apparently Gardlund is right that Wicksell reached this conclusion independently. When intermediation was discussed, the loan and profit rates were assumed to be equal, thus avoiding disequilibrium in the commodities market known as Say's Law.

Did the classicals have an intermediation sphere? Did they properly analyze the saving-investment process? The answer to both questions is, only very rarely. One of the studies that focuses on this question is Corry's (1962) *Money, Saving and Investment in British Economics 1800–1850*. In his third chapter, entitled "The Monetary Aspects of Classical Theory," he addresses the "idea that the bank creation or destruction of credit would upset the 'natural' equilibrium of savings and investment" (p. 60). The idea is discussed by Joplin who, like Wicksell years later, thought that the banking system might prevent the rate of interest from equalizing savings and investment. The reason for this possible failure was that banks could issue credit that did not represent "genuine savings" (p. 61). "In Wicksellian terminology," writes Corry, "what in fact Joplin argued was that if the money rate of interest did not reflect the real rate, a cumulative upswing or downswing would occur." But even Joplin, possibly the most advanced classical thinker on the issue, did not realize that the disequilibrium can result from distortions that begin in the money market.

Laidler (1991), in a section entitled "The Cumulative Process and the Quantity Theory" (pp. 135–139), turns to the different consequences of the Quantity Theory under pure credit and cash economies. In a pure credit economy, the theory does not hold. Furthermore, Laidler makes a distinction between Wicksell's thinking in *Interest and Prices* and in the *Lectures*; in the latter, Wicksell's conclusion is restricted to "a monetary system of unlimited elasticity" (Wicksell 1906, p. 197). But for Wicksell, unlimited elasticity is a pure credit system. The impact of additional gold ("superfluity") on prices raises an important aspect of the trichotomy. Higher prices depend on whether gold enters as a loan or as payments for imports; in the former case, there will be an impact through the usual Wicksellian mechanism, and in the latter, through direct impact on commodity prices. As we have seen, the former entails the possibility of an inverse relation between interest rates and prices (*Lectures*, pp. 197–198). What is crucial is that one channel leads to the exchange sphere whereas the other leads to inter-mediation. We disagree with Laidler's claim that Wicksell "by 1915 [had] become less dismissive of the importance of gold, and hence currency sup-ply changes" (p. 138). Laidler explains the apparent change in the empir-ical evidence, but the fundamental position, in our view, did not change. Wicksell sees gold as having an impact only in a less than pure credit econ-omy, whereas the strength of the impact and the transmission depend on the sphere that is pushed out of equilibrium. This last distinction, one that Wicksell struggles with throughout his various writings, is not always clear. The empirical evidence was significant for Wicksell; he explained the price phenomena during the nineteenth century in terms of the two rates. The moving variable was not the quantity of money (currency), but the natural rate and maybe sometimes the loan rate.

EIGHTEEN

The Puzzling Slow Rise of a Theory of Central Banking

Between Lender of Last Resort, Defensive, and Active Monetary Policies[1]

Introduction

As the story told in this book has shown, monetary theorists from the mid-eighteenth century to the 1870s, with a few exceptions, focused on analyzing what they perceived as the preferred structure of the monetary system – a system founded on convertibility of bank notes to the precious metals – and how that system could best support the real economy. A critical issue – explicit or sometimes implicit – was the attitude of scholars toward interventions in the monetary system and in the financial sector more generally. The very idea of intervention contradicted, of course, the invisible hand approach to money and banking so typical of the founders of classical monetary theory, David Hume and Adam Smith. Hence, a detailed assessment of the few proposals in favor of intervention may help identify early thoughts about alternatives to the invisible hand – alternatives that came to be known in the twentieth century as monetary policy or central banking. One has to remember that, to the surprise of many modern economists, there was no accepted theory of central banking even as late as 1873, when Walter Bagehot first attempted to develop one with the publication of *Lombard Street*. We will argue in this chapter that his theory was not a fully developed theory of central banking. Such a theory had to wait for Knut Wicksell's path-breaking 1898 text, *Interest and Prices*, and his later *Lectures on Political Economy*.

The rise of a theory of monetary policy during the nineteenth century was very slow and encountered many difficulties; yet it is important to

---

[1] An earlier draft of the chapter was presented at the Thirty-sixth Annual Meeting of the **History of Economics Society,** *June, 2009* at the University of Colorado, Denver. I would like to thank Mauro Boianovsky for his discussion and David Laidler, Neil Skaggs, Jerome de Boyer, and other participants for their helpful comments. The usual caveat holds.

remember that just such an alternative to Hume's and Smith's rejection of intervention in money, banking, and finance had been offered in Henry Thornton's *Paper Credit* in 1802, long before Bagehot and Wicksell. A well-known puzzle in the history of monetary theory concerns the disappearance of Thornton's name from the literature toward the 1870s, just when the British monetary orthodoxy was being formed (see Friedrich A. Hayek [1939], Frank Fetter [1965], and David Laidler [1988, 2004]).[2] In this chapter, we will seek to shed some light on the reasons for the objections to and ultimate rejection of both Thornton's innovative theory of monetary policy and his support of discretion and interventions in the monetary system. As for Thornton's puzzling personal disappearance from the literature, that remains an intriguing question that deserves further exploration; we will offer some tentative and speculative explanations. Thus, in this chapter we will reassess the obstacles that delayed the birth of a theory of monetary policy for almost one hundred years after Thornton.

Money and monetary policy play a role in both exchange and intermediation. These dual roles were addressed by Thornton, who did not think that money could be left to regulate itself in both spheres. Analyzing intermediation was not the focus of classical monetary thinking in the nineteenth century; this place was reserved for the exchange process and the determination of absolute prices. Throughout this book, we have distinguished between the roles of money in exchange and in intermediation, and have argued that the focus of monetary theory on exchange may partly explain the delay in the rise of a proper theory of monetary policy. In this context, we will explain the inclusion of Bagehot's less than fully developed 1873 theory of monetary policy in the British monetary orthodoxy. This discussion may shed some light on the objections to intervention in banking and, more broadly, in finance, that are frequently found in present-day debates.

While explaining the puzzling delay in the formation of a theory of monetary policy – although there is no question that in practice such a policy had been used from time to time – we will further distinguish between two forms of central banking: defensive and active. The defensive form of central banking consists of those interventions in the monetary system made when the monetary authority – for example, the central bank – acts to rescue the system. The active form of central banking relates to actions aimed at improving the performance of the real economy via monetary instruments. Defensive central banking is by definition a responsive intervention;

---

[2] The reemergence of Thornton's name and the recognition of his seminal contribution in the twentieth century are due to Hayek (1939) and Viner (1924).

in many cases, it is a response to a crisis in the banking system brought on by the central bank's attempts to address the demands of institutions and individuals. Active intervention is initiated by the monetary authority, which usually decides to act on its own accord, rather than under the pressures from a looming crisis. These two forms of central banking are not necessarily mutually exclusive.

In the history of the theory and practice of central banking, and in the secondary literature over the last twenty years, the concept of the Lender of Last Resort is often the focus of the discussion, sometimes as a synonym or substitute term for central banking.[3] Though the defensive form of central banking is closely intertwined with that of the Lender of Last Resort, the two are not identical. The active, full-fledged modern form of central banking is clearly different from that of the Lender of Last Resort. As the term suggests, Lender of Last Resort refers to cases where an emergency in the monetary system causes a strong institution – for example, the Bank of England in nineteenth-century Great Britain[4] – to function outside its normal day-to-day operations and address the crisis as a measure of last resort. Defensive central banking, on the other hand, refers to more than just undertaking rescue measures when an emergency is already apparent. Defensive central banking, known also as defensive monetary policy, aims to implement appropriate (defensive) policy in normal times in order to prevent the conditions that might lead the system into crisis in the first place.

The concept of the Lender of Last Resort had been the focus of much debate in the British monetary thinking that led to the famous monetary orthodoxy in the 1870s. As we have seen in Chapter 6, the term had already been used toward the end of the eighteenth century by Francis Baring, who discussed the Restriction and the possibility of intervention by the Bank of England under extreme conditions. In case of an extreme alarm, writes Baring, the Bank is "not an intermediate body, or power; there is no resource on their refusal, for they are the *dernier resort*," (Baring 1797, p. 22). This is the French forerunner term for what became the Lender of Last Resort.[5] As we have seen in Chapter 7, Thornton went further than Baring; Thornton

---

[3] See Humphrey (1989), O'Brien (2003), Laidler (2004), and many references therein.
[4] See Clapham (1944), Capie (2007), Wood (2007).
[5] The term *dernier resort* appears again in Baring (1797): "the merchants, manufacturers, etc. can pay no more than 5 per cent. Per annum, and as money was not to be obtained at that rate in the market, they were driven once more to the Bank as a *dernier resort*" (p. 47). The term probably comes from the French legal structure, referring to the concept of no further appeals. (see Capie 2007, p. 311).

clearly understood the role that the Bank of England could and, in his view, should play in the banking system in normal times as well as in times of crisis. What is unique in Thornton's analysis, what made him so far ahead of his time, is that he did not restrict intervention to solving crises in times of emergency, like a run on the banks or possible exhaustion of reserves. He extended the intervention to times of normalcy in order to create conditions that would help prevent crises. Thus, his monetary policy was not only that of a Lender of Last Resort in an emergency, but aimed more generally at defensive policy.

Furthermore, there are suggestions in Thornton's writings for more ambitious interventions in the monetary system than those that defend stability – interventions that are intended to do more than just save the system from reaching extreme conditions and possible financial crisis. Such interventions are more active in nature; they are attempts to affect the real economy. These interventions were usually described in the twentieth century as (active) monetary policy. The puzzling rejection of all three theories of monetary policy – Lender of Last Resort, Defensive Central Banking, and Active Central Banking – by the monetary hegemonic view during the first three-quarters of the nineteenth century, although not always their rejection in practice, will be addressed in this chapter.

Humphrey, in his (1989) paper "Lender of Last Resort: The Concept in History," emphasizes in the definition of the Lender of Last Resort its role in averting banking panics and crises; he describes the Bank of England in the last third of the nineteenth century as "the lender of last resort par excellence. More than any central bank before or since, [the Bank] adhered to the strict classical or Thornton-Bagehot version of the LLR concept" (p. 8). That version, argues Humphrey, aims at an aggregate money stock that the central bank supports by accommodating banking institutions.[6] The Bank does so by using its accumulated reserves and its ability to produce more of its own notes; its major function is to defend the system, and its activity will help to avoid unnecessary fluctuations. It is not a policy directed at smoothing business cycles. The apparent contradiction between the Bank's status as a private profit maker and its public responsibility calls for attention.

---

[6] "That version, named for its principal framers Henry Thornton and Walter Bagehot, stressed (1) protecting the aggregate money stock, not individual institutions, (2) letting insolvent institutions fail, (3) accommodating sound institutions only, (4) charging penalty rates, (5) requiring good collateral, and (6) preannouncing these conditions well in advance of any crisis so that the market would know what to expect" (Humphrey 1989, p. 8).

In Humphrey's 1989 opinion, which restarted a lively debate about the history of central banking, Thornton was the pioneer who created the concept of the Lender of Last Resort at the turn of the nineteenth century, whereas Bagehot was the person who reintroduced the concept in *Lombard Street* and gave it broader exposure. This leaves a lengthy gap in the history of the theory of central banking. O'Brien (2003), who generally agrees with Humphrey's interpretation, argues that there was more continuity in the history of the concept through the activities of Thomas Joplin, another of the concept's advocates, who promoted it and who may have had some indirect influence on Bagehot. O'Brien agrees with Humphrey that Thornton was the first to make "the crucial point that providing last-resort facilities was perfectly consistent with monetary control" (O'Brien 2003, pp. 3–5). However, as I will argue, neither Humphrey nor O'Brien distinguishes between the more defensive role that Bagehot later adopted and Thornton's much broader and more active approach to monetary policy. Surveying the history of the Lender of Last Resort, O'Brien mentions the Bullion Report, which "endorsed" the LLR in the limited version advocated by Bagehot and "supported this general position," but adds that "most accounts of subsequent developments focus on Walter Bagehot."[7] O'Brien talks in passing (in brackets) about some historical accounts of the concept that mention the Banking School, but he does not say more about other possible contributors except for one, Thomas Joplin, who in O'Brien's view is the missing link in the history of the concept between Thornton and Bagehot, and who may have had some indirect influence on the development of Bagehot's monetary theory.

In Laidler's (2004) "Two Views of the Lender of Last Resort: Thornton and Bagehot," he agrees with the claim that the two titular theorists were the pioneers of discretionary monetary policy, but emphasizes the differences between their theories. Bagehot accepted the historical development that shaped the structure of the British system as a fact that should be respected and preserved, and as a result, supported the LLR; Thornton, on the other hand, saw discretion as desirable. For Bagehot, the British system might not be the optimal one, and free banking was a theoretical option; for Thornton, the one-reserve system and the pivotal place of the Bank of England were not deficiencies. But, as I will argue, there were other important differences between the two and between them and Wicksell.

---

[7]   See O'Brien (2003, p. 4), where the Bullion Report (Cannan 1919, pp. 57, 59–60) is mentioned. We will not elaborate on the Bullion Report on the LLR here beyond emphasizing the distinction of internal and external demands and the defensive role of the Bank under the former.

In our following discussion, we will first briefly present the policy con-clusions of classical monetary theory – or in fact the lack of such con-clusions, as classical monetary theory avoids the concept of monetary policy altogether as it was articulated by Hume and Smith. Against the background of these conclusions, we will present Thornton's theories con-cerning the Lender of Last Resort, defensive monetary policy, and active monetary policy, as well as the reasons underlying his rejection of Hume's and Smith's approaches. We will argue that the neglect and almost com-plete disappearance of all of these three forms of monetary policy from monetary discussions during the first three-quarters of the nineteenth century is primarily another reflection of the fact that monetary theory came almost completely under the influence of the Currency Principle and the Currency School. We will then present the dissenting view of the los-ing Banking School, which argued after 1844 for some form of defensive monetary policy. That line of thought is commonly attributed to Bagehot, who helped add it to the monetary orthodoxy of the 1870s and rehabili-tated defensive monetary policy. Bagehot was most probably influenced by the repeating financial crises and possibly also by the Banking School. Wicksell's views concerning active monetary policy will be discussed next. We will argue that his work, at long last, rehabilitated Thornton's active monetary policy in more ways than one. The final section will summarize by speculating on possible explanations for the repeated failure to rein-troduce a theory of active monetary policy from the time of Thornton's disappearance until 1898.

Hume and Smith: Neither Defensive Nor Active Monetary Policy

Hume and Smith provide the benchmark mode of thinking about money and banking during the classical period. They both argue that a system in which many banks issue convertible notes that circulate side by side with coins would regulate itself. There was no need even to supervise the compet-ing banks because, guided by their self-interest, they would always behave in a way that serves society's best interests. The competing banks would contribute to the best overall real economic performance by saving capital and by strengthening the flexibility of the monetary system, enabling it to expand and contract its supply of notes so that the supply would always match the demand; there would never be a need to depart from laissez-faire. According to Hume and Smith, banking was just another trade where competition should rule. Hence, the issue of a unique role for the Bank of England or the advantages of a monetary authority did not come up.

The mechanism that guarantees the right quantity of money in circulation, an obvious concern for both other classical political economists and modern scholars, was that of the convertibility of the banks' notes to gold or silver. According to Hume, this mechanism performs well because the internal banking system was perceived to be part of a global monetary system wherein the value of the precious metals played a self-regulating role, guaranteeing the balance of trade as well as the internal supply of money. This Price-Specie-Flow argument was clearly the foundation of Hume's conclusion, but Smith's monetary theory also relied on convertibility. Individual bankers who issued their own convertible notes would shape their balance sheets, their assets and liabilities, by deciding what assets to discount and how many of their own convertible notes to issue, trying to remain solvent while maximizing profits. These bankers never worried about the overall monetary aggregates in the economy when they made their decisions. Smith clearly believed in free banking[8]; he thought that the monetary aggregates that were not part of the individual bankers' considerations were properly determined by the forces that controlled the international distribution of precious metals, even though he avoided explicit use of the famous Price-Specie-Flow mechanism.

Thus, for Hume and Smith, the monetary system was another domain where competition should rule. In their view, the banking system functions so that the demand for money is supplied via the balance of payments and the competing banks, a method known in the secondary literature as "demand-determined." Thus, the actual quantity of money, defined as coins and convertible bank notes, was always the right one. In Smith's celebrated formulation, as long as the banks acted in line with their best interests and discounted only "real bills," they could not err.[9] The Real Bills Doctrine made the supply of money follow the "needs of trade" and turned any worries about the quantity of money into a nonissue. Hence, a monetary authority is absent as a matter of principle from both Hume's and Smith's monetary thinking. The convertibility of notes and competitive banking are all that is needed to supply a country with an appropriate monetary system, assuming of course that the invisible, long-term international mechanism is holding.

---

[8] See Laidler (1981). His only proposed "intervention" was to disallow low-denomination notes so as to save the poor from the recurring experience of bank failures.

[9] See Laidler (1981) on Smith's Real Bills Doctrine and some recommendations to restrict the denomination of notes so that the poor will not carry small-denomination notes and lose in case of bankruptcy.

Thornton: An Early Advocate of Active Central Banking

Thornton's seminal and only book on monetary theory, *An Enquiry into the Nature and Effects of the Paper Credit of Great Britain* (1802), was written, as we have seen in Chapter 7, after a monetary crisis shuttered the British system in 1797; in it, he explicitly rejects Hume's and Smith's approaches to money and banking. Thornton does not accept the self-regulating idea about banking that lies behind Hume's and Smith's thinking; he argues that neither the Price-Specie-Flow mechanism nor competitive banking provide an appropriate banking system. These two modes, in Thornton's view, did not work under the Restriction. However, his monetary theory goes further; he does not demand a quick return to convertibility as a cure for the crisis; in fact, in 1802, he supports the inconvertible regime of the Restriction (see Arnon 2009). Thornton believes that any monetary system, convertible or inconvertible, calls for discretion and is *not* self-regulating. He argues that the outcome of any competitive banking process cannot be trusted even under convertibility, and that a body representing the best interests of the public should lead the way in determining the relevant aggregates.

According to Thornton, a monetary authority's discretion should go beyond acting just as a Lender of Last Resort and should include implementing active monetary policy. Moreover, Thornton understood the importance of banking beyond its impact on the exchange process and the determination of the price level. He understood the critical role of the monetary system in intermediation and its impact on the real economy. This led Thornton to radical conclusions on the scope of monetary policy.

Thornton's innovative – some would say early Wicksellian – ideas were not accepted by either his contemporaries or later nineteenth-century scholars. Why was his influence so minimal for such a long time? What led important monetary scholars to reject his views on policy? This rejection is particularly intriguing because Thornton was well known by his contemporaries, was often quoted as an authority, and clearly influenced many thinkers for at least fifty years after *Paper Credit*.[10] He contributed to shaping the British monetary orthodoxy in the 1870s, although only indirectly through his impact on the Banking School and the latter's influence on Bagehot[11]; by this time, he himself had already sunk into anonymity. Monetary policy at the beginning of the nineteenth century, therefore,

[10] One can find repeated references to Thornton during the Restriction; J. S. Mill referred to Thornton in his writings, including 1848's *Principles of Political Economy*. But in the 1850s and 1860s, such references disappeared.

[11] See Skaggs (2003).

was in a state of tension between Hume and Smith on the one hand and Thornton on the other. This tension, and the subsequent adherence of so many of the nineteenth-century scholars to the view of Hume and Smith, will be discussed later in the chapter.

In *Paper Credit*, Thornton concludes that the Bank of England is not only practically the pivot of the banking system, but functions as the regulator of the monetary system. In a famous statement, Thornton makes it clear that he has (monetary) policy in mind while talking explicitly about the "true policy of the directors of an institution circumstanced like that of the Bank of England" (p. 259). He emphasizes the "principle of restriction," meaning limiting the quantity of money, but goes beyond it to explain the need to control and direct the monetary system. Thornton claims that there is a need to act according to the prevailing general economic circumstances, and argues against leaving the monetary aggregates to the determination of market forces, the demands of borrowers, or a rule. It is the Bank directors' responsibility to assess the economic conditions and decide which course to take. Thornton defines, again in very modern terms, the conflicting targets of monetary policy.

The belief that a competitive banking system would provide the environment for prosperity was supported, as we have seen, by Hume in 1752 and Smith in 1776, but was put to the test again and again in the coming decades. The instability in the economy, including the recurring incidents of financial as well as more general, real crises had been blamed, at least in part, on the monetary system. The most dramatic incident, in February 1797, resulted in the suspension of cash (specie) payments throughout Great Britain until 1821, but crises also occurred before that year (1783, 1793) and after (1825, 1836, 1847–1848, 1857–1858). Thus, the theoretical discussions about the fragility of the financial arrangements during the Restriction Period of 1797–1821 intertwined with monetary policy arguments beyond just that of the return to gold.

The adherence to Humeian and Smithian monetary thinking during the Restriction implied a return to convertibility and continued laissez-faire in banking. This view came to characterize the group of pamphleteers known as Bullionists (Viner 1937, Fetter 1965). The theoretical doctrine upon which this view depended came under severe attack; one of the better-known criticisms of the Real Bills Doctrine and the Smithian approach to money and banking was provided by Thornton in *Paper Credit*.[12] In the study, which was often cited by Thornton's contemporaries and clearly

---

[12] Thornton's criticism of Smith's formulations can be found throughout the book; see in particular chapter 2 pp. 82–89.

influenced the Banking School,[13] Thornton explains why it is impossible to leave control of the quantity of notes in circulation to the competitive mechanism, even if that mechanism functions under a rule such as convertibility. The right quantity of notes in circulation, he argues, depends on various economic conditions which the Bank of England has to assess; as a result of this assessment, the Bank has to do what is necessary to reach the right quantity. Thus, the Bank of England has to control the quantity of money, taking into consideration more than a responsible lending policy like Smith's Real Bills Doctrine. That Thornton was a pioneer of the modern concept of central banking and stood in clear opposition to the application of laissez-faire in banking can be seen in the following:

> ... we derive a material advantage from the power enjoyed by the Bank of England of exclusively furnishing the paper circulation of the metropolis. To this very circumstance the bank stands indebted for its faculty of regulating all the paper of the kingdom. ... If a rival institution to the Bank of England were established, both the power and the responsibility would be divided; and, through the additional temptation to exercise that liberality in lending, which it is the object of competition to promote, the London notes, and also the country bills and notes, would be more liable to become excessive. Our paper credit would, therefore, stand in every respect on a less safe foundation. (Thornton 1802, pp. 228–229)

Thus, the Bank of England can and should direct the system according to public, not just private, considerations. Monopoly has some advantages because the existence of rival institutions restricts the power of the Bank and increases instability. This modern analysis of the role of the Bank stood in clear contrast to the passive Smithian tradition.[14] Thornton's discussion "Of Country Banks – Their Advantages and Disadvantages" in *Paper Credit* is carried out within the framework of an organized banking system, where the Bank of England plays a central role. The country banks contribute of course to the wealth of society, but according to Thornton, they cannot regulate themselves. His position on this issue is explicitly different from that of Smith, whose view is the target of his criticism.

Part of the explanation for the many differences between Smith and Thornton can be found in the changes in the structure of banking. During the last quarter of the eighteenth century, there were many more country banks; the London bankers stopped issuing notes; the usage of checks

---

[13] Concerning the neglect and rediscovery of Thornton, see Hayek's introduction to the reissue of *Paper Credit* in 1939/1978. For another view concerning Thornton's role in the development of classical monetary theory, and in particular his influence on the Banking School, see Skaggs (1995).

[14] See also Hicks (1967, chapters 9 and 10).

increased; and a clearing house was established in London. In addition, the Bank of England established itself as the banker's bank. Moreover, the disturbing phenomena of crises, which was not central to Smith's theory, became the focus of many nineteenth-century economists, among them Thornton (see Hayek 1939, pp. 37–38). Thornton's criticism of Smith addresses these changes. He argues that in the act of circulation, payments can be made through credit and debt mediums, and not just in gold and notes. The use of these credit and debt mediums is founded on *confidence*, which enables them to perform payments. Thus, both bills of exchange and bank deposits should be considered part of the mediums in circulation.[15]

In his activities, the banker accumulates information about his customers through "[the] bill transactions of the neighbourhood [that] pass under his view: the knowledge, thus obtained, aids his judgment." As a result, the country bankers who "view" the credit given to "surrounding traders" manage to contribute to society by increasing the confidence in the system. In a similar fashion, as the country banks direct credit in their areas, the London banks supervise the country banks and the Bank of England overviews the London banks (p. 176).

Thornton, as we have seen in Chapter 7, offers an illuminating analysis of a typical financial crisis, one that starts in the peripheral counties and ends in the metropolis in "a general failure of commercial credit." Thornton hypothesizes a situation to illustrate such a crisis, and concludes: "It is an evil which aught to be charged not to any fault in the mercantile body, but to the *defects of the banking system*" (p. 186; my emphasis). Furthermore, Thornton argues that Smith has been "inaccurate" in explaining the process whereby an individual bank "persists in the false policy of issuing more paper than is sufficient to fill the circulation of the neighbouring district." The mechanism that will discipline the banks, argues Thornton, is the need to keep funds in London to cover excessive circulation. Thus, if country bankers were to understand their best interests, the existence of a financial metropolis would cause them to "[limit] their issues." The competitive system is thus ruled by the interplay of various demands and supplies of notes, so that "the quantity of the one, in comparison with the demand for that one, is the same, or nearly the same, as the quantity of the other in proportion to the call for the other" (p. 215).

Both before and after 1797, the Bank of England was a major force in influencing the country banks' circulation. However, contrary to conventional thinking, it had not done so through the convertibility of country

---

[15] See Thornton (1802, pp. 100–101); quoted in full in Chapter 7.

bank notes into gold coins but rather through their convertibility to the Bank of England's notes:

> If, then, the directors of the bank [Bank of England] were used before the suspension of their cash payments to limit their issues through a necessity which sometimes urged them, and if thus they limited the paper of the country in the manner which has been described, it follows that, supposing them after the event to have restrained their issues in like manner, though through a somewhat less urgent motive, the general effect must have been the same. (p. 219)

Thornton concludes that the Bank is the regulator of the monetary system and explains why the directors limited their weekly loans to merchants (p. 258). In an oft-quoted statement that we have seen at length in Chapter 7, Thornton emphasizes the "principle of restriction" and the need to control the monetary system:

> To limit the total amount of paper issued, and to resort for this purpose, whenever the temptation to borrow is strong, to some effectual principle of restriction; in no case, however, materially to diminish the sum in circulation, but to let it vibrate only within certain limits; to afford a slow and cautious extension of it, as the general trade of the kingdom enlarges itself; to allow of some special, though temporary, encrease in the event of any extraordinary alarm or difficulty, as the best means of preventing a great demand at home for guineas; and to lean to the side of diminution, in the case of gold going abroad, and of the general exchanges continuing long unfavourable. (p. 259)

Thus, the Bank has to form policy based on the directors' assessment of the conditions in the economy. Based on these circumstances, the Bank has to increase or diminish the "sum in circulation" and do so without causing extreme vibrations. Clearly, the cause for the necessary action depends on whether the demand is internal or external. That is active, not just defensive, monetary policy.

The Bullionists and the Currency School: Rules, Without Monetary Policy

The first call for reform during the Restriction came from the Bullionists, who advocated a return to convertibility and, as we have argued earlier, supported leaving the competitive banking system to regulate itself. This reflected their belief that the Humean or Smithian theories of money hold under convertibility; some accepted a form of the Price-Specie-Flow mechanism, whereas others supported a competitive banking system that would be directed by an invisible hand.

David Ricardo's famous pamphlets on monetary issues were mostly written during the Restriction Period, when notes were inconvertible.[16] As we remember from Chapter 8, Ricardo's first appearances on the public scene and his first steps as an influential political economist began with his articulation of a Bullionist position. In the *High Price of Bullion* (1810), his first published work, he advocates an extreme version of Bullionism that remained his basic position to the end of the Restriction Period in 1821. He modified this extreme Bullionist position dramatically in his last paper written just before his death in 1823.

The belief that convertibility is an adequate and sufficient regulatory device gave way in the 1820s to the rise of a new concept known as the metallic fluctuations principle. One of the first formulations of this principle can be found in Ricardo's last text, the posthumously published pamphlet, *Plan for a National Bank* (1824).[17] This pamphlet had an enormous influence on the famous Currency School of the 1840s and stands in clear contradiction to Ricardo's earlier views.

In *Plan for a National Bank*, Ricardo distinguishes for the first time between the two functions of a bank: to issue notes and to act as an intermediary. Furthermore, Ricardo believes that these functions should be carried out by two distinct bodies directed by quite different principles. The first body, called the Issuing Department (known also as the Currency Department) of the Bank of England would be the sole issuing bank responsible for the creation (and destruction) of convertible notes. This new institute would be guided by a strict rule: Always exchange gold for notes and notes for gold at a given, never-changing rate of exchange. The commissioners in charge of the Issuing Department are not supposed to lend to the government or satisfy its demands. Ricardo proposes that country banks' notes be withdrawn from circulation as part of the reform, turning the Issuing Department of the Bank of England into a monopoly in note-issuing.

Thus, in 1823, and for the first time since Ricardo started writing on monetary issues, he clearly rejects competition in issuing notes and departs from the Humean and Smithian approaches. He now argues that even under convertibility, profit making is not the appropriate guide for note-issuing. However, the Banking Department – the second department proposed

---

[16] Ricardo's most important texts on monetary questions during the Restriction were: *The High Price of Bullion* (1810, III, pp. 45–127); *Reply to Mr. Bosanquet* (1811, III, pp. 45–127); *Proposals for an Economical and Secure Currency* (1816, IV, pp. 43–141); all in the *Collected Works and Correspondence* edited by P. Sraffa in collaboration with M. Dobb.

[17] *Plan for the Establishment of a National Bank* (1824, IV, pp. 271–300). See also Sayers (1953) and Arnon (1987).

by Ricardo – would be free to act as any nonissuing bank under this new approach: that is, to maximize profits by lending the funds it raises. Ricardo's proposals in *Plan for a National Bank* call for a reform in the institutional framework under which the banking system then operated. It seems that the directors of the new Issuing Department monopoly, who were to be guided by these rules, were to have no discretion; and indeed, the Currency School interpreted Ricardo's 1824 text in this way. However, in this last text, Ricardo went a few steps further and discussed the possibility of having the Bank's directors implement monetary policy.[18] Whereas Ricardo's proposals are known for paving the way to the monopolization of note-issuing, he went beyond the simple rule for the determination of the quantity of notes. In his 1824 text, Ricardo discusses not only the responses to developments in the gold market, but also interventions aimed at influencing the quantity in circulation according to overall macroeconomic circumstances.

Thus, as is clear from Ricardo's discussions, he recommends not merely a defense of convertibility, but control of the money supply.[19] Ricardo's position in this last text differs significantly both from his own earlier views and from those of the Currency School. He explicitly rejects both competition and a strict rule as the right methods for determining the quantity of notes, and he openly recommends discretion. His new 1824 theory is closer to what we would call central banking than it is to the automatic mechanism characteristic of the Currency School's proposals, which left almost no place for discretion. Thus, Ricardo was moving toward a rejection of the application of the invisible hand mechanism to money, and adopted a basically visible hand theory. One should note that this visible hand position was contrary to Ricardo's own writings on monetary issues before this text; moreover, this new view was not accepted. What people usually described as Ricardo's monetary positions were either his basically Smithian position before his *Plan for a National Bank* or his recommendation to concentrate issuing in the hands of a single bank. As we shall see, contemporaries, and in particular the Currency School, noticed the change in Ricardo's approach.

The Currency School, as we have seen in Chapter 11, rejected both the concept of a Lender of Last Resort and also, naturally, the more ambitious concept of discretionary monetary policy. Their assumption was that it was enough to restructure the monetary system by making the supply of money correspond to that of the imagined pure circulation. Failing to achieve that correspondence in a competitive banking system, Loyd, Torrens, and

---

[18] See Arnon (1987).
[19] For a detailed study of the changes in Ricardo's views, see Arnon (1987).

Norman advocated the monopolization of the money supply, that is, the supply of Bank of England's notes, making it behave as would a pure circulation. The Currency School argued that the Currency Principle, on which the 1844 Bank Act had been based, guarantees that the money (coins plus notes) supply would be the right one, and that no additional measures were needed.

The Banking School on Monetary Policy after 1844

The rejection by the Banking School Trio of the Currency Principle on theoretical grounds as well as its policy consequences, as described in Chapter 12, made the Banking School authors natural candidates for reviving a theory of central banking in the tradition of Thornton. This is especially true because they were well aware of Thornton's views on the subject. Clearly, their criticisms were a far cry from the simplistic Bullionist and Currency School analysis that attempts to make the monetary system behave as a pure circulation, and to rely for that on the power of gold. The Banking School Trio understood the intricate structure of banking, the many mediums used as assets and liabilities, their complex links, and the unsatisfactory nature of the Bank Act's simple rule as a guide for the monetary system. Thus, the Trio rejected the Currency School proposals to regulate what they defined as "money." They believed that the best way to deal with the supply of money was to leave it to market forces as they operated in the prereformed system. However, because they also recognized the important role that other instruments played in the economy, they needed to answer a simple question: Could the supply of those instruments be left to market forces in the prereformed banking system as well? Their various answers to this important question were far from complete and satisfactory.

For example, we have seen that Tooke's 1844 pamphlet explicitly recognizes the importance of credit instruments. Price levels and other economic aggregates depend on credit to a much greater extent than most people think; when discussing major factors that determine the price level, Tooke shifts his emphasis from the "Seasons" to "Credit." This change probably reflects not only the changing focus of his inquiries, but also the rise in the importance of credit from the 1820s to the 1840s (see 1844, pp. 86–87).

Tooke's analysis of the three different functions fulfilled by banks is of great interest in this regard. The first function, which is carried out only by the issuing banks, is to issue "promissory notes on demand." The second function is to "receive deposits of the incomes of their customers, and to pay out the amount, as it is wanted for expenditure." The third function "is to collect capital from those who have not immediate employment for it, and to distribute or transfer it to those who have" (ibid., p. 36). The second function, carried out "over the counter," is responsible for the circulation of currency, whereas the third one, carried out "behind the counter," is relevant to the circulation of capital and reflects the role of banks in what is known as "intermediation." Tooke claims that this distinction is identical to the distinction between the two types of transactions: those between dealers and those between dealers and consumers. Thus, banks deal with two different subjects beyond issuing: One is the collection of capital from those who have no use for it and its transfer to those who do have use for it; the other is the acceptance of deposits and, through transfers of those deposits, management of payments.

Tooke recognized that banks do have a limited influence on advances and thus on the creation of credit instruments. Through the use of their own capital, though not through their notes, they could make advances in the hope of getting a bigger share of the market. Those advances were not always made against good securities and were considered dangerous to the smooth functioning of the banking system. Taken together with Tooke's assumption that credit influences other variables in the economy, the natural consequence of this observation is to either explain how market forces will determine the right quantity of credit or to suggest some control of credit. Tooke, however, does neither. His silence on the determination of the quantity of credit in the 1844 text remains the weakest point in his analysis.[20]

The 1847 crisis brought the question of the right policy the Bank's directors should adopt back to the forefront. However, this time it was much clearer to the participants that they were in fact debating the desired level of discretion, if any, that the Bank's directors should be allowed, as well as the best tools to be used by them. Instead of the strict rules of the 1844 Bank Act, Tooke continued to support a more flexible banking system stabilized by and based on a big reserve of bullion. This would leave the Bank's directors much broader margins within which they would remain passive in the face of (transitory) gold drains. The directors would react to a drain that went on longer than what was considered "transitory" by increasing the rate of interest, which was their first policy tool. If this discretionary action should prove insufficient and the drain continued, a "corrective measure" would be taken (see Chapter 12). The Bank's directors would be responsible for choosing the course of action and so defending the stability of the system.

---

[20] The determination of the rate of interest, whether in the banks' second role of giving credit or in its third role, intermediation, receives proper and outstanding treatment by Tooke.

Thus, Tooke's policy recommendations after 1844 were clearly in line with what we have described as defensive monetary policy, very close in its main tenets to the future Bagehot Rule that we saw in Chapter 14. According to the Banking School, there was nothing to be gained from the additional regulations and stricter rules that the Currency School advocated. The best way to improve the banking system was to let a monetary authority direct it, and to do that efficiently, the authority's management had to itself be improved. So much was at stake and so much depended on the correct judgments of the directors, in Tooke's view, that it is logical to find Tooke's only recommendations for reform – beyond those of a big reserve and the repeal of the 1844 Bank Act so that his defensive monetary policy could be implemented – directed at the qualifications of the directors and their terms in office. He recommended that the directors be "elected from the leading merchants, traders and manufactures of London" as was then the custom, but with fewer changes in the compound of this body than before. This experienced body should be exclusively responsible for the management of the banking system, and the government should not be superior to the Bank's directors in any decision. When asked in the 1848 Committee about the "Relaxing Clause," a clear rule that would dictate exactly when the Bank Act was to be relaxed in the future, Took again put it to the directors, not the government, to decide. "The difficulty of framing any satisfactory Regulation upon the Subject [the Relaxing Clause] leads me to suppose that upon the whole you must at last leave it to the Responsibility of the Directors. I cannot see any better Course" (Parliamentary Papers [1848b], Q. 3155, p. 354). Tooke returned to this crucial issue in his last writings.

In 1856, Tooke published a pamphlet *On the Bank Charter Act of* 1844, a retrospective on the previous twelve years of Bank of England behavior.[21] In this pamphlet, Tooke discusses the facts during the twelve years before publication, and evaluates both Peel's and the Currency School's views on banking. The pamphlet was written under the shadow of the defeat of the Banking School in 1844; Tooke was naturally trying to vindicate the Banking School's principles as they were confirmed, in his view, by the new facts.

A point of interest is Tooke's critique of the "dogma of the Currency School" concerning note-issuing, which they consider to be the prerogative

---

[21] Many of the arguments were repeated in 1857 when the last two volumes of *History of Prices* appeared. These volumes were written in collaboration with William Newmarch. In the introduction, Tooke explains that they wrote different parts, with Tooke writing the first part on the prices of corn and the seasons in the years 1842–1856 and the fifth part entitled "On the Management and Policy of the Bank of England during the period 1844–1856"; this part was mainly a repetition of his 1856 pamphlet.

of the state. As we know, this belief results from their (to Tooke's mind erroneous) theory that to defend convertibility one has to create a system wherein the quantity of convertible notes and coins would equal the quantity of coins that would have circulated in a "pure" circulation; that would be the case according to the Currency School Trio only if one issuer would follow the Bank Act. The Currency Principle, relating to a desired correspondence between "money" and gold, was the result of the Currency School's assumption that a purely metallic circulation is the perfect currency. However, argues Tooke, there are several assumptions about such a "pure" circulation, from the simple case where payments are executed through the exclusive usage of coins with no credit to the existence of banking, that need to be addressed. Analyzing the latter, one should distinguish between at least three possible banking regimes. In the first case, one has a 100 percent reserve system where the bank keeps all the deposited gold; credit is used among individuals, but is not created by the banks. In the second case, many banks exist, as in the 1850s, but without note-issuing and with no "central quasi-national" bank. Third is the case where "a large Central Bank, such as the Bank of England now is" exists, again without note-issuing by either the Bank of England or the other banks (Tooke and Newmarch [1857], p. 533). These three possible regimes are, of course, very different from each other. The Currency School advocates probably had the third regime in mind; the main point of difference concerns the role played by "Hoards or Reserves in the hands of bankers" when a panic develops:

Suppose, for instance, that in the confidence engendered by an easy state of the money market of long continuance, some of the more enterprising and less wealthy of the banks might invest too large a proportion of their deposits in securities not readily convertible, or of doubtful solidity; and then, supposing a sudden extra demand for coin, whether for export or for internal purposes, these weaker banks might simultaneously fail. These failures would inevitably engender a panic among the depositors in the more wealthy banks, causing a run upon them; and as runs in such cases are infectious, they might extend to the greater number of the banks in the kingdom, who might thus be obliged to suspend their payments. ... Such a catastrophe would be much less likely to occur if ... there were Central Bank possessing a large reservoir of coin, which would enable it to come in aid of such banks as might, although of undoubted solidity, be tottering in a time of panic. (Tooke and Newmarch [1857] vol. V, pp. 535–536)

Beyond the clear description of the central bank's defensive role as a Lender of Last Resort, this passage and the situation analyzed in it pull the rug out from under the most important assumption about the perfect circulation. In the more advanced regimes, where banks exist, the necessary links between gold drains and the circulation are clearly broken. Thus, the perfect circulation under those conditions is far from perfect. Basically, the same reason for rejecting the supposed perfection of the simple, first model – the role played by hoards of gold outside circulation – is used in the other cases. The fact that the Bank of England played such an important role in the banking system through functions besides its note-issuing practically destroyed the Currency School's case. They assumed that a rule, in the form of the 1844 Bank Act, would answer the most urgent question: What should the Bank's directors do under certain specific circumstances? The answer was clear and simple. The directors should issue notes against gold and, beyond that, should behave like any other bank. Thus, the Bank of England should not by any means try to regulate any of its assets or liabilities according to considerations other than simple profit maximization. In other words, the directors were to behave like all other bankers, not interested in the implications of their decisions beyond their own business.

Thus, while Tooke was disillusioned with the quality of the Bank's management and expressed some reservations about their complete discretion, his proposals, in fact, supported their total power. Moreover, it was now made explicitly clear that Tooke well understood the importance to the public of the operations of the Bank's Banking Department. Thus in the fourteenth of the 23 Conclusions of 1857, probably his last published notes, Tooke concluded: "14. That a great mistake was committed by the framers of the Act of 1844, in the assumption, that the Banking Department of the Bank of England admits of being conducted in the same way, and with the same effects on the interests and convenience of the Public, as any other non-issuing Joint-Stock Bank" (ibid., pp. 636–637). The natural conclusion, one might think, was to move on and recommend some ways of dealing with these public interests; however, no such recommendations can be found. Tooke's only, repeated answer was to improve the management of the Bank; however one understood it.[22] This certainly leaves a gap between Tooke's theories of money and credit and his proposed banking regimes. Money should not be controlled, but rather should be left to the

---

[22] The last conclusion of the twenty-three, published a year before Tooke died, reads as follows:

"23. That next, therefore, to the abrogation of the Act of 1844, as it relates to the division of the Departments of the Bank of England; and to restrictions on the Circulation of Bank Notes; the most important question relating to the Currency which can occupy the attention of Parliament, will be the application of a remedy to the obvious faults in the Constitution, and Rules of Management, of the Governing Body of the Bank of England" (Tooke and Newmarch [1857] vol. V, 639).

discretion of the competitive bankers. Credit should be regulated by the Bank of England, but Tooke never specifies exactly how.

Bagehot and Defensive Monetary Policy in the 1870s

Bagehot followed the British financial system closely from three perspectives: that of the editor of the *Economist* for many years; as a discrete counselor to many persons in power; and as one who might one day hold power himself. The British financial system was highly centralized and unstable. As we have seen in Chapter 14, Bagehot's policy prescriptions addressed the system as it was; maybe a better system was possible in theory, but in practice, one has to accept what one has and improve upon what exists. Changing the system to a decentralized one, which does not rely on one reserve and is thus closer to free banking was not a real option for this practical person. One has to appreciate that the assets accumulated over so many years, in the form of trust in and reputation of a working financial system, may be lost in an attempt to radically reform the system.

The actual British banking system of the 1870s, with its high level of concentration and interdependencies and heavy reliance on one pivot in the form of the Bank of England, was not, as many still believed, self-regulating. The banking system was unstable and fragile. Bagehot's analysis is directed first and foremost at those who still hold to the idea that no policy is necessary. He tries to convince his readers that the idea, still common among the Bank directors, that the Bank has nothing to worry about and no responsibilities, was ill-conceived. The system was unstable and dangerous and had to be managed; Bagehot's proposals seek to improve the system by delegating to the Bank the role of the responsible adult.

Like almost all of his predecessors, Bagehot supported convertibility. He worried about the instability of the banking system; his nightmare scenario was a run on the banks when the reserves were insufficient to answer the demand for gold. The possible causes of such a run might have varied, but the basic threat remained the same: Insufficient reserves to support a potential sudden demand. The policy rule that Bagehot formulates in *Lombard Street* articulates a defensive monetary policy; it gives a general plan of action – not too specific, because he believed that it's impossible to provide exact guidelines – for what the Bank directors should do to try to prevent a crisis and, if a crisis should occur, what the directors should do while it continues. The lack of understanding about the dangers of a financial crisis and the rejection of defensive monetary policy, even the denial of its legitimacy, especially by the Bank directors, were Bagehot's main reasons for writing *Lombard Street*.

Bagehot's recommendation, his well-known Rule, is simple: the Bank should extend loans at the start of a crisis, but at escalating interest rates. The exact quantity of the prepared reserve and the schedule of such interest-rate increases should be the prerogative of the Bank directors. The directors were not yet fully ready to fulfill the responsibility, though, because they did not recognize that they had a responsibility. Thus, although the Bank actually made substantial advances[23] and behaved properly during the panic years of 1847, and even more so in 1857 and 1866, it did not yet acknowledge the principle for doing so. Hence, wrote Bagehot, one should be very worried about the Bank despite its reasonable behavior.

Twenty-five years before publishing *Lombard Street*, in a paper entitled "The Currency Monopoly,"[24] Bagehot surveyed works published in the context of the 1847 monetary crisis.[25] At this stage, Bagehot supported the Bank Act. He did not support the claims made by Tooke and Wilson that assign responsibility for the crisis to the Bank Act, nor did he accept Tooke's view that the crisis proved the case against the Bank Act. Although supporting monopoly in note-issuing on the grounds that this was not a proper field for competition,[26] he was already then less clear as to how to address departures from the strict rule embodied in the Bank Act. That is, Bagehot in 1848 raised the possibility of defensive monetary policy under the conditions prevailing in October 1847: A threat to the Bank of England that could bring insolvency in the banking system and "might lead … to a national bankruptcy" (Bagehot, vol. 9, pp. 268–269, quoting Torrens):

> No government would be justified in allowing this to come about while there remained a chance of preventing it by the use of any means whatever. That the Bank directors were excessively to blame, we have no doubt at all. They ran a risk of failure which might have injured the proprietors of Bank Stock, whose agents they are.

---

[23] See *Lombard Street* table on p. 64.

[24] The paper was first published in the *Prospective Review* for 1848, vol. IV, pp. 297–337. See the *Collected Works* vol. 9, pp. 235–271. It is Bagehot's first paper, written when he was only twenty-two years old.

[25] Wilson (1847), Torrens (1848), Tooke (1848).

[26] "But first we shall sum up what have already advanced in the assertion, that the issue of money is a fit case for a government monopoly, because the object aimed at is not to reduce cost price, but to render it fixed: because fluctuations in value are attended with a great derangement of internal commerce; because the interests of individual coiners and issuers are at variance with the interest of the community, and because as a result of the whole, the principle of individual self-interest cannot here be trusted to as a security for the welfare of the community" (vol. 9, pp. 259–260).

... No doubt this interference of government to support the banking department is very different from the currency regulations of which we have spoken before. It goes far beyond the intervention of government to give fixity to the standard of value; it amounts to the admission that government may settle when money of fixed value shall be lent to one man and borrowed from another. A person well instructed in the principles of free trade will be apt to wonder at this. (ibid., p. 269)

The answer, so the young Bagehot tells his readers, is that for historical reasons the banking industry is not a model of competition but rather of monopoly.[27] In this case, the government has helped to create the monopoly and the Bank is "obviously a τυραννος [28], who has obtained aid from without to overthrow the constitution and establish his own rule." Bagehot criticizes Tooke at this point, blaming him for his call for a big reserve in both departments as an almost permanent law:

[Tooke] wishes it to be a law, or almost a law, that there should always be a reserve of £10,000,000 in both departments. This, it seems to us, is perpetuating that system of government interference with banking from which so many evils have arisen. We quite admit that it may be necessary to interfere again because we have interfered before; but a permanent system should, in our judgment, be founded on permanently right principles: the effects of past misconduct will wear out in the course of time: but Mr Tooke proposes to found a lasting system on the rotten basis of antiquated errors; to transmit unimpaired to posterity the evils which we have, to our misfortune, inherited from our fathers. (p. 270)

Although Bagehot states strongly in *Lombard Street* that he plans to run away from the 1840s debates, he comes back to them. However, now he is on the side of history, arguing that they have to fix what they have and not aim at an ideal, competitive banking system. He also argues in 1873 for a structure of interventions very close to what Tooke had praised in the 1848–1858 period after the new crises occurred. Thus, Bagehot's Rule is closer to Tooke and the Banking School than to the ideal – no monetary policy regime – favored by the Currency School. It is defensive monetary policy, but not as yet a fully developed, active monetary policy.

Wicksell and the Reemergence of Active Monetary Policy

Knut Wicksell, the Swedish economist writing at the turn of the nineteenth century, brings our story of the slow rise of central banking theory to a close.

---

[27] This is the case in England with the Bank's monopoly in London; Bagehot is careful to draw a distinction concerning the Scottish experience.

[28] Tyrant, ruler, oppressor; in the *Collected Works* 9, pp. 270 n15.

Although he had not read Thornton and did not even know about his existence until after he had devised his own theory, Wicksell unintentionally revived many of Thornton's ideas on both defensive and active monetary policies. He also rehabilitated and legitimized the idea of nonconvertible paper money, an idea that Thornton thought a feasible alternative to a system based on commodity-money. As we have seen in Chapter 17, Wicksell's views on monetary policy should be understood within the general monetary analysis he proposed. After an in-depth study of the difficulties and advantages of the British monetary system and the contradicting interpretations of what went wrong in times of crisis, Wicksell proposed his innovative monetary theory and balanced view of policy. He considered the monetary authority the defender of the system but also the body that can improve real economic performance; thus, he supported defensive as well as active monetary policy.

The complicated link between the price level and interest rates, an issue that bothered many scholars who studied the British system, led Wicksell to propose a totally new analysis, presented in his monumental *Interest and Prices* of 1898. The new approach brings together a systematic analysis of the real economy and the monetary system. Wicksell argues that the "real rate," defined as the real profit rate in production, is determined by the marginal product of capital. The market rate of interest, defined as the rate paid by loan takers, is determined in the credit market. Any changes in the loan market or in the production sphere will make the market rate of interest unequal to the real or "natural" rate and will trigger a process of price changes. Prices will continue to change as long as the market rate stays below or above the natural one. Hence, as long as the gap is not closed, the economy will experience continuous price changes, a process that Wicksell terms "the cumulative process."

As we have seen in Chapter 17, Wicksell presents a thorough discussion of policy in *Interest and Prices*, in a chapter entitled "Practical Proposals for the Stabilisation of the Value of Money" (chapter 12). Wicksell's proposals are directly derived from the theoretical framework just discussed and aim at stabilizing the price level. Stable prices, the objective – or one of the objectives – of monetary policy, can be reached "through the monetary institutions of the various countries." Wicksell did not trust free banking, which was by then even less appealing than before, and rejected both the Humean and Smithian approaches that made policy thinking void and the preference for a strict rule expressed by the Currency School. Wicksell developed a strategy that calls for action by the monetary authorities in different countries and for international coordination between central banks. The central banks should use their rates of interest as instruments in an attempt to match the average money rate worldwide with the natural rate worldwide. One does not have to know the natural rate, which is hard to calculate nationally and certainly globally, in order to achieve such an ambitious, general objective. It would suffice to look at world prices and determine if they are either rising or falling (Wicksell [1898], p. 189).

We have called this global policy rule "Wicksell's Rule"; like other monetary policy rules we have encountered, it intends to promote the public good. It provides general guidelines for action whose implementation may naturally contradict the private interests of the banks involved. The banks may lose profits if, as recommended, they decrease the interest rate while prices are falling; and in the opposite case, they may lose customers. But, writes Wicksell in *Interest and Prices*, the "banks' prime duty is not to earn a great deal but to provide the public with a medium of exchange – and to provide this medium in *adequate measure*, to aim at stability of prices. In any case, their obligations to society are enormously more important than their private obligations, and if they are ultimately unable to fulfil [sic] their obligations to society along the lines of private enterprise – which I very much doubt – then they would provide a worthy activity for the State" (p. 190). Thus, the banking sector has to serve society and function with an eye for general welfare, not private profit; if this is not true for banks in general, this is true for the central bank.

Thus, Wicksell's policy proposal calls for cooperation between the central banks of the world, or at least between those of the gold-standard countries. Each central bank fixes its interest rate not only according to whether prices are falling or rising in the world but also with an eye on the balance of trade and the exchanges. Central banks prefer to be independent and would not agree to others fixing their rates; they prefer, writes Wicksell, to "retain a free hand to be used *in the last resort*, if not earlier, over bank-rate policy" (p. 191). Such a bold proposal for international cooperation, based on a theory that systematically links intermediation and exchange, the rate of interest and the level of prices, was an innovation. Wicksell first maintains the assumption of the gold standard although, as we have seen, in the pure credit economy its role is less and less important. However, while assessing the role of gold flows in the discussion of international cooperation on policy, Wicksell introduces some intriguing reservations on the gold standard.

In Wicksell's second major work on monetary theory, *Lectures on Political Economy* (in short, *Lectures*), the basic theoretical message remains the same.[29] *Lectures*, however, elaborates on Wicksell's proposals for monetary

---

[29] As stated in Chapter 17, the English translation is of the revised 1915 edition and appeared only in 1936, a year after *Interest and Prices* was translated.

policy. In the *Lectures*, Wicksell expands his criticisms of those who represented the two opposing views in the British classical debates, Ricardo and Tooke. His detailed critique of their respective errors is a prelude to his own policy rule as we have seen in Chapter 17.

The "Positive Solution" Wicksell proposes in the *Lectures*, which both Ricardo and Tooke failed to provide, elaborates on monetary policy. The market rate is determined by savers and investors in the process of intermediation, whereas the real rate on the free, notional capital functions like an anchor. The market rate of interest will settle sooner or later at this real rate, but the process is complex and dependent on the specific payments system. In the case of a simple credit market, in which individuals make loans to each other, one can see a direct and relatively simple mechanism that brings the two rates together. In an "organized credit" system that includes banks, the "connection between loan interest and interest on capital will become much less simple." The reason for the complexity is due to the fact that, unlike individuals who can loan only their available free funds, banks "possess a fund for loans which is always elastic and, on certain assumptions, inexhaustible" (p. 194). As a result, the relationship between the natural rate (on capital) and market-loan rate will be established "by virtue of the connecting link of price movements" (p. 194). To recapture, this is the essence of the two-rates approach: If and when the loan rate departs from the real, normal rate on capital, prices will move.

However, in the *Lectures*, as we have seen, Wicksell addresses monetary policy also when the system departs from the gold standard and assumes inconvertibility. Countries that decide to take this path can create an internal stable system by managing their currency along the lines just outlined. Wicksell believes in the feasibility of a working international paper currency, issued by one global central bank, that uses interest rates as an international policy tool. As we have seen, Wicksell refers in this context to a policy that has "*two degrees of freedom*": cooperation between the central banks of the world responsible for balancing their credits and debits and also for fixing world prices.

Thus, like Smith more than one hundred years before him, he complains about the "pure waste" of using gold as the foundation for the stable monetary system. But that is not the main point; the emphasis is placed on the advantages an inconvertible monetary system has: "As an independent measure of value, independent of material substance, whether gold or silver, and kept stable in value both in space and time in the manner described above, the banknote, or in more general terms bank money, is undoubtedly the ideal which currency systems should endeavor to approach" (p. 224). That calls for an ambitious reform in international monetary arrangements.

Summary

The resistance to central banking has deep roots in preclassical and classical monetary thinking. It was embedded in the analyses of Hume and Smith, which relied on international equilibrating mechanisms to take care of the money supply or on a belief in a competitive banking system, respectively. In both cases, the role of gold as the foundation for all other assets and liabilities was crucial. Real and financial crises played important roles in changing banking theory, but the actual experience of inconvertibility during the Restriction Period did not suffice to change the overall resistance to or avoidance of central banking, as expressed by most of the Bullionists and anti-Bullionists who debated the return to gold in that period. The only exception was Thornton, who rejected Hume's and Smith's analysis of money and banking and was the first theoretician to develop a comprehensive theory of central banking, which in our analysis is a theory that incorporates both defensive and active central banking. Thornton argued for discretion in determining the money supply, including not only bank notes, but also other forms of credits and debits. He clearly understood that an inconvertible monetary system not linked to commodity-money can work efficiently, but argued that discretion is also essential in such a system.

A central question addressed in this book is why Thornton was rejected and why Humean and Smithian anti-central-banking theories continued to prevail. Our analysis of the main schools and theoreticians of the period has identified the ways in which they tried to remain faithful to the principle of nonintervention during, and despite, recurring financial crises. The Bullionists continued to believe that there was nothing wrong with the pre-Restriction monetary system; they attributed the difficulties during the Restriction only to the departure from gold and thus recommended a return to convertibility. When reoccurring crises proved this view wrong, common wisdom embraced the Currency Principle, which did not contradict Hume's and Smith's rejection of central banking. The Currency School added the metallic fluctuations principle discussed in Chapter 11, but continued to reject any form of central banking. The Banking School rejected the proposals of the Currency School and advocated measures designed to avoid the collapse of the banking system. We have characterized such measures as defensive central banking; theirs was a Lender of Last Resort or defensive central banking at best. More crises led to the implementation of defensive central banking in practice and to Bagehot's famous Rule. However, although Bagehot is often presented as the father of central banking, we argue in Chapter 14 that his analysis followed that of the Banking School in laying the foundations for a theory of defensive monetary policy. It was not yet Thornton's active central banking approach.

The monetary difficulties in the 1880s and 1890s led Wicksell to a radical departure from anticentral-banking conceptualizations. For the first time since Thornton, we see the reemergence of an analysis that considers the possibility of a systemic failure in the financial system. We also see the return of an analysis that consistently addresses intermediation, not just exchange, and incorporates the crucial role of finance in intermediation. The Currency School also rejected free banking in all its forms, but they opposed discretion and introduced a strict rule (the metallic fluctuations principle and the monopolization of note-issuing) as a solution to the danger of instability. Wicksell, like Thornton one hundred years earlier, went further. Wicksell, like Thornton, rejected free banking and advocated an active role for the visible hand.

Why had Thornton been rejected for close to a century? Why did he disappear from the canon for so long? The story told in this book can shed some light on these intriguing questions, although the answers cannot be summarized in one sentence. Certainly, some could not accept Thornton's reasoning for what can be described as "ideological" reasons: They really believed in the power and justice of applying the invisible hand to finance. When they were reluctantly forced to acknowledge the existence of recurring failures in reality or, more disturbing for theoreticians, of gaps in theory, they searched for solutions that would not contradict their basic ideology. This is clear in the case of the Bullionists during the Restriction and of the Currency School before and after the 1844 Bank Act. But we have also seen that ideology was not the only reason why monetary theorists of the time missed Thornton's significance.

Thornton, like Wicksell one hundred years later, departed from the common tendency among the classicals to focus almost exclusively on the exchange process and on the mechanisms that transformed barter into a monetary economy. The analysis of intermediation was weak and partial among mainstream classical theorists, who thus did not really understand Thornton's path-breaking thoughts about the importance of credits, debits, and, more generally, intermediation. The frameworks of both Thornton and Wicksell depart from "monetary theories of credit" and approach "credit theories of money." In this context, Sir John Hicks once wrote to me in a letter: "I believe credit comes before money, before hard money that is; not only logically, but also historically."[30] That credit is more basic than money is indeed a radical notion; an idea that is very difficult to accept. This difficulty played an important role in accounting for the slow rise of a theory of active central banking. Following Wicksell, today the notion of active central banking is almost universally accepted. That credit theoretically takes precedence over money remains a controversial idea that was not fully absorbed in twentieth-century monetary theory. Following the development and impact of credit theories of money since Wicksell is an intriguing endeavor that must wait for another book.

[30] Letter from J. Hicks to A. Arnon, December 20, 1988.

Epilogue

The financial crises that started in 2007 in the United States and rapidly spread throughout the world economy have proved yet again that crises are part and parcel of the economy, and that the debate between visible and invisible hands is far from over. Those who attribute zero probability to the reoccurrence of such dramatic events, and they are the clear majority when the economy functions properly, as it does most of the time, prove that the human mind has infinite capacity to delude itself. The belief that we have learned the lessons of the past and have managed to put in place the mechanisms that will ensure that the fragile system will not break again characterizes conventional wisdom in common times. Those who remember the years before the current fragility certainly are aware that most observers thought that, "It cannot happen again." "It," the great depression, happened over seventy years ago, and policy makers, so conventional wisdom argued, had long since drew the conclusions.

In this book, we have shown how the simple truths known to Thornton more than two hundred years ago – that the system is fragile and prone to severe collapses, that convertibility to gold is no defense in itself, that discretionary policy is always necessary but cannot always guarantee society against a crisis, that one has to manage the complex system that connects the decentralized economic units and makes up the financial system – went against the beliefs of most of the classicals. Those few who absorbed the lessons, even if only partially, carried the debate through the nineteenth century, but not until Wicksell close to one hundred years later did these truths become conventional wisdom.

However, the history of the twentieth century has clearly shown that the temptation to reject the necessity for interventions in the rapidly changing financial system is very strong. Whether this temptation reflects the same forces that accounted for the very slow rise of a theory of central banking is a question that we still have to answer. We could argue that the fundamental belief in the invisible hand combined with a strict rule – whether that of the convertibility of bank notes to gold or that of the metallic fluctuations, which was probably the major obstacle on the path to a theory of monetary policy in the nineteenth century – did not disappear. Rather, it presented itself time and again in the twentieth century, not only in banking, but also in the many other facets of finance. As we have seen throughout this book, crisis can play an important role in sharpening critical faculties. One may hope that the present crises will also produce innovative new ideas on managing finance and banking. Indeed, if not, the future prosperity of humanity is in some danger.

Bibliography

Primary References

Attwood, T. (various years), *Selected Economic Writings of Thomas Attwood*, edited with an Introduction F. W. Fetter, London: LSE Series of Reprints # 18.

Bagehot, W. (1873), *Lombard Street: A Description of the Money Market*, London: Kegan Paul, Trench, Trubner & Co. [1896].

—— (1978), *The Collected Works of Walter Bagehot*, The Economic Essays (vols. 9–11), N. St John-Stevas (ed.), London: The Economist.

[Bailey, S.] (1840), *A Defense of Joint Stock Banks and Country Issues*, London: James Ridgway.

Baring, F. (1797a), *Observations on the Establishment of the Bank of England and on Paper Circulation of the Country*, London: Minerva Press [1993].

—— (1797b), *Further Observations on the Establishment of the Bank of England and on Paper Circulation of the Country*, London: Minerva Press [1993].

—— (1801a), *Observations on the Publication of Walter Boyd*, London: Minerba Press.

—— (1801b?), *A Twelve-Penny Answer to a Three Shillings and Six-Penny Pamphlet, Intitled "A Letter on the Influence of the Stoppage of the Issue in Specie at the Bank of England, on the Prices of Provisions and other Commodities,"* London: J. Stockdale.

—— (1801c?), *A Second Twelve-Penny Answer to a New (and Five Shillings) Edition of Three Shillings and Six-Penny Pamphlet, Intitled "A Letter on the Influence of the Stoppage of the Issue in Specie at the Bank of England, on the Prices of Provisions and other Commodities; with additional Notes and a Preface,"* London: I. Walter and Son.

Boase, H. (1804), *A Letter to the Right Hon. Lord King, in Defence of the conduct of the Directors of the Banks of England and Ireland*, London: Bulmer.

Bosanquet, C. (1810), *Practical Observations on the Report of the Bullion-Committee*, 2nd edition, corrected with a supplement, London: Richardson.

Boyd, W. (1801a), *A Letter to the Right Honourable William Pitt on the Influence of the Stoppage of Issues in Specie at the Bank of England on the Prices of Provisions and Other Commodities*, London: Wright.

—— (1801b), *A Letter to the Right Honourable William Pitt on the Influence of the Stoppage of Issues in Specie at the Bank of England on the Prices of Provisions and Other Commodities*, (2nd edition, with additional Notes and a Preface containing remarks on the publication of Sir Francis Baring), London: Wright and Mawman.

Checkland, S. G. (1948), "The Birmingham Economists, 1815–1850", *The Economic History Review*, (New Series), Vol. 1, No. 1, pp. 1–19.

Horner, F. (1957), *The Economic Writings of Francis Horner in the Edinburgh Review 1802–1806*, Edited and with an Introduction by F.W. Fetter, New York: Kelley & Millman.

(1994), *The Horner Papers: Selection from the Letters and Miscellaneous Writings of Francis Horner, M.P. 1795–1817*, Edited by K. Bourne and W. B. Taylor, Edinburgh: Edinburgh University Press.

Hume, D. (1752), *Political Discourses* in Rotwein, E. (1955), *David Hume Writings on Economics*, Madison: University of Wisconsin Press.

Huskisson, W. (1810), *The Question Concerning the Depreciation of Our Currency Stated and Examined*, third edition-corrected, London: John Murray.

Fullarton, J. (1844), *On the Regulation of Currencies*, London: John Murray, (2nd edition 1845).

Jevons, W. S. (1875), *Money and the Mechanism of Exchange*, London: Kegan Paul [1899]. (1884), *Investigations in Currency and Finance*, H. S. Foxwell (ed.), New York: A. M. Kelley [1964].

Joplin, T. (1823a), *An Essay on the General Principles and Present Practice of Banking in England and Scotland*, London: Baldwin, Cradock and Joy, reprinted together with *Outline of a System of Political Economy* (1823b), New York: Kelley 1970.

(1823b), *Outline of a System of Political Economy*, London: Baldwin, Cradock and Joy, reprinted New York: Kelley 1970.

(1832), *An Analysis and History of the Currency Question*, London: Ridgway.

(1840), *On Our Monetary System &c. &c., with an explanation of the Causes by which the Pressures on the Money Market are Produced, and a Plan for their Remedy, which can be carried into immediate effect, without any derangement, and with the appro-bation of the banks, both private and public, by which the currency is issued*, second edition, London: Ridgway.

(1844), *An Examination of Sir Robert Peel's Currency Bill of 1844, in a Letter to the Bankers of the United Kingdom*, London: Richardson.

Keynes, J. M. (1923), *A Tract on Monetary Reform*, London: Macmillan. (1925), "Alfred Marshall, 1842–1924," in *Memorials of Alfred Marshall*, A.C. Pigou (ed.), pp. 1–65, London: Macmillan.

(1930), *A Treatise on Money*, (two volumes) London: Macmillan.

(1936), *The General Theory of Employment, Interest and Money*, London: MacMillan.

King, P. [Lord] (1803), *Thoughts on the Effects of the Bank Restrictions*, (2nd edition, 1804), London: Taylor.

Loyd, S. J. [Lord Overstone] (1857), *Tracts and other Publications on Metallic and Paper Currency*, London: Harrison.

Loyd, S. J [Lord Overtone] and R. Torrens (1847), *The Petition of the Merchants, Bankers and Traders of London Against the Charter Act; With Comments on Each Clause*, in Loyd, S. J. (1857), *Tracts and other Publications on Metallic and Paper Currency*, London: Harrison.

Loyd, S. J [Lord Overstone] (1971), *The Correspondence of Lord Overstone*, (Three Volumes), Edited and Introduction by D. P. O'Brien, Cambridge University Press.

Loyd, S.J. (1832) Evidence in the 1832 Parliamentary Committee.

Malthus, T.R. (1811), "Review of the Controversy Respecting the High Price of Bullion", *Edinburgh Review*, 18 pp. 448–470.

(1823), "[A Review of] Thoughts and Details on the High and Low Prices of the Last Thirty Years" [by Thomas Tooke], *Quarterly Review*, 29, pp. 214–239.

Marshall, A. (1867), "Money," in *The Early Economic Writings of Alfred Marshall*, J. Whitaker (ed.), vol. 2 pp. 277–278, London: Macmillan (for the Royal Economic Society).

(1871?), "Essay on Money," in *The Early Economic Writings of Alfred Marshall*, J. Whitaker (ed.), vol. 1 pp. 164–177, London: Macmillan (for the Royal Economic Society).

(1886), "Answers to Questions on the Subject of Currency and Prices Circulated by the Royal Commission on the Depression of Trade and Industry," in *Official Papers by Alfred Marshall*, J. M. Keynes (ed.), pp. 1–16, London: Macmillan for the Royal Economic Society [1926].

(1887a), "Remedies for Fluctuations of General Prices", *Contemporary Review* (March), Reprinted in *Memorials of Alfred Marshall*, A.C. Pigou (ed.), pp. 188–211, London: Macmillan [1925].

(1887b), "Memoranda and Evidence before the Gold and Silver Commission", in *Official Papers by Alfred Marshall*, J. M. Keynes (ed.), pp. 17–195, London: Macmillan for the Royal Economic Society [1926].

(1890), *Principles of Economics*, Eighth Edition, London: Macmillan.

(1923), *Money, Credit and Commerce*, New York: A. M. Kelley [1965].

Marshall, A.. and Marshall, M. P. (1879), *Economics of Industry*, London: Macmillan.

Marx, K. (1847), *The Poverty of Philosophy*, New York: International Publishers [1963].

(1857), *Grundrisse: Foundations of the Critique of Political Economy* (Rough Draft), Translated and Foreword by M. Nicolaus, Middlesex: Penguin edition [1973].

(1859), *A Contribution to the Critique of Political Economy*, with an introduction by M. Dobb, Moscow: Progress Publishers [1970].

(1867), *Capital, Volume I*, Chicago: C. H. Kerr [1907].

(1885), *Capital, Volume II*, Chicago: C. H. Kerr [1907].

(1894), *Capital, Volume III*, Chicago: C. H. Kerr [1909].

Marx K. and F. Engels. (1934), *Correspondence 1846–1895: A Selection*, New York: International Publishers.

(1963), *Marx-Engels Werke (M.E.W.)*, Vols. 27–29. Berlin: Dietz Verlag.

[McCulloch, J. R.] (1831), *Historical Sketch of the Bank of England*, London: Longmans.

Mill, J. S. (1826), "Paper Currency and Commercial Distress", in *The Collected Works of John Stuart Mill*, J. M. Robson (ed.), vol. IV pp. 71–124, Toronto: University of Toronto Press.

(1844a), *Essays on Some Unsettled Questions of Political Economy*, in *The Collected Works of John Stuart Mill*, J. M. Robson (ed.), vol. IV pp. 289–340, Toronto: University of Toronto Press.

(1844b), "The Currency Question" [Review of Tooke's and Torrens' Inquiries of 1844], *The Westminster Review*, Vol. 41 pp. 579–598; also in *The Collected Works of John Stuart Mill*, J. M. Robson (ed.), vol. IV pp. 341–362, Toronto: University of Toronto Press.

(1848), *Principles of Political Economy*, seventh edition [1871], in *The Collected Works of John Stuart Mill*, J. M. Robson (ed.), vol. II & III, Toronto: University of Toronto Press.

Mushet, R. (1811), *An Inquiry into the Effects Produced on the National Currency and Rates of Exchange by the Bank Restriction Bill; Explaining the Cause of the High Price of Bullion; With Plans for Maintaining the National Coins in a State of Uniformity and Perfection*, Third Edition, London: Robert Baldwin.

Norman, G. W. (1833), *Remarks upon Some Prevalent Errors with Respect to Currency and Banking and Suggestions to the Legislature as to the Renewal of the Bank Charter*, London: R. Hunter.

——— (1838), *Remarks upon Some Prevalent Errors with Respect to Currency and Banking and Suggestions to the Legislature and the Public as to the Improvements of the Monetary System*, London: Pelham Richardson.

Palmer, J. H. (1837), *The Causes and Consequences of the Pressure upon the Money-Market*, London: Pelham Richardson.

Parliamentary Papers. (1793), *Report from the Select Committee appointed to take into Consideration the Present State of Commercial Credit* [Reprinted in P.P. 1826].

——— (1797), *Report from the Committee of Secrecy On the Outstanding Demands of the Bank of England*, in British Parliamentary Papers, The Bank of England and Commercial Credit, Monetary Policy, General I, Irish University Press.

——— (1804), *Report from the Select Committee on the Circulating Paper, the Specie and Current Coin of Ireland* [see also Fetter (1955)].

——— (1810), *Report from the Select Committee on the High Price of Bullion*, [see also Cannan (1919)].

——— (1819a), *Report from the Secret Committee on the Expediency of the Bank Resuming Cash Payments*, P.P. 1819, (202, 282), III.

——— (1819b), *Lords Committees Appointed a Secret Committee to enquire into the State of the Bank of England, with respect to the Expediency of the Resumption of Cash Payments*, P.P. 1819 (291) III.

——— (1832), *Report from the Committee of Secrecy on the Expediency of renewing the Charter of the Bank of England, and on the system on which Banks of Issue in England and Wales are conducted*, P.P. 1831–1832, (722) VI.

——— (1836–1837), *Report from the Select Committee on Joint Stock Banks*, P. P. 1836 (591) IX and 1837 (531) XIV.

——— (1840), *Report from the Select Committee on Banks of Issue*, P. P. 1840 (602) IV and 1841 (366) V.

——— (1847–1848), *Report from the Secret Committee on Commercial Distress*, First and Second reports, P.P. 1848 (395, 584).

——— (1848), *Report from the Secret Committee of the House of Lords appointed to inquire into the causes of the distress which has for some time prevailed among the commercial classes and how far it has been affected by the laws for regulating the issue of banks notes payable on demand together with the Minutes of Evidence*, P.P. 1848, (565) VIII, pt. iii.

——— (1857–1858), *Report from the Select Committee on Bank Acts*, P. P. 1857 (220) X, and 1857–1858 (381) V.

Parnell, H. (1804), *Observations upon the State of Currency in Ireland and upon the Course of Exchange between Dublin and London*, third edition, Dublin: Mahon.

——— (1827), *Observations on Paper Money, Banking and Overtrading*, London: James Ridgeway.

(1832), *A Plain Statement of the Power of the Bank of England*, London: James Ridgeway.

Pennington, J. (1827), *Memorandum* [to Huskisson], Goldsmiths' Library, University of London, Goldsmiths'-Kress Number 25312 Microfilm Numbers 2421.

(1829), *Paper Communicated by Mr. Pennington* [to T. Tooke] Appendix in Tooke, T., *A Letter to Lord Grenville on the Effects Ascribed to the Resumption of Cash Payments on the Value of the Currency*, London: Longman, Brown, Green, Longmans.

Ricardo, D. (1951–1973), *Works and Correspondence of David Ricardo*, edited by P. Sraffa, 11 volumes, Cambridge: The University Press.

(1932), *Minor Papers on the Currency Question, 1809–1823*, Edited with an Introduction and Notes by Jacob H. Hollander, Baltimore: John Hopkins Press.

Senior, W. N. (1829), *Three Lectures on the Value of Money*, London: B. Fellowes [1840].

Simon, H. C. (1936), "Rules versus Authorities in Monetary Policy." *Journal of Political Economy*, Vol. 44, pp. 1–30.

Smith, A. (1776), *An Inquiry into the Nature and Causes of the Wealth of Nations*, edited by E. Cannan, Chicago: The University Press [1994].

(1762–1766), *Lectures on Jurisprudence*, the Glasgow Edition of the works and Correspondence of Adam Smith, Vol. 5, Oxford University Press [1978].

Smith, M. (2001),"Endogenous Money, Interest and Prices: Tooke's Monetary Theory Revisited", *Contributions to Political Economy*, 20, pp. 31–55.

(2003), "On Central Banking "Rules": Tooke's Critique of the Bank Charter Act of 1844, *Journal of the History of Economic Thought*, 25, pp. 39–61.

Thornton, H. (1797), *Evidence before the 1797 Parliamentary Committee*, in Thornton (1802\1939), New Jersey: A. M. Kelley [1978].

(1802), *An Enquiry into the Nature and Effects of the Paper Credit of Great Britain*, (with an introduction by F.A. von Hayek, 1939), New Jersey: A. M. Kelley [1978].

(1804), *Notes on King* in Thornton (1802\1939), New Jersey: A. M. Kelley [1978].

(1811), *Speeches 1811* in Thornton (1802\1939), New Jersey: A. M. Kelley [1978].

Tooke, T. (1823), *Thoughts and Details on the High and Low Prices of the Last Thirty Years* (2 vols), London: John Murray.

(1824), *Thoughts and Details on the High and Low Prices of the Last Thirty Years*, (2nd edition, in one volume), London: John Murray.

(1826), *Considerations on the State of the Currency*, (2nd edition), London: John Murray.

(1829a), *A Letter to Lord Grenville on the Effects Ascribed to the Resumption of Cash Payments on the Value of the Currency*, London: Longman, Brown, Green, Longmans.

(1829b), *On the Currency in Connection with the Corn Trade and on the Corn Laws, to which is added a Postscript on the Present Commercial Stagnation*, (second letter to Lord Grenville), London: Longman, Brown, Green, Longmans.

(1838), *A History of Prices and of the State of the Circulation from 1793 to 1837*, (Volumes I and II), London: Longman, Brown, Green, Longmans.

(1840), *A History of Prices and of the State of the Circulation from 1838, 1839*, (Vol. III), London: Longman, Brown, Green, Longmans.

(1844), *An Inquiry into the Currency Principle: The Connection of the Currency with Prices and the Expediency of a Separation of Issue from Banking*, London: Longman, Brown, Green, Longmans.

(1848), *A History of Prices and of the State of the Circulation from 1839 to 1847*, (Vol. IV), London: Longman, Brown, Green, Longmans.

(1856), *On the Bank Charter Act of 1844, its Principles and Operation, with suggestions for an improved administration of the Bank of England*, London: Longman, Brown, Green, Longmans.

Tooke, T. and Newmarch, W. (1857), *A History of Prices and of the State of the Circulation from 1848-1856*, Vols. V, VI, London: Longman, Brown, Green, Longmans.

Torrens, R. (1812), *An Essay on Money and Paper Currency*, London: Johnson.

(1819), *A Comparative Estimate of the Effects which a Continuance and a Removal of the Restriction upon Cash Payments are Respectively Calculated to Produce: with Strictures on Mr. Ricardo's Proposal for Obtaining a Secure and Economical Currency*, London: R. Hunter.

(1837), *A Letter to the Right Honourable Lord Viscount Melbourne on the Causes of the Recent Derangement in the Money Market and on Bank Reform*, London: Longman, Rees, Orme, Brown & Green.

(1840), *A Letter to Thomas Tooke Esq. In Reply to His Objections Against the Separation of the Business of the Bank into A Department of Iwssue and a Department of Deposit and Discount with a Plan of Bank Reform*, London: Longman, Hurst, Orme and Brown.

(1844), *An Inquiry into the Practical Working of the Proposed Arrangements for the Renewal of the Charter of the Bank of England and the Regulation of the Currency with a Refutation of the Fallacies Advanced by Mr. Tooke*, second edition, London: Smith, Elder & Cornhill.

(1848), *The Principles and Practical Operation of Sir Robert Peel's Act of 1844 Explained and Defended Against the Objections of Tooke, Fullarton and Wilson*, London: Longman, Brown, Green and Longmans.

(1857), *The Principles and Practical Operation of Sir Robert Peel's Act of 1844 Explained and Defended*, (second edition) London: Longman, Brown, Green, Longmans and Roberts.

Wheatley, J. (1803), *Remarks on Currency and Commerce*, London: Burton.

Wicksell, K. (1889?/2001), "Bank Rate of Interest as the Regulator of Prices", Edited and translated by M. Boianovsky and H. M. Trautwein, *History of Political Economy*, vol. 33, pp. 509–516.

(1893), *Value, Capital and Rent*, New York: A. M. Kelley, [1954/19??].

(1898), *Interest and Prices: A Study of the Causes Regulating the Value of Money*, [Translated by R. F. Kahn; Introduction by B. Ohlin] New York: A. M. Kelley, [1936/1965].

(1906), *Lectures on Political economy Vol. II* [Edited with an Introduction L. Robbins], New York: A. M. Kelley, [1935/1978].

(1907), "The Influence of the Rate of Interest on Prices," *Economic Journal* 17, pp. 213–220.

(1925), "The Monetary Problem of the Scandinavian Countries," in *Interest and Prices*, Appendix pp. 199–219

(1958), *Selected Papers on Economic Theory*, E. Lindahl (ed.), with an Introduction, New York: A. M. Kelley [1969].

(1999), *Selected Essays in Economics*, B. Sandlin (ed.), volume two, London: Routledge.

Wilson, J. (1839), *Influences of the Corn Laws as affecting all Classes of the Community and Particularly the Landed Interests*, London: Longman, Orme, Brown, Green and Longmans.

(1840), *Fluctuations of Currency, Commerce and Manufactures; referable to the Corn Laws*, London: Longman, Orme, Brown, Green and Longmans.
(1947), *Capital, Currency, and Commerce*, London: The Economist.
[Wright, T. B. and Harlow, J.] (1844), *The Gemini Letters*, London: Simpkin, Marshall.

Secondary References

Angell, J. W. (1926/1965), *The Theory of International Prices: History, Criticism, and Restatement*, New York: A. M. Kelley.
Arnon, A. (1984), "The Transformation in Thomas Tooke's Monetary Theory Reconsidered," *History of Political Economy*, 16, pp. 311–326.
(1984), "Marx's Theory of Money – The Formative Years," *History of Political Economy* 16, 555–575. Also in Wood, J.C. (Ed.), *Karl Marx's Economics: Critical Assessments*, Croom Helm, 1988.
(1987), "Banking Between the Invisible and Visible Hands: A Reinterpretation of Ricardo's Place within the Classical School," *Oxford Economic Papers*, 39, pp. 268–281.
(1989), "The Early Tooke and Ricardo: A Political Alliance and First Signs of Theoretical Disagreements," *History of Political Economy*, 21, pp. 1–14.
(1991), *Thomas Tooke: Pioneer of Monetary Theory*, Ann Arbor: Michigan University Press.
(1993), "Discussion" of Laidler, D., "Was Wicksell a Quantity Theorist?", in Barkai, H., S. Fischer, and N. Liviatan, (Eds.) *Monetary Theory and Thought: Essays in Honour of Don Patinkin*, Ch 8 pp. 178–181, London: MacMillan Press.
(1997), "Thomas Tooke, The Currency Principle and The 1844 Bank Act", Introductory Essay to Tooke's "An Inquiry into the Currency Principle", re-issued in 'Klassiker der Nationalokonomie' series, B. Schefold, (Ed), Dusseldorf, Germany: Verlag Wirtschaft und Finanzen.
(1999), "Free and Not So Free Banking Theories Among the Classicals or Classical Forerunners of Free Banking and Why They Have Been Neglected," *History of Political Economy*, Volume 31, pp. 79–107.
(2009), "Reexamination of Thornton's Innovative Monetary Analysis: The Bullion Debate during the Restriction Once Again," *History of Political Economy*, Vol. 41, pp. 545–574.
Ashton, T. S. and Sayers, R. S. (eds.) (1953), *Papers in English Monetary History*, Oxford: Clarendon Press.
Atack, J. and Neal, L. (2009), *The Origins and Development of Financial Markets and Institutions: from the Seventeenth Century to the Present*, Cambridge: Cambridge University Press.
Atack, J. (2009), "Financial Innovations and Crises: The View Backwards from Northern Rock", in Atack, J and Neal, L. (eds.), *The Origins and Development of Financial Markets and Institutions: from the Seventeenth Century to the Present*, Ch. 1 pp. 1–31, Cambridge: Cambridge University Press.
Barkai, H. Fischer, S. and Liviatan, N. (1993), *Monetary Theory and Thought: Essays in Honour of Don Patinkin*, Hampshire: Macmillan.
Beaugrand, P. (1982), "Henry Thornton: a mise au point" *History of Political Economy*, vol. 14, pp. 101–111.

Berdell, J. F. (1995), "The Present Relevance of Hume's Open-Economy Monetary Dynamics", *The Economic Journal*, vol. 105, pp. 1205–1217.

Black, F. (1970), "Banking and Interest Rates in a World without Money: The Effects of Uncontrolled Banking," *Journal of Bank Research* vol. 1, pp. 9–20.

Blaug, M. (1958), *Ricardian Economics: A Historical Study*, New Haven: Yale University Press.

Blaug, M. Eltis, W. O'Brien, D. Patinkin, D. Skidelsky, R. and Wood G. E. (1995), *The Quantity Theory of Money from Locke to Keynes and Friedman*, Cheltenham: Elgar.

Boianovsky, M. (1995), "Wicksell's Business Cycle", *European Journal of the History of Economic Thought*, vol. 2 pp. 375–411.

——— (1998), "Wicksell, Ramsey and the Theory of Interest," *European Journal of the History of Economic Thought*, vol. 5 pp. 140–168.

Boianovsky, M. and Trautwein, H. M. (2001), "An Early Manuscript by Knut Wicksell on the Bank Rate of Interest" *History of Political Economy*, vol. 33, pp. 486–507 [the manuscript Wicksell (1889/2001)].

Bonar, J. (1923), "Ricardo's Ingot Plan," *Economic Journal*, 33, pp. 281–304.

Boot, H. M. (1983), "James Wilson and the Commercial Crisis of 1847", *History of Political Economy*, vol. 15, pp 567–583.

Bridel, P. (1987), *Cambridge monetary thought: the development of saving-investment analysis from Marshall to Keynes*, London: Macmillan.

Brunhoff, S. de (1973), *Marx on Money*, New York: Urizen Books [1976].

Buchan, A. (1959), *The Spare Chancellor: The life of Walter Bagehot*, London: Chatto and Windus.

Caffentzis, C. G. (2008), "Fiction or Counterfeit? David Hume's Interpretations of Paper and Metallic Money," Chapter 8 in Wennerlind, C. and Schabas, M. (eds.), *David Hume's Political Economy*, Abingdon: Routledge.

Campbell, R. H. and Skinner, A. S. (1982), *The Origins and Nature of the Scottish Enlightenment*, Edinburgh: John Donald.

Cameron, R. E. (1967), *Banking in the Early Stages of Industrialization: A Study in Comparative Economic History*, with the collaboration of Crisp, O. Patrick H. T. and Tilly, R., New York: Oxford University Press.

Cannan, E. (1919), *The Paper Pound of 1797–1821*, London: P.S. King [with The Bullion Report – 1810].

Capie, F. and Wood G. E. (eds.) (1986), *Financial Crises and the World Banking System*, London: Macmillan.

——— (eds.) (1991), *Unregulated Banking: Chaos or Order?* New York: St. Martin's Press.

Capie, F. (ed.) (1993), *History of Banking: 1650–1850*, (ten volumes of selected readings), London: William Pickering.

Capie, F. and Wood G. E. (eds.) (2007), *The Lender of Last Resort*, London & New York: Routledge.

Cassidy, M. (1998), "The Development of John Fullarton's Monetary Theory," *European Journal of the History of Economic Thought*, vol. 5, pp. 509–535.

Cesarano, F. (1998), "Hume's Specie-Flow mechanism and Classical Monetary Theory: An Alternative Interpretation," *Journal of International Economics*, vol. 45, pp. 173–186.

Checkland, S. G. (1944),

——— (1975), *Scottish Banking: A History 1695–1973*, Glasgow: Collins.

Chiodi, G. (1991), *Wicksell's Monetary Theory*, New York: St. Martin's Press.

Clapham, J. H. (1944), *The Bank of England: H History*, (2 volumes: I 1694–1797; II 1797–1914), Cambridge: Cambridge University Press.

Coleman, D. C. (ed.) (1969), *Revisions in Mercantilism*, London: Methuen.

Collins, M. (1988), *Money and Banking in the UK: A History*, London: Croom Helm.

Collins, M. and Baker, M. (2003), *Commercial Banks and the Industrial Finance in England and Wales, 1860–1913*, Oxford: Oxford University Press.

Corry, B. A. (1962), *Money, Saving and Investment in English Economics 1800–1850*. New York: St Martin's Press.

Cowen, T. and Kroszner, R. (1989), "Scottish Banking Before 1845: A Model of Laissez Faire?" *Journal of Money, Credit and Banking*, vol. 21 pp. 221–231.

Daugherty, M. R. (1942), "The Currency-Banking Controversy: Part I," *Southern Economic Journal*, Vol. 9 (2), pp. 140–155.

(1943), "The Currency-Banking Controversy: Part II," *Southern Economic Journal*, Vol. 9 (3), pp. 241–251.

Davis, T. (2005), *Ricardo's Macroeconomics: Money, Trade Cycles, and Growth*, New York: Cambridge University Press.

de Boyer des Roches, J. (2007), "Cause and Effect in the Gold Points Mechanism: A Criticism of Ricardo's criticism of Thornton," *European Journal of the History of Economic Thought*, vol. 14, pp. 25–53.

Diatkine, S. and de Boyer J. (2008), "British Monetary Orthodoxy in the 1870s: A Victory for the Currency Principle" *European Journal of the History of Economic Thought*, vol. 15, pp. 181–209.

Dorn, J. A. and Schwartz A. J. (eds.) (1987), *The Search for Stable Money: Essays on Monetary Reform*, University of Chicago Press.

Dow, S. C. and Smithin J. (1992), "Free Banking in Scotland, 1685–1845," *Scottish Journal of Political Economy*, vol. 30, pp. 374–390.

Dow, S. C. (2002), "Interpretation: The Case of David Hume" *History of Political Economy*, vol. 34, pp. 399–420.

Duke, M. I. (1979), "David Hume and Monetary Adjustment," *History of Political Economy*, vol. 11, pp. 572–587.

Eagly, R. V. (1970), "Adam Smith and the Specie-Flow Doctrine," *Scottish Journal of Political Economy*, pp. 61–68.

Fama, E. F. (1980), "Banking in a Theory of Finance," *Journal of Monetary Economics* vol. 6, pp. 39–67.

Feavearyear, A. E. (1931), *The Pound Sterling: A History of English Money*, second edition revised by E. V. Morgan, Oxford: Clarendon Press [1963].

Fetter, F. W. (1955), *The Irish Pound*, Evanston: Northwestern University Press.

(1959), "The Politics of the Bullion Report," *Economica*, New Series, Vol. 26, pp. 99–120.

(1965), *Development of British Monetary Orthodoxy, 1797–1875*, Cambridge, Mass: Harvard University Press.

(1965), "The Influence of Economists in Parliament on British Legislation from Ricardo to John Stuart Mill," *Journal of Political Economy*, vol. 83 pp. 1051–1064.

Fisher, I. (1911), *The theory of interest*, New York: Kelley & Millman, 1954.

Foley, D. K. (1983), "On Marx's Theory of Money," *Social Concept* 1, pp. 5–19.

(2005), "Marx's Theory of Money in Historical Perspective" in *Marx's Theory of Money: Modern Appraisals*, F. Moseley (ed.), New York: Palgrave Macmillan.

Frenkel, J. A. and Johnson, H. G. (1976), *The Monetary Approach to the Balance of Payments*, Toronto: University of Toronto Press.

Friedman, M. and Schwartz A. J. (1986), "Has Government Any Role in Money?" *Journal of Monetary Economics* 17, pp. 37–62.

Gardlund, T. (1958), *The Life of Knut Wicksell*, Translated by N. Adler from the Swedish, Stockholm: Almqvist & Wiksell.

(1978), "The Life of Knut Wicksell and Some Characteristics of His Work," *Scandinavian Journal of Economics*, pp. 129–134.

Gayer, A. D., Rostow, W. W. and Schwartz, A. J. (1953), *The Growth and Fluctuations of the British Economy, 1790–1850*, (two volumes), Oxford: Clarendon Press.

Gherity, J. A. (1994), "The Evolution of Adam Smith's Theory of Banking," *History of Political Economy*, vol. 26, pp. 423–441.

Glasner, D. (1985), "A Reinterpretation of Classical Monetary Theory", *Southern Economic Journal*, vol. 52, pp. 46–67.

(1989), "On Some Classical Monetary Controversies" *History of Political Economy*, vol. 21, pp. 201–229.

(1992), "The Real-Bills Doctrine in the Light of the Law of Reflux", *History of Political Economy*, vol. 24, pp. 867–894.

(2000), "Classical Monetary Theory and the Quantity Theory" *History of Political Economy*, vol. 32, pp. 39–59.

Green, R. (1992), *Classical Theories of Money, Output and Inflation*, London: Macmillan.

Greenfield, R. L. and L. B. Yeager (1983), "A Laissez-Faire Approach to Monetary Stability," *Journal of Money, Credit and Banking*, 15, pp. 302–315.

Gregory, T. E. (1928), *An Introduction to Tooke and Newmarch's A History of Prices and the State of the Circulation from 1792–1856*, London: L.S.E. Series of Reprints of Scarce Works on Political Economy Mo. 16.

Gregory, T. (1929), *Select Statutes Documents & Reports Relating to British Banking 1832–1928* (two volumes), New York: Kelley [1964].

Grubel, H. G. (1961), "Ricardo and Thornton on the Transfer Mechanism," *Quarterly Journal of Economics*, vol. 75, pp. 292–301.

Gurley, J. G. and Shaw E. S. (1960), *Money in a Theory of Finance*, Palo Alto: Brooking Institution.

Haavelmo, T. (1978), "Wicksell on the Currency Theory vs. The Banking Principle," in *The Theoretical Contributions of Knut Wicksell*, S. Storm and B. Thalberg (eds.), pp. 81–87, London: MacMillan.

Harris, L. (1997), "Corporate Finance and Capital Accumulation" in Arestis P., G. Palma and M. Sawyer (eds) *Markets, Unemployment and Economic Policy: Essays in Honor of Geoff Harcourt*, Vol. II, Chapter 10 pp. 107–120.

Hayek, F. A. (1929a/1991), "The Period of Restriction, 1797–1821, and The Bullion Debate in England," in W.W. Bartley and S. Kresge (eds.), *The Collected Works of F.A. Hayek*, volume 3, Ch. 11, pp. 177–215, Chicago: The University Press.

(1929b/1991), "The Dispute Between the Currency School and the Banking School, 1821–1848," in W.W. Bartley and S. Kresge (eds.), *The Collected Works of F. A. Hayek*, volume 3, Ch. 12, pp. 216–244.

(1939), *Introduction* to the republication of H. Thornton (1802/1939) *Paper Credit*, New Jersey: A. M. Kelley [1978].

Hayek, F. A. von (1976), *The Denationalization of Money*, London: Institute of Economic Affairs, second edition, 1978.

Heertje, A. (2004), "The Dutch and Portuguese-Jewish Background of David Ricardo," *European Journal of the History of Economic Thought*, vol. 11, pp. 281-294.

Hetzel, R. L. (1987), "Henry Thornton: Seminal Monetary Theorist and Father of the Modern Central Bank," *Federal Reserve Bank of Richmond Economic Review*, 73 (4), pp. 3-16.

Hicks, J. (1967), *Critical Essays in Monetary Theory*, Oxford: The Clarendon Press.

(1982), "The Foundations of Monetary Theory," in *Collected Papers in Economic Theory*, Volume II, Oxford: Basil Blackwell.

(1989), "LF and LP" in Tsiang, S.C. *Finance Constraints and the Theory of Money*, edited by M. Kohn, with contributions by J. Hicks, D. Laidler and A. Stocktman, London: Academic Press.

(1989), *A Market Theory of Money*, Oxford: The Clarendon Press.

Hirsch, F. (1977), "The Bagehot Problem", *The Manchester School of Economics and Social Studies*, vol. 45, pp. 241-257.

Hollander, J. H. (1911), "The Developments of the Theory of Money from Adam Smith to David Ricardo," *Quarterly Journal of Economics*, Vol. 25, pp. 426-470.

Hollander, S. (1973). *The Economics of Adam Smith*, Toronto: University of Toronto Press.

Hollander, S. (1979), *The Economics of David Ricardo*, Toronto: University of Toronto Press.

(1985), *The Economics of John Stuart Mill, Volume I Theory and Method, Volume II: Political Economy*, Toronto and Buffalo: University of Toronto Press.

(1987), *Classical Economics*, Oxford: Basil Blackwell.

Hont, I. and Ignatieff, M. (1983), *Wealth and Virtue: The Shaping of Political Economy in the Scottish Enlightenment*, Cambridge: Cambridge University Press.

Horsefield, J. K. (1944), "The Origins of the Bank Charter Act, 1844," *Economica*, vol. 11 pp. 180-189; also in Ashton, T.S. & Sayers, R.S. (eds.) (1953), *Papers in English Monetary History*, pp. 109-125.

(1949a), "The Opinions of Horsley Palmer: Governor of the Bank of England, 1830-33," *Economica*, New Series, Vol. 16, pp. 143-158.

(1949b), "The Cash Ratio in English Banks before 1800," *Journal of Political Economy*, Vol. 57, pp. 70-74.

(1952), "British Banking Practices," *Economica*, New Series, Vol. 19, pp. 308-321.

Humphrey, T. M. (1981), "Adam Smith and the Monetary Approach to the Balance of Payments", *Federal Reserve Bank of Richmond Economic Review*, 67 pp. 3-10.

(1982), "The Real Bills Doctrine", *Federal Reserve Bank of Richmond Economic Review*, 68(5) pp. 3-13.

(1989), "Lender of Last Resort: The Concept in History," *Federal Reserve Bank of Richmond Economic Review*, 75(2) pp. 8-16.

(1990), "Ricardo versus Thornton on the Appropriate Monetary Response to Supply Shocks," *Federal Reserve Bank of Richmond Economic Review*, 76(6) pp. 18-24.

(1999), "Mercantilists and Classicals: Insights from Doctrinal History", *Economic Quarterly Federal Reserve Bank of Richmond Economic Review*, 85(2) pp. 55-82.

(2003), "Knut Wicksell and Gustav Cassel on the Cumulative Process and the Price-Stabilizing Policy Rule," *Journal of the History of Economic Thought*, 25 pp. 199–220.

(2004), "Alfred Marshall and the Quantity Theory of Money," Federal Reserve Bank of Richmond, Working Paper 10–04.

Hutchison, T. W. (1988), *Before Adam Smith: The Emergence of Political Economy, 1662–1776*, Oxford: Basil Blackwell.

Ingham, G. (2005), *Concepts of Money: Interdisciplinary Perspectives from Economics, Sociology and Political Science*, Elgar.

Kareken, J. H. and N. Wallace (eds.) (1980), *Models of Monetary Economics*, Federal Reserve Bank of Minneapolis.

Kindleberger, C. R. (1978), *Manias, Panics, and Crashes: A History of Financial Crises*, London: Macmillan.

Klein, B. (1974), "The Competitive Supply of Money," *Journal of Money, Credit and Banking*, 6, pp. 423–453.

Laidler, D. (1972), "Thomas Tooke on Monetary Reform" in M. Peston and B. Corry, (eds), *Essays in Honour of Lord Robbins*, London: Weidenfeld and Nicolson.

  (1981), "Adam Smith as a Monetary Economist", *Canadian Journal of Economics*, 14, pp. 185–200.

(1984) "Misconceptions about the Real-Bills Doctrine: A Comment on Sargent and Wallace" *Journal of Political Economy*, vol. 92, pp.147–155.

(1990), "Alfred Marshall and the Development of Monetary Economics", in *Centenary Essays on Alfred Marshall*, J. K. Whitaker (ed.), pp. 44–78, Cambridge: Cambridge University Press; also in *Macroeconomics in Retrospect: The Selected Essays of David Laidler*, Cheltenham: Elgar [2004].

(1991), *The Golden Age of the Quantity Theory*, Princeton: Princeton University Press.

(1993), "Was Wicksell a Quantity Theorist?" in Barkai, H., S. Fischer, and N. Liviatan, (Eds.), *Monetary Theory and Thought: Essays in Honour of Don Patinkin*, Ch. 8 pp. 178–181, London: MacMillan Press.

(2000), "Highlights of the Bullionist Controversy", Research Report #13, Stockholm School of Economics, Institute for Research in Economic History.

(2002), "Rules, Discretion and Financial Crises in Classical and Neoclassical Monetary Economics," *Economic Issues*, vol. 7 pp. 11–33; also in *Macroeconomics in Retrospect: The Selected Essays of David Laidler*, pp. 17–39, Cheltenham: Elgar [2004].

(2004), "Two Views of the Lender of Last Resort: Thornton and Bagehot," in *Macroeconomics in retrospect: The selected essays of David Laidler*, pp. 40–56, Cheltenham: Elgar.

(2006), "Woodford and Wicksell on Interest and Prices: The Place of the Pure Credit Economy in the Theory of Monetary Policy," *Journal of the History of Economic Thought*, vol. 28, pp. 151–159.

Leijonhufvud, A. (1981), "The Wicksell Connection: Variations on Theme" in *Information and Coordination: Essays in Macroeconomic Theory*, New York: Oxford University Press.

Lindahl, E. (1958), "Wicksell's Life and Work," Introduction to K. Wicksell (1958), *Selected Papers on Economic Theory*, New York: A. M. Kelley [1969].

Link, R. C. (1959), *English Theories of Economic Fluctuations 1815–1848*, New York: Columbia University Press.

Magnusson, L. (1994), *Mercantilism: The Shaping of an Economic Language*, London: Routledge.

McCallum, B. T. (1985), "Bank Deregulation, Accounting Systems of Exchange, and the Unit of Account: A Critical Review," in *Carnegie-Rochester Conferences Series on Public Policy*, 23, pp. 13–46.

Mints, L. W. (1945), *A History of Banking Theory*, Chicago: The University Press.

Mises, von L. (1912), *The Theory of Money and Credit*, translated from the German by H. E. Batson, Introduction L. Robbins, New York: The Foundation for Economic Education [1971].

Mitchell, B. R. with the collaboration of P. Deane (1962), *Abstract of British Historical Statistics*, Cambridge: Cambridge University Press [1971].

(1988), *British Historical Statistics*, Cambridge: Cambridge University Press.

Monroe, A. E. (1923), *Monetary Theory before Adam Smith*, Cambridge: Harvard University Press.

Mokyr, J. (ed.) (1985), *The Economics of the Industrial Revolution*, Totowa, NJ: Rowman & Allan.

(1993), *The British Industrial Revolution: An Economic Perspective*, Boulder: Westview Press.

Morgan, E. V. and Thomas, W. A. (1962), *The Stock Exchange: Its History and Functions*, London: Elek Books.

Munn, C. W. (1981), *The Scottish Provincial Banking Companies, 1747–1864*, Edinburgh: John Donald Publishers.

(1991), "Comment" [on White 1991a], in Capie F. and Wood, G.E. (eds.) *Unregulated Banking: Chaos or Order?* pp. 63–67.

Murphy, A. E. (2003), "Paper Credit and the Multi-Personae Mr. Henry Thornton," *European Journal of the History of Economic Thought*, vol. 10 pp. 429–453.

(2005), "Rejoinder to Skaggs's Treating Schizophrenia: a comment on Antoin Murphy's diagnosis of Henry Thornton's Theoretical Condition," *European Journal of the History of Economic Thought*, vol. 12 pp. 329–332.

Nakano, T. (2006), "'Let Your Science be Human': Hume's Economic Methodology," *Cambridge Journal of Economics*, vol. 30, pp. 687–700.

Neal, L. (1990), *The Rise of Financial Capitalism: International Capital Markets in the Age of Reason*, Cambridge: Cambridge University Press.

(1998), "The Financial Crisis of 1825 and the Restructuring of the British Financial System," *Federal Reserve Bank of St. Louis Review*, Vol. 80 (3) pp. 53–76.

Nelson, A. (1999), *Marx's Concept of Money: The God of Commodities*, London and New York: Routledge.

Niehans, J. (1978), *The Theory of Money*, The Johns Hopkins University Press.

O'Brien, D. P. (1965), "The Transition in Torrens' Monetary Thought," *Economica*, vol. 32, pp. 269–301.

(1971), "Introduction" in *The Correspondence of Lord Overstone*, (Three Volumes), vol. 1 pp. 12–144, Cambridge University Press.

(1993), *Thomas Joplin and Classical Macroeconomics: A Reappraisal of Classical Monetary Thought*, Aldershot: Elgar.

(1995), "Long-run Equilibrium and cyclical disturbances: the currency and banking controversy over monetary control," in M. Blaug, et.al. also in O'Brien (2007) Ch. 5.

(1997), "Monetary Base Control and the Bank Act of 1844", *History of Political Economy*, vol. 29, pp. 593–633, also in O'Brien (2007) Ch. 6.

(2001), "Bagehot's Lombard Street and Macroeconomic Stabilisation", *The Scottish Journal of Political Economy*, vol. 48, pp. 425–441, also in O'Brien (2007) Ch. 8.

(2003), "The Lender-of-Last-Resort Concept in Britain", *History of Political Economy*, vol. 35, pp. 1–19, also in O'Brien (2007) Ch. 7.

(2004), *The Classical Economists Revisited*, second revised edition, Princeton: Princeton University Press [first edition 1975].

(2007a), *The Development of Monetary Economics: A Modern Perspective on Monetary Controversies*, Cheltenham: Elgar.

Ohlin, B. (1936), *Introduction to Wicksell, K. Interest and Prices*, Kelley [1965].

Paganelli, M. P. (2009), "David Hume on Monetary Policy: A Retrospective Approach," *The Journal of Scottish Philosophy*, Vol. 7, pp. 65–85.

Patinkin, D. (1952), "Wicksell's Cumulative Process," *Economic Journal*, vol. 62 pp. 835–847.

(1961), "Financial Intermediaries and the Logical Structure of Monetary Theory," *American Economic Review*, pp. 95–116.

(1965), *Money, Interest and Prices* (2nd Edition), New York: Harper & Row.

Peach, T. (2004), "David Ricardo" in *Oxford Dictionary of National Biography*, Oxford: Oxford University Press.

Peake, C. F. (1978), "Henry Thornton and the Development of Ricardo's Economic Thought", *History of Political Economy*, 10, pp. 193–212.

(1982), "Henry Thornton: An Accurate Perspective *History of Political Economy*, 14, pp. 115–120.

(1995), "Henry Thornton in the History of Economics: Confusions and Contributions," Manchester School of Economic and Social Studies, 63, pp. 283–296.

Perlman, M. (1986), "The Bullionist Controversy Revisited," *Journal of Political Economy*, vol. 94, pp. 745–762.

(1987), "Of a Controversial Passage in Hume," *Journal of Political Economy*, vol. 95, pp. 274–289.

(1989), "Adam Smith and the paternity of the Real Bills doctrine," *History of Political Economy*, Vol. 21, pp. 77–90.

Petrella, F. (1968), "Adam Smith Rejection of Hume's Price-Specie-Flow Mechanism: A Minor Mystery Resolved," *Southern Economic Journal*, vol. 34, pp. 365–374.

Pigou, A. C. (1917), "The Value of Money," *Quarterly Journal of Economics*, Vol. 32, pp. 38–65.

Pocock, J. G. A. (1985), *Virtue, Commerce and History: Essays on Political Thought and History, Chiefly in the Eighteenth Century*, Cambridge: Cambridge University Press.

Poitras, G. (1998), "Robert Torrens and the Evolution of the Real Bills Doctrine," *Journal of the History of Economic Thought*, Vol. 20 pp. 479–498.

Pressnell, L. S. (1956), *Country Banking in the Industrial Revolution*, Oxford: Clarendon Press.

Quinn, S. and Roberds, W. (2009), "An Economic Explanation of the Early Bank of Amsterdam, Debasement, Bills of Exchange, and the Emergence of the First Central Bank" in Atack, J and Neal, L. (eds.) *The Origins and Development of Financial Markets and Institutions: from the Seventeenth Century to the Present*, Ch. 2, pp. 32–70, Cambridge: Cambridge University Press.

Reed, M. (2004), "Loyd, Samuel Jones, Baron Overstone (1796–1883)," *Oxford Dictionary of National Biography*, Oxford University Press, Sept 2004; online edn,

Jan 2008 [http://www.oxforddnb.com/view/article/17115, accessed type="text/javascript"document.write(printcitationDate()));24 March 2008]

Reisman, D. A. (1971), "Henry Thornton and Classical Monetary Economics," *Oxford Economic Papers*, 23, pp. 70–89.

Ricardo, D. (1951–1973), *Works and Correspondence of David Ricardo*, edited by P. Sraffa, 11 volumes, Cambridge: The University Press.

Rist, C. (1940), *History of Monetary and Credit Theory from John Law to the Present Day*, New York: A. M. Kelly [1966].

Robbins, L. (1958), *Robert Torrens and the Evolution of Classical Economics*, London: Macmillan.

Roberts, R. and Kynaston, D. (eds.) (1995), *The Bank of England: Money, Power and Influence, 1694–1994*, Oxford: Clarendon Press.

Rockoff, H. (1986), "Walter Bagehot and the Theory of Central Banking," in F. Capie and G. F. Wood, *Financial Crises and the World Banking System*, pp. 160–180, London: Macmillan.

Rosdolsky, R. (1968), *The making of Marx's Capital*, London, Pluto Press [1977].

Rothbard, M. N. (1995), *Classical Economics: An Austrian Perspective on the History of Economic Thought*, Vol. II, Aldershot, U.K.: Edward Elgar Publishing.

(1997), *The Logic of Action I: Method, Money and the Austrian School*, Cheltenham, U.K.: Edward Elgar Publishing.

Rotwein, E. (1955), *Introduction to David Hume: Writings on Economics*, Madison: University of Wisconsin Press.

Salerno, J. T. (1980), *The Doctrinal Antecedents of the Monetary Approach to the Balance of Payments*, Ph. D. Thesis, Rutgers University.

Santiago-Valiente, W. (1988), "Historical Background of the Classical Monetary Theory and the 'Real Bills' Banking Tradition," *History of Political Economy*, vol. 20, pp. 43–63.

Saville, R. (1996), *The Bank of Scotland: A History 1695–1995*, Edinburgh: Edinburgh University Press.

Sayers, R. S. (1953), "Ricardo's Views on Monetary Questions," *The Quarterly Journal of Economics*, Vol. 67, pp. 30–49 also in T. S. Ashton and R.S. Sayers *Papers in English Monetary History* pp. 76–95.

(1963), "The Life and Work of James Pennington," in *Economic Writings of James Pennington*, London, LSE.

(1976), *The Bank of England, 1891–1944*, (three volumes) Cambridge: Cambridge University Press.

(1978), "Introductory Essay" in *The Collected Works of Walter Bagehot*, N. St John-Stevas (ed.), Vol. 9, pp. 27–43.

Schumpeter, J. A. (1954), *History of Economic Analysis*, London: Allen & Unwin.

Schwartz, A. J. (1987), "Banking School, Currency School, Free Banking School" in *The New Palgrave: A Dictionary of Economics*, (eds.) Eatwell, J., Milgate, M. and Newman P. London: MacMillan.

Sechrest, L. J. (1991), "Free Banking in Scotland: A Dissenting View," *Cato Journal*, vol. 10, pp. 799–808.

Selgin G. A. and White, L. H. (1994), "How would the Invisible Hand Handle Money?" *Journal of Economic Literature*, vol. 32, pp. 1718–1749.

Silberling, N. J. (1919), "British Financial Experience 1790–1830," *The Review of Economic Statistics*, vol. 1 pp. 282–297.

(1924), "Financial and Monetary Policy of Great Britain During the Napoleonic Wars," *The Quarterly Journal of Economics*, parts I and II, Vol. 38, pp. 214–233 and 397–439.

Simon, H. C. (1936), "Rules versus Authorities in Monetary Policy," *Journal of Political Economy*, Vol. 44, pp. 1–30.

Siven, C. H. (2006), "Monetary Equilibrium," *History of Political Economy*, 38, pp. 665–709.

Skaggs, N. T. (1991), "John Fullarton's Law of Reflux and Central Bank Policy", *History of Political Economy*, 23, pp. 457–480.

(1994), "The Place of J. S. Mill in the Development of British Monetary Orthodoxy, "*History of Political Economy*, 26, pp. 539–567.

(1995), "Henry Thornton and the Development of Classical Monetary Economics", *Canadian Journal of Economics*, vol. 28, pp. 1212–1227.

(1999), "Changing Views: Twentieth-Century Opinion on the Banking School – Currency School Controversy," *History of Political Economy*, vol. 31, pp. 361–391.

(2003), "Thomas Tooke, Henry Thornton and the Development of British Monetary Orthodoxy," *Journal of the History of Economic Thought*, vol. 25, pp. 177–197.

(2005) "Treating Schizophrenia: a comment on Antoin Murphy's diagnosis of Henry Thornton's Theoretical Condition," *European Journal of the History of Economic Thought*, vol. 12 pp. 321–328.

(2008), "An Inquiry into the Nature and Effects of Henry Thornton's Christian Faith on the Existence and Contents of his Economic Writings", *History of Political Economy*, vol. 40 (annual supplement), pp. 168–188.

Skinner, A. S. (1993), "David Hume: Principles of Political Economy" in D. F. Norton (ed.), *The Cambridge Companion to Hume*, Cambridge: Cambridge University Press.

(1996), "David Hume: Economic Writings" in *A System of Social Science: Papers Relating to Adam Smith* (2nd edition), Oxford: Clarendon Press.

Skinner, A. S. and Wilson, T. (1975), *Essays on Adam Smith*, Oxford: Clarendon Press.

Smith, B. D. (1988), "Legal Restrictions, 'Sunspots,' and Peel's Bank Act: The Real Bills Doctrine versus the Quantity Theory Reconsidered," *Journal of Political Economy*, 96, pp. 3–19.

Smith, V. C. (1936), *The Rationale of Central Banking*, London: P.S. King.

Sylla, R. (2009), "Comparing the UK and US financial systems, 1790–1830," " in Atack, J. and Neal, L. (eds.) *The Origins and Development of Financial Markets and Institutions: from the Seventeenth Century to the Present*, Ch. 7 pp. 209–234, Cambridge: Cambridge University Press.

Taylor, W. L. (1965), *Francis Hutcheson and David Hume as Predecessors of Adam Smith*, Durham: Duke University Press.

Thornton, M. (2007), "Cantillon, Hume, and the Rise of Antimercantilism," *History of Political Economy*, 39(3), pp. 453–480.

Tsiang, S.C. (1989) "The Monetary Theoretic Foundations of the Modern Monetary approach to the Balance of Payments" in *Finance Constraints and the Theory of Money*, edited by M. Kohn, with contributions by J. Hicks, D. Laidler, and A. Stocktman, London: Academic Press.

Uhr, C. G. (1960), *Economic Doctrines of Knut Wicksell*, Berkeley: University of California Press.

Vickers, D. (1959), *Studies in the Theory of Money, 1690–1776*, London: Peter Owen.

(1976), "Adam Smith and the Status of the Theory of Money," in Skinner, A.S. & Wilson, T., *Essays on Adam Smith*, pp. 428–503, Oxford: Clarendon Press.

Viner, J. (1924), *Canada's Balance of International Indebtedness, 1990–1913*, Cambridge: Harvard University Press.

(1937), *Studies in the Theory of International Trade*, New York: A. M. Kelley [1975].

Wennerlind, C. (2000), "The Humean Paternity to Adam Smith's Theory of Money", *History of Economic Ideas*, Vol. 8, pp. 77–97.

(2001), "The Link between David Hume's *Treatise of Human Nature* and His Fiduciary Theory of Money", *History of Political Economy*, vol. 33 pp. 139–160.

(2005), "David Hume's Monetary Theory Revisited: Was He Really a Quantity Theorist and an Inflationist?", *Journal of Political Economy*, vol. 113 pp. 223–237.

(2008), "An Artificial Virtue and the Oil of Commerce: A Synthetic View of Hume's Theory of Money" in Wennerlind, C. and Schabas, M. (eds.) (2008), *David Hume's Political Economy*, Chapter 6, pp. 103–126, Abingdon: Routledge.

Wennerlind, C. and Schabas, M. (eds.) (2008), *David Hume's Political Economy*, Abingdon: Routledge.

Whitaker, J. K. (ed.) (1975), *The Early Economic Writings of Alfred Marshall, 1867–1890*, two volumes, London: Macmillan (for the Royal Economic Society).

White, L. H. (1984), *Free Banking in Britain: Theory, Experience and Debates, 1800–1845*, Cambridge: The University Press.

(1989), *Competition and Currency: Essays on Free Banking and Money*, New York: New York University Press.

(1991a), "Banking without a Central Bank: Scotland Before 1884 as a Free Banking System," in *Unregulated Banking Chaos or Order*, edited by Forrest, C. and G. E. Woods, New York: St. Martin's Press, pp. 37–62.

(1991b), "Free Banking in Scotland: Reply to a Dissenting View," *Cato Journal*, vol. 11, pp. 809–810.

Wood, E. (1939), *English Theories of Central Banking Control: 1819–1858*, Cambridge, Mass: Harvard University Press.

Wood, J. H. (2005), *A History of Central Banking in Great Britain and the United States*, Cambridge: Cambridge University Press.

Author Index

Arnon, 68, 97, 148, 211, 212, 213, 219, 225, 234, 240, 256, 259, 309, 356, 377, 382–383, 397, 407

Attwood, 174, 176, 202, 283, 401

Bagehot, 1, 4, 5, 217, 245, 248, 251, 274, 277–308, 337–339, 343, 365–377, 386, 389, 390, 391, 396, 401, 408, 411, 412, 414, 415

Baring, 3, 73–77, 88–94, 98, 124, 283, 372

Beaugrand, 97

Black, 259

Blaug, 126, 413

Boase, 75, 401

Boianovsky, 344, 366, 370

Bonar, 126, 146, 147

Bosanquet, 126, 127, 134–144, 352, 360, 361, 382, 401

Boyd, 3, 73–98, 102, 121, 127, 401

Brunhoff, 309–310

Caffenzis, 12

Cairnes, 336

Cameron, 26

Campbell, 33, 408

Capie, 89, 372, 408, 413, 415

Checkland, 28, 269, 408

Clapham, 28, 64, 66, 71, 96, 119, 182, 372, 409

Davis, 126, 146

Dobb, 126, 382

Eagly, 45, 47

Fama, 259

Feavearyear, 27, 28, 31, 55, 63, 69, 71, 163, 175, 185

Fetter, 25, 28, 64, 66, 67, 74, 89, 96, 97, 122, 123, 133, 134, 144, 173–178, 188, 190, 206, 209, 219, 228, 246, 248, 270, 278–283, 288, 371, 378

Fisher, 330

Foley, 309, 310

Fullarton, 4, 209, 211, 220, 227–229, 241, 298, 324, 326, 327, 352, 360

Gardlund, 343–344, 365–366, 368

Gayer, 67–68, 212

Gherity, 33, 101, 321

Gilbart, 240, 273

Gregory, 52, 212, 246

Gurley, 154, 356

Haavelmo, 355

Hankey, 288

Hawtrey, 52, 56, 156, 284

Hayek, 74, 96–98, 106, 120, 209, 219, 247, 259, 272, 371, 379, 380

Hicks, 1, 51, 53, 98, 168, 356, 379, 397

Hirsch, 278

Hollander, 33, 35, 97, 126, 127, 247, 248

Hollander S, 33

Hont, 33

Horner, 74, 97, 122–123, 125, 132–133, 231

419

Subject Index

Printed in the United States
By Bookmasters